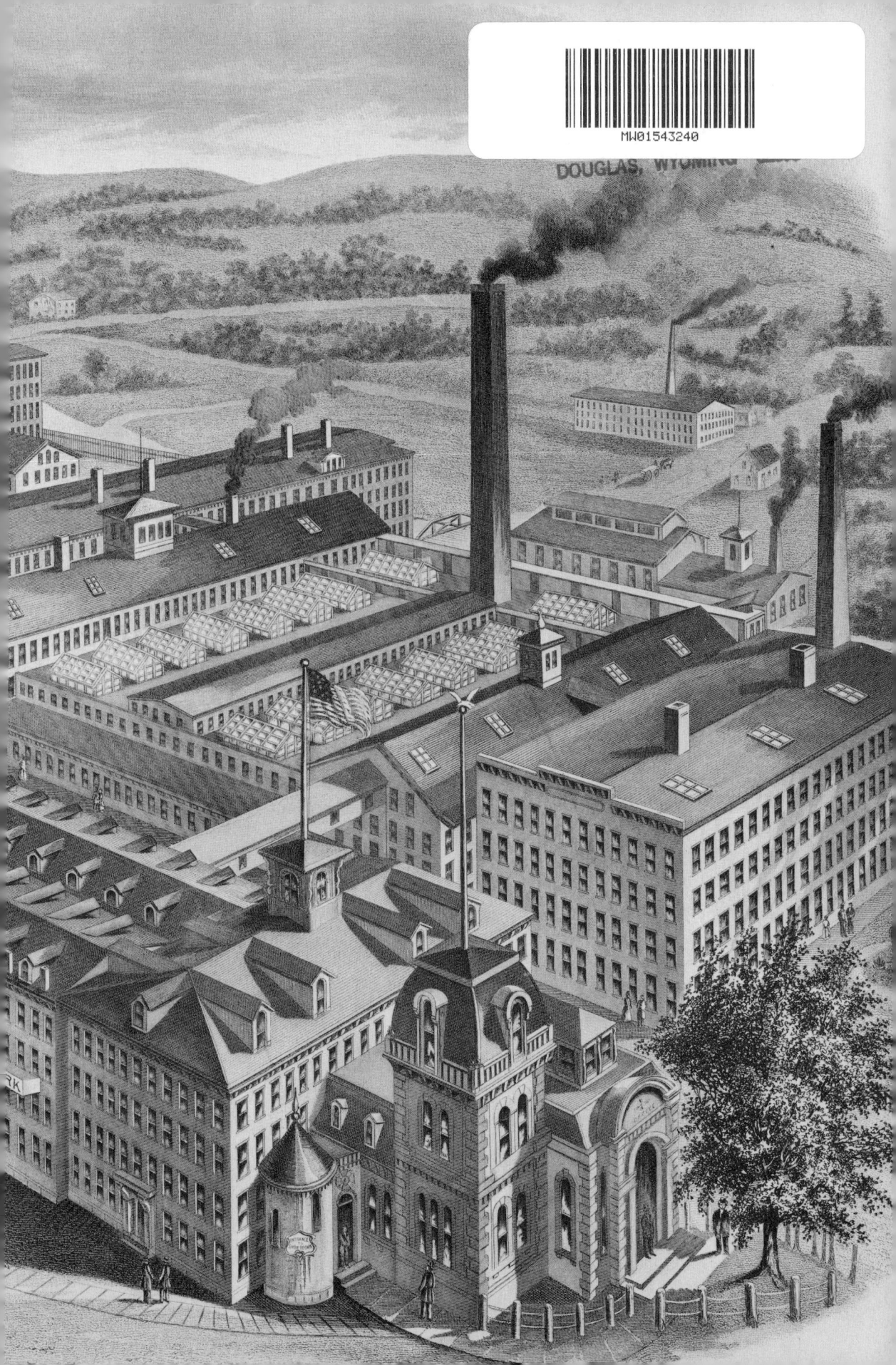

American Silverplate

American Silverplate

by

Dorothy T. and H Ivan Rainwater

Thomas Nelson Inc.
and
Everybodys Press

© 1968 by Dorothy T. and H Ivan Rainwater

Jointly published by Thomas Nelson Inc., Nashville, Tennessee,
and Everybodys Press, Hanover, Pennsylvania
and simultaneously in Canada by
Thomas Nelson & Sons (Canada) Limited, Don Mills, Ontario.
Design by Harold Leach

ISBN 0-8407-4322-X

Library of Congress Catalog Card Number: 72-7998

Printed in the United States of America

Acknowledgments

The most rewarding aspect of doing the research for this volume has been the opportunity to become better acquainted with the collectors, dealers in antiques, and the people affiliated with the silverware industry. Among these, our very special thanks go to E. P. Hogan of the Historical Library, The International Silver Company. His encouragement and enthusiasm have been unlimited. No mere expression of thanks is adequate for his invaluable assistance. We also wish to express our special gratitude to John B. Stevens, President; Stuart C. Hemingway, Executive Vice-President and General Manager; William T. Hiller, Superintendent (Div. III); and Richard Croteau, Photographer, all of The International Silver Company.

Our sincere thanks and appreciation also go to the following of Reed & Barton Silversmiths: Roger H. Hallowell, President; John I. Riddle, Sales Promotion Manager; Stuart Fraser, Photographer; René LaFrance, Repair Shop; and Lorraine Brennan, Photography Department.

For the gift of research materials we are deeply indebted to Dr. Elliot A. P. Evans, Piedmont, California.

Special acknowledgment is made to A. Christian Revi, Editor, *Spinning Wheel* magazine, for the personal interest shown in this project and also for permission to reprint certain materials from that publication.

The writers are indebted to Harold Leach, Production Manager and Art Director, and to Bernice Rich, Editorial Assistant, both of Thomas Nelson Inc.

They also wish to express their deep gratitude to the individuals and institutions mentioned below for their generosity in loaning articles to be photographed, for photographs, and for information and other assistance.

Mr. and Mrs. Carl Almgren
American Heritage Publishing Co.
   Marshall B. Davidson
   Geoffrey Clements
Antiques, Inc.
   Ralph M. and Terry H. Kovel
Mrs. George R. Bradbury
Chatillon-DeMenil House Foundation
   A. S. Bland, Jr.
Chicago Historical Society
   Barbara Denemark
Christofle at Baccarat, Inc.
   William B. Riordan
John Crerar Library
Dr. Elliot A. P. Evans
Ellis-Barker Silver Companies
   Adele Ferber
Mrs. Carl B. Felger
Charles H. Fuller, Old Silverplate, Antiques
Mr. and Mrs. Howard Gianotti
The Gorham Company
   Brendon J. Murphy
W. J. Hagerty & Sons
   William P. Gaffney
Louise Hart Antiques
The International Silver Company
   John B. Stevens

Stuart C. Hemingway
William T. Hiller
E. P. Hogan
Richard Croteau
Sal Crescimanno
Ruth Liedtke
Edward J. Conroy
Malcolm A. Orr
Kensington Galleries
  Alys Spealman
King's Things
Samuel Kirk & Son
  S. Kirk Millspaugh
Lunt Silversmiths
  R. A. Davis
Moore County Historical Association
  Helen K. Butler
Annabelle Mowrey
State of North Carolina
  C. F. W. Coker
Mrs. Loe H. Pardee
Poole Silver Company
  Charles R. Rodgers
Marguerite Pursell, Antiques
Reed & Barton Silversmiths
  Roger H. Hallowell
  Anthony LaChapelle
  John I. Riddle
  Stuart Fraser
  René LaFrance
Lorraine Brennan
Milton Hannah
John Gilroy
A. Christian Revi
F. B. Rogers Silver Company
  Bernard Bernstein
Mrs. Arthur Schuster
Sheridan Silver Company
Grace Smith
Smithsonian Institution
  Barbara J. Coffee
Spinning Wheel
  A. Christian Revi
The Stieff Company
  Gideon N. Stieff, Sr.
  Charles C. Stieff, II
Sussman-Ochs
United States Department of Commerce
  Clarence A. Kalk
  C. E. McMullan
  Lamont V. Gould
  Joel Spearman
United States Department of the Interior
  Charles D. Hoyt
Wallace Silversmiths
  Carol Nixdorf
Renee Williams

Picture Credits

The location of objects and pictorial materials belonging to individuals and institutions is listed below. For simplification, the following abbreviations are used:

INSILCO   The International Silver Company. All the photographs credited to INSILCO, black & white as well as the color transparencies, were taken by Richard Croteau.

R&B   Reed & Barton Silversmiths.

II. EARLY ELECTROPLATING AND THE RISE OF FACTORIES
3, 5 INSILCO; 8 R&B; 12 Samuel Kirk & Son; 13, 14 E. A. P. Evans, photo by Roy D. Graves.

III. MANUFACTURING AND MARKETING
3–20 INSILCO; 21–23 R&B; 24 INSILCO; 26 Mrs. Arthur Schuster; 27–29 Mrs. Carl B. Felger; 33, 34 Mrs. Arthur Schuster; 36 Renee Williams.

IV. PATENTED PROCESSES
7 INSILCO

V. DEVELOPMENT OF STYLES
3, 4 R&B; 7–11 INSILCO; 12 Chatillon-DeMenil House Foundation; 13 A. Christian Revi, photo by Poist's Studio; 15 INSILCO; 16 Kensington Galleries; 17–19 INSILCO; 20 Louise Hart Antiques; 21 INSILCO; 22 Louise Hart Antiques; 23, 24 R&B; 26–28 INSILCO; 28a E. A. P. Evans, photo by Roy D. Graves; 32–35, 35a, 36, 37 INSILCO; 39 E. A. P. Evans; 40–42 The Gorham Company; 43, 43a E. A. P. Evans; 45 The Gorham Company; 46 INSILCO; 48 R&B; 49, 50 The Gorham Company; 53–56 INSILCO; 57a A. Christian Revi, photo by Poist's Studio; 65–67 INSILCO; 68–72 R&B.

VI. EXHIBITION AND PRESENTATION SILVER, AND ORNAMENTAL ART WORK
5 R&B; 6–8 INSILCO; 9, 10 John Crerar Library; 11 *Spinning Wheel* magazine; 16, 18 INSILCO; 19–21 Smithsonian Institution; 23 R&B; 24 Mrs. George R. Bradbury, Jim West Photo; 25 INSILCO; 27–30 R&B; 32–34, color plate E, 38 INSILCO; 39a, 42a, 43 A. Christian Revi, photo by Poist's Studio.

VII. SILVERPLATE FOR TABLE AND HOUSEHOLD USE
1 Privately owned, photo courtesy Ralph M. and Terry H. Kovel; 1b Mrs. Loe H. Pardee, photo by Mulholland Studio; 2–5 INSILCO; 11 E. A. P. Evans, photo by Roy D. Graves; 12–15 R&B; color plate B, 24, 25 INSILCO; 26 A. Christian Revi; 27 Grace Smith; 28, 29 E. A. P. Evans; 33, 34 INSILCO; 35 R&B; 36 INSILCO; 37 R&B; 38, 47–49 INSILCO; color plate A top American Heritage Publishing Co. and INSILCO; color plate A bottom INSILCO; color plate D American Heritage Publishing Co. and INSILCO; 52 INSILCO; 53 Annabelle Mowrey; 54, 62–65, 67–70, 73, 77–80, 82, 83 INSILCO; 83a Mrs. Carl B. Felger; 85 E. A. P. Evans; 86 A. Christian Revi;

91, 92 R&B; 93 INSILCO; 107, 108 *Spinning Wheel* magazine; 111, 112, 114 INSILCO; 115 E. A. P. Evans; 117 King's Things; 121, 121a, 121b INSILCO; 123 E. A. P. Evans; 132 Mr. and Mrs. Howard Gianotti, photo by Poist's Studio; 135–137 INSILCO; 139 R&B; 143 E. A. P. Evans; 147 Mrs. Carl B. Felger; 148–150, 153 INSILCO; 158 R&B; 162, 162a, Mrs. Carl B. Felger; 166, 167 INSILCO; 171 Sheridan Silver Company; 175 Mr. and Mrs. Carl Almgren; 183, 187, 191, 193, 194 INSILCO; 200–202 R&B; 203–205, 212, 214 INSILCO; 218 Mr. and Mrs. Carl Almgren; 219, 220 INSILCO.

VIII. SMALL SILVERWARES AND NOVELTIES

1–4, 6 INSILCO; 13 A. Christian Revi, photo by Poist's Studio; 14–17 INSILCO; 23–27 R&B; 28–31, 33–34 INSILCO; 35 *Spinning Wheel* magazine, photo by Poist's Studio; 37–44 INSILCO; 45, 47, 50 Chicago Historical Society; 51 INSILCO; 54 Mrs. Arthur Schuster; 55–61 INSILCO; 65 Chicago Historical Society; 67, 73–74 INSILCO; 76 A. Christian Revi; 77 INSILCO; 81 Mrs. Carl B. Felger; 86 INSILCO; 92 Mrs. Carl B. Felger; 97 Kensington Galleries; 99 Chicago Historical Society.

IX. LIGHTING DEVICES

1–11, color plate C INSILCO; 17 A. Christian Revi, photo by Poist's Studio; 21 INSILCO; 22 Marguerite Pursell.

X. FLATWARE

1, 1a INSILCO; 2 E. A. P. Evans; 7 INSILCO; 8, 9 Oneida Ltd. Silversmiths; 10, 11 INSILCO; 12 A. Christian Revi; 13 R&B.

XI. CARE AND RESTORATION

1–4 W. J. Hagerty & Sons; 5 R&B.

Contents

	ACKNOWLEDGMENTS	5	
	PICTURE CREDITS	7	
I.	HISTORICAL BACKGROUND	13	

Metallurgy *17;* Uses for Silver *17;* Silverplating *18;* Sheffield Plate *19;* Britannia *20*

II. EARLY ELECTROPLATING AND THE RISE OF FACTORIES   21

International Silver Company *26;* Reed & Barton *27;* The Gorham Company *31;* Wallace Silversmiths *32;* Oneida Silversmiths *32;* Tiffany & Company *33;* Homan Manufacturing Company *33;* Other Manufacturers *33*

III. MANUFACTURING AND MARKETING   39

Base Metals Used in Silverplating *39;* Production Methods *41;* Plating of Colored Gold *58;* Casting *59;* Dutch Reproductions *60;* Advertising *60;* Marketing Methods *63;* Distribution Practices *64;* Premiums and Advertising Pieces *66;* Trade Practices Pertaining to Marketing *72*

IV. PATENTED PROCESSES   75
V. DEVELOPMENT OF STYLES   91
VI. EXHIBITION AND PRESENTATION SILVER AND ORNAMENTAL ART WORKS   133

Exhibition Silver *133;* Presentation Silver *147;* Ornamental Art Work, Vases, and Decorative Articles *154*

VII. SILVERPLATE FOR TABLE AND HOUSEHOLD USE   171

Castors *171;* Centerpieces, Fruit Dishes, Berry Bowls, and Brides' Baskets *184;* Card Receivers *205;* Cake Baskets *221;* Waiters, Bread Trays, and Special Purpose Trays *232;* Butter Dishes *236;* Ice-Water Pitchers *248;* Pitchers *269;* Dessert Services *273;* Punch Bowls, Wine Coolers, Wine-Bottle Cases, Liquor Labels *273;* Cups and Goblets *278;* Chafing Dishes, Baking Dishes, and Other Containers *287;* Spoon Holders *302;* Celery Stands *315*

VIII. SMALL SILVERWARE AND NOVELTIES   321

Self-Pouring Teapots and Coffeepots *321;* Dainty Services for the Proper Eating of the Orange *321;* Salts *326;* Spoon Warmers *334;* Napkin Rings *334;* Knife Rests *348;* Sardine Boxes *348;* Miscellaneous Small Tablewares *348;* Match Safes, Pocket Match Boxes, and Toothpick Holders *354;* Sewing Birds *361;* Boudoir Acces-

sories *367;* Vinaigrettes and Chatelaines *389;* Personal Accessories for Gentlemen *392;* Desk Accessories *398*
IX. LIGHTING DEVICES 407
X. FLATWARE 429
XI. CARE AND RESTORATION 447
Care *447;* Restoration *451*
GLOSSARY 455
BIBLIOGRAPHY 461
INDEX 467

American Silverplate

CHAPTER I

Historical Background

The collecting of American plated silver becomes daily more widespread because of the scarcity of handwrought silver and its increasing cost. Antique-market values of plated wares have also risen but it is still possible for the collector of modest means to assemble a tea service for use at home or for the collector of Victorian novelties to find a variety of articles.

The plated ware found in antique shops today is from those days we now call Victorian and Edwardian. It is a product of men and machines of the machine age and cannot be judged by the standards applied to handwrought silver.

About 1870, following the discovery of the Comstock Lode in Nevada, which made large quantities of silver available for silverplating, an electicism of style prevailed. Derivative elements from Elizabethan, Gothic, Louis XIV or rococo, Egyptian, Oriental, Assyrian, Persian, and Indian styles were blended. Often two or more of these were applied to the same piece—with startling results. The quantities of such pieces which have survived give mute testimony to their popularity and to their acceptance at the time they were made. The hope, expressed by the Commissioners on Art and Industry of the London Crystal Palace Exhibition, 1851, that "an alliance between the fine arts and manufacture would promote public taste" was seldom realized.

With this understanding and with some background knowledge of silver production and the basic principles of the manufacturing of plated-silver wares the collector should be able to choose with care and discrimination.

Silver, the "shining metal" the "Queen of Metals," has through the centuries determined the destinies of men and changed the shape of nations.

The word itself comes from the Old English *seolfor*. The Greeks called the metal ἄργυρος (*argyros*), which is derived from ἀργός "bright" or "shining," and has *argentum* as its Latin cognate.

It is generally conceded that the first metals discovered and used by early man were gold, copper, and silver, in that order. Silver was probably discovered after gold and copper since it is less abundant in the native metallic state. It often is not easily recognizable, being normally found as a sulphide in ores.

After gold and platinum, silver is the most unchangeable of metals because of its resistance to oxidation. This resistance to corrosion, as well as its scarcity and beauty, have made silver highly regarded for personal ornaments.

Discoverers of gold associated its yellow color with the sun and related the brilliant white of silver to the moon. By alchemists it was accepted as the emblem of the place "Silvery" moon, under the name of Luna or Diana, and some of the salts of silver are called "lunar" to this day.

There are numerous early references to silver. Biblical references to silver most often mention it in connection with the decoration of the tabernacle in the wilderness (Exodus), in the building of King Solomon's temple (I Kings), and in the temple of Jerusalem (Ezra). Many references are made to the raising of idols of silver (Judges, Isaiah, Ezekiel, Daniel, Hosea, Acts) and offerings of silver chargers, bowls, candlesticks, and other treasures for the temples are also mentioned. Silver shekels * were mentioned many times (Exodus, Numbers, Judges, II Kings, I Chronicles, Nehemiah, Zechariah, Luke, Acts) in addition to the well-known "thirty pieces of silver" for which Judas betrayed Christ (Matthew). Silver is mentioned as part of the wealth of Abram, later called Abraham (Genesis), and of King Solomon (II Chronicles). The arts of the silversmith were well known as were the techniques used in refining the metal. The fining pot for silver is used as a familiar image (Proverbs 17:3). The variety of silver articles mentioned includes not only the temple ornaments already listed but also such things as trumpets (Numbers 10:2), a palace (Song of Solomon 8:9), chains (Isaiah 40:19), and plates (Jeremiah 10:9).

That silversmithing was an honored craft is demonstrated by Solomon's command (II Chronicles 2:7) on the building of the temple to "Send me now therefore a man cunning to work in gold, and in silver. . . ."

Two silversmiths are identified for us by name. In Acts 19:24 we read, "For a certain man named Demetrius, a silversmith, which made silver shrines for Diana. . . ." In Exodus 31:1–5, Bezaleel was commanded by Moses to "work in gold, and in silver" for the tabernacle.

We are admonished (Psalms, Proverbs, Ecclesiastes, Isaiah, and Jeremiah) that wisdom and understanding are to be chosen rather than silver. (See especially Proverbs 3:13–14.)

The Code of Menes, founder of the First Dynasty in Egypt, around 3500 B.C., sets the value of silver as two-fifths that of gold; Chinese and Persian classics, dating before 2500 B.C. refer to silver; and the historian Diodorus Siculus, who wrote in Greek in the last century B.C., says, "These places being covered with woods, it is said that in ancient times these mountains [the Pyrenees] were set on fire by shepherds and continued burning for many days and parched the earth so that an abundance of silver ore was melted and the metal flowed in streams of pure silver like a river." (*Historical Library*, Book V, Chapter 2.)

From archaeological evidence as well as the earliest records it is known that man in southern Europe and the Near and Middle East used silver as a medium of exchange, for personal adornment, for useful vessels, and as a token of wealth. Silver buttons and a pin have been unearthed at Sialk, Iran, from strata dating from 4500–4000 B.C. The Sialk pin had evidently been worked, annealed, and extensively reworked–revealing that metallurgical art had progressed from the earliest techniques of cold hammering.

A silver vase now in the Musée du Louvre, Paris, but once belonging to Entemena, King of Lagash, Mesopotamia, about 2800 B.C., was formed from an ingot of silver which had been hammered into a sheet, with frequent annealings, and raised by hammering on a stake into its present magnificent form, and then decorated and inscribed with lines by a chasing tool.

Present studies indicate that the earliest known metal work was conducted by the pre-Hittites in Cappadocia in the eastern part of Asia Minor apparently some time in the fourth millennium B.C. The not-always-accidental forest-fire type of production had been replaced by mining operations, probably at first of an open-cast nature but followed by underground work. Smelting in furnaces with controlled cupellation

---

* Not a monetary unit, but pieces of silver of a certain weight.

to produce pure metal would have been required for the quantities of silver exported to Assyria.

Later, mining spread eastward with ore deposits being exploited in Armenia and later in Bactria, and also westward to the Aegean Sea. About 500 B.C. the important Laurium silver-lead mine in Greece, at Laurium, southeast of Athens, became one of the rich mines of antiquity. The size of the slag dumps and the quality of the ore still mined in the region indicate that the Greeks, from 600 to 300 B.C., may have mined about 30 tons of silver a year. These mines were important in the development of Athens; they were its mainstay for three centuries and the chief support in the Persian Wars. They were worked until the first century A.D. and were shut down until about 1861. Modern workmen, on exploring the old shafts and tunnels, found picks and hammers just as Greek miners had dropped them almost 2,000 years before. The wealth of these mines was recorded by Xenophon and Aristotle and about 30 B.C. Strabo told of their being exhausted.

In *De re metallica*, published by Agricola in 1556 and translated by former President and Mrs. Hoover, many quaint drawings show the old-time methods of silver mining, with ore in pigskin sacks being carried on dogs' backs.

The exploitation of mines was done under cruel conditions of slavery. The Spanish silver-lead mines, developed first by the Carthaginians and continued by the Romans after their victory in the Punic Wars, were worked by black slaves imported from Africa.

The development of the spice trade with India created a new demand and silver flowed from Spanish mines. The fall of Western Rome (A.D. 476) and the Arab conquests put an end to this trade until it was restored by Venice about A.D. 1200. From that time it flourished until the Turks captured Constantinople in A.D. 1453. This, along with Vasco da Gama's discovery of the Cape of Good Hope route to the East, put both the spice trade and the silver that paid for it on the seas—where both have continued ever since.

Spanish mining was halted by the Moorish invasion of the eighth century. From that time until the fifteenth century some silver became available from Bohemia and Transylvania. This was mostly from a redistribution by means of war and plunder rather than from the earth.

In 1160, teamsters hauling salt along a road through the Harz Mountains found silver ore and brought about the opening of silver mines in Germany.

The vast quantities of silver found near Joachimsthal, in Bohemia, in the sixteenth century led to the opening of a mine. Coins were struck there and called "Joachimsthaler" which was shortened to "Thaler," from which our word dollar is derived.

From the Isle of Man to the Mediterranean silver was mined in ancient times, with the Roman mines in what is now Spain being the richest. However, these finds paled beside those of the New World.

Spanish discoveries after 1520 of silver in their new empire in Central and South America came in time for great developments in world trade in the sixteenth and seventeenth centuries, and possibly were in part a cause of them. Not only were the mines of Mexico, Bolivia, and Peru much larger but the ore was richer in silver than the European. It was not primarily a lead ore and could be yielded directly to cupellation.

Large quantities of silver were obtained for seventeenth-century Europe from Japan. The Portuguese first developed this trade but their later unpopularity caused their expulsion in 1624 and the trade was taken up by the Dutch who continued it until well into the nineteenth century.

With these exceptions, the world silver supply came from Spanish America until the revolt of the colonies, 1800–1820. During the 300 years from 1521 to 1821, when Spain ruled over Mexico, a steady stream of silver flowed to the mother country. Only the existence of reserves, increased use of gold, and the development of banking systems averted a crisis made imminent by the disruption of silver export. The situation was finally resolved by the discovery of tremendous new silver sources in the Sierra Nevada in the United States.

Soon after the accidental discovery, in 1859, of the colossal Comstock Silver Lode, on the eastern slope of Mount Davidson, in Nevada, the United States was established as the largest producer of silver—a position it retained until about 1900. The Comstock Lode was discovered by two Irishmen, O'Riley and M'Laughlin, who had been lured west after the California gold rush of 1849. As they worked for gold on the claim along the Carson River, they tossed aside some odd-looking, heavy blue rock as worthless. Henry Comstock, trapper and fur trader, recognized the blue rock and staked a claim adjacent to theirs and by "pure bluff induced them to waive their rights to the rock and be content with the surface gold they found." Rich silver ore, the blue rock assayed almost $4,000 a ton.

In February 1873 men struck that giant ore body, the Big Bonanza. It was in the district of the "silver mountains" in the California and the Consolidated Virginia mines. No single silver ore body has ever poured forth wealth at such an astounding rate; in a single month ore valued at six million dollars was mined.

Discoveries of new silver sources followed one another until Idaho, Utah, Arizona, Montana and other western states were among the big silver-producing regions.

According to mining experts, the "Big Bonanza" silver finds in the United States are a thing of the past. Much silver is still mined in this country but it comes mostly from mines which are worked primarily for their lead, copper, zinc, and gold—silver is a by-product.

The most common ore is called "Argentite"; another is called "red silver ore" and is abundant in Mexico, California, and Europe.

Today, most of the world's silver comes from mines in the North American Cordillera where it is associated with Tertiary intrusive volcanic rocks. Included in the rich belt which extends from Utah and Nevada through Mexico to Honduras are the rich districts in the United States of Comstock, Tonopah, and Tintic. In Mexico there is Pachuca, Guanajuato, Real del Monte, San Luis Potosí, Zacatecas, Fresnillo, Mapimí, Parral, Sierra Mojada, Santa Eulalia, and in Honduras the El Rosario Mine. The Coeur d'Alene district in Idaho and nearby areas in British Columbia are in another belt. Another well-known silver-producing belt lies in Colorado. The Cobalt District in eastern Ontario, Canada, is famous for its fabulously rich deposits of native silver.

From Peru through Bolivia and Chile to Argentina, in the South American Andes, lies a belt of rich deposits which, including Potosí in Bolivia, is the most productive district in the world.

Among the approximately sixty best-known silver minerals, the most important are native silver, argentite (Ag_2S), cerargyrite ($AgCl$), polybasite ($Ag_2S \cdot Sb_2S_3$), proustite ($3\ Ag_2S \cdot As_2S_3$), pyrargyrite ($3\ Ag_2S \cdot Sb_2S_3$), stephanite ($5\ Ag_2S \cdot Sb_2S_3$), and sylvanite ($AuAgTe_4$). Native metallic silver is ordinarily found alloyed with another metal such as antimony, copper, gold, mercury, or platinum. The natural alloy of silver and gold is called "electrum." Argentite, also called "silver-glance," is the commonest of silver minerals and contains 87.1 percent silver. It is black with a metallic luster. Horn silver, or cerargyrite, contains 75.3 percent silver and occurs in gray masses which turn black on exposure to light.

Metallurgy

Archaeological finds of silver ornaments and utensils attest to the antiquity of silver processing technology. Native silver ores were undoubtedly found by prehistoric man who may even have discovered that the metal could be reduced from silver chloride ores in a charcoal fire.

The earliest method of extraction of silver can be traced back to the Chaldeans of 2500 B.C. The commonest ore, consisting of silver and lead, was melted in a furnace called a cupel, from which is derived the name "cupellation process." A strong draught of air was allowed to strike the surface of the molten metal. The lead, or any other base metals present, oxidized through contact with the air, while silver did not. The resulting oxides formed on the top and could be removed by skimming. Repetition of this process exposed fresh surfaces of impure metal, which in turn delivered up the base metal as oxides, leaving relatively refined silver. The cupellation process is still used by native silversmiths in the Orient and by modern refineries when it suits the ores.

Silver-bearing lead ores of Mount Laurium, Greece, were concentrated by washing, reducive smelting, and cupellation by 1000 B.C.

A later process, used for centuries, by which silver was recovered from its ores, is amalgamation with mercury. Sometimes called the "patio" process, it was first used in 1557 at Pachuca, Mexico, and continued there until about 1925. It was carried out by the treading of mules all day long in a courtyard or *patio*, until their feet had broken up the ore and allowed the mercury to amalgamate with the silver. The mercury was then volatilized off by heating, leaving metallic silver as a residue.

At one time, silver was recovered from rich, yet simply structured oxidized ores by relatively crude methods. As these ores became scarcer and it was necessary to resort to the more complex and leaner ones, improved extractive technology was developed. Only about 1 percent of the present domestic silver production comes from the amalgamation and cyanidation of silver ores proper, the remaining being a by-product of base metal ores processed by flotation and smelting.

These processes produce a crude metal which needs refining. About 1400, alchemists discovered that silver could be separated from base metals with nitric acid. All metals, except gold, when placed in nitric acid go into solution. The addition of some copper returns the silver to solid form as a precipitate. This method, used until 1800, resulted in the purest silver then known. In the seventeenth century it was discovered that sulphuric acid could also be used. This process was first used on a large scale in Paris by D'Arcet in 1802 and later in London by Johnson, Matthey in 1871.

At the beginning of the twentieth century, electrolysis, the principle on which the plating of base metals is founded, was also adapted to the refining of silver and replaced the sulphuric-acid process. The crude silver plate (anode) is electrolyzed in a bath of dilute solution of silver nitrate depositing a crystalline silver on a second plate (cathode). This process produces a refined silver with a purity of more than 999 parts per thousand.

Uses for Silver

Though there is a great difference in the discovery of silver and the invention of uses for it, the art of working it must be almost as old as its discovery. For centuries, silver has been used for coinage and more recently as a monetary reserve as bullion to support paper currency. The principal consumer, however, is the silverware industry where it is used mostly in the fabrication of tableware of sterling silver—with lesser quantities being used to make jewelry, insignia, and novelties. The photographic industry ranks second as a consumer, with electroplating being third. Silver solders and brazing alloys containing 10 to 80 percent silver, are of increasing importance, and silver compounds, used for caustic, astringent, and antiseptic purposes in medicine are also invaluable. Silver has its uses as dental fillings and in surgery as suture plates and wires. While the addition of small amounts of copper to impart hardness to silver is well known, the addition of small amounts of silver to copper to impart hardness to commutator bars is less well known.

Domestic uses for silver increased rapidly as soon as it was available in large quantities. For centuries it had been a status symbol of the wealthy. It was not until the introduction of electroplating in the middle of the nineteenth century, when silverplated flatware became practical, that iron forks and knives were virtually banished from domestic tables. The widespread popularity of tea and coffee services and other hollow ware had to wait for the exploitation of silver from the Comstock Lode.

Silverplating

"Plate" strictly speaking, means, "wrought," or "flattened" silver and is derived from the Spanish *plata* and the Old French *plate*—the feminine form of *plat*. It is considered to be traceable to the Greek πλατύς.

Thus, the term "silverplate," though its use has long been sanctioned by custom, is actually incorrect—a tautology, or needless repetition. British usage of "plate" or "silverplate" is confined to solid silver, while in this country, when we speak of "silverplate," we ordinarily refer to electroplated wares formed of base metals and overlaid with silver.

The imitation of gold and silver by overlaying baser materials is an art practiced from earliest times. Ancient Egyptians were especially skilled in gilding. Assyrian metalworkers were successful in overlaying iron with bronze; their methods now are lost.

The Romans decorated their harness and armor with ornaments of silver copper, and copper vessels coated with silver have been found at Herculaneum. Mirrors of silvered tin were used by Roman ladies and were described by Pliny in his *Natural History.* He describes the method of applying gold or silver to articles of tin or copper. It is similar to the amalgamation process in that the precious metal was applied by an amalgam of mercury. He says, "The most convenient method for gilding copper would be to employ quicksilver [mercury]. The copper must first be well hammered, after which it is subjected to the action of fire. It is then cleansed of all extraneous substances, it being known by its brightness when it has been sufficiently purified. This done, it is again heated by fire in order to enable it when thus prepared, with the aid of an amalgam of pumice, alum, and quicksilver, to receive the gold leaf when applied." Silver was applied in the same way. He also says that a mixture of lead and tin, called "stannum," was used to cover copper drinking vessels since when "copper vessels are coated with stannum, they produce a less disagreeable flavour and the formation of verdigris is prevented."

Silversmiths of ancient Mexico and Peru were quite advanced in their knowledge and were masters in working gold and silver and in their imitations. Articles found in Peru are silverplated on copper by a process similar to "Old Sheffield Plating"—the two metals being fixed together by the action of heat *before* "making up." Among the relics of old Celtic days are ornaments discovered in Ireland of bronze inlaid, or "plated," with gold by a process which also must have been closely allied to "Old Sheffield Plate."

In Saxon times, when the goldsmiths' craft received support from Alfred the Great, English metalworkers practiced the art of overlaying baser metals with gold by amalgamation.

Though little remains of goldsmiths' work of Norman England, the names of goldsmiths have come down to us. For instance, the Monk Anketil was sent to the Danish Court to "Show and impart his skill in silver, gilding and jewellery." Through the centuries the art of gilding was practiced and by the fifteenth century the art of imitating silver had reached a high state of perfection. This trade had become so successful that it had to be controlled by law. Still later, the art of gilding and silvering baser metals was used and abused until, during the reign of James I, an Act of Parliament was passed to control the use of "gold and silver foliate" (*i.e.*, leaf).

Another method of silvering copper was employed about this time. A silver paste was rubbed onto copper without the application of heat. It was used especially for silvering the breastplates for coffins, as lack of durability for this purpose was of little importance.

Close-plating was usually employed in the covering of steel blades of knives. It was practiced in Sheffield but the center of the industry was Birmingham.

Articles to be close-plated were thoroughly cleaned, then immersed first into a solution of sal-ammoniac which acted as a flux, then immersed in molten tin. Thin silver foil was then applied and heated by means of a soldering iron, which caused the tin to melt and fuse the silver. The whole surface was then smoothed, burnished, and polished.

The two disadvantages to close-plate are that it is affected by heat and moisture. If placed in contact with a flame, the silver would disappear. In damp conditions the steel might rust and the plating peel off.

French plating, which originated in France, is often confused with close-plating. It differs only in that no intermediate solder is necessary, the silver being applied directly to the base metal. French plating was frequently employed in the manufacture of "Old Sheffield Plate" as a means of repairing a spot where the silver of the fused plate was accidentally rubbed away during the process of "making up."

Sheffield Plate

During the eighteenth century there was a growing desire for finer domestic vessels and tableware among the middle classes in England. Wooden or "treen" vessels had been replaced by pewter, which, in turn, was replaced by "China" ware. Silver was a great luxury, its value then being many times that of the present. What we now call "Old Sheffield Plate" had probably been known in England for a long period but in 1724 it was rediscovered by Thomas Bolsover and brought to public notice. Two or more ingots, silver and copper, were bound together with a small quantity of borax, placed in a furnace and heated until the exact moment of the union of silver and copper. This was then carefully and quickly withdrawn and allowed to cool. After cleaning, the resulting "sandwich" was reduced to the desired thickness by hammering or rolling. One basic difference between "Old Sheffield Plate" and electroplate is that the articles were formed *after,* not before, plating.

Articles made of "Old Sheffield Plate" were formed as was solid silver; many of the makers being silversmiths who continued to work in the traditional methods of "raising" the body of an article into shape from a flat sheet of metal by the use of mallets and hammers. Such hand-raised articles in "Old Sheffield Plate" are tempered by the constant alternation of hammering and annealing and will survive an astonishing amount of wear.

Today the market is flooded with supposedly genuine Sheffield Plate which is in reality copper electroplated with silver. Some pieces are marked "Sheffield Plate." Without exception, any piece so marked is NOT true "Old Sheffield" or fused plate.

Britannia

From the middle of the seventeenth century to the middle of the nineteenth, pewter was known as the "poor man's silver" in America. About 1820 some of these fragile vessels were replaced by the inexpensive and colorful earthenware Staffordshire dishes and by "Old Sheffield Plate." But the perfection of a "new" metal closely related to pewter created a new household ware and produced the men who were to found the electroplating industry in this country. This metal was called "Britannia."

Pewter and britannia have been confused since britannia's first introduction, but they differ substantially in composition of the metal, in methods of manufacture, and in appearance. Both are always composed principally of tin, copper, and antimony. Lead was an ingredient of most pewter while true britannia contains none. Pewter of good quality is bright but does not have the lustrous silvery sheen of britannia. Pewter is fabricated almost solely by casting in molds while britannia is also formed by stamping and spinning. Harder than pewter, britannia can be made with thinner walls. Stamping and spinning make feasible the production of shapes not possible by casting.

Britannia metal was an improvement on "white metal" first given commercial value by James Vickers, Sheffield, England, about 1769. This alloy consists mainly of tin hardened with antimony and a little copper.

Factory production methods and equipment used in the production of the new britannia wares lent themselves to electroplating. In fact, many early pieces of electroplate were on a britannia base.

The natural process of the electrodeposit of one metal upon another had been noted in ancient times and it was believed that transmutation of metals had occurred. Later, it was learned that silver could be deposited from solutions of its salts upon some other metals simply by immersing them and the process of "water silvering" was practiced in a small way. Not until the beginning of the nineteenth century were the laws regarding the deposition of metals by natural forces thoroughly explored. At that time the forces of electricity were studied and applied in science and manufacturing. The science of chemistry began to emerge from alchemy and the chemist ceased to be regarded as a sorcerer.

CHAPTER II

Early Electroplating and the Rise of Factories

Unlike the invention of fusion plating ("Old Sheffield Plate"), the beginnings of electroplating cannot be traced to one individual. The process was derived from a series of discoveries made early in the nineteenth century. As early as 1801, experiments in England established that a current of electricity passing through a conducting liquid decomposed the ingredients of that liquid and caused their elements to be set free at the two immersed electric poles. Perhaps Dr. Alfred Smee, who had done much early experimenting with electricity and who invented the battery bearing his name, had the earliest conception of the idea of the power of his galvanic battery to collect or disperse the invisible atoms of pure metal held in solution and to direct them for disposition on other metals. Application of this principle led to the birth of the electroplating industry.

At first regarded as a curiosity, no commercial application of electroplating seems to have been made for a number of years. But between 1836 and 1838 the English firm of G. R. & H. Elkington, of Birmingham, took out various patents, including one for "electro-gilding." Therefore, they are usually credited with the invention of electroplating. By 1838 they were electroplating buttons. John Wright, a surgeon and native of Sheffield, but practicing in Birmingham, discovered the need for cyanide of potassium in the plating solution. He submitted his process to the Elkington company who embodied it in their patent of 1840.

A representative of the Elkington firm came to the United States and attempted to interest New York firms in the possibilities of their new process but found little interest in it.

There can be no doubt that the Elkington firm was the first to make practical use of the new process, both by their patent, taken out in 1840, and by buying up other related patents. This firm secured almost all such patents so that anyone wishing to obtain instruction in the new process and to apply this method in plating his wares had to go to study in Birmingham, pay the firm a royalty of £150, and guarantee that he would not deposit less than 1,000 ounces of silver per year.

Several other English firms later profitably engaged in electroplating and exported vast quantities to this country. Among them were James Dixon & Sons, William Hutton & Sons, Mappin & Webb, Joseph Rodgers & Sons, John Round & Son, and Walker & Hall, all of Sheffield, and R. Pringle & Sons of London.

The Christofle firm of Paris was the first to apply the electroplating process to articles for household use in France. One patent for this method was purchased by them in 1840 from a chemist named Rouby. They also manufactured under a royalty owned by the Elkington company.

Much uncertainty surrounds the beginning of electroplating in this country. John O. Mead, britannia-ware manufacturer of Philadelphia, Pennsylvania, is generally credited with being the first.

Around 1830–1835 Mead was in charge of the silverplating and gilding work at the N. P. Ames Manufacturing Company of Chicopee, Massachusetts, using the old mercury-and-acid process. He went to England to learn the new plating technique and brought back a Smee battery and continued his experiments on his return. By 1845 he developed the first successful plating techniques. That same year he also formed a partnership in Hartford, Connecticut, with William and Asa Rogers under the name of Rogers & Mead. This company was soon dissolved. Mead returned to Philadelphia in 1846 and reestablished his business under the name John O. Mead, later Mead & Sons, while William and Asa Rogers founded the firm of Rogers Bros. early in 1847.

Other early experimenters in this country were numerous. Among them were James H. Isaacson, William H. Pratt, Sumner Smith, and William B. Cowles.

Shortly after Elkington's visit to New York, the *Journal of the Franklin Institute and Mechanics' Register* carried an article, taken from a British publication, outlining the method of electroplating by use of galvanic batteries. Sumner Smith, a member of the Institute, apparently read and profited by the article for in 1842 he advertised in the *Hartford Times* that he had discovered the "art of Gilding, Silvering, etc., by Galvanism, and any person wishing information in this beautiful art may obtain it of the subscriber for a moderate compensation." Immediately, several Hartford people began to experiment with the process, evidently having secured information from Smith. William H. Pratt in 1842 and Horace Goodwin, Smith's father-in-law, in 1844 advertised that they were doing silverplating.

Reverend Whitfield Cowles, pastor in Granby, Connecticut, added to his duties as minister and farmer and became a manufacturer in 1808. He made wire and was a peppermint distiller. He is also credited with making the first cotton cloth in that vicinity. In 1832 Cowles took his sons into business under the name of Whitfield Cowles & Sons. This business led to the first real development in commercial silverplating in this country. Whitfield Cowles died in 1840 and one or more of his sons continued the business under the name of Cowles & Company. In 1843 Asa Rogers, Jr., and James H. Isaacson joined the Cowles company and began silverplating spoons. Records show that the plating was being done at the Cowles plant in the latter part of 1843, and that by 1844 plated goods were being manufactured and sold in considerable quantities. Some, if not all, carried the Cowles name as a trademark. They were so successful that it was decided to organize a new company under which the spoon business would be further developed. This took place November 13, 1845, when the Cowles Manufacturing Company was formed by William B. Cowles, Asa Rogers, Jr., James H. Isaacson, and John D. Johnson. William Rogers gave financial assistance to the new firm and in the Hartford newspaper in 1846 he advertised that he was selling to the trade the products of the Cowles Manufacturing Company.

The Cowles factory in Spoonville (Granby, Connecticut) between 1843 and 1846 was a veritable training school for workers in the new process of silverplating as well as the making of German silver blanks for plating. Scores of men who had some previous experience in the making of coin-silver spoons as well as many young men with no previous training were employed there.

The Sperry brothers, Egbert W., Albert A., and William, and Alfred W. Sperry, a son of Egbert W., who were associated from time to time with the Rogers brothers, were there.

Andrew W. and Horace Fox, before and after their Granby association, were silversmiths in Hartford. In 1846, Marshall Forbes, then only 16 years old,

II. EARLY SILVERPLATING AND THE RISE OF FACTORIES 23

was learning how to plate and burnish silverware in Granby. A few years later he left, going to Wallingford, Connecticut, where he worked for Samuel Simpson. By 1854 he was in Meriden, Connecticut, working in the plating room of the Meriden Britannia Company being placed in charge of that work a short time later where he continued as superintendent the remainder of his life.

There were many others who had their first instructions in silverplating under the supervision of Asa Rogers, Jr., and Isaacson but the list is too long to include here. The Cowles plant in Granby was undoubtedly the first place where the experimenting that had been going on in Hartford was put to practical use and enabled the producer to supply spoons and forks of uniform quality.

During this time William Rogers with his brother Simeon maintained a jewelry and silversmith's shop in Hartford. Before that, William as well as Asa, Jr., had been making coin-silver spoons starting about 1825. They had built up a solid reputation for the quality of their coin-silver spoons and did not wish to risk their reputation by sponsoring the sale of silverplate until they determined that it was of good quality. In 1846 Asa Rogers, Jr., and Isaacson left the Cowles firm and moved all their activities to the basement of William Rogers' store in Hartford (Fig. 1). There, in 1847, they began to plate and sell their spoons under the mark "Rogers Bros."

The three Rogers brothers were all, at one time or another, associated with or partners in various concerns making silverplated goods. It was they, more than any others, who established the silverplating industry in this country (Fig. 2).

Though the silverplated-ware industry in this country goes back to 1847

1. Rogers Bros. store, Hartford, Conn., as it appeared about 1847. *The Silver Standard*, Vol. 1, No. 1, 1905.

SILVER!

Invention studied out by
Rogers Bros.
will be perfected

Improved processes makes
Silver Plate
UNEQUALLED
for actual use

The Rogers Brothers Store, which has been located in State Street and has been headquarters for cutlery as well as making a specialty of silverware made exclusively of dollars, are now producing an entirely new and novel article in silverware. The first pieces were produced early this year. They are importing German silver spoons and forks, which by a new and unique process are coated with pure silver. This is an important discovery, as it is found that goods so treated have all the good qualities of solid silver and are really much stronger and practical for service. Wherever they have been shown they have been easily sold, and the three Rogers Brothers are now making arrangements to properly take care of the new business. To Asa H. Rogers is really due the credit of this new process, although Simeon has also made it a careful study. We predict for this enterprising firm a large measure of success, and shall await further developments with interest. The present place of business, which they now occupy and which undoubtedly be too small for any great period and will necessitate their building on or moving to larger quarters. For the present at least they anticipate still selling the old line which includes table cutlery of the best quality, with ivory, horn and other styles of handles, as well as spoons, forks, ladles, etc., made of pure silver and elegantly finished.

II. Early Silverplating and the Rise of Factories

and the struggles of the Rogers brothers in their little basement shop in Hartford, it was the britannia makers who made their efforts a commercial success. The mechanical genius of the Rogers brothers joined with the practical business ability of the britannia makers constituted the beginnings of plated-silverware manufacture as an industry.

As early as 1852 there were six or seven small britannia-ware manufacturers in Meriden, Connecticut. The idea occurred to one of these pioneers to combine the efforts of these individual makers into what became the Meriden Britannia Company (Fig. 3). The leaders of this new organization were well aware of the great potential value of the electroplating process. The Rogers brothers, though they had been moderately successful, were hampered by lack of capital and someone to market their product. The Meriden Britannia Company had both of these to offer, and an agreement was reached whereby the Rogers brothers produced the goods that were later to be described in the catalog of the Meriden Britannia Company, in 1867, as having "all the advantages of silver in durability and beauty at one-fifth the cost." In 1862 when the Rogers brothers' company had financial trouble, most of its tools, equipment, and the trademarks were bought by the Meriden Britannia Company and the three brothers, William, Asa, Jr., and Simeon went to Meriden to supervise the production of "1847 Rogers Bros." silverplate. All three were em-

2. Rogers Bros. advertisement about 1862, just prior to the taking over of the firm by Meriden Britannia Co. *The Silver Standard*, Vol. 4, No. 2, 1908.

3. The Meriden Britannia Co. in 1856 and 1863.

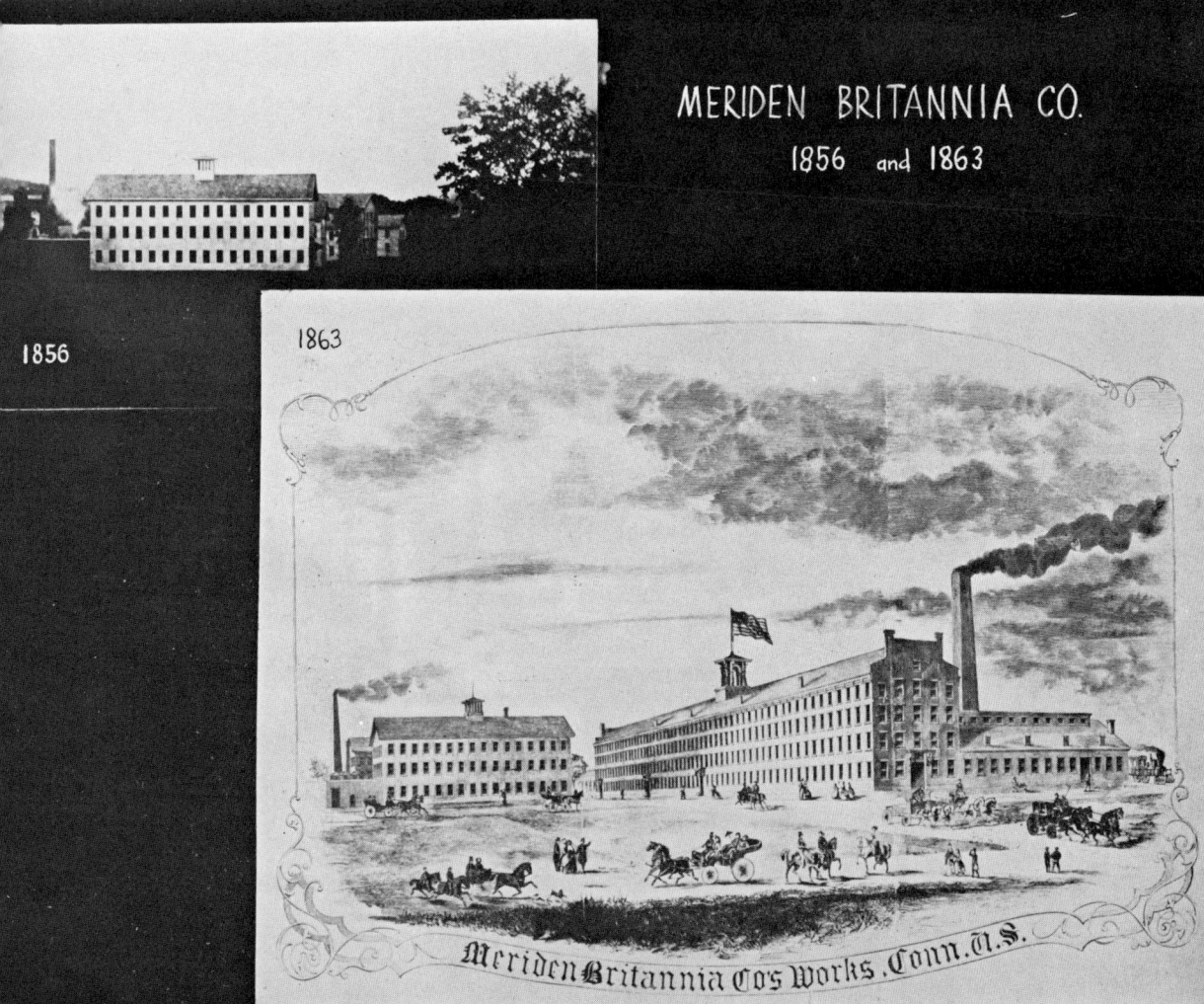

ployed by Meriden Britannia Company when they died. See front endpaper.

International Silver Company

The International Silver Company, Meriden, Connecticut, was incorporated in 1898 by a number of independent New England silversmiths whose family backgrounds began with the earliest American settlers. International has become not only world renowned for the quality of its fine silver, it has also become the world's largest manufacturer of silverware (Fig. 5).

Early records of this enterprise go back to Ashbil Griswold who in 1808 set up his pewter shop in Meriden, Connecticut, soon expanding his business to include britannia ware. Meriden became the center of pewter, britannia-ware, and coin-silver manufacturing through the efforts of Griswold and other independent makers who joined together to finance the Yankee peddlers responsible for selling and bartering these wares.

About the same time, the growing demand for coin-silver ware led the three Rogers brothers, William, Simeon, and Asa, Jr., to open their workshop in Hartford, Connecticut. The high cost of coin silver led to experiments in the new process of electroplating spoons and forks with pure silver.

In 1847 they perfected the process and marketed their first silverware under the trademark "Rogers Bros." Their fine workmanship and high quality material soon established the Rogers Bros. line throughout the country.

Britannia, more brilliant, harder, and more resistant to wear than pewter, was replacing pewter in many American homes. Several small factories in Meriden turned to the production of this new ware, most of which was marketed by Horace C. and Dennis C. Wilcox under the name of H. C. Wilcox & Co. The Meriden Britannia Company, which followed in 1852, offered German silver hollow ware and flatware for silverplating by 1855.

5. Main Office and silverplate hollow ware factory, International Silver Co., Meriden, Conn.

II. Early Silverplating and the Rise of Factories

In 1862 the Rogers brothers, who had been making and selling plated silverware in Hartford, moved to Meriden and joined the Meriden Britannia Company. Their "1847 Rogers Bros." trademark was an important addition to that company.

Others, who had set up small shops in Connecticut, soon realized they could all work more efficiently and supply the demands of the public better by combining into one organization. The scope of the Meriden Britannia Company had become international with the establishment of London and Canadian branches and sales offices in New York, Chicago, and San Francisco. The Meriden Britannia Company was the leading spirit in the formation of the International Silver Company in November 1898.

Among the many independent companies (all in Connecticut except where otherwise listed) which then or later became part of the International Silver Company, either directly or indirectly through the Meriden Britannia Company, were the American Silver Company, Bristol, established in 1901; Barbour Silver Company, Hartford, 1892; Derby Silver Company, whose factory was located in Huntington (later called Shelton), across the Housatonic River from Derby, 1873; Forbes Silver Company, Meriden, 1894; Hall, Elton & Company, Wallingford, 1837; Holmes & Edwards Silver Company, Bridgeport, 1882; Holmes & Tuttle Manufacturing Company, Bristol, 1851; International Silver Company of Canada, Ltd., Inc., 1922; La Pierre Manufacturing Company, New York, New York, 1888; Maltby, Stevens & Company, Huntington (later called Shelton), 1879; Maltby, Stevens & Curtiss Company, Wallingford, 1884; Manhattan Silver Plate Company, Brooklyn, New York, 1877; Meriden Britannia Company, Meriden, 1852; Meriden Britannia Company, Ltd., Hamilton, Ontario, Canada, 1879; Meriden Silver Plate Company, Meriden, 1869; Middletown Plate Company, Middletown, 1864; Norwich Cutlery Company, Norwich, 1890; Parker & Casper Company, Meriden, 1867; C. Rogers & Bros., Meriden, 1866; Rogers Cutlery Company, Hartford, 1871; Wm. Rogers Mfg. Co., Ltd., Niagara Falls, Ontario, Canada, 1911; Rogers Bros., Hartford, 1847; Rogers & Bro., Waterbury, 1858; Rogers & Hamilton Company, Waterbury, 1886; Rogers, Smith & Company, Hartford, 1856; Simpson, Hall, Miller & Company, Wallingford, 1866; Simpson Nickel Silver Company, Wallingford, 1871; Standard Silver Company of Toronto Company, Ltd., Toronto, Ontario, Canada, 1895; Watrous Manufacturing Company, Wallingford, 1896; E. G. Webster & Son, Brooklyn, New York, 1886; E. G. Webster & Bro., Brooklyn, New York, 1863; Webster Manufacturing Company, Brooklyn, New York, 1859; Wilcox Britannia Company, Meriden, 1865; Wilcox Silver Plate Company, Meriden, 1867; Wilcox & Evertsen, New York, New York, 1892; and Wm. Rogers Mfg. Co., Hartford, 1865.

Today the International Silver Company is not only the world's largest manufacturer of silver tableware, it makes a broader variety of products than any other silverware manufacturer. The Hotel Division specializes in flatware and hollow ware designed for use by hotels, restaurants, airlines, railways, steamships, and institutions. About 30 different silverplated flatware patterns are currently produced by the International Silver Company for regular retail trade channels.

It is the only silver manufacturing company to maintain an historical library which houses an extensive collection of silverplated wares made by the company and its predecessors.

Reed & Barton

Other companies were quick to follow the Rogers brothers. Less than a year after they started their operations in

6. Taunton Britannia Manufacturing Co., later Reed & Barton, about 1830.

Hartford, Henry Reed made plans for a plating department and hired Deforest H. Peck, who had learned plating from the Rogers firm. Peck was soon supplanted by M. Brown, a plater from England.

The present firm of Reed & Barton, Taunton, Massachusetts, grew out of the business established in 1824 by Isaac Babbitt and William Crossman for the manufacture of britannia ware. It was first known as Babbitt & Crossman. Little is known of their early products but Edmund Porter, in his "Metallic Sketches" reported on their first teaware that, "The pots were stamped in lead dies under a screw press [not cast, as earlier pewter had been] and the bodies fluted like the English style."

In 1827 William A. West was taken into partnership and the firm name became Babbitt, Crossman & Company. A further change was made two years later when Isaac Babbitt sold his interest and Zephaniah A. Leonard purchased a one-third interest in the britannia works and the partnership of Crossman, West & Leonard was formed. Babbitt remained with the company as plant superintendent. It was also in 1829 that William Porter, the foreman, discovered a means of stamping hollow ware with ring dies, a process which became universal in sheet-metal work. Up to this time all hollow ware had to be shaped by a tedious process involving several dies in order to prevent the edges from wrinkling.

Need for funds for further expansion led to the dissolution of Crossman, West & Leonard in 1830 and to the formation of the joint-stock company, the Taunton Britannia Manufacturing Company (Fig. 6).

A new factory at Hopewell, an outlying section of Taunton on the Mill River, was built and in 1831 the manufacturing of britannia ware was shifted to the new factory. The manufacture of coffin plates, castor frames, tankards, church cups, christening bowls, soup ladles, and candlesticks began and in 1832 toast racks, soda dispensers, and fruit dishes were added. Teaware which had been the mainstay in 1830 declined after 1831. Pewter and britannia lamps, because of the increasing availability of whale oil, were in demand. The sudden popularity of castor sets led to a shift in emphasis in production. English design traditions continued with many pieces patterned after those made by James Dixon of Sheffield, England.

Early in 1832 William Crossman, William West, and Zephaniah Leonard sold their interest in the company to Horatio Leonard. Crossman remained with the company, later becoming superintendent. The new corporation was also called the Taunton Britannia Manufacturing Company. General downward business trends and strong competition from foreign markets led to the complete failure of the company in 1834. Only three people had faith to continue. They were the company sales agent, Benjamin Pratt; Henry Reed, a spinner, and his friend, Charles E. Barton, the solderer. Reed and Barton had both served their apprenticeships in the company and their main asset was their knowledge of britannia manufacturing. To this, Benjamin Pratt contributed his experience in salesmanship and in April 1835 the Taunton Britannia Manufacturing Company opened once again under new management. Reed and Barton rented a few of the tools and equipment of the old company while Pratt sold the wares on hand and tried to collect money owed the company. By the end of 1836, the business had survived and made slight gains. Horatio Leonard transferred to his son, Gustavus, all rights, title, and the stock and tools of the business. Soon afterwards an agreement was drawn up that left ownership of the factory itself in the Leonard family and granted to Reed and Barton one-third ownership each in the tools of the company as well as one-third interest in profits. The new company was known as Leonard, Reed & Barton and began business under the new name in 1837.

The year 1837 brought with it a depression replete with more failures than the country had ever seen, but once again the company managed to survive. Three new teaware patterns, numbers 2700, 2800, and 2900, have been credited for the company's success during this difficult period. These designs were English in origin and had already proven their worth.

By 1840 Henry Reed and Charles Barton purchased Gustavus Leonard's interest in the company. Leonard continued to work for the company as salesman-treasurer and the Leonard, Reed & Barton mark was used on some wares. However, when the company applied for a renewal of their trademark registration in 1886, they claimed that the name "REED & BARTON" had been used since August 26, 1840 (back endpaper). Possibly both marks were used from 1840 to 1847 when Henry H. Fish, brother-in-law of Leonard, purchased a one-third interest. At his entry, the old mark was dropped entirely.

Manufacturers frankly copied English designs, being more concerned with manufacturing problems than style. The introduction of each new Dixon pattern led to a flurry of activity. In the 1830s and in 1840 each new design was marked by an increase in rugged simplicity as thoughts of the gracious Georgian era faded.

Early in the 1830s the new alloy, German or nickel silver, was introduced from England. Henry Reed was among the first American manufacturers to see its advantages and by 1838, almost ten years ahead of the others, Leonard, Reed & Barton were manufacturing nickel-silver castor frames. By 1840 they were also experimenting with some flatware.

By 1848 Reed & Barton were turning their attention to plated silverware. Their first plater, Deforest H. Peck, was with the company only a year, when an expert plater named Brown was brought from England. Henry Reed learned from Brown and for a time did all the plating himself. Reed & Barton applied its plating process to their regular line of britannia ware but nickel silver was found to be more durable and satisfactory and its use spread.

In the late 1850s new types of decoration began to appear. In 1852 Reed &

Barton hired their first chaser and floral patterns were carefully incised on their wares. Engine-turning also became popular and Reed & Barton wares were for some time sent to Boston to be decorated with fine geometric patterns. By 1860 they installed their own lathe for this purpose.

Gradually it was recognized that the design of their products was important and in 1854 William Parkin was brought from England to cut the dies for teaware. Parkin also did some of the designing. Numerous designs were patented by Parkin though the first Reed & Barton patent, a tea-service design, was recorded January 12, 1858, in the name of Henry Reed. *(See Chapter V, Figs. 12, 12a, 12b.)*

The formation of the Meriden Britannia Company in 1852 in Meriden, Connecticut, was to have far-reaching effects, not only on Reed & Barton, but also on the entire britannia and plated silverware industry. Formed by a merger of several small Connecticut firms, the Meriden Britannia Company was essentially a selling organization. Their aggressive marketing program made obsolete former selling practices. They purchased large quantities of goods from other manufacturers in order to present complete lines to dealers. Other companies soon followed suit. This often placed the manufacturer in the position of competing with his own goods. Articles manufactured by Reed & Barton might be sent to Hartford for a coating of Rogers Bros. silverplate and then appear in the market with a "Rogers Bros." mark in competition with the Reed & Barton plated line.

Practically none of the britannia or plated-silver manufacturers could supply a complete line. Reed & Barton and the Meriden Britannia Company offered the greatest assortment, yet Reed & Barton bought most of its flatware from Rogers & Bro. of Waterbury, Connecticut, and the Hartford Manufacturing Company. They produced little of their own flatware except for the hotel trade until the 1860s. On the other hand, Rogers & Bro. in 1865 was one of Reed & Barton's best customers for hollow ware.

The depression of 1866 and 1867 following the Civil War brought about the failure of many jobbing concerns, a large number of which abandoned plating and confined their activities to the wholesale business.

A growing market for hotel ware not only provided in itself a considerable source of sales but also encouraged the development of flatware for domestic use. Reed & Barton manufacturing facilities had been limited to the production of spoons but by 1872 this production was expanded to include other types of flatware.

With the entry of the Gorham Manufacturing Company into the field of silverplated wares in 1865, launched with a vigorous advertising campaign, Reed & Barton the following year submitted their first advertising in the *Dunkley & Woodman Business Directory*. A larger advertising program was launched in *Harper's Weekly* in 1868.

Through the 1860s Henry Reed and William Parkin continued to design Reed & Barton wares. High-footed forms decorated with much chasing were prevalent. In December 1868 Henry Reed secured a patent for the first original Reed & Barton flatware pattern. It was called "Roman Medallion." *(See page 433.)*

On September 13, 1867, Charles Barton died; Henry Reed was at his bedside. In 1868 a new partnership, consisting of Henry Reed, Henry Fish, and George Brabrook, who had long been active in marketing, was formed. Each assumed a third interest. The name of the firm continued unchanged. In February 1888 the company was incorporated.

During the 1870s and 1880s Reed & Barton products were in line with those of other companies in design. The old, gracefully curved teapot handles, for instance, had given way to angular forms. Bodies of the ware were covered with an array of decorative detail, little of which bore any relation to form.

While some of the designs of that period may lack merit, Reed & Barton workmanship, especially in burnishing and casting, exhibited a skill not surpassed by any firm today.

In 1875 W. C. Beattie was brought from England to be Reed & Barton's first full-time designer. He was followed by an increasing number of foreign-trained designers who exerted their influence, with the results being apparent by the late 1880s. From 1890 to 1900, though silverware was characterized by ornateness, decoration was adapted to form and most was in good taste.

From 1911 to 1913 a moderately low-priced line was marketed under the name Reed Silver Company. And in the 1930s the Viking Brand of plated hollow ware was brought out, but terminated in 1941. Both lines were discontinued because they did not come up to the standards expected of the Reed & Barton Company.

The newest facility of the Reed & Barton plant is a modern plated hollow ware department (Fig. 8). The new building replaced seven old ones. Great emphasis has been placed on the handling of materials. Raw materials come in at one end and with continuous, in-line production, finished products come out at the other. Among the new machinery installed is a huge, highly versatile, and efficient plating machine.

The Gorham Company

The Gorham Company, Providence, Rhode Island, showed its first real interest in silverplating when John Gorham, son of the founder, went to England on May 1, 1852, to become an apprentice to the Elkington firm in Birmingham. He also worked with James Dixon & Sons of Sheffield to learn to make white-metal hollow ware. He brought a group

8. Reed & Barton plant with the new plated hollow ware building in the foreground.

of English workmen with him on his return. Then in 1854 George Wilkinson, English silversmith, was lured to the Gorham plant from the Ames Manufacturing Company of Chicopee, Massachusetts, to supervise the silverplating. Technical difficulties encountered and the intervention of the Civil War, which made it necessary to abandon the use of silver as a basic material, delayed the production of their first electroplated wares until 1865.

Little mechanical progress had been made until this time in the manufacture of silverware. The method of making teaspoons at that time was crude and laborious by present standards. An ingot of silver was rolled to a thickness equivalent of the shank of the spoon. The bowl and the upper part of the handle were forged to a proper thickness with a hand hammer. The rolls were revolved by a windlass, and during the process, as the silver became too hard to work, it was necessary to heat it nine successive times on an ordinary blacksmith's forge before the spoons were finished. Two men, by hard work, could make two dozen teaspoons in a working day of ten hours. John Gorham was a pioneer in the fast-moving industrial revolution. He quickly recognized the advantages of machinery and as a result the Gorham Company was among the first to introduce factory methods to augment hand craftsmanship in the production of silverware. He designed and made much of the machinery himself when none was available to suit his purposes.

The Gorham Company ceased production of silverplated flatware May 1, 1962, but their silverplated hollow ware continues to be an important part of their output.

Wallace Silversmiths

Wallace Silversmiths, Wallingford, Connecticut, was founded by Robert Wallace who began making spoons of German silver for Hall, Elton & Company in 1834.

In 1834 when Wallace had been in his small factory about a year, he was shown a spoon by one of his patrons in New Haven. It was made of a metal that was new to both of them. It was called German silver. A Dr. Feuchtwanger, an analytical chemist, was known to have brought a small bar of this metal from Germany. Wallace succeeded in purchasing this bar, took it to Waterbury, had it rolled, and from the sheet made four dozen spoons. While in Waterbury, Wallace purchased the formula for the new metal from a gentleman recently arrived from England. Soon afterwards he moved his factory to Wallingford and enlarged it in order to expand the manufacture of spoons and other flatware. He immediately began the compounding of the new metal, becoming the first to manufacture the new German or nickel silver in this country.

Later, a partnership with Samuel Simpson was formed under the name of R. Wallace & Co. At the end of ten years, in 1865, the firm name became Wallace, Simpson & Co., and this is the first mark to be found on Wallace plated ware. In 1871 the corporate name was changed to R. Wallace and Sons Mfg. Co. and to Wallace Silversmiths in 1956. Since 1861 they have produced large quantities of silverplated hollow ware.

Oneida Silversmiths

The Oneida Company was founded by John Humphrey Noyes in 1848 at Oneida Creek, New York, as an experiment in communal living. It was not until 1877 that the Oneida Community embarked on the manufacture of tableware.

Iron spoons in two patterns, "Lily" and "Oval," were their first tablewares. Production of these eventually led to their line of Community Plate which was introduced in 1902. *(See chapter X, "Flatware," pages 435–436.)*

They began the production of silverplated hollow ware in 1926.

Tiffany & Company

Tiffany & Company, New York City, silversmiths and merchants, was founded in 1837 as Tiffany & Young. The firm underwent several changes in name and was finally incorporated in 1853 as Tiffany & Company. Electroplating was added to their endeavors in 1870.

The Tiffany company had an interest in the Adams & Shaw plated-ware factory, Newark, New Jersey. Caleb Cushing Adams, president, was a silversmith in New York City from around 1876 to 1880. Thomas Shaw, head of the manufacturing, had learned electroplating at Elkingtons of Birmingham, England, and came to America about 1860. He settled first in Providence, Rhode Island, where he worked for the Gorham Company, which was then trying to break into the trade in electroplate. In connection with Tiffany & Company he formed the manufacturing company of Thomas Shaw & Company. By 1876 it was listed as Adams & Shaw. The *Jewelers' Circular & Horological Review*, Vol. VII, August 1876, p. 99, carries a notice of the opening of Adams & Shaw sample offices at No. 1 Bond Street, New York City, for wholesale orders of sterling and electroplate. Following a fire in the Waltham Building, the factory was removed to Newark, New Jersey, and located at Park Street, corner of Mulberry, 1878–1880. Both Adams and Shaw were skilled designers and both had worked for the Gorham Company. Adams was for 18 years the predecessor of Edward Holbrook as general manager of the Gorham Company. Each had relatives associated in silversmithing. John P. Adams, brother of C. C. Adams, was owner of Adams, Chandler & Co., jewelers of New York City. Shaw had a son, Frank, who was also a fine designer. He became tubercular and was sent to Colorado in 1885 to stay with another brother, Walter. He wrote his father from there and sent sketches of designs he was making for him. Frank Shaw was an able draftsman and inventive designer who unfortunately died at the age of twenty-four.

Homan Manufacturing Company

One of the few silverplate-manufacturing companies outside the northeastern part of the country to gain prominence was the Homan Manufacturing Company of Cincinnati, Ohio. It was established in 1847 by Henry Homan and Asa F. Flagg. The Cincinnati city directories of 1842–43 and 1846 list Asa F. Flagg as a britannia manufacturer. Flagg was so devoted to his work that he was known locally as "Pewter" Flagg. The partnership was first formed to manufacture pewter. They also manufactured britannia wares until Flagg's retirement in 1854. About 1864 the company gradually changed from the manufacture of pewter, britannia, and German silver to electroplated silverware. They became especially well known for their ecclesiastical wares, their Mississippi River boat equipment, bar equipment, and articles for domestic use.

While there is extreme doubt in regard to many "manufacturers" of silverplated wares outside the northeastern states, there can be no such doubt about the Homan company. *The Watch Dial*, July 1888, p. 13, carries a detailed description of the factory and describes the manufacturing processes there including the smelting room, casting of handles, spouts, etc., spinning, soldering, plating, burnishing, and chasing.

Around 1896 the name of the firm was the Homan Silver Plate Company which was succeeded by Homan Manufacturing Company between 1904 and 1915. It went out of business in 1941.

Other Manufacturers

Many others became well known as manufacturers of silverplated wares. Additional hundreds entered the business

B. F. NORRIS, ALISTER & CO.,

113 AND 115 STATE STREET, CHICAGO, ILL.

We make a specialty of getting up Outfits that are Practical, Useful and Low in Price. We recommend these Plater's Outfits as being perfect in all respects, and the best ever offered to the trade.

OUR NEW IMPROVED $15.00 AND $25.00 BATTERY AND OUTFITS COMPLETE.

VIEW OF TRAVELING PLATER'S $25.00 OUTFIT IN PRACTICAL OPERATION FOR GOLD AND SILVER PLATING.

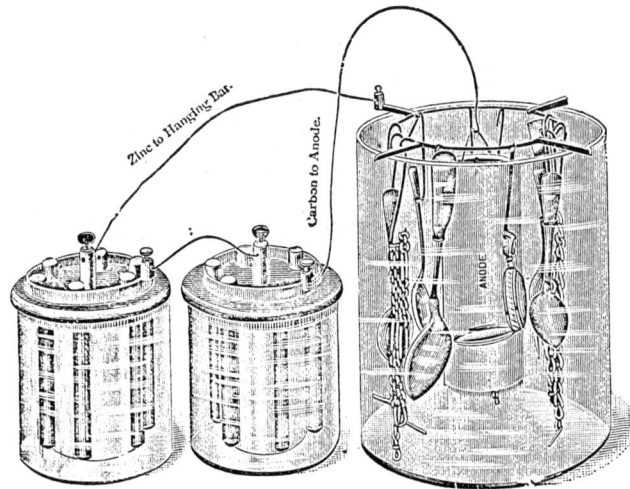

The following is a list of supplies which are included in our new improved $25.00 battery and outfit for gold and silver plating:

2 New Improved Equalizing Batteries.
1½ Gallon Silver Solution.
1 Bath for Silver.
1 Silver Anode.
Hanging Bars.
1 Quart Gold Solution.
1 Gold Anode.
1 Gold Bath.
1 Scratch Brush.
1 Cleaning Brush.
1 Fine Brush.
1 Straight Burnisher.
1 Burnisher for Bowls of Spoons.
1 Box Polishing Rouge.
1 Box Polishing Whiting.
1 Box Pumice Stone.
Copper Wire, Coarse.
Copper Wire Fine.
Hanging Hooks.
Anode Hooks.
Book of Instructions.

This set will plate from 2 to 3 dozen spoons at a time, or a caster.
Boxed ready for shipping

This cut represents the Improved Equalizing Battery of the Traveling Plater's Outfit, with the method of connection.
The glass jar is used to show the articles as they appear in the bath.
The cut is merely to represent methods of connection and arrangement of work in bath.
The tube in the center of hanging Bar is the Anode bent round, so as to give an equal surface to all the work.
To connect the batteries together, run a wire from the carbon of one to the zinc of the other.

OUR IMPROVED $15.00 GOLD, SILVER AND NICKEL PLATING OUTFIT COMPLETE.

The following is a list of supplies included in our improved $15.00 battery outfit;

3 Batteries.
1 Gallon Silver Solution.
1 Bath for Silver.
1 Silver Anode.
Hanging Bars.
Gold Solution, 1 Pint.
1 Bath for Gold.
1 Gold Anode.
Nickel Solution, 2 Gallons.
1 Nickel Anode.
1 Cleaning Brush.
1 Fine Brush.
1 Steel Burnisher.
Copper Wire, Coarse.
Copper Wire, Fine.
Chemicals for Charging Batteries.
Hanging Hooks.
Anode Hooks.
1 Box Polishing Rouge.
1 Box Pumice Stone.
1 Box Whiting.
Book of Instructions.

VIEW OF $15.00 OUTFIT IN PRACTICAL OPERATION.

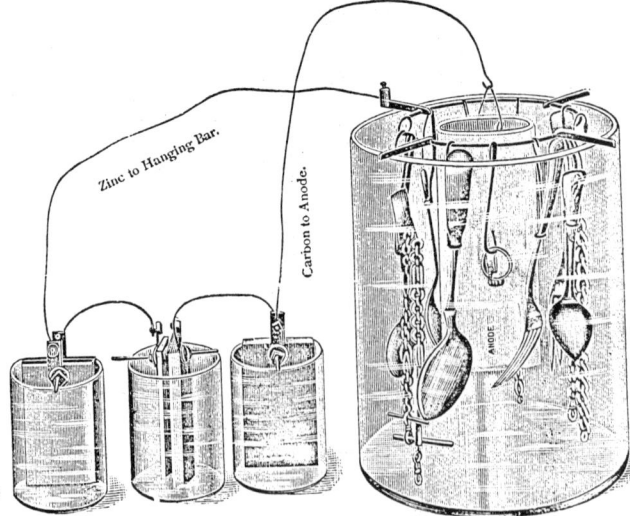

This set will plate from 9 to 12 spoons, knives, forks, etc, such as the case may be, at a time.

This cut represents the method of connecting the three batteries together, also connection with the bath, and the use of the New Improved Hanging Bar, also Hanging Hooks.
The glass jar is used so as to show the articles as they appear in the bath.
The cut is merely to represent methods of connection and arrangement of work in bath.
The Tube in the center of Hanging Bar is the Anode bent round, so as to give an equal surface to all the work.
To connect the batteries together, run a wire from the carbon of one to zinc of the other.

☞ Your orders will be carefully attended to.

B. F. NORRIS, ALISTER & CO., 113 & 115 State Street, CHICAGO.

II. Early Silverplating and the Rise of Factories

as small manufacturers or as silverplaters. For only a modest investment it was possible to set up a silverplating shop (Fig. 9). Many took advantage of this to establish companies which purchased articles "in the metal" to be silverplated and stamped with their own names. Even those who manufactured some wares themselves purchased additional items in order to offer their customers a complete line. This type of cooperation within the industry was especially prevalent in the late 1860s, when even the larger manufacturers engaged in this practice.

In the middle 1860s jobbers and retailers who operated their own plating shops purchased two-thirds of the Reed & Barton factory output. They purchased quantities of wares "in the metal," plated them, and sold them with their own trademarks.

The advantage of the practice of purchasing pieces "in the metal" and plating them was one of economics. There were not any government standards set forth for the amount of silver to be deposited on a piece. In a very short time a coating of silver could be put on by the rankest amateur. The customer had no way of knowing the thickness of the deposit, how clean the pieces had been before plating, or how well the silver deposit was burnished. The companies that have stayed in business have done so because their work has stood the test of time. Cheap plating jobs came off in a short time and the plating business disappeared almost as rapidly as the poor work it had done. Making the dies for original patterns was, and still is, an extremely expensive operation. Only a firm with substantial backing could afford to have dies cut for original patterns. This was especially true until after William Gale invented the double-die process which he patented. The development of the drop hammer and shaped dies brought down the costs. Because of the tremendous expense involved, many of the first patterns sold in this country were produced from blanks made in England and brought here for plating.

9. Advertisement of simple silverplating outfit. With such an outfit even the amateur could go into the silverplating business. *American Jeweler*, September 1892.

10. Waste bowl marked "Kann & Sons Co., Quadruple Plate, Balto."

It is not unusual to find identical pieces bearing different trademarks, or no marks at all.

Most manufacturing was confined to the New England and northeastern states, though a few manufacturers, such as the Homan Manufacturing Company of Cincinnati, Ohio, became known throughout the country. Most of the firms outside the northeastern section (Fig. 10) bought their wares already formed but unplated, and applied their own silverplating and stamped on their own names. *(See spoon holders, Chapter VII, Figs. 196, 197.)*

Examples of this type are numerous. A cake basket, for instance, marked "Springfield Silver Plate Co., Springfield, Massachusetts," is identical to one illustrated in the August 1867 Meriden Britannia Company catalog. *(See also Chapter VII, Figs. 72–73.)* Comparison with old catalogs is not always conclusive evidence of the actual manufacturer since identical catalogs were published bearing names of different "manufacturers."

Baltimore city directories list several "manufacturers of silverplated wares." But Baltimore suffered several disastrous fires with the resultant loss of records, making it difficult to determine if any actual manufacturing was done there. However, the repeated discoveries in the Baltimore area of certain design features on silverplated wares, which repeat designs of the Kirk silversmiths of Baltimore, do cause speculation as to their origin (Figs. 11, 12).

Pieces bearing San Francisco's Haynes & Lawton name *(see castor, Chapter VII, Fig. 11)* also bear a soldered-on mark of the type often used when wares were fabricated by one company to be plated and sold by another. An advertisement of Haynes & Lawton found in the 1869 San Francisco Directory, which describes their silverplating and refers to them as "Agents for Pacific Plate Works" tends to substantiate the belief that they were silverplaters, not manufacturers (Fig. 13). So does the following quotation. "Silverplating under the older methods have been practiced in San Francisco for a number of years, the articles being made of equal quality to the same work imported. During the past year, however, a new branch of the business, viz., electrotyping has been introduced in San Francisco by the Pacific Plate Works, Haynes & Lawton being the agents. By this process excellent work is done, the designs being elegant and the standard coating of metal of a purity and thickness not to be excelled." (Henry Langley, *The Pacific Coast Almanac for 1869*, San Francisco, 1869, p. 69.)

11. Sugar bowl with ram's head handles obviously derived from the Kirk design.

12. Sugar dish made by Samuel Kirk, Baltimore, Md., about 1822.

Silverplating had become an important endeavor in San Francisco by the 1870s as evidenced by the advertisement of the San Francisco Plating Works found in the *Report of the Eighth Industrial Exhibition of the Mechanics,* held there September 1871 (Fig. 14).

13. Haynes & Lawton advertisement, San Francisco City Directory, 1869.
14. Advertisement of San Francisco Plating Works. *Report of the Eighth Industrial Exhibition of the Mechanics,* September 1871.

HAYNES & LAWTON,

THE OLDEST ESTABLISHED

CROCKERY HOUSE

IN CALIFORNIA,

Offer to the inspection of the Public, the largest and best selected Stock of

English Earthenware, French Porcelain,

AMERICAN AND FRENCH GLASSWARE,

Ivory Handle Table Cutlery, Elegantly Decorated Dinner, Tea, Dessert and Toilet Sets,

Ever exhibited on this Coast, at their Spacious Warerooms,

516, 518, 520 and 522 SANSOM ST.

SAN FRANCISCO.

PACIFIC PLATE WORKS,

Established with the view of furnishing a Reliable Article of

Silver Plated Ware,

Which shall be equal in Durability & Finish to the Imported Goods.

The Plating will all be executed upon

NICKEL SILVER

AND

White Metal.

All articles issued from the Works are guaranteed to have the full deposit of Silver. Articles from which the silver has been worn can be re-plated at a moderate charge.

HAYNES & LAWTON,

AGENTS FOR PACIFIC PLATE WORKS

SILVER MEDAL

Awarded at Mechanics' Institute Exhibition of 1871

FOR THE BEST

GOLD & SILVER PLATING,

BY THE

SAN FRANCISCO PLATING WORKS,

655 MISSION STREET,

Between New Montgomery and Third,   SAN FRANCISCO.

Every description of goods, (including Table Ware,) from which the silver is worn, re-plated in the best manner. A large assortment of new styles of Plated Ware and Cutlery on hand and for sale at the lowest rates. New and elegant styles of Door Plates and Numbers furnished. The interests of Manufacturers consulted by plating home-made goods at prices that will compete with the East. A liberal discount made to the Trade. Gold-Saving, Silver-Plated Amalgamating Plates, for Miners' use, furnished to order.

All Goods warranted First-Class in every respect.

EDWARD G. DENNISTON, Proprietor.

CHAPTER III

Manufacturing and Marketing

Base Metals Used in Silverplating

The quality of silverplated ware is dependent in part upon the type of base metal used in manufacturing the blanks to be plated. The metals most commonly used are nickel, tin, antimony, and copper.

Nickel silver is the most satisfactory base metal for silverplated ware. It is of fine, even grain, and is similar to silver in appearance. It is more durable than other alloys, although the degree of durability varies with the proportion of nickel used. This is usually 65 percent copper, 5 to 25 percent nickel, and 10 to 30 percent zinc.

Prior to the early nineteenth century virtually the only metals available for the fabrication of flatware and hollow ware were solid silver and pewter. Metallurgy had not yet developed other suitable alloys.

In 1823 a society devoted to promoting industry in Prussia offered a prize for an alloy which, while similar in appearance to silver, should not cost more than one-sixth as much and should be suitable for tableware. A year later two German scientists, working independently, produced an alloy of nickel which met these specifications. It was called German silver, later to be known as nickel silver.

The formula was kept a closely guarded secret for many years but the metal itself was imported into the United States to be made into flatware and hollow ware. In 1834 A. H. Hagenmacher patented what was at that time described as "a new American silver." It was similar to the nickel alloy developed in Germany, and was used, according to the advertisements in the *Greenfield* [Massachusetts] *Gazette*, for the manufacture of "tea sets, including forks, spoons, etc., usually made of real silver."

About that same time Robert Wallace of Wallingford, Connecticut, and, a bit later, Benedict & Burnham of Waterbury, Connecticut, obtained the formula and began rolling German silver.

Silverplated hollow ware may be divided into two basic classes; that is, "hard metal" ware and "soft metal" ware. The best quality ware is "18 percent" meaning that the alloy is 18 parts nickel, 22 parts zinc, and 60 parts copper. When polished, this alloy is so white it is difficult to distinguish from silver.

"Soft metal" wares are made on a white metal or britannia metal base. The precise composition varies with the individual manufacturer but white metal is an alloy composed principally of tin, antimony, and copper. Lead and bismuth may also be added. Most hollow ware made from soft metal is produced by the spinning process which is why "soft metal ware" is often referred to as "spun ware." Spun ware is turned on a lathe and, while the method requires more operators, the machinery used is less expensive and the heavy die cost of harder metals is eliminated. Among the several disadvantages to soft metal ware are the ease with which pieces are dented and the inability to

40 AMERICAN SILVERPLATE

withstand heat. White metal is easily worked and is now used principally for trim and attached parts.

Copper and brass are used as base metals for many hollow ware articles, particularly in reproduction of antiques and in ecclesiastical ware. They are less expensive and more malleable than nickel silver, but are less durable; also, when silverplating is worn away from edges, they present a sharp contrast.

While nickel silver and white metal are more often used as base metals than copper and brass, between 1931 and 1935 copper and brass were used frequently because of their relative smaller cost. Also, since copper was used in the manufacture of "Old Sheffield Plate," the general public has the impression that it possesses a particularly desirable quality.

Federal specifications call for nickel silver as a base metal for silverplated tableware of all kinds for government use, unless white metal is specifically named.

Flatware blanks, almost without exception, are made of 18 percent nickel silver. Blanks for hotel hollow ware are also made of 18 percent nickel silver, while those for commercial distribution

2. Apple-blossom design for silver mounts. Design Patent No. 36,280; April 7, 1903; Seth H. Leavenworth, Cincinnati, Ohio; Assigned to Homan Silver Plate Co.
1. Trumpet-flower design for "Silversmith's Stock." Design Patent No. 32,331; March 13, 1900; Seth H. Leavenworth, Cincinnati, Ohio; Assigned to Homan Silver Plate Co.

are made of 10 percent nickel silver. Commercial hollow ware of second grade is made on a copper or white-metal base. Mounts or borders are almost always of white metal; these are soldered in place on the blank before plating (Figs. 1, 2).

The silver used for plating is 999/1000 pure.

Production Methods

Each new silver pattern begins in the design department of the silver manufacturer and each is the result of many months of work. New patterns have their beginnings in the creative minds and hands of talented industrial designers who are artists of international reputation (Fig. 3). Dozens of designs are sketched, discussed, drawn, and redrawn while the appearance of each is considered from all angles. Scale and proportion, beauty of line, style and type of decoration, fitness of design, ease of handling, and use are all carefully considered.

After a design is accepted, a master craftsman, who is also a talented artist, carves and hand-chases a sample piece, while a modeler makes a greatly enlarged three-dimensional model in wax (Figs. 4, 5). This wax model is then cast in plaster of Paris. This creates a reverse mold into which melted bronze is poured to make a working enlargement. When completed, these bronze master models are used with a die-cutting machine which operates in principle similar to an artist's pantograph, and roughs out the die in blocks of steel. After this, patient, painstaking hand-

3. A flatware pattern begins with the artist who sketches the design.

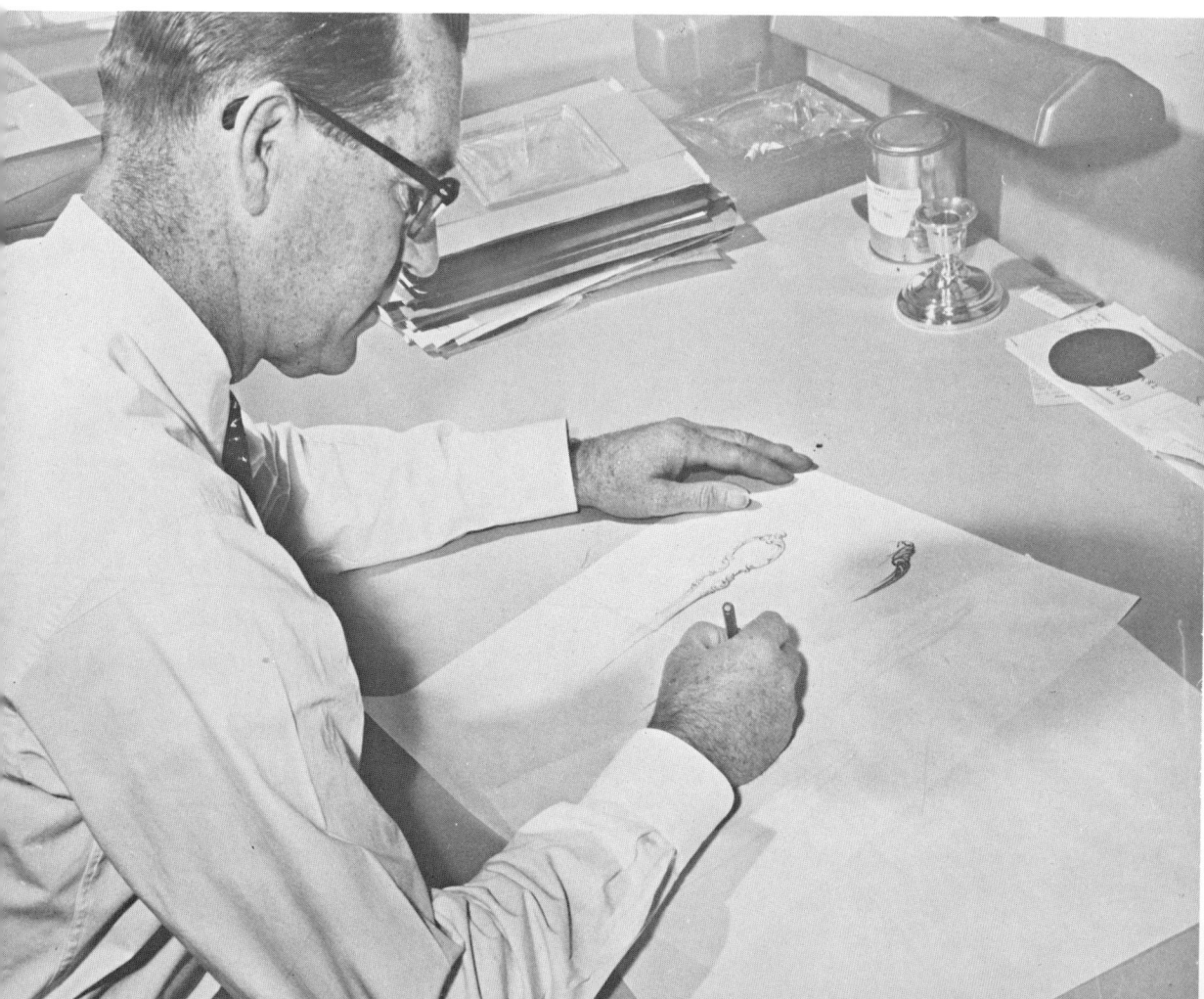

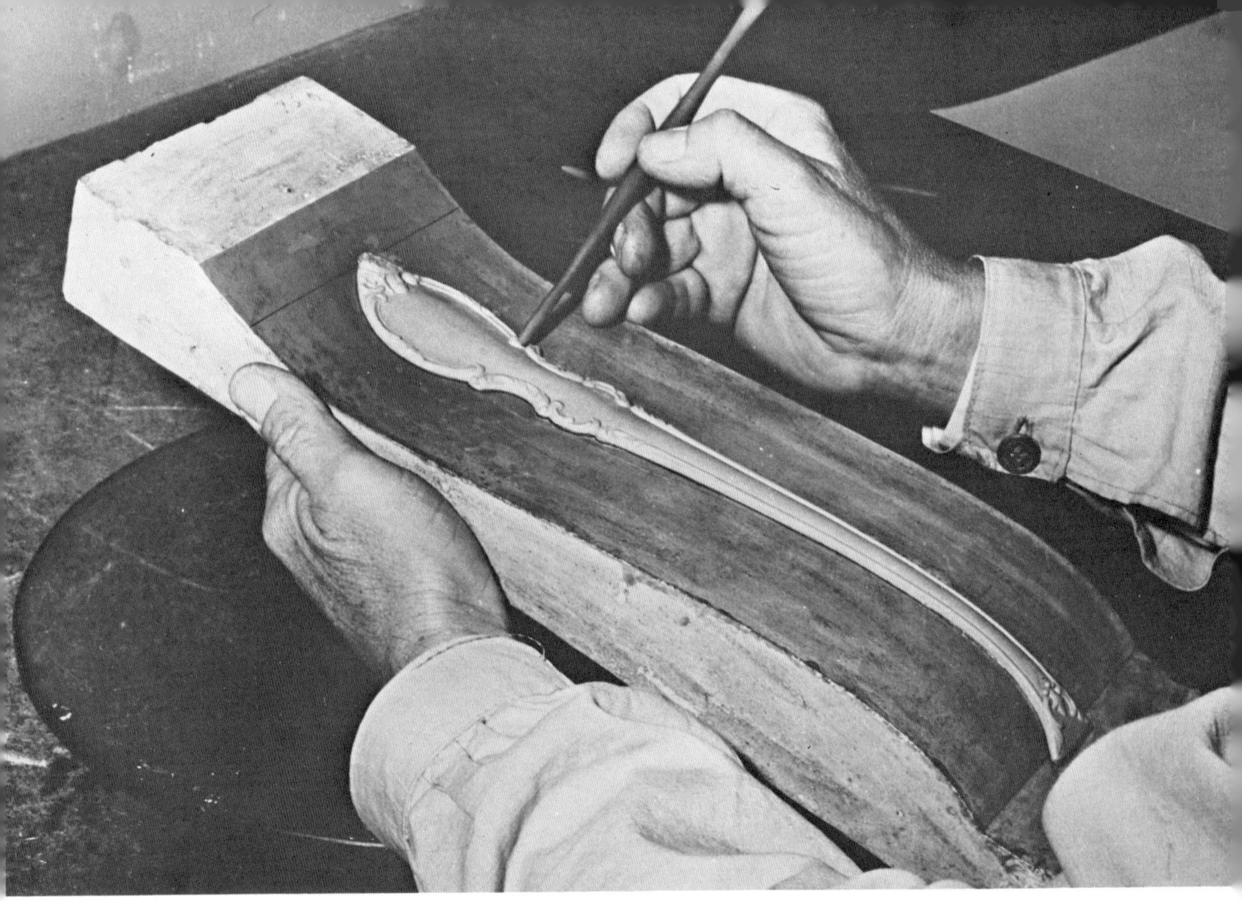

III. Manufacturing and Marketing 43

4. A model of the design is fashioned in red wax about twice the size of the tablespoon to permit every detail of the design to be brought out and perfected.

5. A handmade fork in sterling silver is completely chased by a master craftsman who is a talented artist. The height and depth of the design bring out the shadows and highlights.

6. *Sheet Metal*—The proper proportion of copper, zinc, and nickel are melted together in this electric furnace. The molten metal is then poured into molds where it hardens gradually, forming bars of nickel silver.

work of a highly skilled craftsman transforms the rough die into a finished and highly polished one. When completed, the dies must be hardened in order to withstand the continual pounding of heavy drop presses. They are placed in furnaces and heated completely through to a temperature of 1600° F. The dies are removed from the furnace and quenched in brine, then heated again in a furnace at 400° F and cooled.

In the rolling mill, where actual manufacturing of nickel silver begins, the

correct proportions of copper, zinc, and nickel are melted in huge electric furnaces at a temperature of 2400° F. (Some manufacturers buy their blanks of various alloys already rolled to the required thickness and cut to size.) The molten mixture is poured into iron molds, thus forming slabs or bars of 18 percent nickel. They weigh about 90 pounds each and are 1 1/4 inches thick (Fig. 6). These bars are then rolled between steel rolls, weighing three tons each. The manufacture of various articles requires nickel-silver blanks of various gauges; for teaspoons, for instance, the blanks are about 1/8 to 5/16 inch in thickness. The rolling operation is repeated time and time again with cleaning and annealing in between until the proper gauge is reached (Figs. 7, 8).

7. A view of the casting shop in the rolling mill which produces metal for International products and nonferrous metals for outside commercial use.

The nickel-silver blanks are tested to see that they conform to the standard and are then cut, first into strips, and then into individual pieces of the correct length for various size spoons or forks (Figs. 9–11). These pieces are then squeezed or "upset" in the narrowest part in order to create a stronger shank.

Grade rolling is the next step. This flattens out the blank to varying thickness between two revolving steel rolls; the irregularity of circumference of one of the rolls making this distribution of metal possible.

8. *Rolling*—Bars of nickel silver are rolled down in a series of passes between steel rollers, annealed (heated), and rolled again until required gauge of metal is obtained.

9. *Blanking*—Blanking is the first operation in making spoons and forks. This operation produces a blank of the required size and shape to manufacture a piece of flatware.

46 AMERICAN SILVERPLATE

The metal blank is then placed over a steel die which has been cut the shape of the desired spoon. This metal blank is then stamped with a blow from the steel upper die, called the force, which is of the same shape in the convex, thus forming the bowl of the spoon (Fig. 12).

The design of the handle is struck in a drop press with the aid of two steel dies into which has been cut the pattern. The lower die produces the design on the front of the spoon handle, and the upper die makes the design on the back of the handle (Fig. 13). At this stage, even the smallest particle of dust could spoil the work, so a strong current of air is blown across the top of the die to keep it dust free.

10. *Cutting to Outline*—Flat rolled blanks are fed to a machine which punches out the piece in practically its final shape and outline.

The spoon bowl is then subject to "facing" in which the edges are smoothed on a coarse emery belt (Fig. 14).

The cut and stamped blanks are smoothed through sixteen separate operations to give them the proper finish (Fig. 15). The tip of the handle, the edge of the handle, shoulder of the bowl, the facing top edge, inside and outside of the bowl, and back and front of the handle must all be "sand" buffed in separate operations. This "sand" is in reality a finely ground pumice.

The making of the blank is followed by six inspections before the spoons are ready for silverplating.

After a thorough cleaning the nickel-silver blanks are ready for silverplating and are placed in the tanks on racks. Bars of pure silver are attached to the anodes while the blanks act as the cathodes. An electric current passing through the silver cyanide solution, or electrolyte, in the tanks decomposes the

11. *Cross Rolling* — Blanks are passed between heavy rollers to distribute the metal in correct proportions for length, width, and thickness.

12. *Bowl Forming* — Bowl forming is accomplished by stamping the bowl or tine portion of the article in a contour die designed especially for each piece.

silver anode and carries the silver to the blanks where it is deposited in a closely adhering layer. During the transfer of the metal, the composition of the silver solution or electrolyte remains unchanged. Usually the articles to be plated are rotated in the tanks, keeping the solution agitated and assuring an even distribution of silver during the plating process (Fig. 16). The length of time the pieces remain in the tank, the quantity of silver in solution, and the amount of electrical current used determine the thickness of the silver deposited. The plating of flatware requires about 60 minutes. Parts of pieces that are subject to heavy wear, such as the bottoms of spoons, are subsequently given an additional coating of silver by suspending those parts in the electroplating solutions. In some plants elaborate equipment is employed in an effort to place the deposit so that the heaviest coating of silver will adhere to points that receive the greatest wear (Fig. 17).

Often a preliminary or "strike" of other metal is used prior to the deposition of silver.

Regulation of the amount of silver applied is of great concern. According to an article in *Harper's Monthly*, September 1868, p. 445, one of the earliest means of accomplishing this was a device purchased at the Paris Exposition of 1867. Unfortunately, the writer neglected to reveal the nature of the device.

In 1872 Henry Wilde, an Englishman who had participated in the original Elkington experiments in Birmingham,

13. *Stamping*—Striking the design on front and back of handle.
14. *Edge Polishing*—Fine abrasive belts are used to polish edge surfaces of spoons and all other articles of flatware to a smooth finish.
15. *Finishing*—A smooth surface is given the spoon handle with fine abrasive on a high-speed revolving buffing wheel.

III. Manufacturing and Marketing   51

refined the procedure whereby an article to be plated would be rotated in the plating bath, with better and more uniform results. One of Wilde's machines was imported by the Meriden Britannia Company. Within a short time virtually all American firms were using this process.

Prior to this, however, the Meriden Britannia Company had developed a method of "Sectional Plating," or plating several layers of silver on those areas of flatware which would be subject to most wear (Fig. 20).

The quantity of silver liberated from the anodes and deposited on the cathodes depends chiefly upon the quantity of silver in solution and the amount of electricity passing through the electrolyte. Silverplating solutions differ in their ability to deposit silver uniformly on irregularly shaped articles. These solutions also differ in their chemical composition with the type of deposit desired. The current and voltage also differ. For white and bright deposits the current density varies from 3 to 25 amps per square foot of surface to be covered and the voltage from 3/4 to 1 volt. Temperature has an important ef-

16. *Silverplating*—Forks rotate in plating tank containing a silver cyanide solution and bars of pure silver. Amount of electric current, quantity of silver in solution, and length of time pieces remain in tank determine amount of silver deposited on each piece.
17. *Spot Plating*—Backs of forks are placed on rack so that most-used sections are in a silver cyanide solution giving the wear points overlaid reinforcing with pure silver.
20. Model of "Sectional Plating" or "XII Plating" machine developed by the Meriden Britannia Co. Meriden Britannia Co. catalog 1877.

MODEL OF ELECTRO-PLATING MACHINE.

The Sectional or XII process will *add three times to the durability* of goods so plated.

fect on the distribution of the deposit and also on the maximum current density permissible. A temperature of 75° F is commonly used.

Some of the finest grades of silverplated flatwares receive sterling silver inlays which reinforce points that will receive the greatest wear. Recesses are made at these points in the base-metal blanks and blocks of silver inserted and melted to fill the recesses, the articles are then shaped and plated.

Where large quantities of articles are silverplated, they are kept in constant motion during the plating process in order to obtain a quicker and more uniform deposit. The newest techniques employ continuous conveyor-belt types of operations in which the unplated articles enter tremendous automatic machines, move steadily through, coming out completely plated and rinsed. In some instances circular tanks are used in which the articles to be plated are revolved in the vat, each article being taken past the various anodes in the plating bath.

After the plating is completed, the articles are washed, dried, and polished or buffed or not, depending on whether a bright or dull finish is desired.

Each piece is given a final inspection and then wrapped in sulphur-free tissue and packaged in tarnish-resistant paper or, more often now, is individually packaged in a plastic wrap.

Several types of finishes may be obtained by using sulphides and then subjecting the articles to scratch brushing, burnishing, and polishing. "Butler's" or "dull finish," "French-grey" and "matte" silver are descriptive terms applied to various effects produced by different methods. The butler or dull finish is produced by brushing with a tampico wheel using pumice and water, then wet scratch brushing, using a fine crimped-wire brass or nickel-silver wheel, followed by drying and lacquering. The French-grey silver finish is produced in a similar manner but the article is first given a light oxidization which is relieved with a steel crimped-wire wheel. The matte finish is produced by matte dipping before silverplating and then, after plating, by scratch brushing lightly with a crimped-wire wheel.

At the International Silver Company a new "Bright Plate" machine has been installed and placed in operation. Bright Plate is a major development in the silverplating process. It produces a better quality plate and, as the name implies, eliminates costly hand-finishing operations almost entirely.

Hollow ware pieces are frequently gold plated on the inside by an electrolytic process. The article to be plated is filled with a solution containing gold. A strip of metal attached to an electrically charged wire is immersed in the gold solution, and the gold is precipitated on the inside of the article.

"Making a Silverplated Teapot," as recorded in *Appleton's Journal,* December 1878, gives a vivid description of the process as applied to the production of collectible silverplate. A condensed version follows.

First, into the modeling room, where soft light streams in from half-curtained windows. The designer draws the design for the teapot. Ornamental portions which are to be cast are carefully modeled in wax; and from the wax, plaster casts are taken from which are made the molds. Designers working slowly and patiently, putting a bit of soft red wax here, carefully molding it and then cutting it away again with the steel tool until the shapeless lump of wax grows into a perfect ornament. Another workman with ready pencil is tracing the pattern of the teapot upon paper, limning the gracefully curved outlines carefully, and tracing the lines to be engraved clearly, until the design for the teapot is drawn and the ornaments modeled.

The raw materials or metals from which the teapot is to be made come in pigs from the mines, the rest of the work is done at the factory. The white metal on which they plate the silver is composed of tin, copper, and antimony. The exact proportions

III. Manufacturing and Marketing   53

used of these metals vary slightly with different manufacturers. The metals, having been bought in pigs, are broken up with a hammer, put into a furnace, and smelted, after which the metal is transferred to a caldron set in a brick furnace, where it is maintained at a temperature of about 500° F. This is the point at which they find they can best work it and keep it clear of dross or impurities. The contents of the caldron are stirred with a pitch-pine stick which is thought to have some good qualities as a collector of impurities. The workman has a row of iron molds with wooden handles, which look very much like square sadirons with hollow bases. Into these molds he pours the molten white metal through a narrow opening at the end. The metal contracts as it cools and shrinks away and leaves a small cavity in the center, which he fills up with a second ladleful of metal, and the top is lifted off the mold and another is added to the pile of finished plates at his side. The plates of metal are about seven inches long by five wide, and about three-quarters of an inch in thickness, while at one end is a little stub where the metal was poured into the mold. This serves to catch the impurities which rise to the surface.

In the next room the plugs or stubs containing the dross are cut off and the plates are then rolled until they are of the required thickness. They are fed through rollers five times and are reduced from three-quarters of an inch to three-eighths of an inch in thickness and increased from seven inches in length to twenty-six inches.

The plates are then taken across the room to a machine which removes a thin shaving from the surface, and thus brings out the clear, silvery appearance of pure metal. This removes from the surface of the metal the dross which the pressure of the rollers has brought to the surface of the plate.

Some of the plates are then cut into strips about three-quarters of an inch in width by being run through two revolving steel disks placed so that their edges are in contact much as are the edges of a pair of shears, except that these disks have a cir-

21. The teapot whose production is described in the excerpt from *Appleton's Journal*. It was designed and patented by William C. Beattie, February 1, 1876, for Reed & Barton.

cular instead of a lateral motion. The strips are then passed under a roller and emerge bearing a continuous raised pattern. These strips are called "trimming" and are used for decorations by being soldered upon the ware, or inserted into it.

The rest of the rolled plates are cut into circular disks by a wheel similar to the one which cuts the other plates into strips. The plates are then fashioned into "shells." The machine for this purpose is a stamp resembling a pile driver. The disks of metal are placed over a steel die, which is cup-shaped, and are held in place by an iron ring that catches and binds the edges, and which is secured to the die by thumbscrews. A rope attached to a belt running over a friction-pulley is pulled, raising a plunger of several hundred pounds' weight. Fastened to this plunger is a piece of steel which exactly fits the cup-shaped die below, across the mouth of which is fastened the metal disk. The weighted die is raised about three feet and allowed to drop upon the disk and force it down into the cup below, stretching out the elastic metal, and molding it into the shape of a high-crowned hat with a very narrow brim. An imitation of repoussé work may be added at this stage. For a teapot, the shell would be cut into four or five sections, struck with a die and then resoldered.

Die work is not struck with just one decisive blow, as this would tear the metal. A series of blows, eight or ten, are struck in the same way that shells are formed, until the metal is forced well down and is in contact with the inner surface of the engraved die. Then a die, or force, which is made of a hard composition metal and fits exactly into the steel die below, falls upon the metal with a weight of from six hundred to thirteen hundred pounds. In this way machinery and mechanical appliances are made to do the work that it would require countless thousands of blows with the hammer to do by hand. The spouts of the teapots are made in the same manner; two pieces of a spout are struck by a die and then are soldered together.

In the spinning room the shells are placed upon a wooden mold, or chuck, and set spinning at a tremendous rate. The spinner then presses a wooden stick along the outside of the shell. The shell is no longer hat-shaped, but like a perfect cup, the soft-metal brim having been pressed and whirled down into place. The shells are then taken to another lathe and placed over a sectional chuck. The lathe is set in motion and a stick used to press down the soft metal until it assumes all of the curved lines of the steel chuck. The core or center piece of the chuck is removed and then the chuck falls into pieces or sections which are easily removed from the interior of the teapot through its narrow neck. The shell is then placed on another lathe and cut into three parts, and the trimming or bands of repoussé work are soldered into the openings thus made. On still another lathe the shell is smoothed to give the surface a very high finish.

After being polished with a smooth steel and soap-and-water, the teapot shell comes out looking as if it had already been plated with purest silver.

The shell is then sent to the fitter's bench to have a spout-hole cut in it and is again polished.

The teapot is now nearly ready to receive its legs and handle. These indispensable portions are made in an adjacent building where the furnace and caldron of liquid metal attract attention. Here a workman is engaged in pouring the hot metal into a mold, and then immediately pouring it out again, in this way casting hollow handles. The metal which comes in contact with the steel sides of the mold is almost instantly chilled into solidity, and the metal in the center, being poured out again before it has time to cool, leaves a hollow shell within the mold, thus forming the teapot handle. The mold is made in two parts, each of which has a wooden handle, and is fastened together temporarily by a large iron pin, shaped like a hairpin. When ivory rings are inserted in the handle, as non-conductors, they are placed in the mold before the hot metal is poured in, and thus they become a part of the handle. The legs are cast solid, and all of the ornaments except figures which are cast hollow. Every casting is made with a certain amount of waste attached to it, which has afterward to be cut off. This is called "sprue." When the piece to be cast is large, there are several ducts or entrances to the mold through which the metal is poured. These give opportunity for the

III. Manufacturing and Marketing

air to escape, so that the mold will fill up solid, and are each filled with the sprue, which gathers the impurities.

The trimmings made, the spout, the legs and handle are carefully fitted to the shell. The waste is cut away and the various parts passed along to be soldered together.

The shell is fastened to a frame, and the trimmings placed against it and soldered on. A compound blow-pipe is used, with air and illuminating gas forced through it. The solder used is simply a little strip of white metal about the size of a straw and softened by the admixture of a little lead, so that it will melt more easily than the castings.

The teapot has now reached its final form but still more ornamentation is to be added. Three different types of ornamentation are used—hand-engraving, chasing, and machine-engraving, or engine-turning, as it is called. In the engraving rooms the ware is placed upon a circular pad that revolves and there the engravers, with their sharp, steel points, trace upon it the patterns or designs which are furnished them. With a firm hand they spin the ware around on the pad, and trace vines and leaves, curling tendrils and intricate arabesques, in lines of light, while a delicate thread of metal falls away from the tool, showing that these lines are cut into the surface. Thence, into the chasing-room, where this delicate work is done mostly by women. The teapot is filled full of pitch, which is melted and poured into it, and which, when it hardens, gives a perfectly solid lining to resist the blows of the chaser's hammer. Then it is placed on a pad on the bench, and one of the girls takes up a steel point and traces upon it the lines of the pattern by repeated blows with a small hammer. The difference between the chasing and engraving is that, while one cuts away the metal, the other forces it in.

Next we see the method of producing genuine repoussé work, and are able to make the contrast between the amount of labor involved in decorating a vessel by this process and that of stamping it with a die. A steel arm or stake is fastened firmly in a vise, and the round point is upturned so that when the vessel is drawn over the arm this point is in contact with the interior. The article already having been engraved, the workman grasps it firmly in the left arm and hand, and then, pressing it against the steel point, strikes the end of the arm which is outside a smart blow, causing it to vibrate through its length, and the point to strike against the inner surface, and force it out little by little. Hundreds of strokes must be made to perfect the design of a little spray of roses.

The third process is engine-turning. It is by this machine that the wonderful imitation of delicate tracery is produced. In front of the operator is a stationary, steel-pointed graver, while the article to be decorated is placed in front of it and fastened to a movable frame which passes up and down in contact with the point of the graver. The frame which holds the work has at one side an iron point which is pressed by a spring on the other side of the frame, against an upright brass cylinder, on which are indentations—a little suggestive of a pattern as the notes on the cylinder of a music-box. The principle is much the same, for, as the frame is moved up and down, this point follows the indentations on the cylinder, and the movements of the work against the cutting-tool are guided by it, and the result is that the pattern is cut in waved lines.

Another process is called satin finish. This is done by means of a revolving spindle, around which is a mass of jointed steel wires which hang loosely upon the spindle, each having at its end a steel point. The rapid motion given to the spindle throws out these wires, and when the article to be finished is brought within range of their points, it receives millions of little blows, each one of which leaves an almost imperceptible mark upon the soft metal, but their accumulation gives it the peculiar soft sheen of satin, and the surface is then finished by a revolving wire brush.

All decoration having been placed on the teapot it is then cleansed with warm water and potash to remove any grease. After being dried it is polished by being held against a rapidly revolving wooden wheel covered with a brush made of leather. It is now ready to be plated.

The electroplating is done in a separate building. Every piece to be plated is weighed on a pair of troy scales. After being plated, one piece of each pattern is again weighed in order that the quantity of silver which has been deposited may be computed. The teapot is then scoured again with pumice-stone dust and water and then hung in fresh water until ready to go into the bath.

The "bath," as it is called, is a double cyanide of silver and potassium contained in a large wooden vat. The articles to be plated are hung by copper wires from brass rods laid crossways on the copper-covered edges of the vat, and, this being done, the connection is made with the battery; the result being that the silver held in solution is released in minute particles and attaches itself to the surface of the metal article. The strength of the solution is kept up by plates of solid silver which are suspended in the vat.

The first step is to place the teapot in the "striking" bath, where a light but perceptible coating of silver is almost instantaneously deposited on it. It is then hung in an ordinary bath, where it remains about an hour, more or less, according to the thickness of the plating of silver which it is designed to receive.

Until a comparatively recent date, the electricity used in this operation was generated by means of a galvanic battery, but a great improvement has now been made by employing instead magneto-electric machines. Most of the unhealthy and disagreeable features of the plating-room are overcome by discarding the old galvanic battery with its paraphernalia of jars, plates, acids, mercury, and the like, and economy is also gained.

The process of plating the interior of hollow vessels with gold is also done in this room. The vessel is made to serve as a vat, and is ladled full of a double cyanide of gold instead of silver, and the connection with the battery is made by holding one pole against the outside of the cup and stirring about the solution in it with a piece of gold attached to the other pole. In a few moments the gold is deposited evenly on the interior. If, as in the case of the lip of a vase, the solution will not reach as far as is desired to plate or gild the interior, a bit of fine sponge fastened on the end of a stick is used to wash the parts with the solution. Various shades of color in gold are secured by an admixture of copper and silver, thus producing red, pink, and green shades, as well as the pure golden yellow.

If it is desired to plate one portion of an article with silver and another with gold, or with two shades of gold, one part is painted with a "resist," of black varnish. After the exposed part is plated the varnish is easily removed; the plated portion is then covered with resist in the same way, and the area first covered by resist receives another color.

The teapot which was bright and shining when it entered the bath has now emerged a soft, opaque white. It is plunged into cold water for a moment, then into hot water, and then handed over to a polisher, who holds it for a moment against a rapidly revolving fine-wire brush, which partially removes the white bloom from its surface, and it is then ready to be burnished.

The process of plating table-forks differs in one respect from other articles, because instead of hanging quietly in the bath, they are suspended from a frame and kept gently agitated all the while they remain in the solution. This is to prevent the silver from depositing upon them unevenly or in current marks, as the currents of electricity are divided and broken somewhat by the pointed tines of a fork.

In the burnishing-rooms the greater portion of the work is done by women. Here the teapot is rubbed all over its surface with a set of polished steel tools so formed as to fit into all of the intricate curves in the ornamentation. The surface of the article is kept wet with soap and water. Spherical articles having a considerable plain surface are placed upon a lathe and burnished while in rapid motion. In this case the burnishing-tool is a piece of highly-polished bloodstone cemented into a wooden handle, and the article is kept wet with stale beer.

One more operation and the teapot is complete [Fig. 21]. In still another room, the teapot is given a final polish with revolving disks made of cotton rags and filled with rouge.

In the papering-room, the finished ware is wrapped in several thicknesses of tissue paper, marked with the pattern and other data. At last they are entered in the stock books and placed in ware rooms, and when sold are packed in tin-lined wooden cases and shipped to all parts of the world.

The making of hard-metal or nickel-silver goods differs in several essentials. Spoons, forks, salvers, and plain hollow ware for the use of hotels, are all articles liable to receive rough usage, and accordingly have to be made of some more durable material than white metal. Nickel silver is composed of copper, zinc, and nickel. In rolling the plate and in working the metal, at times it becomes hard and brittle, and has to be annealed several times in what are called "muffle-furnaces." The machinery employed is heavier but in other respects resembles that used for making white or soft metal ware.

Modern manufacturing methods place great emphasis on quality control, efficiency of operation, and better working conditions for employees. Modern methods have brought about a revolution in the industry. Machinery operated now by skilled workmen accomplishes in minutes what took the work of days under old conditions. The new system basically is an "in-line" organization, with raw materials coming in at one end with continuous production coming out at the other. In the new, highly versatile plating machines unplated articles move through a closed system on conveyor belts. Rectifiers assure the proper amount of silver deposit. Modern systems of lighting and air control assure the best working conditions.

Operations in the new plated hollow ware plant of Reed & Barton serve to illustrate the great difference in this century and the last (Fig. 22).

22. Reed & Barton's new plated hollow ware operations. Photographs courtesy of Reed & Barton. From *The Silver Lining*, November-December 1969.
Raw Material Storage Area—The design of racks allows for the immediate selection of proper metal specifications.
Pneumatic Drop Hammer Area—The conveyor shown to the left of hammers delivers completed work to automatic washing machines.
Hollow Ware Press Area—Proper spacing between presses accelerates changing of large dies, making for greater efficiency.

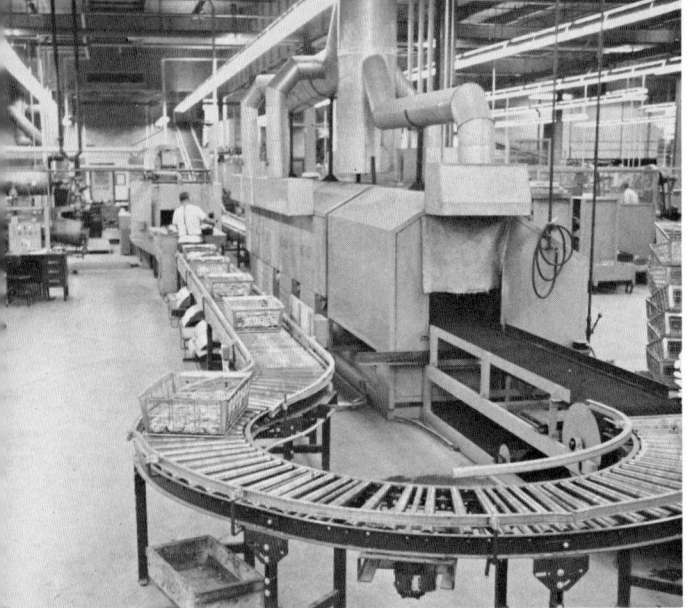

Plating of Colored Gold

Hollow ware and flatware of all types could be obtained, at extra cost, decorated in "XX Gold Inlaid," "Gold Variegated," and "Gold Inlaid," all of which produced articles in silverplate with fruit, flowers, and other ornamental motifs in gold and natural colors. None of these processes, whose name varied from one manufacturer to another, were actually inlay. All were electroplating processes accomplished by means of painting the parts to remain silver with a resist and by electrodeposit of gold alloys to produce the various colors. This resist had to be removed and reapplied for each color deposited. The *Jewelers' Circular and Horological Review*, July 1876, lists the following gold alloys:

Yellow Gold
    Pure or fine gold, 24 parts
Red Gold
    18 parts fine gold, 6 parts copper
Green Gold
    18 parts fine gold, 6 parts silver
Blue Gold
    18 parts fine gold, 6 parts iron
White Gold
    12 parts fine gold, 12 parts silver

Other alloys used for the plating of colored gold included adding a trace of silver cyanide to the gilding bath to produce green gold and copper cyanide to make a red-gold deposit. White gold could be produced by a gold-nickel and gold-tin binary deposition. Gold-zinc

22 continued.
Washing and Annealing Area—The large conveyor delivers the output of the washing machine directly to the annealing furnace.
Spinning Area—The conveyors are used to move spun or turned work to the washing-machine area.
Conveyors—Conveyors from soldering and sand-polishing areas allow greater efficiency by washing work within five minutes of completion.

alloys ranged in color from yellow, through white, to lavender.

This selective plating process required much careful handwork. Painting on the resist was a tedious task and one which had to be repeated for each color deposited. Platers and gilders were faced with the problem of depositing a coating of gold thick enough to withstand wear. Prolonging the time an article was in the plating bath did not solve the problem as the deposit tended to build up in an uneven, crystalline manner. Scratch-brushing was then used to reduce the irregular surface, after which plating was repeated. Alternate brushing and plating might be repeated several times. Always an expensive process, it has for many years been prohibitive.

Gold plating of this type, being much softer than silverplate, has seldom survived rigorous polishing. Only rarely, except on trays which have protective glass inserts, are pieces found with more than a trace of colored gold decoration.

Casting

Casting is one of the many processes involved in the making of fine silverware. This aspect of fine craftsmanship may be illustrated by the operations at Reed & Barton where it is done in three different departments; the foundry, the white-metal casting department, and the centrifugal casting department (Fig. 23).

Britannia metal, or white metal, is basically a tin alloy, used in the manu-

22 continued.
Plating Machine—A new addition. Rectifiers along wall assure the proper amount of silver deposit.
Automatic Plating Machine—Another view of the new machine shows pieces of plated hollow ware as they are coming out of the last rinse.
Automatic Polishing Machines—These are partially shown above. Various other types of polishing machines are also installed here.

facturing of trimmings such as handles, spouts, finials, feet, hinges, and various mounts to be applied to hollow ware stampings. All casting in the white-metal department is done in bronze molds. There are two methods of molding used, "slush" and "solid" molds.

In the foundry, molds are made of a special kind of sand, which holds the shape impressed into it, even when the molten metal is poured into it. Each mold is destroyed in the process of removing the casting so that new molds are constantly needed. The sand, however, can be used again and again.

Foundry work also includes an operation called "snagging," or removing excess metal from the castings. Castings of brass are cleaned in the wheelabrator, a machine that tumbles the pieces in a revolving drum where steel abrasives wear away unwanted parts.

Centrifugal casting is done mainly on sterling items which have fine detail. A Cerro-Bend metal mold is made from the master pattern. From this a wax pattern is made. The wax patterns are embedded in plaster. The sterling is poured with a centrifugal force into this plaster impression.

Dutch Reproductions

Dutch reproductions had a vogue from about 1910 to 1930 (Fig. 24). Those made by the Barbour Silver Plate Company division of the International Silver

22 continued.
Inspectors—In one of the final inspecting areas the inspectors receive hollow ware delivered by conveyor from buffers prior to plating process.

Company were made by a process no longer used, called "copper deposit." An impression of the design was made in red wax, then this wax form was hung in a plating tank and plated with copper until the desired thickness had been obtained. The wax was afterwards melted away and the piece silverplated. Such things as handles, spouts, bases, and covers were attached and were not made as part of the original piece.

Advertising

Silversmiths from earliest colonial times were aware of the value of advertising. Frequent notices by individual craftsmen appeared regularly in newspapers.

When electroplating became commercially feasible, the Connecticut manufacturers advertised in local newspapers.

Between 1858 and 1860 Rogers Bros. Mfg. Co. and Rogers, Smith & Company each published a small catalog containing price lists and a few woodcuts of

23. *Casting.* Photographs courtesy Reed & Barton. From *The Silver Lining*, March-April 1970.
Mold being closed in the foundry. Master patterns have made impressions on the sand. Mold will then be baked for casting.
Casting is removed from mold after it has been baked. It will be brushed, "gates" sawed, filed, and sent to the silver room.
Ready to pour off a mixture of white metal into ingots for white-metal hollow ware trimmings.
Casting a pitcher handle. The ladle holds metal which is poured into a bronze mold, fastened with C clamps.
"Dress off" operation for white-metal castings.
Centrifugal casting, involves first making a wax pattern. The tank holds hot wax, which is then poured into a Cerro-Bend mold.

flatware. With this small beginning, the growth of catalogs in both size and quality was rapid.

Photography had been discovered but had not been perfected sufficiently for the portrayal of silverplated goods. Its use was severely limited because of the lack of quality in the negatives and the limitation of means whereby prints could be reproduced in newspapers and periodicals.

The electrotype process was the subject of intense interest during the Crystal Palace Exposition in London in 1851. The perfection of electrotypography made possible the large-scale commercial application of relatively inexpensive wood engravings. Its appearance was timed to coincide with the tremendous expansion of markets and led to the publication of illustrated catalogs in the late 1850s.

Much rivalry in the trade resulted in the publication of increasingly larger and more elaborate catalogs as each company endeavored to outdo the other. Reed & Barton, in 1877, published a magnificent volume of two hundred and twenty-four pages illustrating their entire line in finely executed woodcuts. The Meriden Britannia Company published a similar one in 1878 and an even larger edition in 1883. This was followed in 1885 by a still larger catalog by Reed & Barton. Though the size of catalogs declined after this period, they remain an important source of study material for the serious collector and the student of American nineteenth-century silver.

The major silver manufacturers still publish catalogs. These are supplemented by pamphlets illustrating individual patterns or particular lines and by national advertising in leading monthly periodicals.

24. Dutch reproductions made about 1920 to 1931. Basket on right by E. G. Webster & Son of Brooklyn, N.Y., others by Barbour Silver Plate Co.

III. Manufacturing and Marketing

Marketing Methods

Most manufacturing of silverplated wares was originally confined to the New England and northeastern states, principally Connecticut, New York, and Massachusetts. Silverplating soon followed in Illinois, Indiana, Maine, Maryland, New Jersey, Ohio, Pennsylvania, Rhode Island, and Wisconsin, and as far west as California. The merchandising of manufactured ware was for many years on a more or less free and easy basis, the day of the peddler's wagon having barely closed. The ideas and efforts of two Meriden, Connecticut, pewterers and britannia makers, Asbil Griswold and Horace Wilcox had been to equip wagons, which were sent out for trips of greater or lesser length. Their own manufacturing of pewter and britannia wares had filled the local markets and Wilcox had loaded a wagon with the products of local makers and peddled it from house to house and town to town. This method had already proven so successful that when silverplated articles were made, they too were added to the "Yankee Peddler's cart." These traveling merchants were accustomed to accept various kinds of merchandise instead of money, which was not plentiful. From door-to-door peddling they branched out to store-to-store selling and finally set up district sales offices and went into wholesale merchandising.

Complete lines of silverplated wares in several different grades are made by large manufacturers. The better grades are sold through jewelry stores and the jewelry departments of large department stores. Large quantities of low-priced wares are sold in chain stores and department-store basements. Some lower priced wares are marketed unbranded or under trade names unlike those of better quality made by the same company.

All the silverplate with standard trademarks, from reputable companies,

clubs, steamships, railroads, and restaurants is generally of good quality. Products for this trade are usually manufactured by a few large companies on special order and constitute an important outlet.

Distribution Practices

Silverplate was distributed through mail-order catalogs at prices that seem incredible today. Feature pickle castors at 75¢, combination sugar bowl and spoon holder for $2.18 with 12 spoons or $1.69 without the spoons. Compare present-day prices with "fruit stands [brides' baskets] at $3.98, for a thirteen-inch-high quadruple silverplated large massive frame, hand burnished with fancy ornamental handle and feet . . . bowl of pink and white glass, eleven inches in diameter, with hand painted decoration in colors and gold." That was the highest priced model, others were as little as $2.35. These are among the prices quoted in Sears, Roebuck & Company catalogs in the years between 1889 and 1909.

There can be little doubt that some mail-order houses undercut prices in a way that jewelry stores and some manufacturers considered unfair competition. The very nature of silverplated wares makes them especially subject to the abuse of unscrupulous manufacturing and marketing practices. On new articles a thin coating of silver looks no different from one of an adequate thickness to give good wear. Unfortunately, most of the buying public is not suffi-

25. Advertisement of Rockford Silver Plate Co. of Rockford, Ill., whose manager was a firm supporter of the Jewelers' Crown Guild. *The Keystone,* August 1906.

is the same regardless of distributor. For instance, the "1847 Rogers Bros." brand offered as premiums by some stamp-redemption centers is the regular product. This is also true of distribution by mail-order houses.

Occasionally special lines have been made for premium use but were usually marked with a different mark or trade name.

Silverplated ware made for hotels,

26. Advertisement of Larkin Soap Mfg. Co., Buffalo, N.Y., dated July 1, 1893.

ciently acquainted with the other indications of quality workmanship which are evident to the naked eye. Reliance on trademarks and the company name is still the best guide.

As a result of unfair price competition the trade journals carried numerous complaints and "letters to the Editor" from jewelers who felt that mail-order houses were distributing low-quality goods at prices with which they could not compete.

The Watchmakers' and Jewelers' Guild of the United States was organized in Chicago in 1870 or 1880 (records do not agree on the date) to combat the "catalogue nuisance," as it was then called. Later, the object of this group was to adopt a distinctive mark, or marks, which were to be stamped on the goods of certain manufacturers, who bound themselves to produce goods of specified quality, and not to sell those goods to other than Guild members, under penalty of a monetary forfeit and loss of trade sufficient to keep the goods in their legitimate channels, and prevent ruinous competition from outside sources.

Two trademarks were used. One was two doves perched on a man's hand. The other was "U S Guild" the letters being intertwined. This latter mark of fine lines often broke the plating on certain qualities of goods, consequently the Guild adopted the device of two doves on an open hand.

In 1892 another organization replaced the earlier Guild. The new group was incorporated as the Jewelers' Crown Guild, of Rockford, Illinois. Their intention was to follow the plans and objects of the old United States Jewelers' Guild. They redefined the type of distributors who would qualify as legitimate retail jewelers. A legitimate jeweler, from the Guild standpoint, was a practical bench-worker, or he who had a bench-worker in his employ. The Guild believed that the retail dealer was the educator of the consumer concerning the quality of goods sold, and that the class or brand of goods the retail jewelers united in recommending to the people would be the brand people would buy. Directors stated that the organization was in the interests of the craft and not for any pecuniary gain to

27. Advertisement from *Ladies' Home Journal*, June Supplement, 1891.

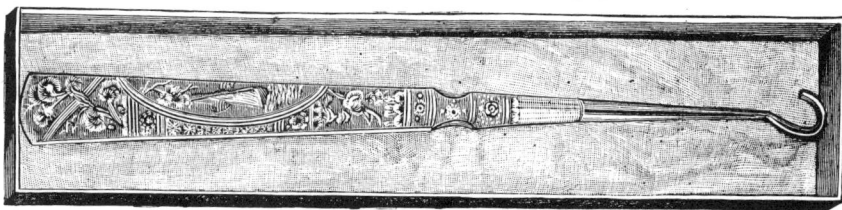

A Beautiful Oxidized Silver-Plated Button-Hook
IN A SATIN-LINED BOX

To any one who will, before July 1st, 1891, send us One Dollar for a new Yearly Subscriber (not their own name), we will mail, postpaid, this Button-hook, thousands of which we have used, and which appears to be very popular with the ladies. It measures 7½ inches long and is beautifully chased. It is of the best quality and triple-plated. It will be found to be extremely convenient on account of its length, and would be an ornament to any lady's dressing-table. We send it out in a Satin-lined Case. Price, 35 cents, postpaid.

the association. The stamp of the Jewelers' Crown Guild was a crown with the words CROWN and GUILD superimposed.

The manager of the Rockford Silver Plate Company was a director of the new Guild and one of its firm supporters. The company's advertising reflected his stand (Fig. 25). In spite of those who believed in the principles advocated by the Guild, it survived only a few years.

Premiums and Advertising Pieces

Because silverplated articles are relatively inexpensive and readily available in quantity and in a variety of styles, they were widely used as premiums and for advertising.

The Larkin Soap Manufacturing Company of Buffalo, New York, regularly published premium lists of articles which could be obtained by persons who sold their soap from door-to-door (Fig. 26). A number of these articles were silverplated wares. A "ladies' silver, quadruple plated, cut glass inkstand—The daintiest and prettiest inkstand we ever saw" could be obtained free by the patron who secured two orders of soap. The regular price, according to a supplementary price list, published July 1, 1893, was $3.75.

The *Ladies' Home Journal* also catered to the individual who would solicit subscriptions. Rewards for these subscriptions could bring the 1891 solicitor such items as a "Beautiful Oxidized Silver-Plated Button-Hook" in a satin-lined box for only one new yearly subscriber at one dollar a year (Fig. 27). More diligent solicitors were rewarded with a silverplated memorandum tablet, sent postpaid, as a premium for 12 three months' subscriptions at 25 cents each, or, for eight subscribers and 50 cents extra (Fig. 28). Similar offers were made for several years and the

28. Memorandum tablet given by *Ladies' Home Journal* as premium. May Supplement, 1891.

Memorandum Tablet
Sent, postpaid, as a Premium for a Club of 12 Three months' Subscribers at 25 cents each; or, for 8 Subscribers and 50 cents extra.
Price, $1.75, postpaid.

Finest quality of quadruple Oxydized Silver-plate; Artistic ornamentation. Celluloid Leaves—one for each day in the week. Guaranteed to please.
Price, $1.75, postpaid.

III. Manufacturing and Marketing 67

TOY DISHES.
Children's Britannia Tea Set.
Given for a club of only 5 yearly subscribers; or, for only 3 yearly subscribers and 25 cents extra.

A delightful premium for the girls and one that is always acceptable. This set is very pretty in design, brightly polished, and hard to break, can be sent safely through the mails. You can judge of the size of the dishes when we say the teapot is 3½ inches high. We will send above set postpaid to any address for 75 cents, if you wish to purchase instead of securing it free of cost by sending subscribers.

29. Toy dishes given as premium by *Ladies' Home Journal,* May 1889.

variety of articles included silverplated salt and pepper "sprinklers," napkin rings, "Royal Ooze Calf" purse with silverplated mountings, chatelaine bag and chain, mirror, brush and comb sets, silver jewel caskets, teaspoons, tablespoons and forks, sugar shell or butter knife, and toy dishes of britannia (Fig. 29).

The *Overland Monthly* also rewarded those who secured subscribers to their magazine. A cold-meat fork, sugar shell, gravy ladle, cheese server, or cream ladle in the "Raphael" pattern, made by Rogers & Hamilton, was offered for only two subscriptions at one dollar each (Fig. 30).

Some idea of the extent of this type of solicitation of magazine subscriptions and payment in premiums may be gained from an April 1905 advertisement in the *Peoples' Home Journal.* The silverplated fruit dish, offered for five yearly subscriptions at 35 cents each or ten at 25 cents each, was their 987th premium (Fig. 31).

The Herbene Pharmacal Company, New York City, published an eight-page premium list in 1903, "To encourage our agents to make all the sales possible, premiums are offered in addition to the regular agent's profits." The list of premiums offered included a coffee or tea pot, cake basket, spoon holder, bread tray, sugar dish and cover, cream pitcher, sugar bowl and cover, syrup pitcher with plate, silver tray or waiter, pickle castor, fern dish (Fig. 32), cup and saucer, fruit or berry dish, cake basket, set of six nut picks and one nut cracker, flatware of all kinds, or a dinner castor.

While much of the silverplated ware offered as premiums was obtained from

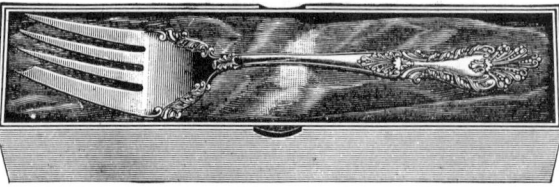

COLD MEAT FORKS.

The Raphael Pattern.

The "Rogers, Hamilton" Brand.

Superiority in Workmanship, Style, Durableness.

All pieces heavily coated in parts most exposed to wear.

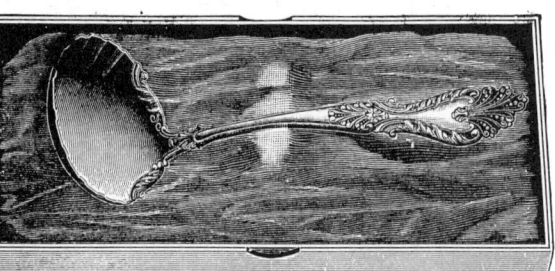

GRAVY LADLES.

The National Magazine Premium Offers.

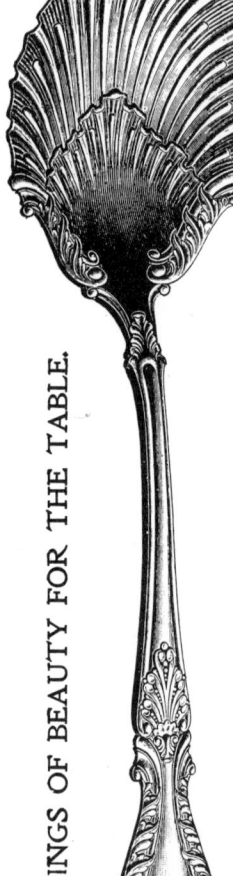

SUGAR SHELL
Exact Size.

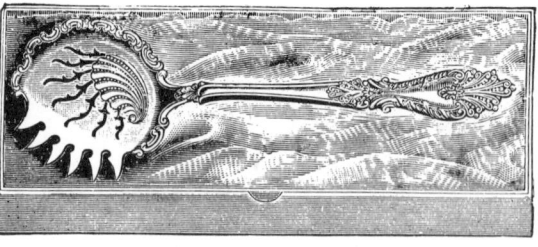

CHEESE SERVERS.

For Only 2 Subscribers

You Send two Subscriptions

Of One Dollar each and you have a choice of either of these Silver Pieces. Sent by mail in boxes immediately on receipt of subscriptions.

The W. W. POTTER CO., 91 BEDFORD ST., BOSTON, MASS.

CREAM LADLE, Exact Size.

For Only 2 Subscribers

THINGS OF BEAUTY FOR THE TABLE.

STYLE, FINISH AND LASTING QUALITIES.

III. Manufacturing and Marketing   69

31. Premium offered by *People's Home Journal,* April 1905.

regular manufacturers of silverplate, some of it was from firms such as Kelley & McBean, Niagara Falls, New York, who specialized in the manufacture of aluminum, silverware novelties, and advertising specialties. One of their catalogs, published about 1894, contains 20 pages of silverplated articles available for use as premiums. The attention of advertisers was called to a paper knife on which "Any firm or individual name may appear where ours does, on the back" (Fig. 33). Further attention is called to the many ways a spoon may be stamped with a cut of building or scene, thereby adapting it to individual use (Fig. 34).

30. Premiums offered in *Overland Monthly,* December 1897.

Distributors of foods were naturally attracted to silverplated articles to use for advertising and promotion of their products. The Ceylon Tea Company, San Francisco, California, for instance, offered "A Silver Plated Tea Spoon" for

32. Fern dish from premium list of Herbene Pharmacal Co., New York City, 1903.

No. 23.—Fern Dish.

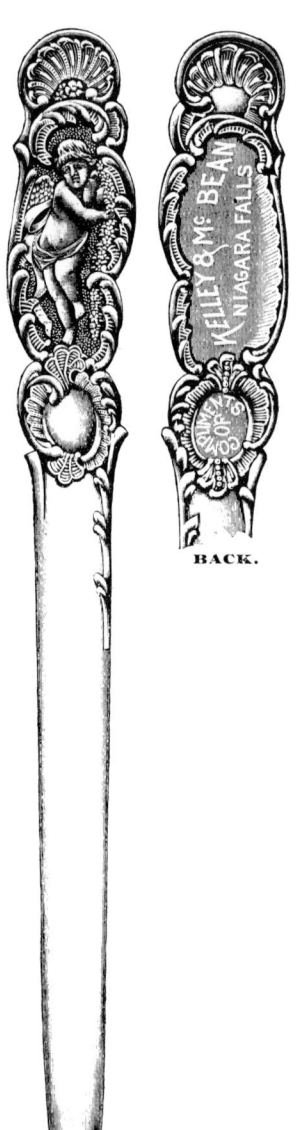

BACK.

only five cents in cash with each purchase of a pound of tea or a one-dollar purchase of coffee, spices, baking powder, flavoring extracts, cocoa, and chocolate (Fig. 35). A special silver coupon was furnished to the customer and punched at the time of each purchase until the required dollar's worth of groceries had been purchased.

In the rather free and easy relationships that existed between merchant and wholesalers of bygone days, substantial gifts were given as evidences of a relationship that somehow seemed to transcend the merely commercial. Typical of these gifts was the jug advertising the Deuster Wine Company (Fig. 36). The daughter of the original owner said of it, "The jug has the name of the company my father worked for, 'Deuster Wine Company.' When Mr. Deuster retired, my father and two partners bought the business and my father was president. It was strictly a wholesale liquor business—no 'saloon'— tho they did sell bottled goods to retail trade. It was perfectly respectable for ladies to go in and order their table wines which were later delivered by horse and wagon (on Sundays my father hitched the horses to a buggy and took the family riding) . . . the jug was given to Mr. Deuster or to my father . . . in the early 1900s."

33. Paper knife made by Kelley & McBean, Niagara Falls, N.Y., for advertising.
34. Spoon bowls to be made for advertising. Made by Kelley & McBean, Niagara Falls, N.Y.

 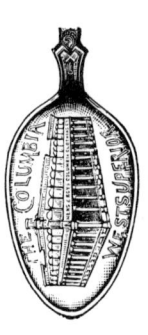     

III. Manufacturing and Marketing   71

35. Coupon to be redeemed for a silverplated teaspoon following purchase of merchandise from Ceylon Tea Co., San Francisco, Cal.

36. Advertisement of silverplated "Old Jug" given to Deuster Wine Co. members, Green Bay, Wis., early 1900s.

The advertising mirror made by James W. Tufts was probably given to a merchant in much the same manner (Fig. 37). Advertising slogans such as "Hard White Metal," "Quadruple Plate of Silver," "Satisfaction Guaranteed in Every Particular," are interwoven into the design.

37. Advertising mirror made by James W. Tufts, Boston, Mass.

Trade Practices Pertaining to Marking

According to the United States Tariff Commission Report in 1940, the National Stamping Law of the United States, enacted June 1906, and effective one year later, does not contain specific regulations with regard to the marking of silverplated ware except that it may not be branded as "sterling" or "coin" silver. Certain standards, however, as to the quantity of silver deposited on silverplated ware are generally recognized in the trade. These standards as applied to teaspoons are given below. The same requirements pertain to other flatware pieces in like proportions.

Standard or grade	Number of ounces of pure silver per gross of teaspoons
A1 or Standard	2
A1 or A1X or Extra	2 plus overlay or 2½ no overlay
AA	3
Double or XX	4
Triple or XXX	6
Quadruple or XXXX	8
F.S.B. (Federal Specifications Board)	9

Silverplated teaspoons manufactured in accordance with the requirements of the Federal Specifications Board Procurement Division are plated with four and a half, and tablespoons with five times as much silver as similar articles manufactured according to the "A1" or "Standard" grade.

Marks used to designate the type of base-metal blank used in fabricating silverplated articles include "EPNS," electroplate on nickel silver; "EPC," electroplate on copper; "EPWM," electroplate on white or britannia metal; "EPBM," electroplate on britannia metal; and "EPNS-WMM," electroplate on nickel silver with white-metal mounts.

The maker's name usually appears on silverplated ware as a designation of quality, except on the cheaper grades of ware. Registered trademarks are often descriptive of the quality of plating or type of base metal used.

In their best grades of silverplated flatware, a few manufacturers utilize sterling silver insets at points of greatest wear. Other manufacturers reinforce their better grade products by an overplate covering points of greatest wear.

The numbers stamped on the bottom of hollow ware do not indicate the year of manufacture but are pattern numbers.

As early as 1867 the Meriden Britannia Company had a system of stamping nickel silver, silver-soldered hollow ware with a cipher preceding the pattern number (i.e., 0256), and by 1893 nickel-silver hollow ware with white-metal mounts had as a part of the number two ciphers (i.e., on a waiter with white metal, 00256). This made it quickly understood by the number whether the piece was nickel silver, silver soldered, or nickel silver with white-metal mounts.

In their catalog for 1861 mention was made only of white-metal-base items but in 1867, when they changed the form of their trademark, they had a mark for items plated on nickel silver and another for those plated on what they called "Superior white metal."

In the first catalog issued by the Meriden Britannia Company in 1855, they offered their wares both plated and unplated. Those items unplated were priced under a column headed, "In Britannia."

White metal was a standard base metal in the various divisions of the International Silver Company until the early 1930s. In 1928, 1929, and 1930, they used 91 percent tin, 7 percent antimony, and 2 percent copper, which is what they use for their present-day pewter.

The pewter they made in 1930, when there was a brief revival, was 80 percent tin, 7 percent antimony, and 13 percent copper.

III. Manufacturing and Marketing

The manufacturing of silverplated ware in this country has always been closely associated with the names of prominent firms. Since the purchaser's only guarantee of the quality of the silverplating and the amount of plating applied has been based on the maker's reputation, the establishment of a firm or brand name has been of paramount importance. Some manufacturers had previously established reputations for the quality of their pewter or copper products. A few were already established as manufacturers of sterling-silver wares.

When silverplated hollow ware was first manufactured, some manufacturers either failed to indicate quality or marked it with their own name and "Triple" or "Quadruple" plate. No federal regulations applied but, as a result of policing within the industry, manufacturers of better hollow ware began imprinting only their name and guarantee. Widespread public acceptance of this practice now makes misleading marking suspect. The Meriden Britannia Company dropped all reference to "Quadruple" plate in 1896, and stated thereafter articles would be stamped "made and guaranteed by the Meriden Britannia Co." However, some other makers continued to use "Quadruple Plate" marking until about 1912.

Manufacturers of silverplated flatware, in addition to their trademark, stamp the quality upon their goods, almost all of them adopting the same signs and figures. These signs and figures are as follows:

AI	Standard Plate
XII	Sectional Plate
4	Double Plate, Teaspoons
6	Double Plate, Dessert Spoons and Forks
8	Double Plate, Tablespoons
6	Triple Plate, Teaspoons
9	Triple Plate, Dessert Spoons and Forks
12	Triple Plate, Tablespoons

Because the base metal and its preparation as well as the proper application of the silverplating are fully as important as the amount of plating applied, the presence of a reputable maker's name or trademark is still the purchaser's only guarantee of quality.

Practically none of the silverplate manufacturers made complete lines of hollow ware and flatware. They purchased large quantities of goods from other manufacturers, plated them, and stamped them with their own trademarks. Reed & Barton and the Meriden Britannia Company offered the greatest assortment, yet Reed & Barton bought most of its flatware from Rogers & Bro. and the Hartford Manufacturing Company. They produced little of their own flatware except for the hotel trade until the 1860s. Flatware of almost all manufacturers turned up in many different catalogs and with many trademarks. Rogers & Bro., in 1865, was one of Reed & Barton's largest customers for hollow ware.

Basic shapes of tea sets were sometimes sold to various companies to have different finials, spouts, or feet attached. Sometimes the chasing varied from one company to another.

The Wm. Rogers Mfg. Co. of Hartford and Rogers & Bro. of Waterbury made no plated hollow ware. The Hartford company issued complete catalogs nevertheless, while the Waterbury firm simply sent dealers portfolios of photographs on request.

Another example is Rogers, Smith & Company who had merchandise identical to that of the Meriden Britannia Company and issued identical catalogs, changing only the firm name.

That is why it is not unusual to find identical pieces of both flatware and hollow ware bearing the trademarks of various companies.

Fig. 1. Fig. 2. 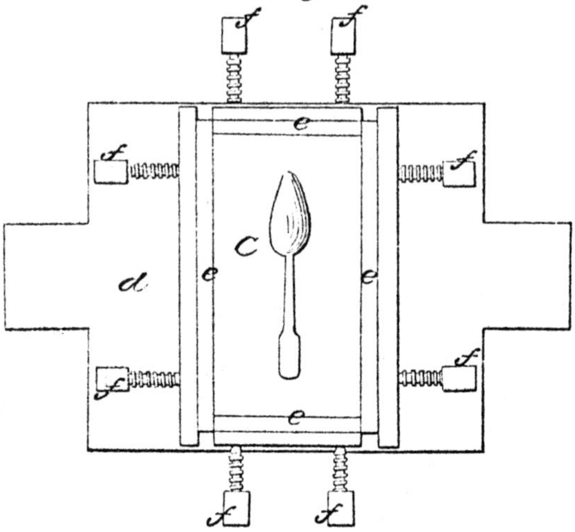 Fig. 3.

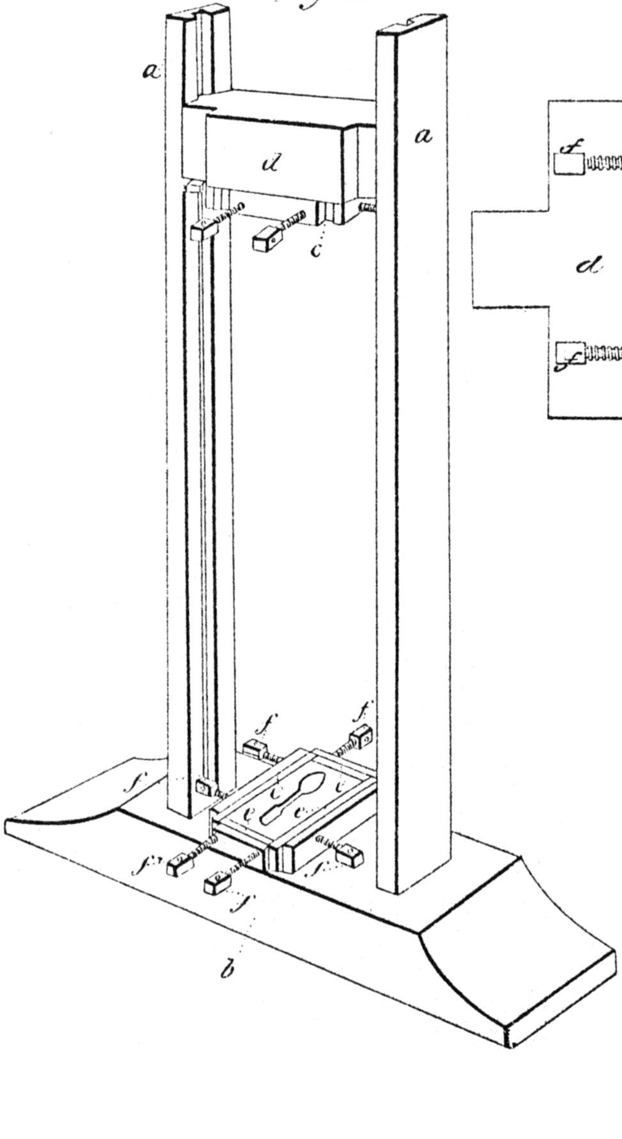

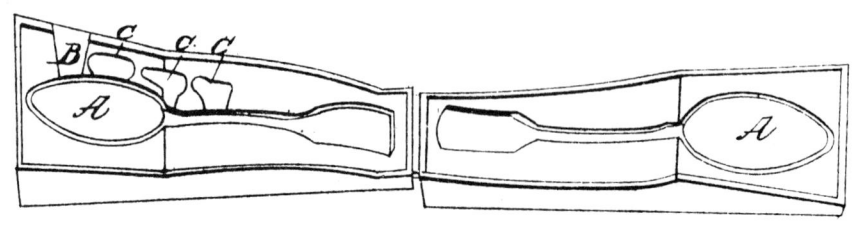

CHAPTER IV

Patented Processes

Silverplating began with experimentation; this experimentation has never ceased. Within the industry there has been a constant search for improved methods and materials.

Spoons were the first silverplated articles made in quantity in this country and even before the discovery of silverplating had been the subjects of some of the first patents.

In 1801, long before electroplating became practical, Thomas Bruff took out the first patent for "Manufacturing Spoons." Some other early patents for the manufacture of spoons were those of I. Bisbee in 1809, J. Perkins in 1813, J. Ridgeway in 1814, and William Gale in 1826. This may be Gale's invention of producing spoons and forks by means of rolls with the patterns for both sides sunk into them. No copies of these patents could be located in Patent Office records.

A. Little, in 1830, took out a patent for "Making Spoons." No printed specifications could be found but the Patent Office drawing shows a swage, or stamping device, for shaping spoons (Fig. 1).

R. Butcher, Philadelphia, took out a patent December 27, 1830, for "Spoons from tin plates, pewter in sheets, sheet-silver, etc." This was followed by patents for "Mfg. spoons" by C. Goodyear, Philadelphia, in 1832, a "Mold for casting metal spoons" by T. Mix, Cheshire, Connecticut, and a patent for "Casting Spoons" by W. Mix, Prospect, Connecticut, in 1836 (Fig. 2).

Unfortunately, most of the records and the specifications concerning these early patents have been lost so that the true nature of most may never be known, though some clues may be derived from the association of their names. J. Perkins, of Newburyport, Massachusetts, who on June 29, 1813, received a patent on a "Spoon," was the silversmith, Jacob Perkins, born July 9, 1766. Perkins was apprenticed to Edward Davis who left him the business when he was only 15 years old. Perkins lived in Newburyport until about 1816 when he moved to Philadelphia. An inventive genius, Perkins was honored in London by the Society of Liberal Arts. He invented a machine to manufacture wire into nails. During the War of 1812 he supervised the restoration of old guns for the government and invented a steam gun to fire 100 balls a minute. He died in London July 13, 1849. While the exact nature of this patent may never be known, we may speculate that, because of Perkins' interest in inventions, it is most likely to have been concerned with the making of spoons rather than with their design. (At that early date *invention* and *design* patents were not listed separately.)

The invention of Josephus Brockway, Troy, New York, was for a "Machine for Manufacturing Silver Spoons" (Fig. 3).

1. Patent for swaging spoons. A. Little; Patent No. 6280x; December 14, 1830.
2. Patent for casting spoons. W. Mix, Prospect, Conn.; Unnumbered Patent; June 28, 1836.

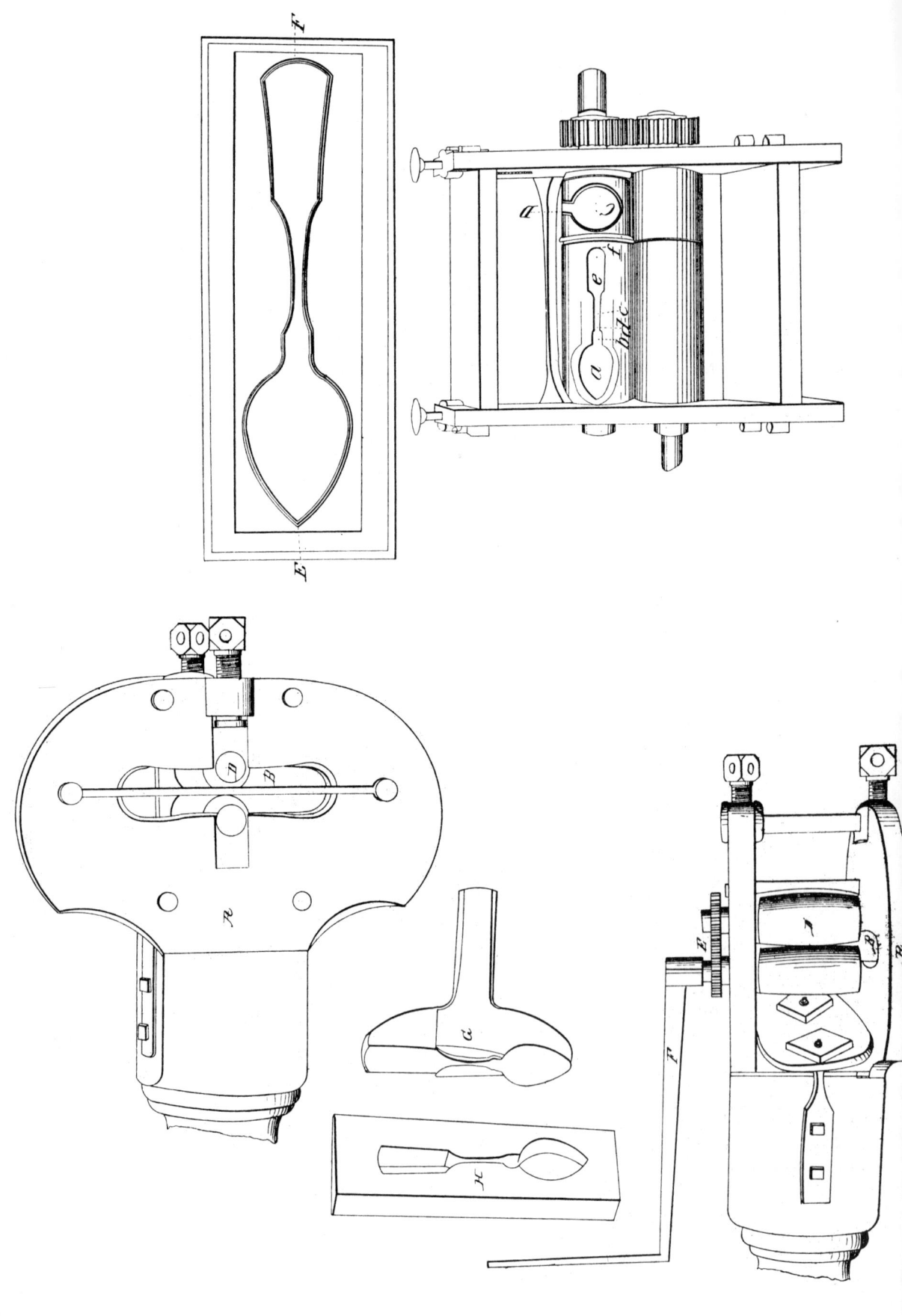

IV. Patented Processes

This was for swaging, or rolling, and the principle involved was: "1. The shaping of a roller of a common plater's mill, so that it shall receive a bar of silver widthwise, and roll it into the shape of a spoon, one end for the bowl, and the other for the handle, leaving the bowl its proper shape with the silver thickest at the edges and thinnest in the middle, and this to be made separate from, though designed for a cutter. 2. The formation of a cutter in the same, or a separate mill, or on a separate piece of steel designed only to cut off the edges, without altering at all the thickness of the silver in the bowl, but to extend the length of the handle, perfect in its proportionate thickness, and cut it to its proper shape."

On July 19, 1838, S. Boon, Hamilton, New York, received a patent for a "Plating-Mill for Making Spoons" (Fig. 4). Sanford Boon was a silversmith who advertised from 1822 to 1844. He is listed from 1832 to 1834 as a member of the firm of Boon & Ormsby of Cortland, New York. This patent was not concerned with electroplating, as one might think from the "Plating-Mill" mentioned. It was another rolling mill with convex rollers "designed to give the silver the different and varied thicknesses required in the different parts of a spoon. . . ."

Some of the early patents were concerned with saving materials used in making spoons and increasing their durability. John Mix, of Cheshire, Connecicut, on March 14, 1848, patented spoons with handles of "iron or composition metal tinned with Britannia metal bowls . . . thereby saving about one-third of the cost of stock for spoons, and makes a stronger and more durable spoon, than those made wholly of Britannia metal, or other metal suitable for such spoons" (Fig. 5).

William Mix of Prospect, Connecticut, was granted a patent on May 23, 1848, for an "improved spoon made of britannia, block-tin, or any suitable metal for casting, with the handle strengthened by wire . . . by casting the handles hol-

5. John Mix, Cheshire, Conn., on March 14, 1848, patented a method of making spoons of iron with britannia handles. Patent No. 5,473.

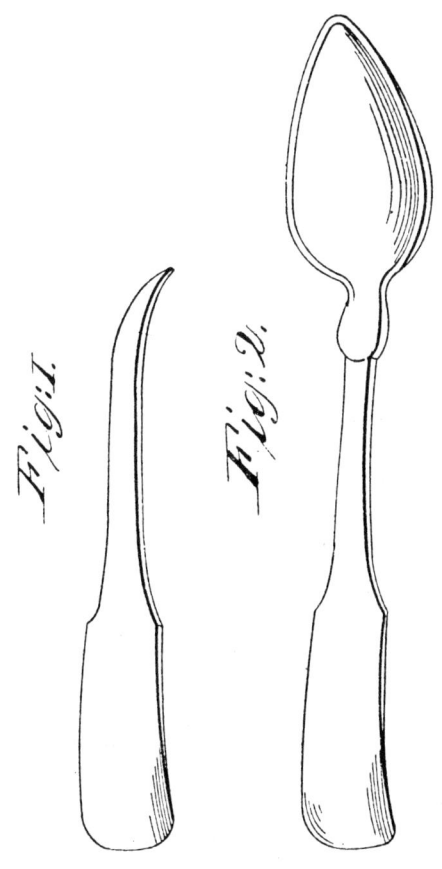

3. Patent for swaging spoons. Josephus Brockway, Troy, N.Y.; Patent No. 26; September 20, 1836. Graded rollers form blanks of thickness proportionate to completed spoon.

4. Patent for swaging spoons. S. Boon's rolling mill was designed to give the silver the different thicknesses required in the different parts of a spoon. Patent No. 848; July 19, 1838.

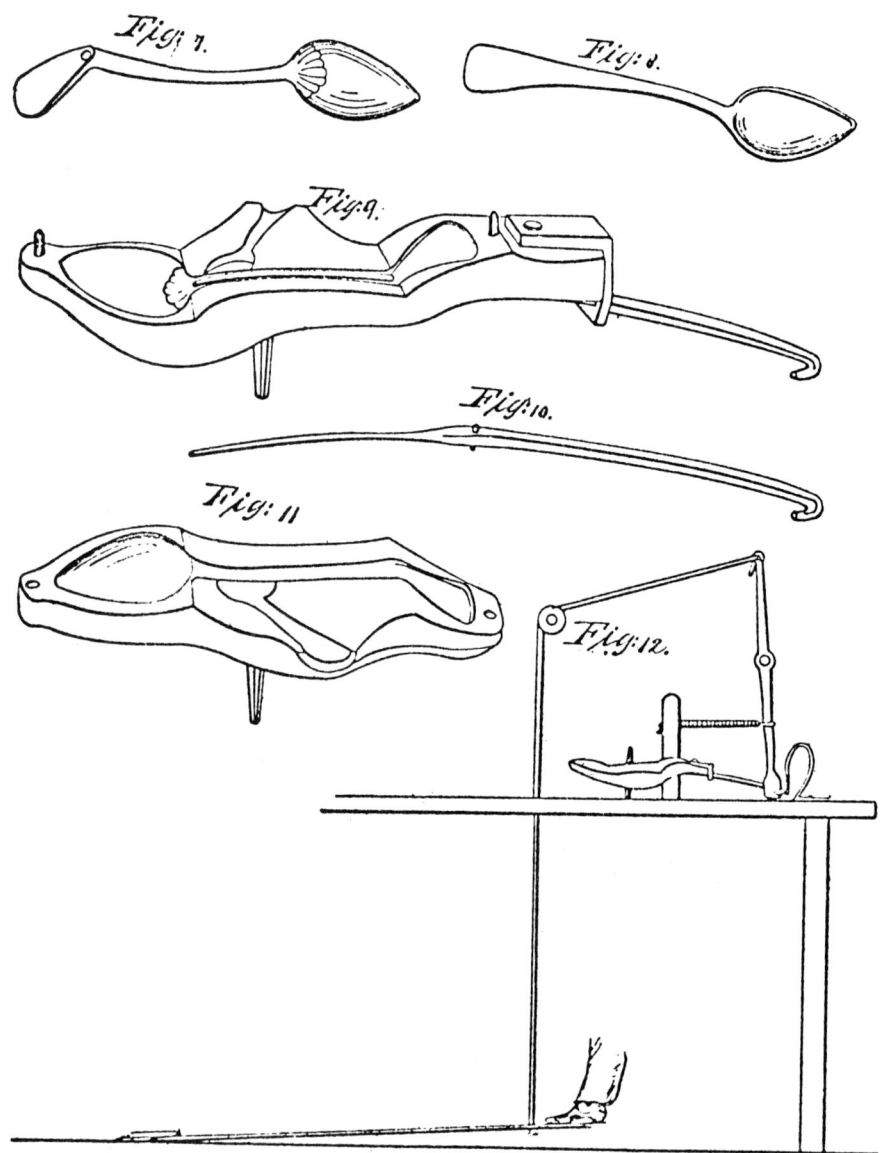

6. Patent drawing for William Mix's wire-strengthened spoons. Patent No. 5,598; May 23, 1848.

low by means of a draw-tap and placing the wire therein, and by means of a drop with suitable dies condensing and closing the metal around the wire with a smooth surface for the last finish. . . ." He maintained that his invention would result in a saving in stock and a spoon of greater strength; a saving of time by the use of the draw-tap as opposed to fixing a wire in place inside the mold for each casting and another saving of time by the use of wire pre-cut to the proper length (Figs. 6, 7). The following year Mix received, on May 1, another patent for a further improvement for his "wire-strengthened spoons." The new process was basically the same.

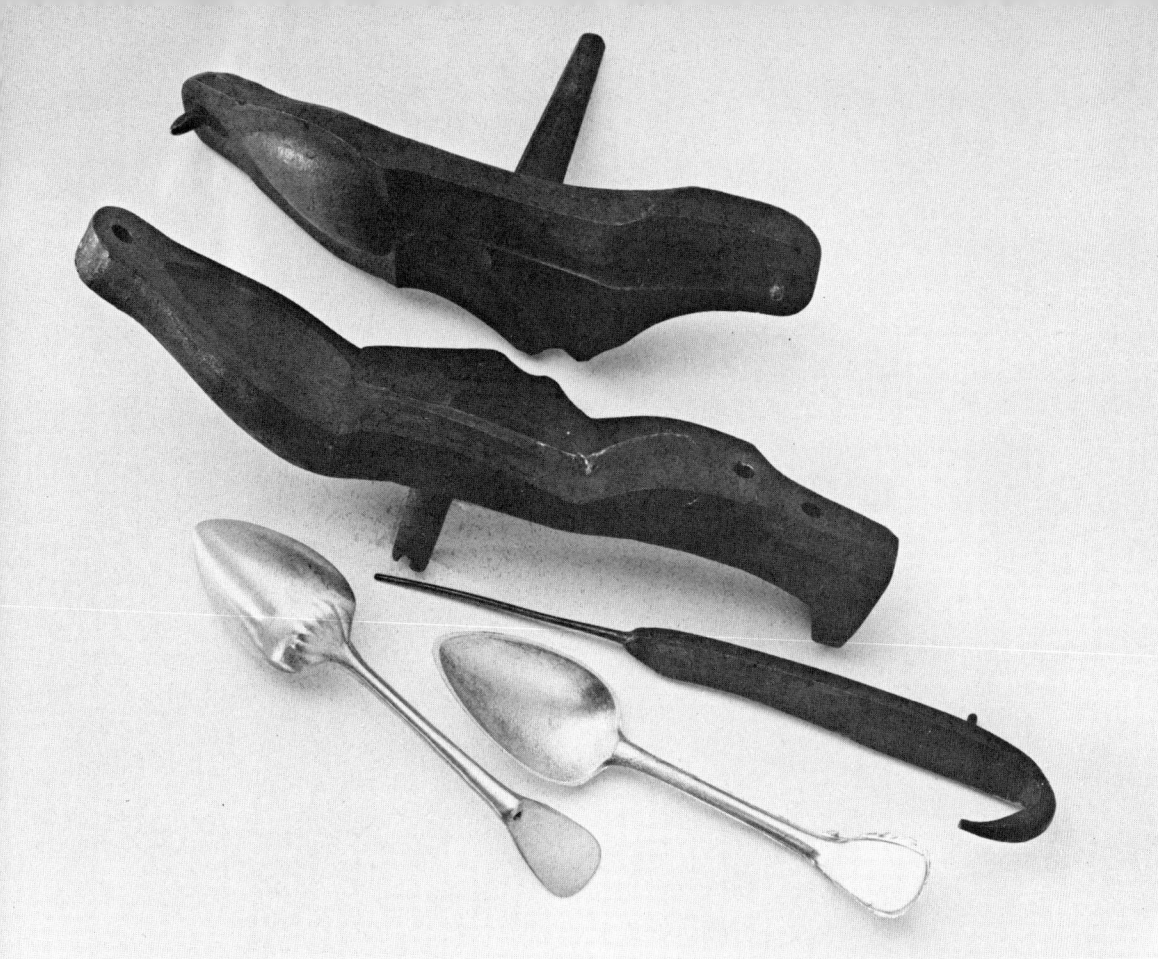

7. Spoon mold with draw tap and two spoons. The mold is attributed to William Mix, Prospect, Conn. The hole from which the draw-tap has been drawn and into which the wire is to be inserted may be seen in the spoon on the left. Length of spoon impression 8 1/8 in.

The mold was altered so that the "spoon handle is cast in a straight or nearly straight, form, and with the end of the handle much larger than ordinary."

In a patent dated June 29, 1886, William Bradel of New York City improved upon Mix's idea with the "insertion of a tinned wire shank the curvature of which corresponds to the curvature of the spoon or fork" (Fig. 8).

Garry I. Mix, Wallingford, Connecticut, nephew of William Mix, obtained several patents for the improvement of spoons (Fig. 9). His first patent was for an iron spoon made in two pieces and fastened together with a rivet, the whole "to be tinned or galvanized." This patent is dated October 27, 1857. Then, like his uncle, he also patented an invention of "a new and useful Improvement in Wiring and Strengthening Cast-Metal Spoons," the wires in this case being flattened rather than round (Figs. 10, 11). This patent is dated February 26, 1861.

Garry I. Mix was also granted two other patents for "the Form of Spoon Shanks," whose purpose was to provide strengthened shanks which would not break so readily. These were Patents No. 1,651, August 19, 1862, and No. 2,249, January 30, 1866.

Lack of strength in spoon handles must have been a continuing problem. Florian Grosjean of New York City sought a solution to the problem by stamping or swaging sheet-metal spoons with a longitudinal ridge for strength-

(No Model.)

W. BRADEL.
MANUFACTURE OF SPOONS.

No. 344,517. Patented June 29, 1886.

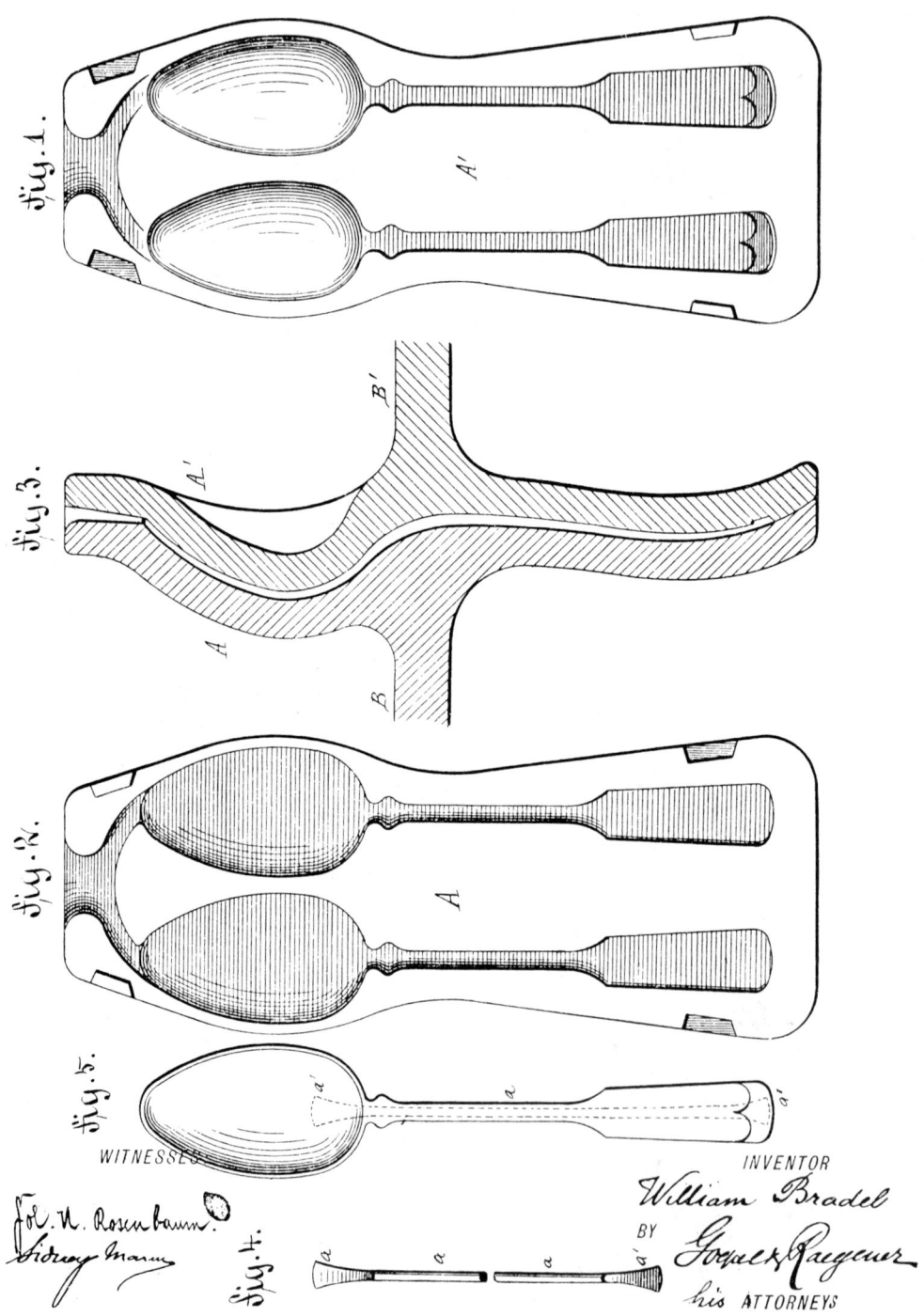

WITNESSES
Sol. N. Rosenbaum
Sidney Mann

INVENTOR
William Bradel
BY
Goepel & Raegener
his ATTORNEYS

Color Plate A. *Right:* Fruit bowl of translucent shaded pink-to-white glass, applied crystal edge, gold decoration. The silverplated stand was made by the Wilcox Silver Plate Co. in 1886; 12½ in. high. *Bottom:* Berry or preserve dish of pressed blue glass in the "Daisy and Button" pattern; silverplated basket made by the Meriden Britannia Co. about 1896; 9 in. high.

Color Plate C. Kerosene lamps with reproduction shades. *Left to right:* Meriden Britannia Co., 1882; Rogers, Smith & Co., 1882.

Color Plate B. (Left page), Pickle Castors. *Back row, left to right:* Blue, Hartford Silver Plate Co., 1890-93; Cranberry, Wm. Rogers Mfg. Co., 1891; Clear, Rogers, Smith & Co., 1896; Green, Derby Silver Co., before 1883. *Front row, left to right:* Cranberry, Wilcox Silver Plate Co., 1886-1897; Double Amber, Meriden Britannia Co., 1878; Blue decorated, Wm. Rogers Mfg. Co., 1891.

Color Plate D. *Left:* Silverplated stand marked "Victor Silver Co." (a division of the Derby Silver Co., Derby, Conn.) with shaded white-to-pink cased glass bowl; multi-colored enamel decoration inside bowl; 8½ in. high. *Right:* Shaded blue-to-white satin glass bowl in a silverplated basket made by the Wm. Rogers Mfg. Co., Hartford, Conn. in 1889; 13 in. high.

Color Plate E. (Next page), *Back row, left to right: Blue edge,* Middletown Plate Co., about 1874; *Crane,* Wm. Rogers Mfg. Co., 1882; *Gold edge,* Meriden Britannia Co., about 1872. *Front row, left to right: Birds,* Meriden Britannia Co., 1878; *Tall,* Meriden Britannia Co., 1868; *Ruby,* Meriden Britannia Co., 1867; *Green,* Hartford Silver Plate Co., about 1880. →

IV. Patented Processes 81

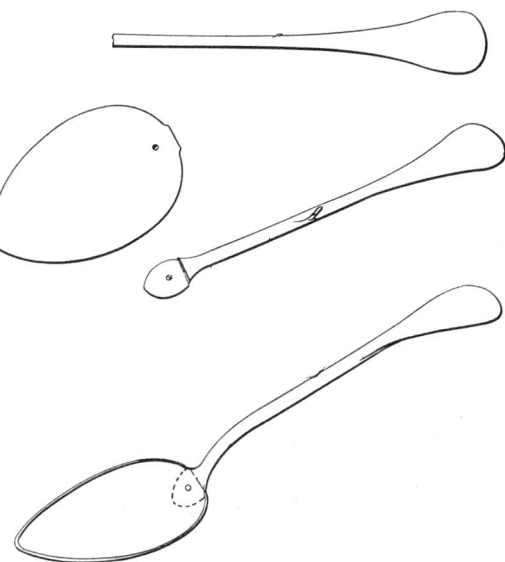

9. Spoon to be made of iron with handle attached by a rivet. The bowl is formed by dies while the handle is made of iron wire. Patent issued to Garry I. Mix, Wallingford, Conn.; Patent No. 18,513; October 27, 1857.

ening (Fig. 12). The original date of this patent was not located but it was reissued under Patent No. 1,509, July 7, 1863.

R. Humphrey, Unionville, Connecticut, and James Fallows, Philadelphia, Pennsylvania, both thought to solve the problem of strengthening spoon handles by stamping the handle blanks wider than normal and turning the edges downward (Figs. 13, 14). Their patents were No. 46,907, March 21, 1865, and No. 54,516, May 8, 1866, respectively.

Maltby Fowler, Northford, Connecticut, in a patent dated September 27, 1881, offered his solution in the form of a spoon blank made of two overlapping pieces of sheet metal riveted together (Fig. 15). In his words, the purpose

10. Flattened, rather than round, wires are used in strengthening spoons made by Garry I. Mix. Patent No. 31,555; February 26, 1861.

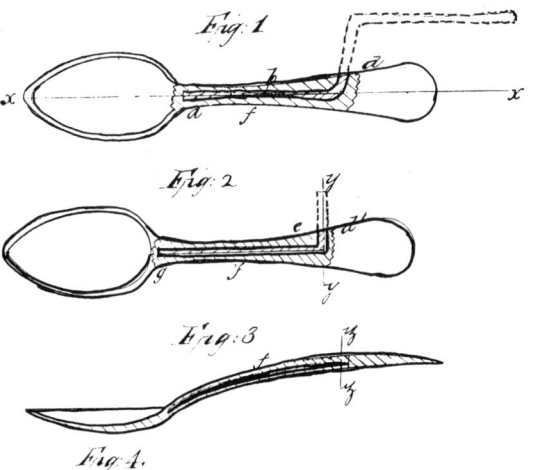

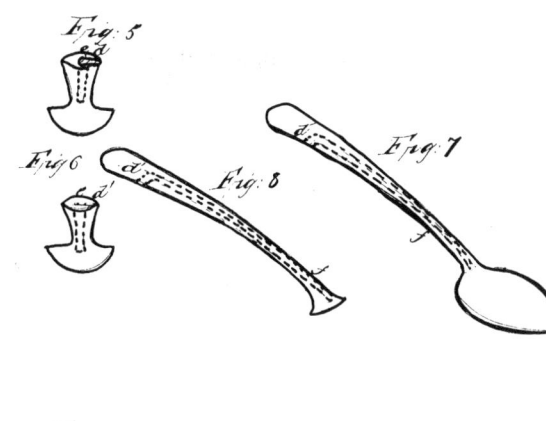

8. An improvement on Mix's idea with the insertion of a curved wire. Patented by William Bradel, New York City; Patent No. 344,517; June 29, 1886.

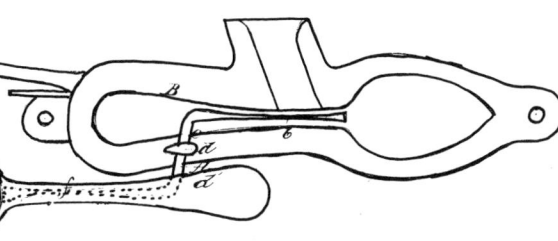

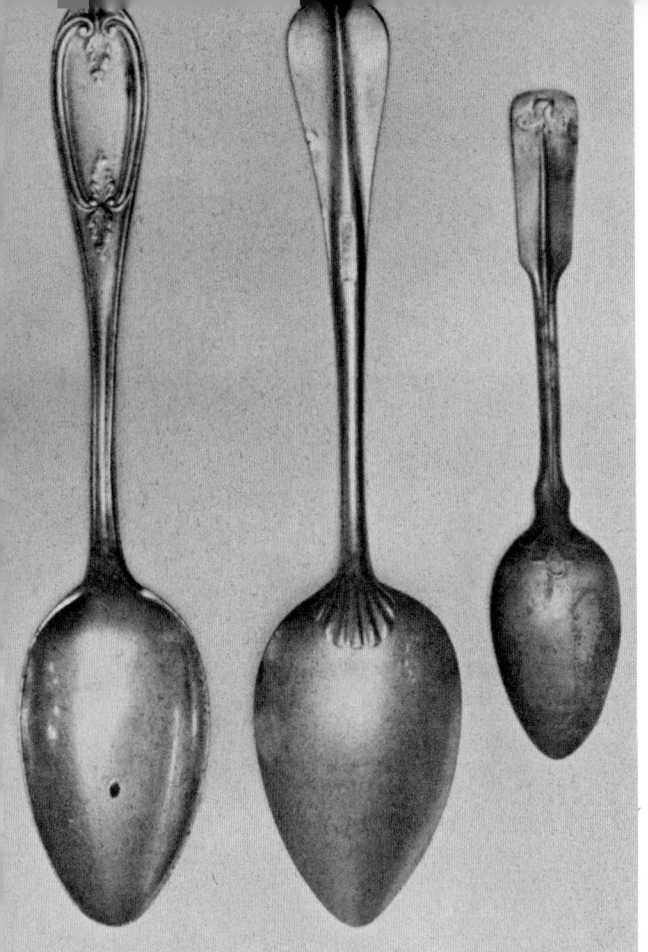

was "to stiffen the narrow parts of their handles."

An important item of expense in the manufacture of spoons is the preparation of the metal for blanks. LeRoy S. White, Waterbury, Connecticut, December 24, 1867, patented a "Spoon blank of such form, and so cut or stamped out of the bar or plate without intervening scrap . . ." which would result in saving the expense of remelting, recasting, and rerolling the metal for blanks. (Fig. 16).

Protection of the points of greatest wear of silverplated flatware has always been of primary concern. Jared C. Blackman, West Meriden, Connecticut, in his patent for the improvement in plated ware, October 29, 1867, stated that "the application of a heavy film of precious metal to the points of greatest

11. Wire-strengthened spoons. *Left to right:* Marked "Pat. Feb. 1861"; "BRIT^A, W."; unmarked.

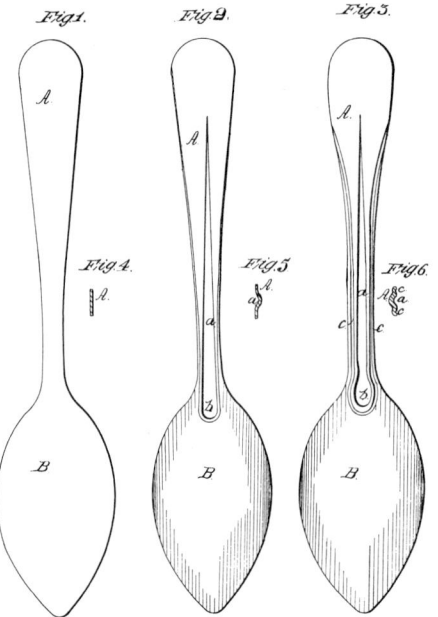

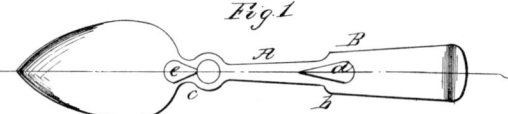

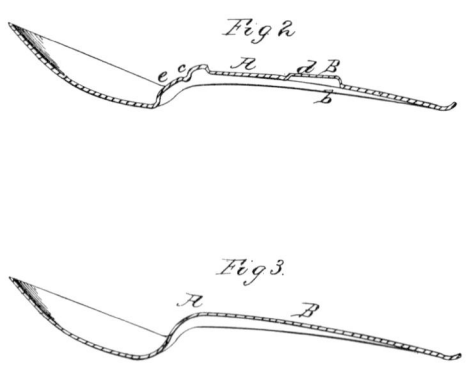

13. Patent for strengthening spoon handles. R. Humphrey, Unionville, Conn.; Patent No. 46,907; March 21, 1865.

12. Spoons swaged with longitudinal ridge for strength. Florian Grosjean, New York City; Patent No. 1,509; reissued July 7, 1863.

IV. PATENTED PROCESSES   83

wear" could be applied "in any suitable manner" (Fig. 17).

George C. Robinson, Cincinnati, Ohio, was also concerned with the points of greatest wear. His approach was different. His patent, dated February 4, 1873, was for the construction of flatware with tiny projections which would receive the wear (Fig. 18), his theory being that "such projections will not look unsightly after the plating upon them is worn off."

The application of small pieces of solid silver to the backs of spoons at critical points is described in the Patent No. 424,503 by William Rogers, Hartford, Connecticut, dated April 1, 1890, Fig. 19). He stated that these pieces were to be made with a design and would serve the purpose of protecting the points of wear as well as adding a decorative touch.

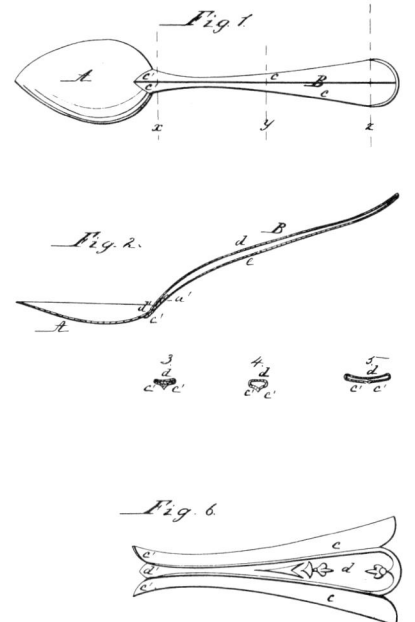

14. Patent for strengthening spoon handles. James Fallows, Philadelphia, Pa.: Patent No. 54,516; May 8, 1866.

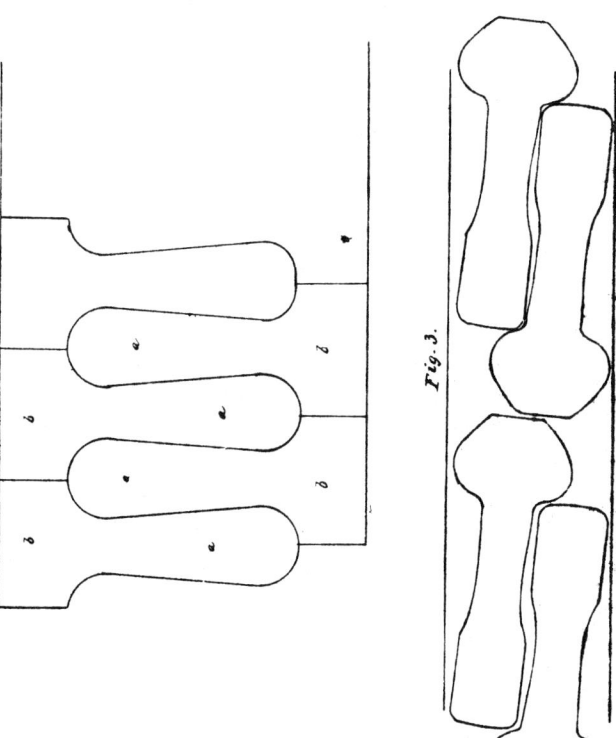

15. Spoon blank made of two overlapping pieces of sheet metal riveted together for strength. Maltby Fowler, Northford, Conn.; Patent No. 247,554; September 27, 1881.

16. Interlocking spoon blanks to save metal. LeRoy S. White, Waterbury, Conn.; Patent No. 72,706; December 24, 1867.

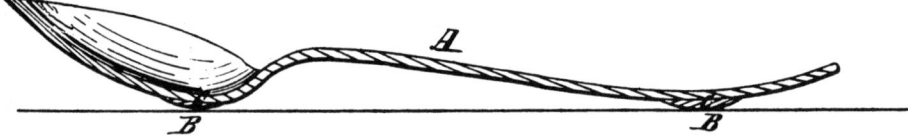

17. Improvement of plated ware by application of heavy film of silver to the points of greatest wear. Jared C. Blackman, West Meriden, Conn.; Patent No. 70,156; October 29, 1867.

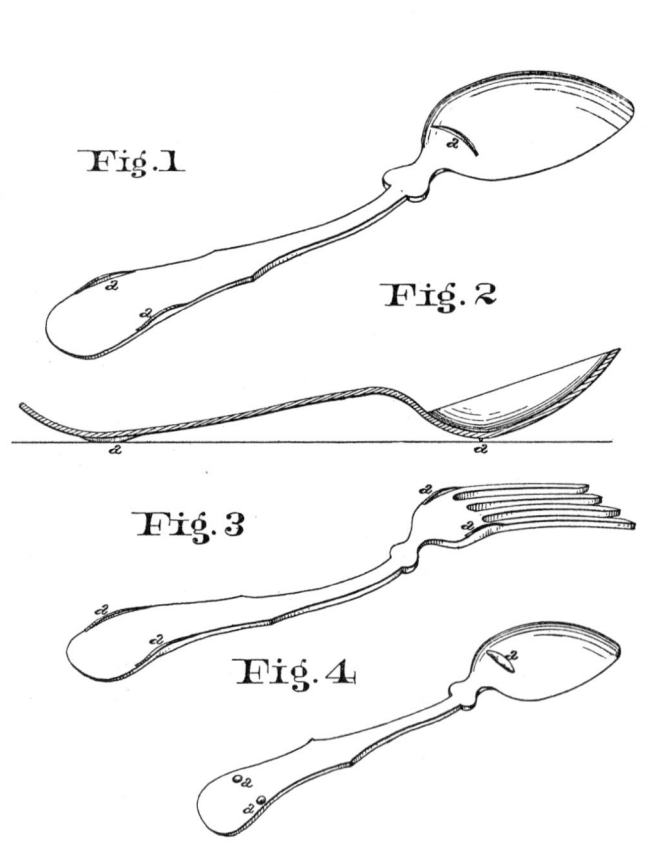

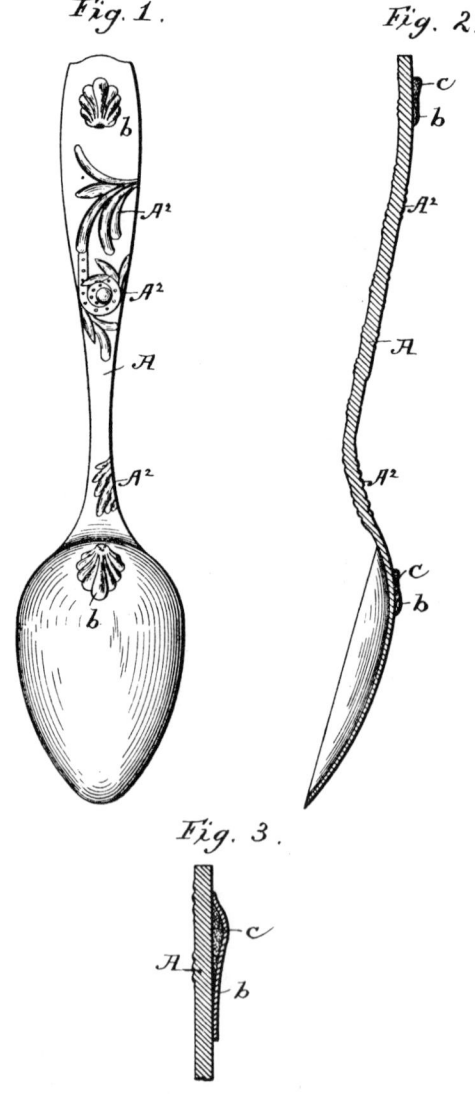

18. Patent for the construction of flatware with tiny ribs or projections which would receive the wear. George C. Robinson, Cincinnati, Ohio; Patent No. 135,590; February 4, 1873.

19. Patent No. 424,503 by William Rogers, Hartford, Conn.; dated April 1, 1890.

IV. Patented Processes   85

Robert Wallace, Wallingford, Connecticut, obtained Patent No. 220,002, September 23, 1879, for the cold-rolling of homogeneous steel to manufacture forks or spoons (Fig. 20). The method entailed cutting the blanks to desired size and form; imparting a smooth surface to the blank; applying an adhesive substance, such as turpentine, to the blanks or rolls, or both, preparatory to rolling, and afterward cold-rolling the blanks to impart the desired thickness to different portions; annealing the cold-rolled blanks in air-tight receptacles; and stamping, shaping, and plating the blanks to form the completed article.

20. Drawing that accompanied Robert Wallace's Patent No. 220,002, dated September 23, 1879, for the cold-rolling of homogeneous steel to manufacture forks or spoons.

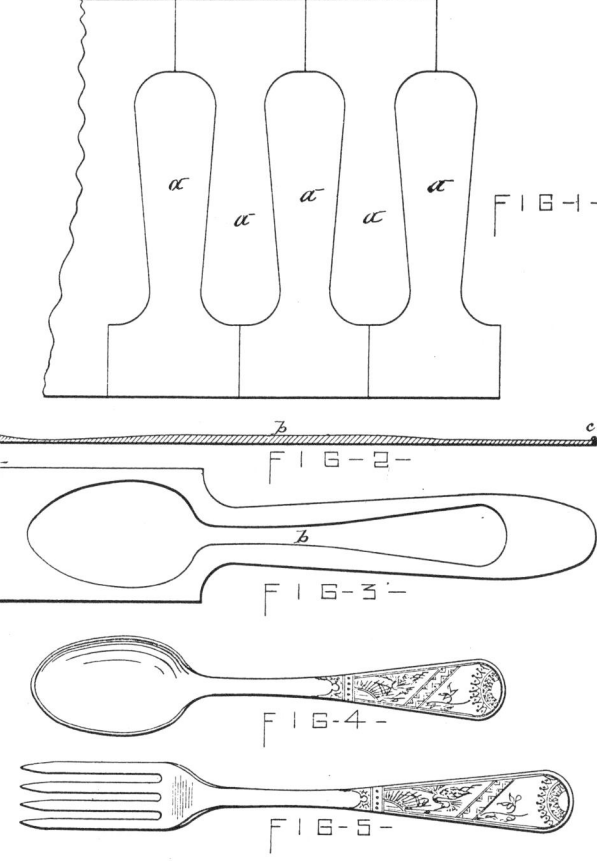

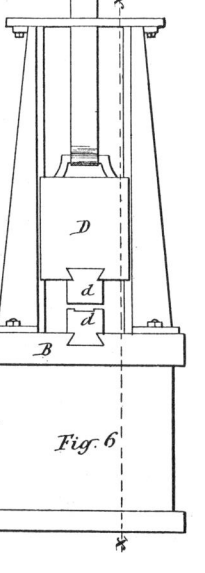

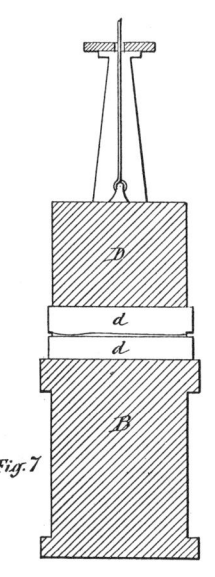

21 and 21a. Drawings which accompanied the specifications for manufacture of spoons and forks by Leonard F. Dunn, Oneida Community, N.Y.; Patent No. 280,918; July 10, 1883.

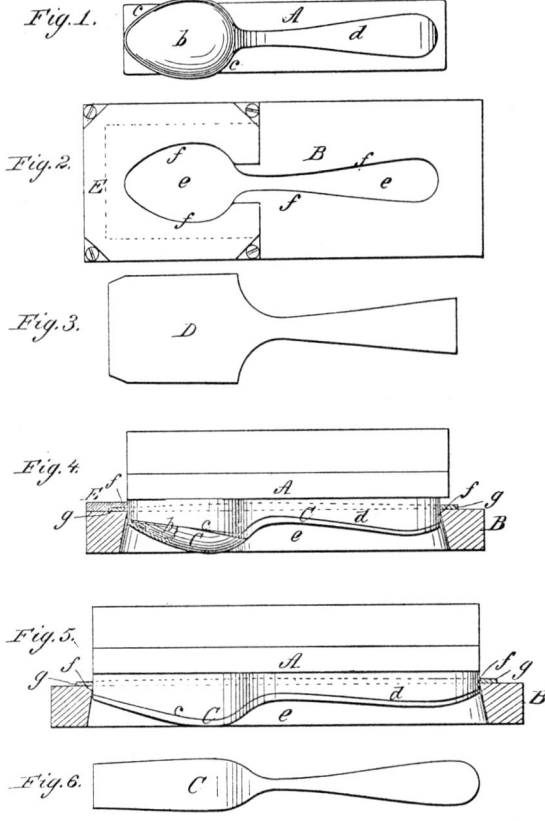

22. Manufacture of spoons and forks with blanks curved to the shape of the curved die in which they are to be stamped with a design. Joseph Sheridan, Jersey City, N.J.; Patent No. 269,726; December 26, 1882.

Leonard F. Dunn, Oneida Community, New York, described his entire process for manufacturing spoons in Patent No. 280,918, granted July 10, 1883 (Figs. 21, 21a). Excerpts from that lengthy description give an idea of the amount of work involved.

This invention consists in a novel process of forming from malleable or wrought-iron, or from ingot-iron, which is sometimes called "homogeneous steel," forks, spoons and analogous table-ware designed to be plated with silver or other precious or desirable metals. . . . Heretofore it has been deemed impractical to form of malleable iron or wrought-iron a fork or spoon susceptible to a perfect plating of silver or other precious metal, owing to the porosity or want of compactness of the base upon which to apply the plating, and in cases where the attempt has been made it was found necessary to first apply to the surface of the article a coating of tin to fill the pores and form a compact and smooth surface. To obviate this expense resort has been had to the use of steel as the material for the blank; but in the employment of this material great difficulties have been encountered in cold-rolling out the blanks into the requisite length and shape. The smooth and hard blanks offered such resistance to the impingement of the rolls as to cause the blanks to slip and receive the wrong impression from the rolls . . . [and] generally presents an uneven surface, and requires grinding or other smoothing operation. Furthermore, the steel blank . . . becomes so hard and compact as to resist the impressions to be subsequently made by the usual dies by which the surface . . . is to receive its ornamentation, and therefore has to undergo an annealing process before the finishing of the surface can be effected. . . .

I form the blanks . . . in any suitable manner, from malleable or wrought-iron, though preferably from wrought-iron, by punching said blanks in the usual manner, out of sheets of such metal . . . which sheets I cleanse or scale, by a scratch-brush or other suitable means, beforehand, so as to save the extra time and labor of so treating the blanks individually. The blanks are made of a form to avoid the waste of material. . . . Said blanks are passed cold between graded rollers, which distend said blanks and impart to them the various thicknesses required at different parts of the spoon. . . .

Although the soft-iron blank is not so liable to slip while passing between the rolls, yet I effectually guard against said accidents by providing the rolls with a transverse crease, which forms across the front end of the blank a bead, c, and thereby obtains a firm hold thereon. The blank thus rolled I cut into the shape of a spoon or fork blank, as represented by the letter b . . . and introduce the same, together with either or both charcoal and cyanide of potassium, into an air-tight muffle and subject it to sufficient heat to partly or wholly carbonize the blank, which by aid of the cyanide, is effected so rapidly as not to change the form of the blank, and while producing a surface which is less liable to corrode . . . and leaves the blank sufficiently soft and in proper condition to receive the subsequent impressions of the dies by which the surfaces are to be ornamented . . . and impart to the blank the requisite tenacity and elasticity. . . . I thoroughly cleanse it, and then smooth and further compact or solidify the surfaces . . . by strokes or impingements of polished planishing dies d d, secured to the bed B and drop D of a suitable press. . . . The dies are finely graded to correspond to the various thicknesses required at different parts of the spoon or fork . . . after trimming and finishing edges . . . by subjecting the blank to the impingement of suitable dies of a drop-press, said dies being formed with cameo configurations, by which they impress on the spoon the desired ornamentation. . . . The spoon is thus prepared to receive the plating . . . and is susceptible of a high finish or polish.

The purpose of the invention patented December 26, 1882, by Joseph Sheridan, Jersey City, New Jersey, was to produce fork and spoon blanks "in the required bent form of the article to be produced, and so that it conforms to the shape of the curved die in which it is afterward struck up or embellished" (Fig. 22).

William A. Warner, Syracuse, New York, acquired two patents (No. 309,013, December 9, 1884, and No. 337,099, March 2, 1886) for a process whereby a solid block of silver was inlaid at the crucial points, affording a positive guarantee against the base metal being exposed through wear (Fig. 23). The patent rights to this process were acquired by Holmes & Edwards and it is still used.

A few years later, Warner, then living in Bridgeport, Connecticut, took out Patent No. 755,727, March 29, 1904, for an improved method of inlaying blanks with blocks of solid silver (Fig. 24). This patent was assigned to the Holmes & Edwards company.

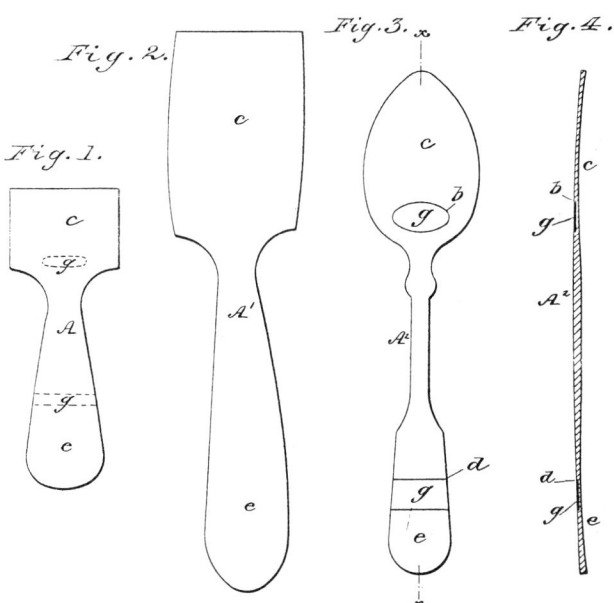

23. Process whereby a solid block of silver was inlaid at the points of greatest wear. William A. Warner, Syracuse, N.Y.; Patent No. 337,099; March 2, 1886.

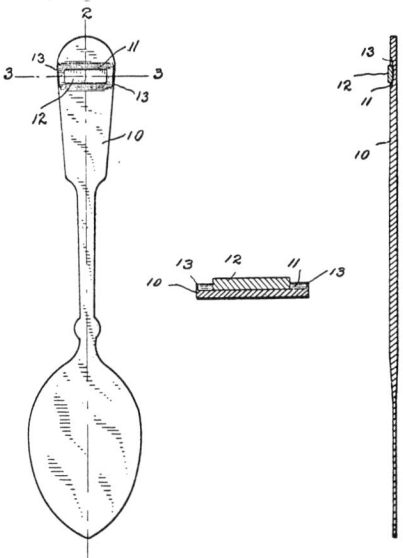

24. An improved method of inlaying solid silver at points of greatest wear. William A. Warner, Bridgeport, Conn. Patent No. 755,727; March 29, 1904; assigned to the Holmes & Edwards Co.

(No Model.)

H. C. HART.
ART OF MAKING SPOONS.

No. 458,168.   Patented Aug. 25, 1891.

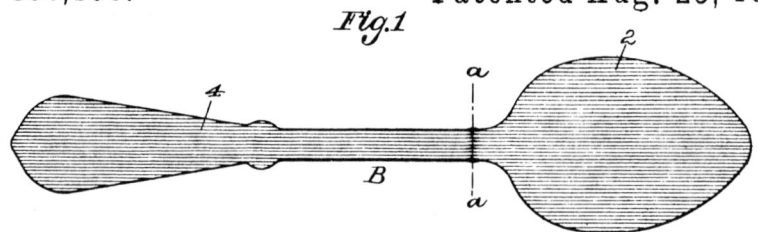

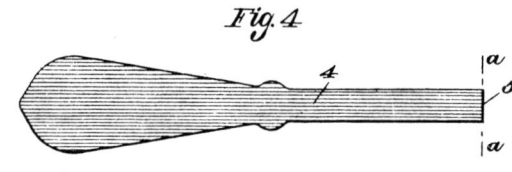 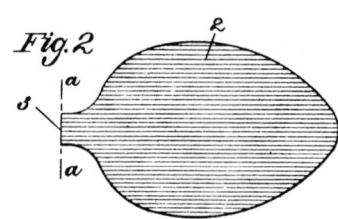

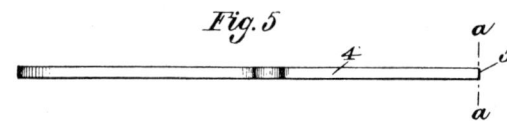 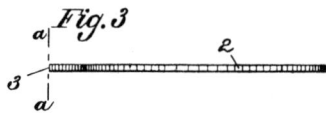

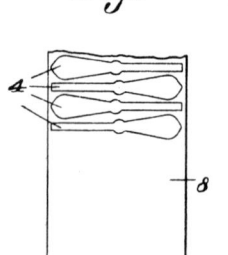 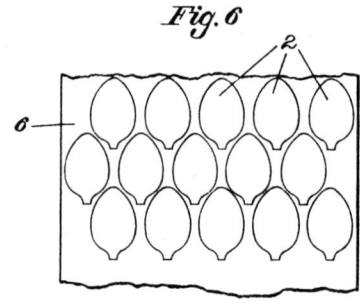

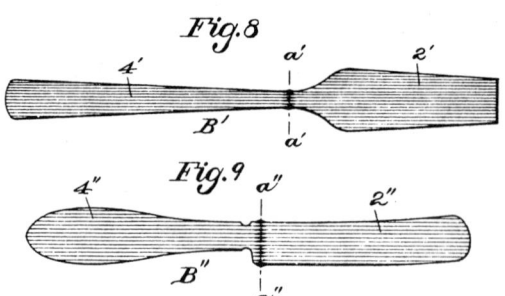

Witnesses: Inventor:
Henry L. Rickard.   Hubert C. Hart,
H. Mallner   By his Attorney
     F. H. Richards

IV. PATENTED PROCESSES   89

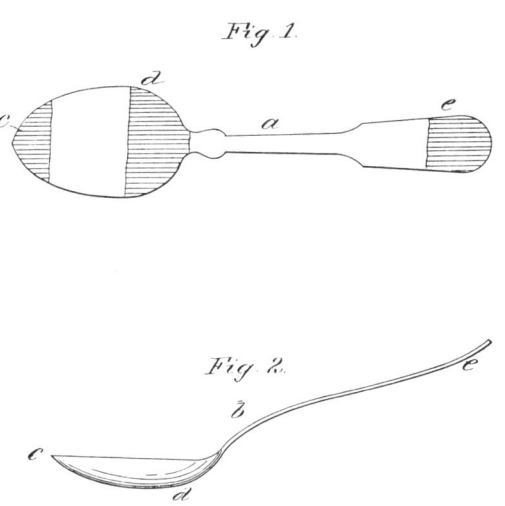

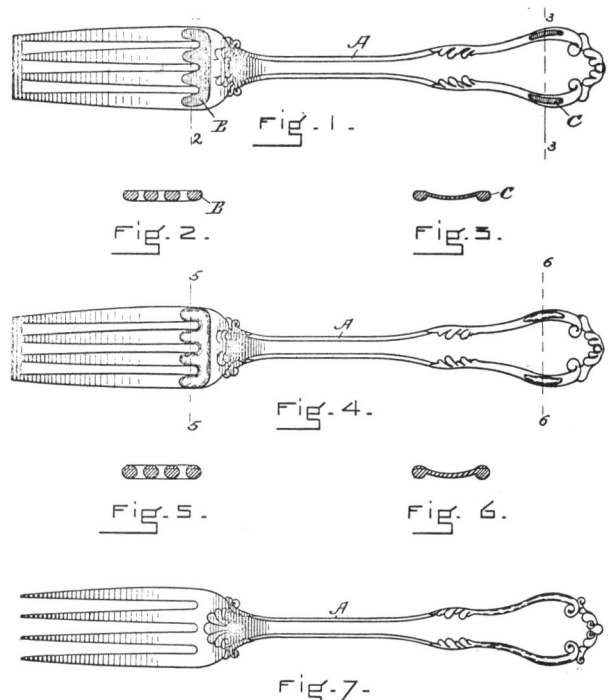

26. Another patent for reinforcing the wearing points. William E. Pleadwell, Bridgeport, Conn.; Patent No. 477,265; June 21, 1892.

The process patented by Hubert C. Hart, Unionville, Connecticut (No. 458,168, August 25, 1891) was for cutting knife, fork, and spoon bowls and handles from different thicknesses of metal and welding them together (Fig. 25). While this would have avoided the use of graded rollers, it would have meant using the time-consuming process of welding each article. The process could not have been judged satisfactory as it is not used.

Another means of reinforcing the wearing points of silverplated flatware was patented by William E. Pleadwell, Bridgeport, Connecticut (No. 477,265, June 21, 1892). Pleadwell's patent called for "electroplating such points in a blank and then subjecting the plated surface to pressure, then forming the article to

25. Process for cutting knife, fork, and spoon bowls and handles from different thicknesses of metal and welding them together to avoid the expense of graded rollers. Hubert C. Hart, Unionville, Conn.; Patent No. 458,168; August 25, 1891.

27. A process of reinforcing points of greatest wear. George Hale Brabrook, Taunton, Mass.; Patent No. 606,183; June 28, 1898; assigned to Reed & Barton.

shape, and finally plating and finishing the surface, including those parts previously plated." A resist of wax or varnish was used to protect the surfaces not to be plated during the first part of the process (Fig. 26).

George Hale Brabrook, on June 28, 1898, patented for Reed & Barton a process (No. 606,183) whereby a portion of the base metal is removed by grinding or filing and replacing the base metal thus removed by silver or other metal and then subjecting the article to the final striking (Fig. 27).

Many other patents have been secured as the employment of improved methods is a continuing process. These later patents apply mainly to various types of machinery used in manufacturing. All have the common aim of producing better flatware.

1. Vase representing the triumph of Science and the Industrial Arts in the Great Exhibition. *Art Journal Illustrated Catalogue of the Industry of All Nations*, London, 1851.

CHAPTER V

Development of Styles

One of the earliest arts practiced in America, silversmithing had its beginnings within a short time after the arrival of the Pilgrims at Plymouth although, undoubtedly, the first silver used in the Colonies was brought here by the settlers.

Two distinct influences helped to determine the styles that American silver followed. By far the greater influence was that of English silver since most of the first settlers were English and were under the political control of England. English silver itself was influenced by the Continent through Dutch sources and immigrant Huguenot silversmiths from France. Then there was a direct impact on American styles through the immigration of Dutch settlers in New York and through Huguenot refugees who settled there.

The earliest American silver, following the then-current English style, was in the tradition of the Renaissance. Basic rectilinear forms were ornamented with paneling or bands of matting. Standing cups with slightly flaring rims were mounted on turned balusters. Dutch styles were more massive and ran to heavy ornament executed in relief by embossing and chasing. Many Dutch Colonial pieces made use of abundant engraved ornamentation.

Colonial craftsmen produced silver that was entirely handwrought; no dies or mechanical tools were employed. The articles they made may be divided into three categories: ecclesiastical or church, domestic, and personal. The scope of this book is concerned mainly with domestic silver. In this class, early silversmiths produced tankards, mugs, beakers, teapots, coffeepots, kettles and urns, tea caddies, sauce boats, punch bowls, pitchers, covered grace or loving cups, saltcellars, casters or shakers, candlesticks and snuffers, braziers, spoons, and knives and forks.

The richness of the baroque style that was introduced in American silver near the end of the seventeenth century featured rich gadrooning, fluting, and embossed ornament. The plainer surfaces and sturdy proportions of what has been called the "Queen Anne period" did not actually appear in American silver until around 1715 to 1720 but it persisted until at least 1750 and was then replaced by the profusion of cast shell, C-scroll ornaments, and pear- and inverted-pear-shape bodies of the rococo period.

About the time of the War for Independence the asymmetry of the rococo was discarded in favor of the classic urn shape. This return to a more orderly style was derived at first from the work of Robert Adam, who, in turn, had been inspired by visits to Roman ruins. Classicism was quickly adopted by American silversmiths for the new republic was being compared to that of ancient Rome. Festooned swags of drapery in bright-cut engraving, applied reeded moldings, beading, and fluting were features of the classic style.

When the War for Independence was won in 1776, because of the intense feelings against everything English, French styles became fashionable. Designs in hollow ware became larger and more elaborate. The simplicity of earlier Colonial days gave way entirely to the highly ornamental styles of the French Empire. Applied bands of laurel, oak leaves and acorn borders, Greek key, and other geometric designs were typical ornament. Ball and winged-paw feet and cast finials and caryatid supports were also featured.

A few years before the accession of Victoria to the throne of England in 1837 romanticism began to replace the Empire style though the latter persisted in combination with romantic features and anticipated the rococo revival. Naturalistic motifs were an important feature in the design of rococo silver in the middle of the nineteenth century. Shapes as well as decoration of articles became naturalistic. Leaf-shaped vessels sprouted rustic twigs or grape vines for handles while finials were acorns, bunches of grapes, birds, or animals. Classic shapes, based on Greek and Etruscan pitchers, were popular. All-over repoussé of floral designs and landscape scenes was one of the most important types of decoration. Gothic design elements and interlaced Elizabethan strapwork were found but did not assume the importance of the pear- and inverted-pear-shaped coffeepots and teapots and pitchers of exaggerated proportions which were encrusted with applied ornaments such as grape vines, oak branches, acanthus leaves, and other rococo features.

Following the successful electroplating experiments of the Rogers brothers in the late 1840s, American-made silverplated wares began to appear on the market. Spoons, at first, were the principle product. The styles followed those of coin silver and were plain or fiddle shapes. "Threaded," "Tipped," "Olive," "Beaded," and other similar patterns were all introduced before 1860.

Britannia makers were quick to realize the appeal of the new silverplated wares and soon were offering their regular britannia line to which a coating of silver had been applied. Because of the britannia tradition and because of the restrictions imposed by the methods of forming britannia wares, these articles, especially the tea sets, were simpler in design than the then-current styles in solid silver.

The catalog of the Crystal Palace Exhibition, held in London in 1851, was replete with elaborate designs, massive in scale and weighed down with detail. Flatware handles of twisted branches and curling vines were teamed with spoon bowls in the form of flowers and leaves. Tazzas and flower baskets whose supports were writhing snakes or fanciful foliage received great praise. Centerpieces combined statuettes symbolizing the exploits of historical figures with palm trees, lotus plants, banyan trees, and sacred moon plants. Classic shapes were sometimes used for tea services but were so encrusted with cherubs, animals, gargoyles, dragons, sea horses, birds, and grapevines with clusters of grapes that the original shape was almost obscured. The firm of Elkington, Mason & Co. exhibited a number of their electroplated wares (Fig. 1). Among the most striking of these was "a vase intended to represent the triumph of Science and the Industrial Arts in the Great Exhibition; the style is Elizabethan enriched. Four statuettes on the body of the vase represent Newton, Bacon, Shakespeare, and Watt, commemorating Astronomy, Philosophy,

2. Service of solid gold presented to Edward K. Collins by the Citizens of New York as a tribute for his establishment of an American line of transatlantic steamers. The service was made by Ball, Black & Co., by whom it was exhibited at the Crystal Palace Exhibition in London in 1851 and again at the New York Crystal Palace in 1853–54. *The World of Art and Industry,* New York, 1854.

3. First pewter tea set made by Reed & Barton.

4. First plated silver tea set made by Reed & Barton.

Poetry, and Mechanics respectively. On the four bas-reliefs, between these figures, the practical operations of Science and Art are displayed, and their influences typified by the figures on the base, indicating War, Rebellion, Hatred, and Revenge, overthrown and chained. The recognition and the reward of peaceful industry are symbolized by the figure of Prince Albert surmounting the composition, who, as Patron of the Exhibition, is rewarding the successful contributors. The height of the vase is four feet; it was designed and modelled by Mr. W. Beattie."

Silverplated articles from several British manufacturers were illustrated. Tea sets and centerpieces, revolving liquor stands, and fish slices were among the exhibits. Dixon & Sons of Sheffield exhibited a tureen and dish described as "examples of the plain but truly elegant Grecian style adapted to objects of ordinary use, and it is certainly not a little refreshing to the eye, somewhat overwearied with the constant recurrence of the elaborate and often over-decorated patterns of the Italian style, and those founded upon it. The absence of a *plethora* of ornament is amply atoned for by the simple beauty of that which appears in these designs."

No American silverplate manufacturers are mentioned in the 1851 catalog but the influence of this Great Exhibition was evident in the New York Crystal Palace Exhibition, held two years later, in 1853. The Collins solid gold service (Fig. 2) and the castor by the Ames Manufacturing Company (*see Chapter VII, Fig. 1*) are ample proof.

International exhibitions have long been a source of inspiration. In 1854 Commodore Matthew Galbraith Perry opened Japan to the western world but the impact of this new design source was not fully felt until after 1862, when the first important exhibit of Japanese art and artifacts was shown at the International Exhibition held in London.

By 1860 the population of this country had increased enormously and many people had money to spend on more than the bare necessities. The relatively low cost of silverplate made it available to a large sector of the population that was untutored in artistic values. The beauty of hand craftsmanship was set aside for quantity production. Machines had largely replaced handwork in silversmithing, and while great progress was made in technique, artistic taste did not keep pace. The 10 or 15 years following the close of the Civil War was a period of chaos in art in this country. From about 1865 to 1880 the general taste was at a lower standard than at any time before or since.

Quantities of silverplate appeared on Victorian tables. It became the true status symbol of the period. A complete tea and coffee service was the goal of every housewife. Most sets included three pots, sugar bowl, creamer, and waste bowl. The largest of these pots

5. Design Patent No. 657; granted to William Hattersley and Charles Dickinson, Newark, N.J.; July 4, 1854.

The above Cuts are only intended to represent a few of the great variety of Goods manufactured at this Establishment.

Dealers will find it convenient to be able to obtain at one place nearly every article in Silver, desired either for ornament or utility. Prices low as work of equal merit can be obtained in the country.

was the coffeepot which, in addition to the trademark and style number, was sometimes stamped "7." The teapot was stamped "6," and the third pot, for hot water, stamped "5." This denoted the capacity in half-pints. Matching pieces such as swing kettles for hot water, coffee urns, spoon holders, butter dishes, cake baskets, syrup pitchers, and trays were available as adjuncts to the tea table and for display on the sideboard.

Tea sets are among the comparatively few of the many types of articles made in silverplate whose popularity continues. For this reason, they may be used to trace the development of design from almost the very beginning of electroplating to the present.

While some of the first plated tea sets were the regular line of britannia makers to which silverplating had been applied, it was not long until the manufacturers of silverplated wares were marketing specially designed tea services (Figs. 3, 4).

The earliest patent for a design for a tea or coffee service was granted to William Hattersley and Charles Dickinson, Newark, New Jersey, July 4, 1854 (Fig. 5). Although the patent papers fail to specify the material to be used, William Hattersley is listed in the Newark city directories of 1849–50, as a silversmith. He also worked with britannia metal. The cast grapes and leaf decorations of the handle, spout, and finial have a sculptural quality and yet they conform to the body shape and would in no way interfere with function. Both shape and decoration are related to the Collins solid gold service exhibited at the Crystal Palace Exhibition in New York in 1853. However, the pedestal-footed teapot by Hattersley and Dickinson shows considerably more restraint than the overly exuberant decoration of the Collins ware.

No such restraint was used in the

6. Advertisement of Gorham Co. *Illustrated American Advertiser*, Boston, Mass., 1853.

7. Coffee urn made by Rogers Bros. Mfg. Co. between 1853 and 1862.
8. Teapot of classic urn shape, made by Rogers Bros. Mfg. Co. about 1855.

1862 (Fig. 7). This urn, of vase shape with fluted lower body and fluted, high-domed cover, is decorated with bands of guilloche, a classic Greek architectural ornament. The stand rests on paw feet and is enriched with beading, scrolls, and modified palmettes. The finial is a squat vase shape.

A teapot, also of classic urn shape, made by Rogers Bros. Mfg. Co. about 1855 is decorated with bands of beading and Greek key (Fig. 8). The urn finial repeats the shape of the body.

Another teapot, made about 1857, by Rogers Bros. Mfg. Co. has a strawberry

9. Teapot made by Rogers Bros. Mfg. Co. about 1857.

production of the "Testimonials in silver, richly embellished with Appropriate Designs," in an advertisement of 1853 (Fig. 6).

The coffee urn, made by Rogers Bros. Mfg. Co., can be dated within a few years by the mark which was used by them when they were in business in Hartford, Connecticut, from 1853 to

10. From the first illustrated Rogers Bros. Mfg. Co. catalog, 1860.

10a. Patent Office drawing of tea set patented by A. Leonard, February 23, 1858, and assigned to the Rogers Bros. Mfg. Co.

V. Development of Styles 99

11. Swing kettle and coffee urn. Rogers Bros. Mfg. Co. catalog, 1860.

12. Reed & Barton's first patented design for a teapot. This five-piece set, whose original design was patented January 12, 1858, is displayed in the dining room of the Chatillon-DeMenil Mansion, St. Louis, Mo.

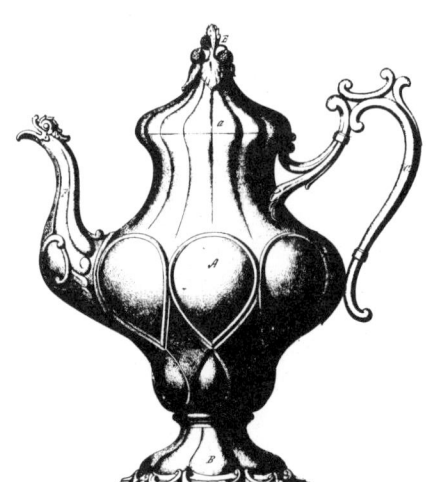

12a. Patent drawing of Reed & Barton's first patented design for a teapot. Design Patent No. 981; January 12, 1858; designed by Henry G. Reed.
12b. Trademarks on Reed & Barton's first patented design for a teapot.

finial and leafy scroll and floral engraving (Fig. 9).

The first illustrated Rogers Bros. Mfg. Co. catalog, published in 1860, depicts a patented tea set plated on German silver (Fig. 10). Patent Office records show that the design was patented by A. Leonard on February 23, 1858, and was assigned to the Rogers Bros. Mfg. Co. (Fig. 10a).

This same Rogers Bros. catalog offered a swing kettle and coffee urn in "Britannia" or "Plated," with the additional choice of "Plain" or "Chased." Presumably, both sets would bear the cast floral decorations (Fig. 11).

On January 12, 1858, Henry G. Reed received a patent for the design of the first Reed & Barton patented teapot (Figs. 12, 12a, 12b). Complete services, consisting of coffeepot, teapot, sugar bowl, creamer, and waste bowl were made. One such set, with its unique wild-strawberry finials, is displayed in the dining room of the Chatillon-De-Menil Mansion, St. Louis, Missouri. The lobes of the bodies of these pieces are reminiscent of the "pineapple" lobing, a typical Germanic type of decoration particularly prevalent in Nürnberg.

A teapot by Bancroft, Redfield & Rice, New York City, was made between 1857 and 1863 and can be dated by changes in the firm name since on March 25, 1863, the company became Redfield & Rice (Fig. 13). Decorations are cast floral and grape designs, applied bands, and embossed and engraved flowers and grapes on matted grounds. The finial echoes the body shape of the teapot.

George W. Smith's patented design for a teapot, dated April 26, 1859, is described in his own words as follows: "The base of the tea-pot is formed somewhat similar to the scotia and upper half of the torus of the composite order of architecture combined; and, in order to accord to the flutes and convex ridges, running into each other, and the embossed quatrefoil and trefoil embellishments in which they terminate, it is ornamented at its lower part with a series of trefoil embossings. . . ." The spout is fluted and ridged to correspond with the body of the pot. The cover is embellished with a finial "formed somewhat similar to a pineapple, and ornamented with inverted leaves and other such elaborate crocket-work. . . ." This fluted design was still being shown in the Meriden Britannia catalog issued August 1867 (Fig. 14). Teapots in two sizes, a coffeepot, sugar bowl, creamer,

14. George W. Smith's design for a teapot, patented April 26, 1859.

A Meriden Britannia teapot with high-domed cover, cast leafy scroll handle, applied egg-and-tongue and beaded borders was made in 1861 (Fig. 15). The same design was also offered

15. Meriden Britannia Co. teapot made in 1861.

13. Teapot made between 1857 and 1863 by Bancroft, Redfield & Rice, New York City.

and waste bowl were illustrated. The design must have been a popular one as it was also used for ice pitchers, double-wall ice urns, water pitchers, and other articles.

16. Tea service made by Rogers & Bro. about 1865.

in the 1867 Meriden Britannia catalog with Grecian Chased or Grecian Engraved as well as Plain or Damask Chased designs as shown here.

A hunting dog appears as the finial on a Rogers & Bro. tea service while his quarry appears as the deer head and feet (Fig. 16). A nearly identical service is in the Museum of History and Technology in Washington, D.C. (*See Chapter VI, Figs. 19–21.*) The tea service in the museum was presented in

17. Medallion design tea service made by Rogers Bros. (West Meriden, Conn.) about 1867.

V. Development of Styles   103

1868 to General Judson Kilpatrick on the occasion of his marriage.

Medallions were a popular Renaissance motif among silver manufacturers. Two tea services, one with the "Rogers Bros." trademark (Fig. 17) and the other with the Meriden Britannia Company mark (Fig. 18), were typical. So popular was the Medallion motif that it was also found on ice pitchers, castors, wine stands, pickle and preserve stands, cake dishes and cake baskets, fruit stands, celery stands, syrup pitchers, goblets and cups, spoon holders, napkin rings, mustard cups, card receivers, vegetable dishes, tureens, and flatware. Illustrated historic design books and manuals of the mid-nineteenth century, in which cameos of Greece and Rome were illustrated, were the principal source of inspiration for these designs.

Medallion patterns, in both flatware and hollow ware, have long appealed to purchasers of silver and presently have great appeal to collectors. The appearance of three "Medallion" patterns by San Francsico manufacturers eight or ten years after their vogue began suggests how popular these patterns were in the Far West and how widespread their distribution.

Pyriform tea services were made throughout the 1860s. Two such services are represented here by the teapots and were illustrated in the 1867 Meriden Britannia catalog (Figs. 19, 20). It is interesting to note that the Grecian engraved was priced at ten dollars while the plain teapot was eight; two dollars then, covered the cost of the handwork of engraving. Being done by machine, the engine-turned design was, fittingly enough, added for a mere dollar and a half. The leafy scrolls on handles, spouts, and finials and the applied borders are typically rococo.

18. Medallion motif tea service made by Meriden Britannia Co. about 1867.

19. Pyriform coffeepot made by the Meriden Britannia Co. 1867.
20. Coffeepot made by the Meriden Britannia Co. 1867. Identical to Fig. 19 except for engraving.

A complete departure in shape is found in the acorn-shaped vessels of the "Charter Oak" pattern (Fig. 21). Made by the Meriden Britannia Company and illustrated in their 1867 catalog, it is one of the few designs of that early period to be named. Naturalism is carried out to the fullest extent in the cast oak leaves and acorns on the handles, spouts, and finials as well as in the embossing and engraving of additional oak designs on the bodies.

Several complete tea services and numerous odd pieces identical, or similar, to the pedestal-footed teapot have been found in the Baltimore, Maryland, area. The ram's head on the squared-off handle was a feature of many pieces made in solid silver by Samuel Kirk of Baltimore (Fig. 22). The finial is a grape cluster and leaves. No marks identify the maker.

The squared-off handle of the teapot designed and patented by William Parkin, January 12, 1869, for Reed & Barton, presages the style that was to dominate teapot handles for a number of years (Fig. 23).

Tea sets of the 1870s may be typified by the "long-legged look," squared-off handles, and ornamentations which, more often than not, bore no relationship to each other nor to the shape of the pots themselves. The angularity of handles was often repeated in supports, in the spout, and in the body of the vessel itself. Straight-sided vessels were engraved and chased with designs of flowers, butterflies, birds, and geometric designs—the latter seldom having any relationship to the shape of the vessel. Supports were often animals, masks, or geometric figures.

George Gill's design for a teapot, patented April 18, 1871, embodies a lion-head finial, cast acanthus-leaf thumb rest, S-scrolls, and neo-Renaissance cast mask supports on a kettledrum shape (Fig. 24). Note that the design as submitted to the Patent Office (Fig. 24a) specified a pedestal base while the man-

21. "Charter Oak" pattern tea set made by the Meriden Britannia Co. about 1867.

ufactured product is supported by four mask feet. Other examples of this same style have been noted with different engraved designs.

Also supported by mask feet is the teapot patented by William Parkin, for Reed & Barton, May 21, 1872 (Fig. 25), and the one made by the Webster Manufacturing Company of Brooklyn, New York, also about 1872 (Fig. 26). The mask on the last-mentioned will immediately be recognized by collectors

22. Coffeepot with ram's head decoration on handle. No marks.

106 AMERICAN SILVERPLATE

23. Teapot designed and patented by William Parkin, January 12, 1869 for Reed & Barton.
24. Teapot designed by George Gill and patented April 18, 1871.

24a. Patent Office drawing of George Gill's teapot.
25. Teapot patented by William Parkin for Reed & Barton, May 21, 1872.

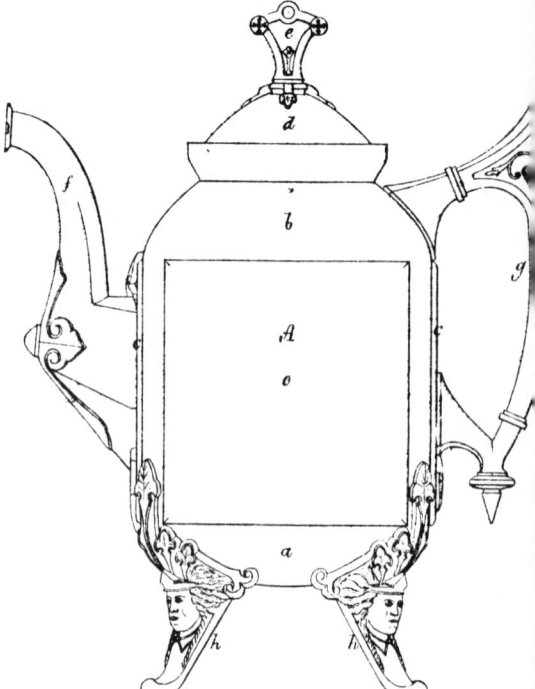

of pressed glass as being the same as Hobbs, Brockunier & Company's "Centennial" pattern, also known as "Viking," and "Bearded Man" or "Bearded Head" (Fig. 27). The design patent for the "Centennial" pattern was registered by John H. Hobbs on November 21, 1876. (See A. C. Revi's *American Pressed Glass and Figure Bottles*, pp. 186 and 187.) An animal head joins the lower part of the angular handle to the body of the post while a bird picking up a pebble forms the finial. Cast acanthus leaves decorate the handle, spout, and lower body. This is an excellent example of unrelated ornamentation.

The ball-shaped teapot, made by

26. Teapot made by the Webster Mfg. Co. 1872.
27. Tea service made by Webster Mfg. Co. 1872.

108 American Silverplate

28. Ball-shaped teapot made by Simpson, Hall, Miller & Co. about 1872.

28a. Ball-shaped teapot and creamer made by Reed & Barton about 1875.

Simpson, Hall, Miller & Company of Wallingford, Connecticut, about 1872 has hoof feet attached to the body with deer heads and a finial in the form of a sphinx (Fig. 28). The engraved strapwork is well adapted to the shape of the vessel—better than many of that period. The designer of this teapot is not known but the design bears much affinity to other designs by that same company which were patented by the designer Herman Vasseur.

A similar ball-shaped set was made by Reed & Barton and was illustrated in their catalog published in 1877 (Fig. 28a).

The tea service patented by George Gill for Reed & Barton, September 17, 1872, is a more complicated form (Fig. 29). The bottom is a section of a sphere from which project the feet. These terminate in a claw which grasps a flattened ball. The upper front face of each foot is ornamented with an elongated stem and sprig of leaves. The handle has a downwardly projecting piece ending in a ball and the figure of a lion at the top. The cover is surmounted by a cone with a twig containing acorn hulls. The spout has a projecting enlargement overhung by a series of pendant acorns.

V. Development of Styles 109

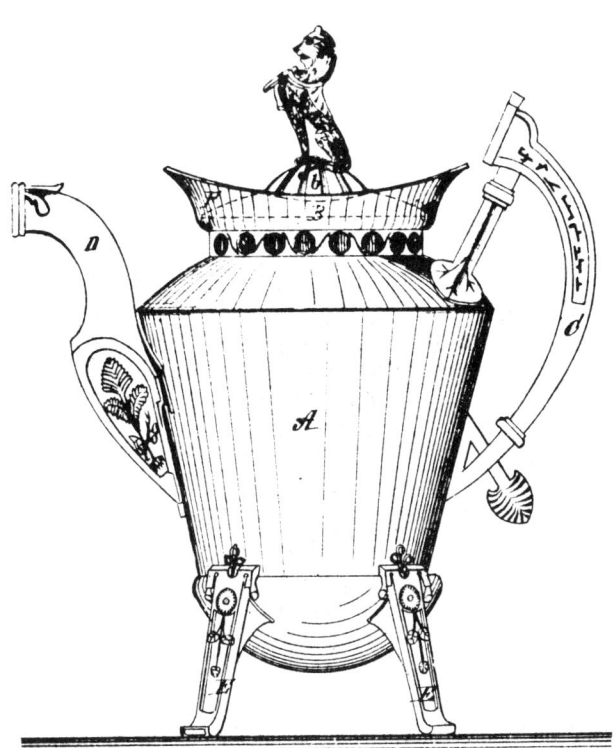

29. Coffeepot patented by George Gill, September 17, 1872; made by Reed & Barton.

30. Coffeepot designed and patented by Henry G. Reed, for Reed & Barton, on April 28, 1874.

31. Teapot patented by George Gill for Reed & Barton on August 12, 1873.

32. Teapot patented by John Jepson, West Meriden, Conn., and assigned to the Meriden Britannia Co., April 14, 1874.

An equally complicated design is the one by Henry G. Reed, also for Reed & Barton, patented April 28, 1874 (Fig. 30). The body of the pot is an egg, truncated at both ends and surmounted by a cylindrical neck. "Antique figures" ornament the band around the neck. The quadrangular feet bear figures of birds standing erect, with the tips of their beaks resting upon the plumage of the breast. This motif, the pelican piercing her breast in order to feed her young, sometimes called "the pelican in her piety," is an ancient Christian sym-

33. Coffeepot of the complete set especially gold plated for showing at the Philadelphia Centennial Exhibition, 1876. Made by the Meriden Britannia Co.

34. Complete tea service in the style gold plated for the Philadelphia Centennial Exhibition in 1876.

bol signifying atonement and piety. The motif is incomplete here as the three infant birds, usually depicted in their nest with mouths open to receive the blood from the wound, are omitted. The teapot spout has a disk supporting two half-figures of similar birds. The diagonal band passing around the body of the pot is a distinctly disturbing element.

Teapots with huge "collars" flaring around the top first appeared about 1868 (Fig. 31). The one patented by George Gill, August 12, 1873, for Reed & Barton has a finial that is a rampant lion holding a shield.

A similar collar is used by John Jepson who patented the egg-shaped teapot whose design patent was assigned to the Meriden Britannia Company April 14, 1874 (Fig. 32). This particular specimen bears the mark of Rogers, Smith & Company.

The Meriden Britannia Company made a tea and coffee service with high flaring collars which was especially gold-plated for a showing at the Philadelphia Centennial Exhibition in 1876 (Figs. 33, 34). It was illustrated in their catalog for 1878.

These high flaring collars continued to be used through the 1870s but virtually disappeared from designs introduced in the early 1880s (Figs. 35, 35a).

Birds holding snakes in their beaks bridge the angle between the body of the vessels and the rustic branch supports the tea service made by the Middletown Plate Company and illustrated in their catalog of 1874 (Fig. 36). A similar bird forms the finial. The placement of another bird just below the spout of the teapot is unusual. Additional birds, over-size insects, pots of flowers, and foliage are found on the band around the body.

The all-over repoussé work, made so popular in this country through the solid silver examples made by Samuel Kirk of Baltimore from about 1824, became popular also for plated ware. The "embossed" tea set, made by the

35. Coffeepot made by Simpson, Hall & Co. of Wallingford, Conn., about 1878.
35a. Coffee urn made by the Meriden Britannia Co. about 1878.

36. Teapot and sugar bowl made by Middletown Plate Company about 1874.

37. Tea and coffee service made by the Meriden Britannia Co. about 1886.

V. DEVELOPMENT OF STYLES   113

38. Tea service made by the Meriden Britannia Co. about 1886.

39. Tea set made by the Pairpoint Mfg. Co. about 1885.

40. Teapot made by the Gorham Co. Gorham Co. catalog, 1884.

40a. Teapot made by the Gorham Co. Gorham Co. catalog, 1884.

41. Teapot made by the Gorham Co. Gorham Co. catalog, 1884.

Meriden Britannia Company illustrates this style (Fig. 37). The decoration of this tea set, while elaborate, is well adapted to the shape.

Early in the 1880s there was a trend away from the long-legged vessels of the 1870s and by the middle of the decade many tea sets were of squat shape and rested on a low rim. The satin or butler's finish, which was produced by a revolving wheel of wire making tiny scratches, giving the article a dull appearance, was introduced. Ornamentation on these sets was often simplified and was well suited to the more restrained shapes. The tea service made by the Meriden Britannia Company and shown in their 1886–87 catalog illustrates this trend (Fig. 38). The same trend is also seen in the tea set made by the Pairpoint Manufacturing Company of New Bedford, Massachusetts (Fig. 39).

In some instances the sole decoration was in the fluting of the body, as illustrated in teapots made by the Gorham Company and shown in their 1884 catalog (Figs. 40, 40a).

A palmette band and palmette thumb rest form the decoration of another Gorham teapot (Fig. 41).

In earlier services there was little difference in the appearance between pots intended for tea and those for coffee. Only a slightly larger capacity identified the coffeepot. This tendency towards a larger coffeepot increased until by the middle of the 1880s the difference was considerable. Not only was there a difference in size but the bodies of coffeepots tended to be more elongated while those of the teapots were more squat. Also, at this time long-necked after-dinner coffeepots made their appearance in silverplate. These exotic forms were adapted from Turkish and Persian designs (Fig. 42). Some had plain surfaces while others bore surface ornament such as the bamboo and the floral designs on the Pairpoint Manufacturing Company sets (Figs. 43, 43a).

Teapots with straight sides were an innovation of the late 1880s, being more squat than the "lighthouse" type of coffeepots in favor more than two hundred years earlier (Fig. 44).

Tea sets of the 1890s were generally smaller than previous ones and followed the squat shapes of the latter part of the previous decade. Some rested on rims, others were raised on low feet. Still others rested flat on the table and must have posed a problem in protecting that surface from the heat.

Compared to the 1870s there was a vast improvement in design. One factor responsible for this improvement was the great influx of trained artists and craftsmen from all parts of Europe. Another factor was the influence of the graduates of several American art schools.

Ornamentation as well as shape of vessels was more restrained than it had been earlier. Examples of this are two tea sets made by the Gorham Company

42. After-dinner coffeepot whose long-necked shape was adapted from Turkish and Persian designs; popular in the 1880s. Gorham Co. catalog, 1888.
43. After-dinner coffee set made by Pairpoint Mfg. Co. about 1885.

43a. After-dinner coffee set made by Pairpoint Mfg. Co. about 1885.

and shown in their catalog of 1888 (Fig. 45). Engraved floral designs and fluting were the only decoration.

Applied bands of leafy scrolls, such as that on a teapot made by E. G. Webster & Son, of Brooklyn, New York, about 1890, were popular (Fig. 46).

Another form of ornamentation is seen on the tea set made by Woodman-Cook, Portland, Maine (Fig. 47). The ornament here is cast and applied to the squat form, not repoussé.

A Reed & Barton set of about 1890–95 is decorated with what is described in their catalogs as "Venetian chased" and is actually a plating process whereby

44. Straight-sided teapot of the late 1880s. Patented by W. H. Sills: Design Patent No. 19,192; July 2, 1889.

V. Development of Styles 117

colored golds are deposited, creating designs in natural colors (Fig. 48).

Beaded borders with shell, scroll, and leaf decorations on spouts, handles, and feet decorate fluted bodies whose shape has long been associated with English designs (Fig. 49). These distinguish a tea set found in the Gorham Company catalogs of 1892 and 1894.

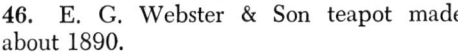
45. Teapots and coffeepots made by the Gorham Co. about 1888–90. Gorham Co. catalog, 1888.

Also in the Gorham Company 1894 catalog is a tea set whose floral decoration is described there as "Repoussé chased" (Fig. 50).

Patent designs by Henry Berry, May 29, 1894, for the Derby Silver Company of Derby, Connecticut (Fig. 51), and by Frederick W. Van Bergh, May 10, 1898, for the Van Bergh Silver Plate Company of Rochester, New York (Fig. 52), show the careful attention given to the details of ornament.

46. E. G. Webster & Son teapot made about 1890.

47. Tea set marked "Woodman-Cook, Portland, Maine." Made about 1890.

48. Reed & Barton tea set of about 1890–95 decorated with "Venetian Chased" designs.

A teapot made by Simpson, Hall, Miller & Company of Wallingford, Connecticut, about 1895, elaborate though it is, consists of harmonious elements in a unified design (Fig. 53).

The swirled and fluted body of the pot made by the Meriden Britannia Company about 1896 is further enhanced by rococo borders and feet (Fig. 54).

V. Development of Styles 119

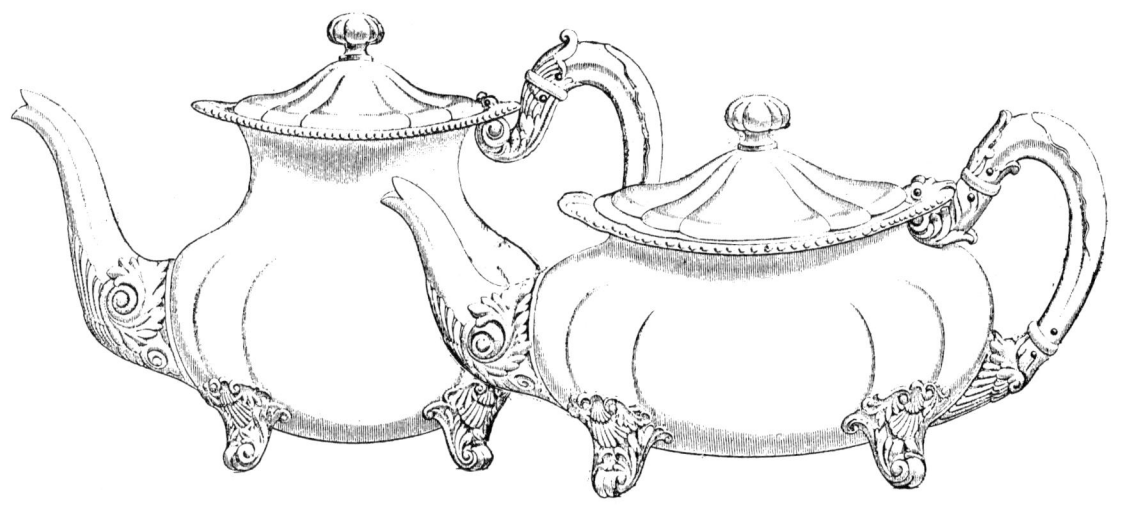

49. Coffeepots and teapots made by the Gorham Co. about 1890–95. Gorham Co. catalogs, 1892 and 1894.

50. "Repoussé chased" coffeepot and teapot made by the Gorham Co. 1894. Gorham Co. catalog, 1894.

Floral chasing almost covers the bodies of pieces in the tea set made by the Meriden Silver Plate Company between 1896 and 1913 (Fig. 55). The finials are berries and leaves. The supports are paw feet.

No one style has ever replaced others completely. Various ones exist side-by-side. And so it was with Art Nouveau, a new concept containing elements of Japanese art, pre-Raphaelite affectation,

120   AMERICAN SILVERPLATE

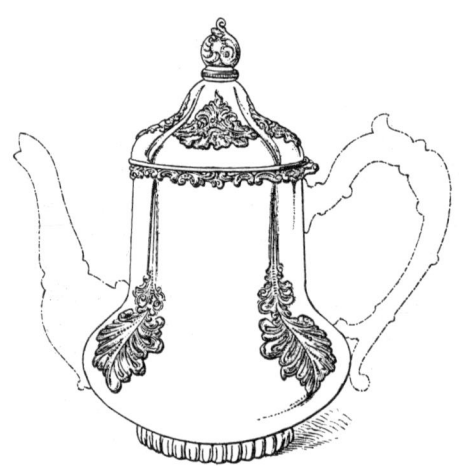

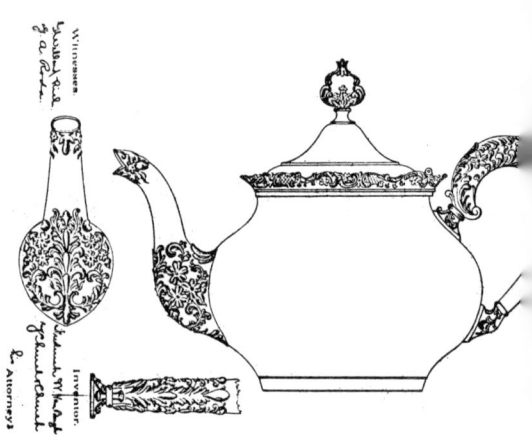

51. Coffeepot designed and patented by Henry Berry; assigned to the Derby Silver Co. Design Patent No. 23,315; Patented May 29, 1894.

52. Teapot or coffeepot designed and patented by Frederick W. Van Bergh; assigned to Van Bergh Silver Plate Co. Design Patent No. 28,610; Patented May 10, 1898.

and motifs derived from ancient Byzantine, Moorish, Egyptian, and Roman cultures (Figs. 56, 57, 57a). It was an attempt to break away from all previous

fetters and conventions of historic styles and to bring the fine arts and the crafts into an overall esthetic unity. The shape or outline is the most important

53. Teapot made by Simpson, Hall, Miller & Co. about 1895.

54. Swirled and fluted design made by the Meriden Britannia Co. about 1896.

55. Tea and coffee service made by the Meriden Silver Plate Co. between 1896 and 1913.

56. "The Marguerite" tea and coffee service made by the Derby Silver Co. about 1900–05.

57. Art Nouveau teapot designed by Albert Steffin, for the Pairpoint Corp. Design Patent No. 37,008, June 28, 1904; Patented spout for teapot designed by Henry Weber. Design Patent No. 36,519; Patented August 25, 1903.
57a. Art Nouveau teapot designed and patented by Albert Steffin for the Pairpoint Mfg. Co. Design Patent No. 36,877; Patented April 12, 1904.

aspect with free-flowing organic lines defining sinuous stems, blossoms, and leaves. The female form, usually with swirling draperies merging with long flowing hair, is a dominant motif in Art Nouveau designs.

Though the movement had its beginnings in the 1880s it did not reach silversmithing in this country until close to the turn of the century when English-born William Christmas Codman was brought here by the Gorham Company to direct their design department and to train a select corps of Gorham silversmiths to produce Art Nouveau designs. The first of these were placed on the market in 1901.

While the first Art Nouveau articles made in this country were handwrought and unique, the designs and motifs were soon adapted to the machine-made products of the manufacturers of silverplated wares.

58. Advertisement of tea set made by the Homan Manufacturing Co. of Cincinnati, Ohio. *The Keystone*, August 1906.

Homan Plate

No. 2264. TEA SET

This service is executed in the burnished finish, and is free from excessive ornament; its beauty and attractiveness consisting in its novel and graceful shape, its unique flutings, and perfect consistency and harmony of design.

"WELCOME TO 'ITS' OWN"

From time immemorial tea services have been conceded the most staple of hollowware productions.

Quite recently there is said to have been some falling off from this standard due to the humdrum sameness and lack of individuality in the patterns offered.

To restore the sale of the teaware to its rightful volume, we have prepared this year seven strikingly handsome new designs, original and full of initiative in every detail.

Do not place your order for hollowware before having seen these.

The Homan Manufacturing Company

New York Salesroom, 32 Park Place
Chicago Salesroom, Silversmiths' Building
Boston Salesroom, Jewelers' Building

Office, Factory and Salesroom

CINCINNATI, OHIO

Made since 1847

The Art Nouveau movement among silversmiths in the United States was of brief duration, being largely phased out about 1910 to 1915. It did not result in the complete upheaval in the silversmithing arts that it did in the art fields whose media were less costly materials. Much Art Nouveau silver was plated ware, usually appearing in the less expensive lines of any given company. Articles for personal use and adornment were far more numerous than tea services or other pieces intended for general household use.

Ornate silver designs of the period between 1890 and 1910 were derived largely from the French Renaissance, but English Georgian was also widely adopted (Fig. 58). Asymmetrical rococo styles thrived alongside "Old English." These were followed by Art Nouveau which served as an inspiration for a true American Renaissance which was clearly reflected in the exhibits of silver seen at the St. Louis Exposition in 1904.

National and international expositions have always reflected current styles in silver as they have the other arts and have, in turn, asserted their influence on further developments. The Hudson-Fulton Celebration held in New York in 1909, with its exhibits of early American silver and furniture was largely responsible for arousing a nationwide interest in Colonial styles. It was not long before silverware was distinctly Colonial in design. This was a complete departure from the highly ornate scroll and shell rococo designs of the

59. 1. Teapot designed by Charles A. Bennett, New Milford, Conn.; assigned to the Bennett-Merwin Silver Co. also of New Milford. Design Patent No. 48,097; Patented November 9, 1915. 2. Coffeepot designed by Grosvenor N. Allen for Oneida Community Silver. Design Patent No. 70,208; Patented May 25, 1926. 3. Teapot designed by Charles H. Greenwood for Albert Pick & Co. of Bridgeport, Conn. Design Patent No. 69,878; Patented April 13, 1926.

60. "Sanderson" tea service. Meriden Silver Plate Co. catalog, 1924.   61. "Adam" tea service. Meriden Silver Plate Co. catalog, 1924.

62. "Chippendale" tea service. Meriden Silver Plate Co. catalog, 1924.

63. "Hammered Grecian" tea service. Meriden Silver Plate Co. catalog, 1924.

V. Development of Styles 127

1890s and the sinuous lines and heavy floral effects of the first few years of the twentieth century.

The continuing vogue for period styles may be traced to the 1910–20 era when practically all of the silverware patterns showed a strong Colonial and early nineteenth-century influence in their designs (Figs. 59–63). This new cycle began with the severe simplicity of the Colonial and evolved through gradual changes to the more ornate periods. Chippendale, Sheraton, Hepplewhite, and Adam were the inspiration for many period designs of the 1920s and 1930s.

Dutch reproductions were made from about 1910 to 1930 (Fig. 64).

64. Dutch reproduction design patented by M. Weintraub. Design Patent No. 41,765; Patented September 12, 1911.
65. "Joanne" service made by Webster-Wilcox division of the International Silver Co.

66. "Paul Revere" service made by Webster-Wilcox division of the International Silver Co.

67. International Silver Co.'s most popular pattern in inexpensive quality silverplate.

V. Development of Styles

In the 1920s a new, modernistic style developed, now called "Art Deco," derived from "Art Decoratif." It might more properly be called "Art Moderne." It is a hard-edged, geometric style which succeeded Art Nouveau. This was the beginning of a whole new era of styling which, while it was not adopted in its entirety by silversmiths, has had some influence.

Five distinctive styles have emerged with a periodic swing between "soft" and "crisp" feeling. These styles cannot be dated accurately as the beginning and end of a style are seldom discernible.

The first of these was the Stepform, from about the mid-20s to mid-30s, often called "skyscraper," and distinguished by set-back shapes with vertical rather than horizontal accent. The vertical lines of tall steel American skyscrapers even found their way into silverwares. Details include zig-zags, lightning bolts, sun rays, reed, and fluting.

Another approach was one of graceful curvilinearity, or Streamform, called "streamlining," when in use from the early 30s to early 40s. "Tear-drops" and horizontal accents of parallel lines and stripes were the motifs used on silver.

Taperform, whose trapezoidal blocks initiated the shift to crisper forms thrived from the mid-40s to mid-50s. Stars, crowns, and faceted light-catching bezels were features of this style.

69. Twentieth-century tea and coffee service made by Reed & Barton; "Denmark" pattern.

70. Twentieth-century tea and coffee service made by Reed & Barton; "Americana" pattern.

71. Twentieth-century tea and coffee service made by Reed & Barton; "Tara Hall" pattern.

V. Development of Styles 131

Sheerform, introduced first through the appliance industry, from the late 50s through the mid-60s, rapidly swept through the whole styling field. The basic boxlike shape was later cluttered with "butterfly" panels, the "bow-tie" shapes in escutcheons, and stars with an even number of points.

Sculptureform first appeared in architecture and transportation in the early 60s. The major shapes are pure and peaked ellipsoids, hyperboloids, paraboloids, and softened "flying wedge" shapes. Some of the familiar devices of previous styles such as vees, crowns, and stars were put into the new "swoop" shapes.

72. Twentieth-century tea and coffee service made by Reed & Barton; "Winthrop" pattern.

A sixth style, which may be designated as Facetform, as exemplified by Olivetti's faceted typewriter, emerged in the late 60s.

Current productions in silverplated tea services are so diverse that it is possible to obtain a service that harmonizes with any setting. Hollow ware is often styled to match or to harmonize with patterns of sterling flatware as well as with silverplated flatware (Figs. 65–67, 69–72).

CHAPTER VI

Exhibition and Presentation Silver and Ornamental Art Work

Exhibition Silver

"The Great Exhibition of Industry of All Nations," was the official title. More familiarly called the "Crystal Palace Exhibition," or simply "The Great Exhibition," it opened May 1, 1851, in London's Hyde Park. The first *international* exhibition, it set the pace for those that have followed. Its avowed purpose was "to exhibit the arts and manufactures of all nations." In this, it was surely successful. From that May opening until closing day in October more than six million people attended. In these days of instant communication it is difficult to comprehend just what this means. For the first time, vast numbers of people from all over the world were brought together in a setting and in an atmosphere where a ready exchange of ideas could take place. It cannot be questioned that the exhibition had a stimulating effect on the movements for formal adult education and led to the development of mechanics institutes. Informal education was also stimulated through the promotion of new museums and art galleries. And, while it may not have understood fully all the complicated workings of electrotyping and electroplating, there can be no doubt that the public saw the "Decorative Arts" and aspired to have the results of "the galvano-plastic Art" at home. Electroplating, although still in its infancy, captured the attention of the whole world through the exhibits of the silverplate manufacturers of Sheffield, Birmingham, London, and Glasgow (Fig. 1).

America's response to the London Crystal Palace exhibition was to open her own in New York in 1853. The New York Exhibition, held in 1853–54, in a cruciform Crystal Palace surmounted by a great glass and iron dome 168 feet high, was international in character. Although plenty of foreign exhibitors took part, the project did not pay; receipts amounted to little more than half the expenditure. While it did not achieve the financial success of its London counterpart, the impact of the silver exhibited was considerable. Electrotype copies, which are made by the electrodeposition of silver, were featured in the exhibition. This relatively simple and inexpensive means of copying ancient works of art made possible the presentation of faithful copies of pieces seen previously only by those who could visit the museums of Europe (Fig. 2). Designers and manufacturers of silverplated wares carried with them the impressions created by these ancient pieces and stimulated the Renaissance Revival which had actually begun some 10 to 12 years earlier. These classical forms and decorations were subsequently copied by manufacturers and called Etruscan, Greek, or Pompeiian.

134   AMERICAN SILVERPLATE

1. Centerpiece by Hawkesworth, Eyre & Co., Sheffield, England. Exhibited at the London Crystal Palace, 1851. *The Art Journal Illustrated Catalogue of the Industry of All Nations*, London, 1851.

2. "Race" plate and "Iliad" salver made by electrotype process from originals in the Musée du Louvre, made by Elkington & Co., Birmingham, England, and exhibited at the New York World's Fair, 1853–54. *The World of Art and Industry*, New York, 1854.

metallic work of which was heavily plated with silver and some portions gilt." Appearing primarily ornamental to our eyes, we are assured that "Its capability of service is shown by being in active use for three months before it was placed in the Crystal Palace."

Reed & Barton was among the award-winning manufacturers of silverplated wares who exhibited at the New York exhibition.

Only two American silver manufacturers exhibited at the Paris Universal Exposition in 1867. The report of the Commissioners is of interest, however, for the commentaries on the silver industry. Though stated largely in connection with foreign industry, most remarks were equally applicable in this

An exhibit, perhaps surprising to present-day readers, was that of the carriage of the Hope Hose Company of Philadelphia (Fig. 4), "the decorative

country. Class 21 of the exposition included gold and silverplate. About this class the Commissioners had this to say:

> This class comprises: 1. Artistic goldsmiths' work; 2. The major part of small table plate in gold, silver, and in alloyed metals, silvered or gilt by electrochemical process; 3. Bronze ornaments for the tables and dessert services; 4. Plated ware; 5. Gold, silver, and church plate; 6. Gold, silver, and copper enameled ware. The goldsmiths' trade is almost entirely concentrated in Paris, but there are some makers of church plate at Lyons. Fine silver is worth an average of 220 francs the kilogram. The law allows the employment of two different standards of alloy for solid plate, but the first of these [.950] is almost exclusively employed. This is worth 212 frances 62 centimes, while the second is worth only 180 francs the kilogram. Silver and gold are applied by the electrochemical process upon articles made either of brass or white metal (maillechort), which is brass with the addition of nickel. The prices of the metals which enter into the manufacture of these alloys are as follows: Copper, 200 to 300 francs the 100 kilograms; zinc, 75 to 80 francs; nickel, 12 francs to 13 francs. The manufacture of plated ware is rapidly disappearing. The operations which contribute to the production of goldsmiths' work are very numerous. The metallic alloys are melted in crucibles; they are afterwards cast in molds of beaten earth and sand. When taken from the mold the articles pass into the hands of the chaser. The chaser's work is, however, economically replaced in the case of stamped work by presses and steel dies. By means of these processes are produced table ornaments, certain objects of art, and various pieces of goldsmiths' work, which are also made by means of the latter, the hammer and stamping. Mounting consists in uniting the various parts of a work together. This is done by means of soldering and also of screws and nuts. Spoons and forks are made by means of

4. Carriage of the Hope Hose Company of Philadelphia. Displayed at the New York World's Fair, 1853–54. *The World of Art and Industry,* New York 1854.

rollers, on which the forms of the articles are engraved. The other processes are hand engraving and biting in with acid, enamelling, engine-turning, and polishing with special lathes; and, lastly, finishing, which includes rouge polishing and burnishing with steel, agate, and other tools. Goldsmiths' work is done almost exclusively in large shops or at the houses of master workmen, employing a certain number of assistants and apprentices; very few work entirely alone. The proportion of men to women in the business is four to one. The number of females engaged has, however, increased since the introduction of electroplated work, the polishing of which is entirely performed by them. The average rate of wages in Paris is 5 francs a day for men and 2 francs (40 cents) for women. The manufacturers generally sell their productions either to retail dealers or to merchants and agents for exportation. The annual value of productions, including plated ware, is 43,000,000 francs, of which only about 4,000,000 francs' worth are exported. —*Translation of the introduction of Paul Christofle, member of the Committee of Admissions of Class 21.*

The oldest establishment in France, the well-known house of Odiot, made a large display. There was nothing, however, that claimed the merit of novelty, unless it was the three massive pieces of plate which were intended in some way to celebrate the fame of the Creusot Iron Works. These were remarkable for the introduction of figures in the ordinary artisan's costume of the day, smiths resting from their toils with their implements in their hands, and cogwheel, piston rods, and cranks filling up the details of the foreground. The idea was an innovation, and the difficulties to be overcome were no doubt great. But in these matters the effect is all that need be judged, and this did not give general satisfaction.

The collection exhibited by the brothers Fannière, besides its high order of artistic merit, had the extremely rare peculiarity of being the work of the hands of the exhibitors themselves. The brothers Fannière, pupils of Vechte, from being art workmen in the employ of others, have risen by their talents and industry to an independent commercial establishment, and in this exhibition carried off the first gold medal awarded to silverplate. Their specialty is a very high perfection of repoussé sculpture. Two shields, one in iron and the other in steel, were the most remarkable of their productions. The amount of relief was considered greater than had ever before been attained in the material, and as steel is not a tractable metal, it was deserving of attention, not only for its great artistic merit, but as defining the limit within which bold embossing, almost amounting to alto-relievo, retains its genuinely metallic character. With silver it is different. If it be burst by forcing it into a relief beyond its powers of expansion, it may be patched up by soldering in new pieces neatly enough to escape observation unless the back be carefully examined, and even the back may be so cleaned up by files and other implements as to show no seams.

The largest collection was by Mr. Christofle, whose innumerable stores all over Paris are easily recognized by the invariable sign of windows filled with tablespoons tossed into confusion with a prodigal hand. The house is one of the largest in the world, employs an enormous number of workmen, and manufactures everything, from the commonest articles of plated ware to the most expensive art productions for the table. The mass of material put on show was of a very heterogeneous character.

A collection of great artistic value and beauty was also exhibited by Mr. Le Pec, whose specialty is enamelling on a solid gold ground—gold being the only metal that can withstand the firing necessary for the superimposed work which Mr. Le Pec employs. When a vase has been thoroughly finished by this elaborate process it looks more like the production of the potter than the goldsmith.

The German collection by Wagner, the court silversmith of Berlin, was well worthy of examination. He exhibited two important works—bucklers—one given to the Prince Royal on his marriage, the other to Francis the Second of Naples, in 1864, in memory of the siege of Gaeta. Both are examples of the art skill for which the house is renowned.

Russia had a superb collection of thoroughly characteristic silverware, mixed with occasional imitations of Arabic and Persian art. The Muscovite style is a combination of the various contrast of whitened silver and oxydized silver, both obtained by the aid of acids and gilding. The designs are striking and, in not a few, inscriptions in the Russian alphabet, either pierced or engraved, are used with quaint effect. The hammered and chased silver work was regarded as the best in the class.

In the English section there were three names that challenged attention—Hancock, Hunt & Roskell; Elkington; and the English Christofle—but only Elkington exhibited silver ware. The collection was exceedingly fine. A silver swan exhibited in one of these cases occasioned a good deal of amusement, and was certainly one of the most ingenious pieces of mechanism in the building. It was of life size, and was gracefully poised on a basin of artificial water represented by revolving spirals of crystal. In this water a shoal of artificial fish were seen swimming. The swan moves the feathers of its neck gracefully, takes a proud and dignified survey of the situation, perceives the fish, seizes one in its bill, and then raises its neck and straightens it so that the fish disappears. Satisfied with this frugal but somewhat indigestible repast, the automaton curls its neck under its wings and goes to sleep. The whole is effected by means of clockwork machinery, which is said to be old, the present exhibitor only having refitted it.

In this class there were but two American exhibitors. A small collection of chased silverware was forwarded by Messrs. Tiffany & Co., of New York, which was good enough of its kind, but inadequate to the occasion. Two pretty models of steamboats in precious metals were much admired. They were from the same house. A collection of Connecticut tableware was shown and used in the American restaurant.

The tableware was silverplate made by the Meriden Britannia Company.

The silver sculptures by Tiffany & Co. were a model of the *America* by Crawford, the statue decorating the cupola of the Capitol Building, Washington, D.C., and models of the steamers *Commonwealth* and *Vanderbilt*. The hull of the model of the *Vanderbilt* was fashioned in frosted or "dead" silver, with a burnished streak for gunwale. The paddles were of burnished silver, tipped with gold; the tops and bottoms of the funnels of gold; the deck of polished silver; the quarter boats of gold.

American manufacturers of silverplate exhibited in other international exhibitions but the next one of great importance to them was the Philadelphia Centennial, held there in 1876, to celebrate the one hundredth anniversary of America's independence.

One special value of international exhibitions is the opportunity for work to be exhibited and seen by people of many nations at one time. It is the host nation, naturally, which usually stands to benefit most. In the various fields of fine arts shown at Philadelphia, this was especially true. This country's concern with carving a new nation out of a wilderness had up to that time compelled it to be largely preoccupied with material things. Though there had been painters of importance, art had not played a significant part in American life. Following the Centennial, numerous schools and societies of art were founded and there was an awakening of national interest in art. There was no great influx of foreign silver exhibits at Philadelphia. From England, for instance, only the Elkington firm contributed. Silver exhibits were not lacking, however, for American silversmiths came into their own.

Silver manufacturers had for previous exhibitions created special displays to demonstrate their craftsmanship. These pieces served as the focal points about which their regular line of goods was placed. The Philadelphia Centennial provided an unprecedented opportunity for publicity—one which the manufacturers used to the best advantage.

Reed & Barton set up an ornate glass cabinet in which they placed 1,040 gilded and silverplated pieces. The center of interest was their "Progress Vase," designed by W. C. Beattie. Four feet long and three feet in height, it depicted the progress of America from its discovery by Columbus to the time of the Centennial. The Gorham Company contributed an even larger work titled "The

5. Reed & Barton tea set displayed at the Philadelphia Centennial and admired by the Japanese Commission who purchased it for presentation to the Emperor of Japan.

Century Vase." This piece was also executed in sterling silver and stood four feet two inches in height, with a base of five feet four inches in extent. It was designed by George Wilkinson and Thomas J. Pairpoint, both designers for the Gorham firm. Its motif was similar to that of the Reed & Barton creation.

These exhibition pieces were not the only wares to receive special attention at the Centennial. One of Reed & Barton's regular tea sets of heavy electroplate, designed and patented by William C. Beattie (July 25, 1876), profusely decorated with repoussé chasing and "oxidized and gold-finished," according to the 1877 Reed & Barton catalog, was admired by members of the Japanese Commission who purchased it for presentation to the Emperor of Japan (Fig. 5).

The Meriden Britannia Company also

VI. Exhibition and Presentation Silver   139

erected a large display booth at the Philadelphia Centennial (Fig. 6). Featured in the front center of this exhibit was "The Buffalo Hunt," designed by Theodore Baur, German-born modeler-sculptor. This handsome piece of statuary was originally cast in bronze and symbolized the "Winning of the West" phase of American life, during which time much emphasis was placed on the vast herds of bison roaming the western plains. Following the Philadelphia Centennial, "The Buffalo Hunt" was exhibited at the International Cotton Exposition in Atlanta in 1881, at the International Exposition in Paris in 1889, the Trans-Mississippi and International Exposition at Omaha in 1898, and in other exhibitions. In 1882, and again in 1886, it was made a standard catalog item, and was priced at $315 in "old silver" finish, and $325 in "gold inlaid," the latter finish being a plating process whereby the Indian's body was plated in red gold, the buckskin breeches in yellow gold, the buffalo (bison) in bronze and the remainder in "old silver." It was also made in a small size, measuring 9 1/2 inches in height, priced at $23.50; the buffalo alone as a paperweight, 4 1/2 inches high, was sold for $5.50.

One of the known examples of this striking group is part of the International Silver Company's historical collection, and is on exhibit in their showrooms at Meriden, Connecticut (Fig. 7).

6. The Meriden Britannia Co.'s booth at the Philadelphia Centennial. Featured in the front center was "The Buffalo Hunt" with monumental pieces of silverplate inside the case.

7. "The Buffalo Hunt," designed by Theodore Baur and made by the Meriden Britannia Co. to be exhibited at the Philadelphia Centennial.

Simpson, Hall, Miller & Company, Wallingford, Connecticut, exhibited a multi-fauceted water cooler with a 21-gallon capacity. It now rests on a marble-top table in the hall of the Connecticut House of Representatives in the state capitol building, Hartford, Connecticut.

The Meriden Silver Plate Company was among the award winners at the Philadelphia Centennial (Fig. 8). They and the Middletown Plate Company both created elaborate centerpieces for their special exhibits. That such elaborate centerpieces and fruit dishes won the acclaim of their day is amply demonstrated by the reception given them at the Philadelphia Centennial in 1876 (Fig. 9). The description of two will suffice:

American art in silver-work had another happy illustration in the large and elaborate *épergne* or centre-piece contributed by the Meriden Silver-Plate Company, of West Meriden, Connecticut. It did signal credit to American design and workmanship, and was one of the most striking objects of this department of art-manufacture at the Exhibition. The graceful conception of the designer, Mr. John Hill, is admirably worked out, and the ornamentation is of an appropriate and chaste character, the whole of it being what is known as chased and applied work. The general motive of the piece, as may be seen from the engraving, is allegorical; and, though not distinctly typical of the growth of the century in the arts of civilization, its symbolism has a recognizable bearing on the sentiment underlying

VI. Exhibition and Presentation Silver 141

8. Medals won by the Meriden Silver Plate Co. at the Philadelphia Centennial. Meriden Silver Plate Co. catalog, 1877.

9. Silver epergne exhibited at the Philadelphia Centennial by the Meriden Silver Plate Co. *Gems of the Centennial Exhibition,* 1877.

142   AMERICAN SILVERPLATE

our centenary. From the centre of the base, which is twenty-seven inches square and four inches in height, rises a dome-shaped pedestal surmounted by a draped figure, supporting a large centre-dish of glass, elaborately cut. Surrounding the pedestal are four figures, symbolizing Music, Art, Science, and Commerce. Outside of these and of the centre pedestal are four columns, but three of which are shown in the engraving, supporting richly-cut glass dishes, similar to the centre glass in design and style. The height of the *épergne* is thirty-eight inches. The artistic effect of this piece of silver-work is heightened by the beautiful and elaborate, though not overwrought, ornamentation of the base, pedestal, and column, with fine engraved work, lightened and varied by sharp yet delicate contrasts of gold and silver. This ornamentation is not often used in silver-plate, but in the present instance it is applied with striking and graceful effect. The draped figure in the centre-piece and the four symbolic figures, like the rest of the metal, are heavily plated, but have their surfaces finished in ivory tint instead of being brightened by the burnisher's tool. The pure, white figures stand out in pleasing and effective relief from the brightly-polished surface. The rich effect of the large oak-leaves in applied work, almost producing the impression of high-relief, and contrasting with the bright surface of the base, is a particularly noticeable feature of the decoration, and lends additional massiveness—a desirable result in the enrichment of the base of the design. The glass dishes deserve special mention, not only for the clear, rich quality of the glass, but also for the admirable finish of the cutting, which evinces skilled workmanship equal to that of the best foreign glass-cutting.

A beautiful design in silver-plate represents an ornamental centre-piece, which was exhibited in the pavilion of the Middletown Plate Company, of Middletown, Connecticut [Fig. 10]. The name given was the "Barge of Venus," and the novel and striking grace

10. "Barge of Venus" exhibited at the Philadelphia Centennial by the Middletown Plate Company. *Gems of the Centennial Exposition,* 1877.

of the design made it the object of much attention at Philadelphia. The barge itself is in the shape of a sea-shell, of much beauty of curve and contour. It is lined with gold, and the outside shows a rich satin finish. Cupid stands on the lofty prow, driving the swans with golden ribbons, and the well-known American water-plant, the cat's-tail springs from the water on either side. The figures of the swans and of the driver Cupid are neatly modeled, and, it must be confessed, in the highest degree artistic in their effect. The execution of the feathery coats of the swans is very elaborate, aiming to be natural, not conventional, and imitating very successfully the appearance of the wings and bodies. It resembles the hand or hammered work as executed in solid silver. The plateau or water-surface is in polished glass, and the border is ornamented with a gracefully-executed wreath of laurel. The base is oblong, and is covered with a looking-glass plate, and the four little figures at the corners are richly gilded, being designed to represent Music. The sides are etched with designs after familiar American plants. The combination of gilded work, burnishing, and chasing, in the production of this piece, is very rich in effect, as well as harmonious.

In connection with this beautiful piece of work we may say a few words about the originality, grace, and boldness, of American art-work in silver-manufacture, though the "Barge of Venus" perhaps illustrates this not a whit better than our other engravings of silver-ware. No branch of art-manufacture has achieved such results, for some manifest reasons which may be briefly glanced at. Honesty of purpose and execution furnishes the true basis of Art, for without it Art is flimsy and shallow, debasing public taste instead of elevating it. The enormous production of silver in America has very much widened its application in all the manifold uses of art-manufacture; and, if it has not cheapened the products themselves much, it has extended the taste for an appreciation of the beauties of silver-work as an ornamental feature in household and social life. Silver-manufacture shows its intrinsic worth and excellence as an art-product with a naked fidelity to truth, which removes that liability to bewilderment and bad taste that enables the manufacturers of gaudy and extravagant furniture to impose their inartistic but high-priced work on those who have acquired wealth too suddenly to use it with correct taste and sound judgment. The silversmith—including in this term the manufacturer of silver-plate—is debarred from bad work, and driven to employ the best artistic talent in his wares. The character of the work and the variety of processes by which it is wrought and ornamented give inviting opportunity for the exercise of inventive genius and skilled workmanship. The largely-augmented number of people either wealthy or in good circumstances within the last quarter of a century, and the peculiar availability of artistic silver-work for gifts, have insured a great and increasing demand for these wares. The manufacturer is thus stimulated to do the best possible work, and the result is that American silver-ware competes very favorably with its foreign rivals. In the purely artistic products of silver, where beauty is entirely divorced from use and it becomes an end unto itself—as, for example, in plaques and statuary—American Art has not achieved so much; but, in all the varieties of vessels and table-ornaments now demanded by the cultivated and wealthy classes, the Philadelphia Exhibition gave honest grounds for national pride.

The centerpiece or epergne made by the Meriden Silver Plate Company was illustrated also in their catalog of 1879 and listed as "No. 1599. With Oxidized Silver and Gold Finish. . . .$750.00."

Another silverplate manufacturer, James W. Tufts, Boston, Massachusetts, erected an entire building at the Philadelphia Centennial (Fig. 11). Tufts' building was 60 by 75 feet, and 70 feet high. It was erected expressly to display the automatic fountains that were a major production of the company. The soda fountain of that time was a magnificent piece of equipment. Many were made of Italian marble and the metal parts silverplated. From the silverplating of fountain parts, Tufts branched out into the manufacture of an extensive line of silverplated items such as pitchers, dishes, and vases which were also exhibited.

144 AMERICAN SILVERPLATE

11. James W. Tufts building at the Philadelphia Centennial. Reprinted from the *Spinning Wheel*, May 1961, with permission.

A silverplated paperweight was made by James W. Tufts as a memento of the Philadelphia Centennial (Fig. 12). Miss Liberty surmounts the tall column on which the Declaration of Independence is recorded. Every word of the Declaration stands out distinctly and can be read easily. Engraved scenes of the Landing of Columbus, the Boston Massacre, and the Signing of the Declaration of Independence are on three sides of the pedestal while the front panel is inscribed "Manufactured by James W. Tufts, Boston, Mass., Design Patented Feb. 22, 1876."

Some contemporary writers, referring to the Philadelphia Centennial Exposition, wrote smugly of the excellence of the American silverwares displayed there, though one of the judges mentioned "the meretricious ornament" of American designs. Fortunately, some of the silver manufacturers compared American products with those from other countries and were shocked out of their complacency and directed their designers along new routes. This exhibition, celebrating the completion of the first century of American independence,

12. Silverplated paperweight made by James W. Tufts as a memento of the Philadelphia Centennial. Height 8 1/4 in.

was the first big factor in the awakening of our nation to its woeful lack of artistic taste. The reaction was not immediate but it could be felt by 1885. Another influence was the increased travel to Europe from where Americans brought home with them objects of art which inspired new concepts of beauty.

Other exhibitions in which manufacturers of American silverplate participated were those held by the American Institute, the Massachusetts Charitable Mechanic Association, the International Exposition of Chile (1875), the two Australian exhibitions held in Sydney (1879) and Melbourne (1880), and the Paris International Exposition held in 1889, winning awards in all. Travel by this time had become possible for greater numbers of people and many Americans visited the Paris Exposition. It was the impression made on them by this 1889 exhibition which led to the organization of the World's Columbian Exposition which was the next exhibition to have an important influence on Americans. While Parisians had transformed the heart of their city with the Eiffel Tower and exotic architecture, Chicagoans literally created a new city in Jackson Park to celebrate the 400th anniversary of Columbus' discovery. It also symbolized the city's rise from its own ashes. The Chicago exhibition is said to have had a more lasting effect on its visitors than any other world's fair before or since. The lavish use of electricity, for instance, impressed upon the people of this country for the first time the importance of this new source of light and power. The dazzling architecture of "The Dream City" with the glittering lights playing on the all-white facades was seen by millions. Appropriately enough, most of the exposition's buildings burned shortly after it closed but the memory of "The Great White City" with its classic columns influenced architecture, painting, sculpture, and the industrial arts. Charles Follen McKim and Stanford White, two pupils of Henry Hobson Richardson, who had been largely responsible for an indigenous American architecture, set off a new trend back toward historical revivalism. Richard M. Hunt's French Renaissance administration building dominated the exhibition grounds just as the neoclassic style of architecture reigned supreme in this country for 50 years afterwards.

Ever since their successful participation in the Paris Exposition of 1867 Tiffany & Company had won high honors and favorable attention from the public by their exhibits. With the introduction of electroplated wares to their products, their million-dollar exhibit at the World's Columbian Exposition included silverplated wares such as candelabra, piano lamps, meat and vegetable dishes, tea sets, and other domestic silver.

All the major silver companies of this country seem to have exhibited in Chicago. Their exhibits were enclosed in massive glass cases. They were not without their problems in arranging these. In June 1893 the *Jewelers' Weekly* tells that the "third pane of curved glass ordered by the Meriden Britannia Company for half of one of the bow windows in its case was received last week broken like its predecessors. Several weeks passed before this broken glass could be replaced."

Among the companies exhibiting was the Wm. Rogers Mfg. Co. Their large ebony-black pavilion was 15 by 25 feet and 35 feet high. An anchor, the trademark of the company, borne aloft, made one of the conspicuous features of the American silverware section in the Manufactures Building. A souvenir spoon, with this same device on the handle, was manufactured and distributed free of charge by the Wm. Rogers Mfg. Co. to visitors to their pavilion (Fig. 13). It was intended as a reminder of the merits of the "Anchor Rogers" brand of silverplated ware. Twenty-five patterns, including all the new patterns of the factory, were displayed in a

13. Souvenir spoon with "Anchor Rogers" trademark, given to visitors by Wm. Rogers Mfg. Co. at the World's Columbian Exposition, Chicago, 1893.

case whose base was yellow China silk. Ladles, fish knives and forks, crumb scrapers, berry spoons, sugar and nut spoons, pickle and oyster forks, cheese scoops, toddy strainers, nutcracks and fruit knives, sugar and bonbon tongs with after-dinner coffees between the prongs, orange spoons, bonbon scoops and ice cream spoons, nut picks, dessert spoons and teaspoons, and hollow-handled, silver-soldered knives and forks were among the flatware items shown. Their "Columbia" pattern was entirely new, having been designed especially in honor of the exposition.

Other late patterns displayed were "Opal," "Armenian," "Rose," "Pequot," "Kings," "Shell," and "Cromwell."

The Rogers company had a special exhibit of flatware, which called attention to their Sectional XII plate. As explained in the exhibit,

. . . after goods receive the regular plate they are again triple plated at all wearing points by the company's new and improved Sectional process, by which their extra plate is more than equal to the regular 12-ounce or triple plate; double plate is more than equal to regular 16-ounce or quadruple plate; triple plate is more than equal to 24-ounce or sextuple plate; extra Sectional XII plate is more than equal to regular 16-ounce or quadruple plate.

In addition to flatware, the Rogers company exhibit also contained hollow ware of nickel silver and a few pieces of sterling. There were six-piece tea sets, four-piece tête-à-tête sets, chafing dishes, mugs and cups, soda-glass holders, and castors. They also exhibited "a most attractive line of novelties and useful articles of the smaller class: including fish sets, children's sets, bread and milk sets, tilting teas, individual butter plates, salts and peppers, individual salt, pepper and butter sets, bonbon dishes, and scoops."

At the west end of the pavilion were shown the processes of manufacture of steel knives, German silver forks and spoons, and handmade solid silver spoons.

No exhibition up to this time had ever brought forth as many silverplate souvenirs. It was a sentimental age in which the collecting of souvenirs of all kinds was in vogue. Typical of these souvenirs was the Columbus match safe and sugar tongs (Figs. 14, 15).

The design and manufacture of these and other such souvenirs caused the creation of numerous small companies to manufacture and market them.

The Panama-Pacific International Exposition, which opened in San Francisco

VI. EXHIBITION AND PRESENTATION SILVER

14. Columbus match safe, souvenir of the World's Columbian Exposition, Chicago, 1893. *Jewelers' Weekly*, Dec. 7, 1892.

February 20, 1915, and closed December 4th of that same year, celebrated the building of the Panama Canal and the rebuilding of San Francisco after the catastrophic earthquake and fire of 1906. Its theme was that of achievement.

One of the achievements of the Meriden Britannia Company, which by then was part of the International Silver Company, was a silver sculpture called "The Spirit of the West" (Fig. 16). It was comprised of the metals used in the silver industry—pure silver, pure gold, white metal, and nickel silver. It was five feet high, seven feet four inches long, and weighed 659 pounds.

15. Sugar tongs, souvenir of the World's Columbian Exposition, Chicago, 1893.

An illustrated folder, distributed at the time, describes the sculpture thus:

On the base are etchings symbolic of the changing conditions which accompanied the transformation of the West. The Indian Council and Buffalo Hunt are memories of a bygone day. The Forty-Niners are represented with their prairie schooners eagerly seeking the land of golden promise, and the miners delving for its generous wealth. At either end are the two figures of Commerce, typifying the Transcontinental Railroad industry and ocean shipping with the waters of the Atlantic and Pacific united through the Panama Canal.

Surmounting the pedestal, upborne by life-like "grizzlies," are images representing the three great sources of western leadership—stock raising, mining, and agriculture—and over all is the spirit of peaceful Victory, which truly belongs to the youth and energy of the conquering West.

The "Spirit of the West" was described in a San Francisco newspaper as "the largest piece of sculptured silver in the world." It was the work of Louis Gudebrod in collaboration with Samuel Stohr of the International Silver Company design staff.

In 1923, by vote of the board of directors of International Silver Company, the silver sculpture was formally presented to M. H. deYoung, founder of the M. H. deYoung Memorial Museum in Golden Gate Park, San Francisco. Some years later it was placed on long-term loan in the "Whitney Museum" near the Cliff House in San Francisco.

Presentation Silver

The nature of its manufacture and consideration of the tremendous expense which would be involved almost pre-

16. "Spirit of the West" silver sculpture made for the Panama-Pacific Exposition, San Francisco, Cal., 1915, by the Meriden Britannia Co.

cludes the making of one-of-a-kind silverplated presentation pieces. Most are adaptations of regular stock items.

The Kalakaua Yacht Cup is an example of this (Fig. 17). One of the most treasured perpetual awards, it is considered to be the oldest trophy in the biennial races of the Transpacific Yacht Club between San Pedro, California, and Honolulu, Hawaii. The Yacht Cup was obtained by King Kalakaua in hopes of establishing transpacific yacht races.

King David Kalakaua, the last of Hawaii's kings, loved ocean travel. Accepting an invitation from the United States government in 1874, he was received with highest honors by President Grant and did much to promote friendship between the Hawaiian Kingdom and the United States. In 1881, he made a trip around the world and thus became the first reigning monarch to circumnavigate the globe.

With his love of the sea and his desire to perpetuate the Polynesian seafaring tradition, it was only natural that Kalakaua should encourage yacht racing.

His hopes of establishing transpacific yacht races were not realized during his lifetime and the trophy remained in obscurity until 1923, when it was presented to Eugene Overton of Los Angeles on the yacht *Spindrift*. Commodore Overton presented the cup to the Transpacific Yacht Club, which in turn placed it in the custody of Bernice P. Bishop Museum in Honolulu, from which it is removed only for presentation to the winner in Class A in the race held in July of each odd-numbered year.

Engraved on the larger dome of the cover is the statement that King Kalakaua had the trophy made in China.

VI. Exhibition and Presentation Silver   149

17. Kalakaua Yacht Cup, perpetual trophy awarded in the biennial races of the Transpacific Yacht Club between San Pedro, Cal., and Honolulu, Hawaii.

18. Original appearance of the Kalakaua Yacht Cup as it was shown in the 1886 catalog of the Meriden Britannia Co.

VI. Exhibition and Presentation Silver

This is in error, however, as stamped on the bottom of the rim is the familiar mark of the Meriden Britannia Company. This is further confirmed by the illustration from the 1886 catalog of that firm (Fig. 18). Some time after the cup was sent to Honolulu, the original figure was removed and the figure of a surfrider was substituted. This figure was eventually replaced by the small yacht. The location of the original figure is not known. The surfrider, however, was located in a Honolulu silversmith's shop which donated it to Bishop Museum. Winners' names are engraved on the silver plates attached to the koa-wood base.

A complete table service made by the Meriden Britannia Company is in the Museum of History and Technology, Washington, D.C. This set, described as "the largest and most elaborate set of presentation silver in the Museum," was given to General Judson Kilpatrick by the Veterans Association of Connecticut on the occasion of his marriage to a Chilean in 1868 while he was serving as U.S. Minister to Chile (Figs. 19–21). Almost identical to the Rogers & Bro. tea service illustrated in Chapter V, Fig. 16, this service differs only in the engraving and in having a jumping-horse finial in place of the dog on the Rogers service. The set is engraved with the emblems of the United States, Chile, the U.S. Army, and the U.S. Navy. The monograms on the individual pieces are in gold of four colors. More than any other silver service in the Museum, this one may be said to epitomize the elaborate realism so popular during the height of the Victorian era.

In a Smithsonian Institution publication the service is described,

19–21. Silver service presented to General Judson Kilpatrick by the Veterans Association of Connecticut. Now in the Division of Political History, Museum of History and Technology, Washington, D.C.

The pieces are marked "Meriden B. Company" in a circle around a shield surmounted by balanced scales. This mark was used in the second half of the nineteenth century by the Meriden Britannia Company for its high-grade silverplated hollow ware made on a base of nickel silver.

There are two trays in the set. The smaller tray is shown. The larger one measures 22½ inches by 38 inches and is inscribed:

The Veteran Soldiers of Connecticut
to Kilpatrick

It is engraved in gold and silver with flags of the United States and Chile crossed with bayonets and spears. On one side there is a center medallion in gold with the monogram "L V K" (for Luisa V. Kilpatrick) in a circle surmounted on a shield of stars and stripes. Above the monogram there is a banner with three stars and a triangle. On the other side of the standing piece two eagles in a fighting position are shown in front of a sunburst design. The motto "Tuebor" is at the top of the sunburst. The entire design is encircled by a ring of stars, and there is a shield of stars and stripes at the top. This same design is repeated on all forty pieces.

The service contains napkin rings, vegetable dishes, syrup jar, spoon holder, large centerpiece, porcelain-lined pitcher, and other miscellaneous pieces of silver used for table service. The pieces of the tea and coffee service are mounted on four feet that are fastened to the bowl with deer heads with branched horns. Each foot stands on a cloven hoof. The knob of each of the pots is a tiny horse jumping over a four-bar hurdle.

Ship's trumpets and firemen's trumpets were often awarded for bravery and valor. The ship's trumpet illustrated here was presented to the missionary ship the first *Morning Star* by children of the missionaries stationed at Constantinople (Figs. 22, 22a). Money for building the *Morning Star* was raised by selling ten-cent shares to children in Sunday schools in many states. She was launched in Boston on December 2, 1856, and served missionaries in Micro-

22. Ship's trumpet presented to the missionary ship *Morning Star* by children of the missionaries stationed at Constantinople.

22a. Ship's trumpet presented to the missionary ship *Morning Star* by children of the missionaries stationed at Constantinople.

23. Ice-water pitcher presented to General James A. Garfield in 1880.

nesia until December 12, 1865. The ship's trumpet is now in the collections of Bernice P. Bishop Museum, Honolulu, Hawaii.

An elegant tilting ice pitcher was presented to General James A. Garfield by the votes of his friends at a fair held by the Junior Hose Company of Chambersburg, Pennsylvania, October 1880—just a month prior to his election to the presidency of the United States (Fig. 23). In 1963 the pitcher was returned to the original makers, Reed & Barton, for refurbishing. Present owners are Mr. and Mrs. James Garfield, Mentor, Ohio.

It was, and still is, the custom for "visiting firemen" to compete for prizes. These competitions, called "musters," are actively promoted by the manufacturers of fire engines. Ice pitchers were often awarded to the winners. A pitcher inscribed "City of Coldwater/July 4, 1872" was won by "The Tempest" of Battle Creek, Michigan, in a competition on that national holiday (Fig. 24).

This particular celebration attracted more attention than usual, as according to the *Coldwater* [Michigan] *Republican,* June 22, 1872, ". . . it was decided to purchase of the Silsby Manufacturing Co., of Seneca Falls, N.Y., one of their third size Rotary Steam Fire Engines."

The History of Branch County Michigan (Everts & Abbott, Philadelphia, 1879) says that the new steam engine was christened "The City of Coldwater." Henry P. Collin, in *A Twentieth-Century History and Biographical Record of Branch County* (Lewis Pub. Co., New York City, 1906) says, ". . . in 1872, this department of public service became 'The City of Coldwater Steam Fire Engine Company' that being the date of the purchase of the first steam fire engine."

Contemporary newspaper accounts told of the "very handsome ice pitcher, tray and goblets" that were awarded to "The Tempest" of Battle Creek, Michigan. The tray and goblets are no longer with the pitcher which turned up at an auction house in Fort Worth, Texas. It is now privately owned.

24. Ice-water pitcher won by "The Tempest" in a "muster" held in Coldwater, Mich., July 4, 1872.

The magnificent model of the famous yacht *The Defender* that defended America's title in the International Cup Race of 1895, is an example of the fine craftsmanship of the Meriden Britannia Company (Fig. 25) which produced these art works in silverplate. The model was made precisely to scale from the original plans of the yacht's designers, Herreshoffs of Bristol, Rhode Island.

The hull is of silverplate, with spars of brass, guard rails of copper, sails of sterling silver, and a gold-plated deck. It was described in the *Jewelers' Cir-*

25. Model of the yacht *The Defender* made by the Meriden Britannia Co. in 1895.

cular and Horological Review, November 6, 1895, as

The handsomest piece of work, without doubt, ever turned out by the Meriden Britannia Co. is now on exhibition at the New York store of the company. It is an exact copy of the yacht Defender. Everything about the model is metal, from the sea that curls away at the bow to the fine rope in the rigging. The workmanship is among the finest and most skillful of its kind that has been seen in New York in many years. Every detail of the boat is carried out with exactness and skill. The miniature craft rests on a base two by four feet. This base is made to represent a choppy sea, and the effect is quite remarkable. Around the base is a border of anchors and chains, set off by unique corner pieces. The hull of Defender rests in the center of the silver sea, and seems to be sailing under great headway. The hull is of silver, the metal being the original color as it comes out, lacquered to preserve the white finish and leave the hull white just as the original appeared. The length of the hull is 30½ inches. The sails are as follows: Mainsail, working topsail, jib, jib staysail and jib topsail. The rigging is exactly the same as that on the original sloop. The miniature was built under the direction of Walker Wilkinson, and the men in the factory were over a month in building it. The model as it stands is valued at about $1,000.

It is on display at the International Silver Company, Meriden, Connecticut.

Ornamental Art Work, Vases, and Decorative Articles

Ornamental works of art, vases, and decorative articles in silverplate have been, and still are, made by all the major manufacturers. Vases of simple shapes were illustrated in the catalogs in the 1860s (Fig. 26). More elaborate vases and figurines were added to their productions somewhat later. A vase,

26. Vase made in the 1860s. Identical to one shown in 1867 Meriden Britannia Co. catalog.

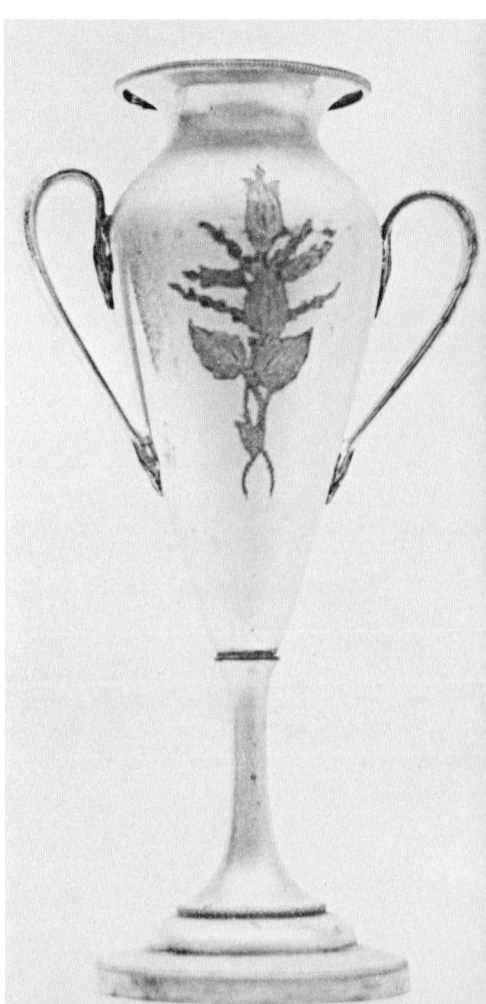

VI. ORNAMENTAL ART WORKS   155

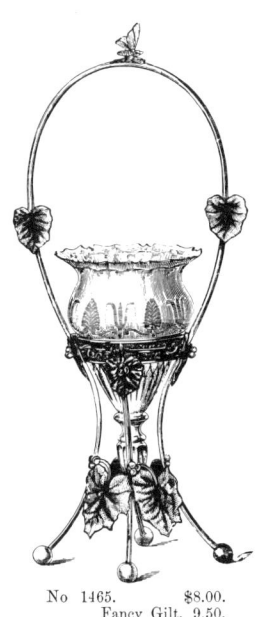

No 1465. $8.00.
Fancy Gilt, 9.50.

No. 1540. $7.50.
Fancy Gilt, 8.50.

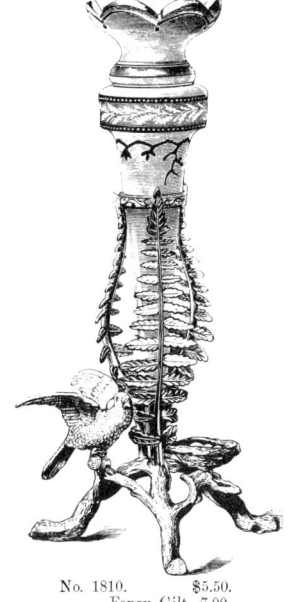

No. 1810. $5.50.
Fancy Gilt, 7.00.

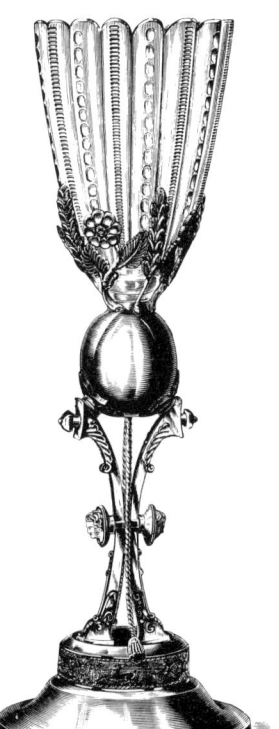

No. 1680. $9.00.
Fancy Gilt, 10.50.
" 1670. Smaller size, 7.50.
Fancy Gilt, 9.00.

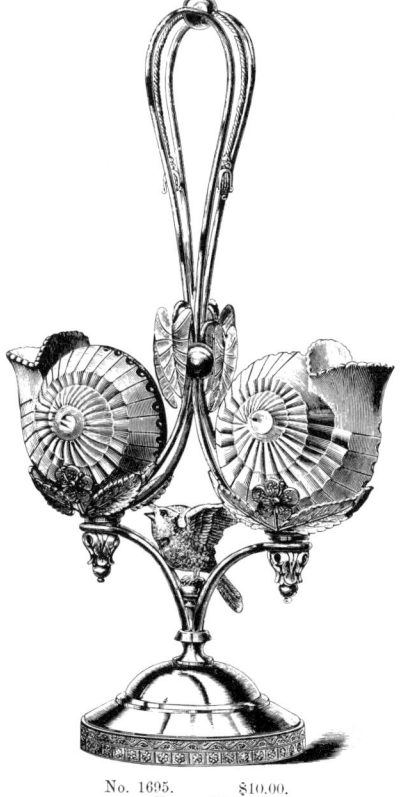

No. 1695. $10.00.
Fancy Gilt, 11.50.

No. 1475. $8.50.
Fancy Gilt, 10.00.
" 1470. Smaller size, 7.00.
Fancy Gilt, 8.50.

VASES.

27. Reed & Barton catalog, 1877.

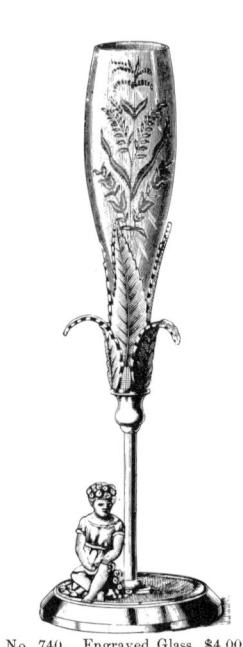

No. 740. Engraved Glass, $4.00.

No. 1915. $9.00 Fancy Gilt, $10.50.
No. 1905. Size smaller, 7.50. " " 8.50.

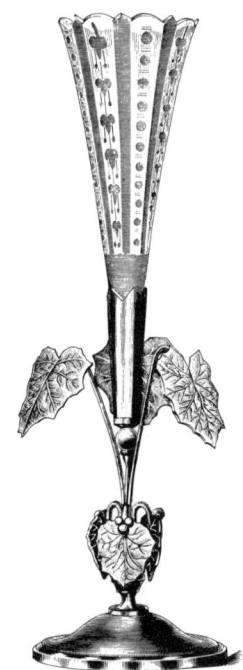

No. 1390. $5.00.
Fancy Gilt, 6.50.

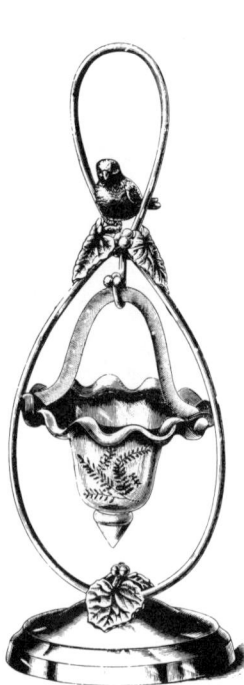

No. 1505. $8.00.
Fancy Gilt, 9.50.

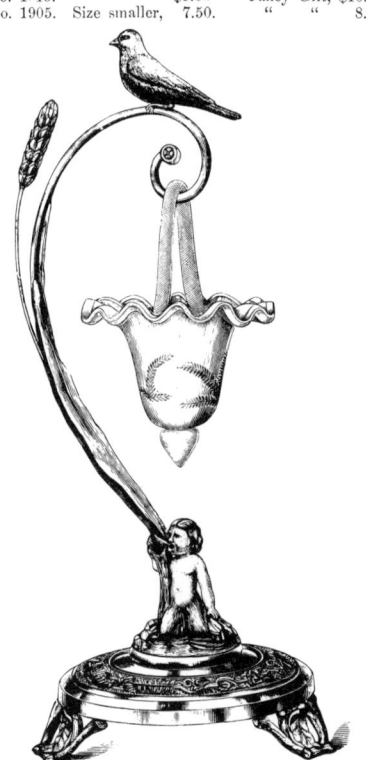

No. 1500. $10.00. Fancy Gilt, $12.00.

No. 1260. $8.50.
Fancy Gilt, 10.00.

VASES.

28. Reed & Barton catalog, 1877.

VI. ORNAMENTAL ART WORKS   157

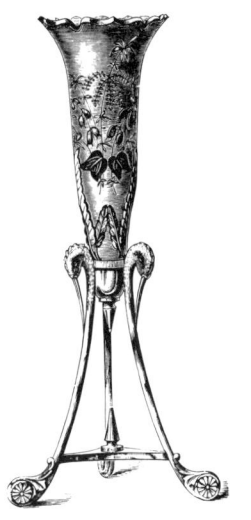

No. 770. $4.50.

No. 01600. $4.00.
Fancy Gilt, 5.00.
" 1600. Same price.

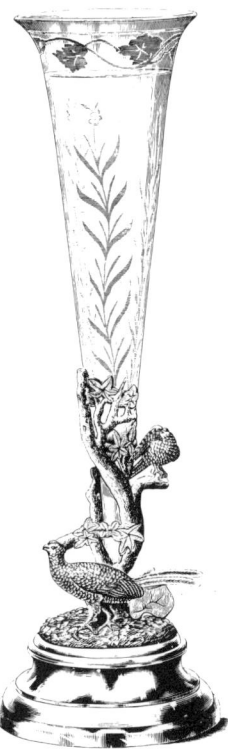

No. 01620. $7.50.
Fancy Gilt, 9.00.

Height, 22 inches.
No. 1530. $20.00.
   Fancy Gilt.   23.00.
" 1520. Two Baskets and Vase, 15.00.
   Fancy Gilt,   17.00.

No. 1620. $7.50.
Fancy Gilt, 9.00.

VASES.

29. Reed & Barton catalog, 1877.

VASES.

30. Reed & Barton catalog, 1877.

VI. Ornamental Art Works   159

No. 6200.   Apollo.
Height, 13 inches.   Size of Base, 5¼ x 5¼ inches.
Old Silver, .   .   . $25.00 Net.

No. 6000.   Mars.
Height, 16 inches.   Size of Base, 6 x 10 inches.
Old Silver, Gold Inlaid, .   . $45.00 Net.

No. 6400.   Indian Chief.
Height, 16 inches.   Size of Base, 4 x 7 inches.
Old Silver, Gold Inlaid, . $50.00 Net.

No. 6300.   Indian Squaw.
Height, 13½ inches.   Size of Base, 4 x 7 inches.
Old Silver, Gold Inlaid,   . $48.00 Net.

32. Meriden Britannia Co. catalog, 1877.

160 AMERICAN SILVERPLATE

No. 3130. QUAIL.
Height, 7½ inches. Size of Base, 3½ x 6½ inches.
Old Silver, ... $6.75 Net.

No. 3120. HUMMING BIRD.
Height, 7 inches. Size of Base, 3½ x 6½ inches.
Gilt, ... $5.00 Net.

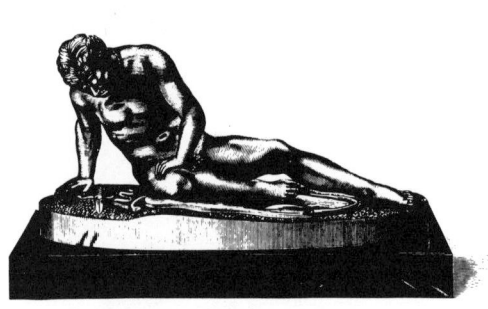

No. 6100. DYING GLADIATOR.
Height, 7½ inches. Size of Base, 12½ x 6½ inches.
Old Silver, ... $24.00 Net.

No. 3110. WOLF AND GROUSE.
Height, 5 inches. Size of Base, 3 x 6 inches.
Old Silver, . . . $5.50 Net.

No. 3140. BUFFALO.
Height, 4½ inches. Size of Base, 3 x 5½ inches.
Gilt, ... $6.75 Net.

No. 3100. SETTER DOG.
Height, 3½ inches. Size of Base, 3½ x 6½ inches.
Old Silver, Gold Inlaid, . . $6.00 Net.

33. Meriden Britannia Co. catalog, 1877.

VI. Ornamental Art Works 161

No. 6500. Egyptian Vase.
Height, 21 inches.
Old Silver, . . . $22.50 Net.

No. 7000. Egyptian Aquarium.
Height, 48 inches.
Cut and Engraved Globe. Capacity 10 gallons.
Oxydized, Gold Inlaid, ... $140.00 Net.

No. 6600. Egyptian Vase.
Height, 21 inches.
Old Silver, . . . $22.50 Net.

34. Meriden Britannia Co. catalog, 1877.

decorated with simple beading and an engraved rose design is marked "J. H. & A. W. Hart/Brooklyn" but is identical to one illustrated in the Meriden Britannia Company catalog of 1867.

Ten years later, in 1877, the Reed & Barton company carried an extensive line of elaborate vases with fancy cut and engraved glass inserts (Figs. 27–30).

One of the art works made by the Meriden Britannia Company and illustrated in their catalog of 1877 was a 16-inch-tall statue of Mars. This statue was made of silverplate and richly ornamented with gold plate. An example is currently on exhibit at the International Silver Company.

Other figurines carried in the 1877 Meriden Britannia Company catalog were a bust of Apollo, an Indian Chief, Indian Squaw, Quail, Hummingbird, Dying Gladiator, Wolf and Grouse, Buffalo, and a Setter Dog (Figs. 32, 33).

Vases and an aquarium, "in the Egyptian style," were also illustrated in this same catalog (Fig. 34). The aquarium, standing 48 inches tall, must have been an impressive piece.

Among the most attractive vases were those made of colored and decorated glass with silverplated mounts (Color Plate E). The black-and-white engravings in early catalogs give no idea of their true beauty. These early catalogs have little to say about the glass, referring to it only as "Ruby," "White," or "Decorated." Because of the glass, these vases attracted the attention of glass collectors years ago and have now become scarce and expensive.

Catalogs of the 1880s abounded in illustrations of vases and flower stands (Fig. 36). Some were small vases suitable for sentimental bunches of violets and pansies. Others were larger and suited to the bouquets so beloved by every true Victorian woman.

An interest in flower growing had been an indulgence of English men and women since early in the nineteenth century. It was not until somewhat later that the average American displayed this same interest. Settlers in a new and hostile land, it was only when freed from this total engrossment in maintaining a family that the urge to add beauty to his surroundings asserted itself in an esthetic interest in flowers. Victorian women were devoted to the decorative art of bouquet-making and manufacturers of silverplate catered to their needs by supplying a wide variety of vases (Fig. 37). Rustic scenes, flowers, birds, and butterflies were among the sentimental motifs employed.

Collectors of Art Nouveau will find vases which are admirably adapted to the shapes and motifs which characterize that style (Figs. 38, 39, 39a). Delicate traceries of flowers often form the ornaments.

One of the most beautiful lines of decorative silverplate ever produced in this country was the "Fine Arts Line" of the Wilcox Silver Plate Company, a division of the International Silver Company, produced briefly prior to

36. Small flower vase made by Wilcox Silver Plate Co. of Meriden, Conn., about 1884.

VI. ORNAMENTAL ART WORKS 163

No. 421.
Silver, . $5.00 (MORIBUND).

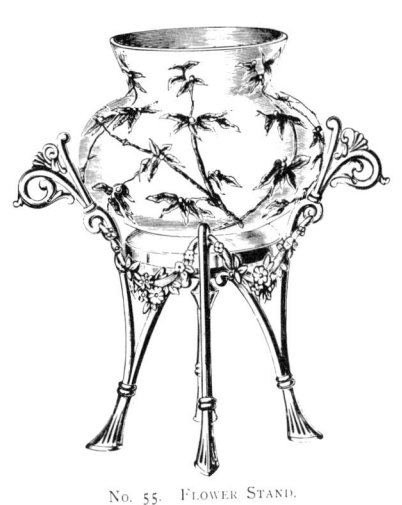

No. 55. FLOWER STAND.
Silver, . $6.00 (KEPT).

No. 408.
Silver, . $5.00 (LEND).
Silver, Gold Inlaid, 6.00 (LENGTH).

No. 307.
Gold and Silver, . $7.50 (LAKE).

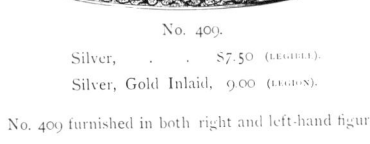

No. 409.
Silver, . $7.50 (LEGIBLE).
Silver, Gold Inlaid, 9.00 (LEGION).

No. 409 furnished in both right and left-hand figure.

No. 283. . $7.50 (LAGOON).

37. Meriden Britannia Co. catalog, 1886.

164 American Silverplate

No. 371. $4.00 (LACONIC).

No. 427.
Old Silver, $4.00 (MODULATE).
Non-Tarnishable.

No. 432.
Old Silver, $5.00 (MOULDING).
Non-Tarnishable.

No. 419.
Old Silver, $3.00 (MOULDER).
Non-Tarnishable.

No. 420.
Old Silver, $3.50 (MODERN).
Non-Tarnishable.

Flower Stand.
No. 41, $4.25 (LANCE).

Flower Stand.
No. 42, $5.25 (LANCET).

Flower Stand.
No. 51, $4.75 (INVADE).

37 continued.

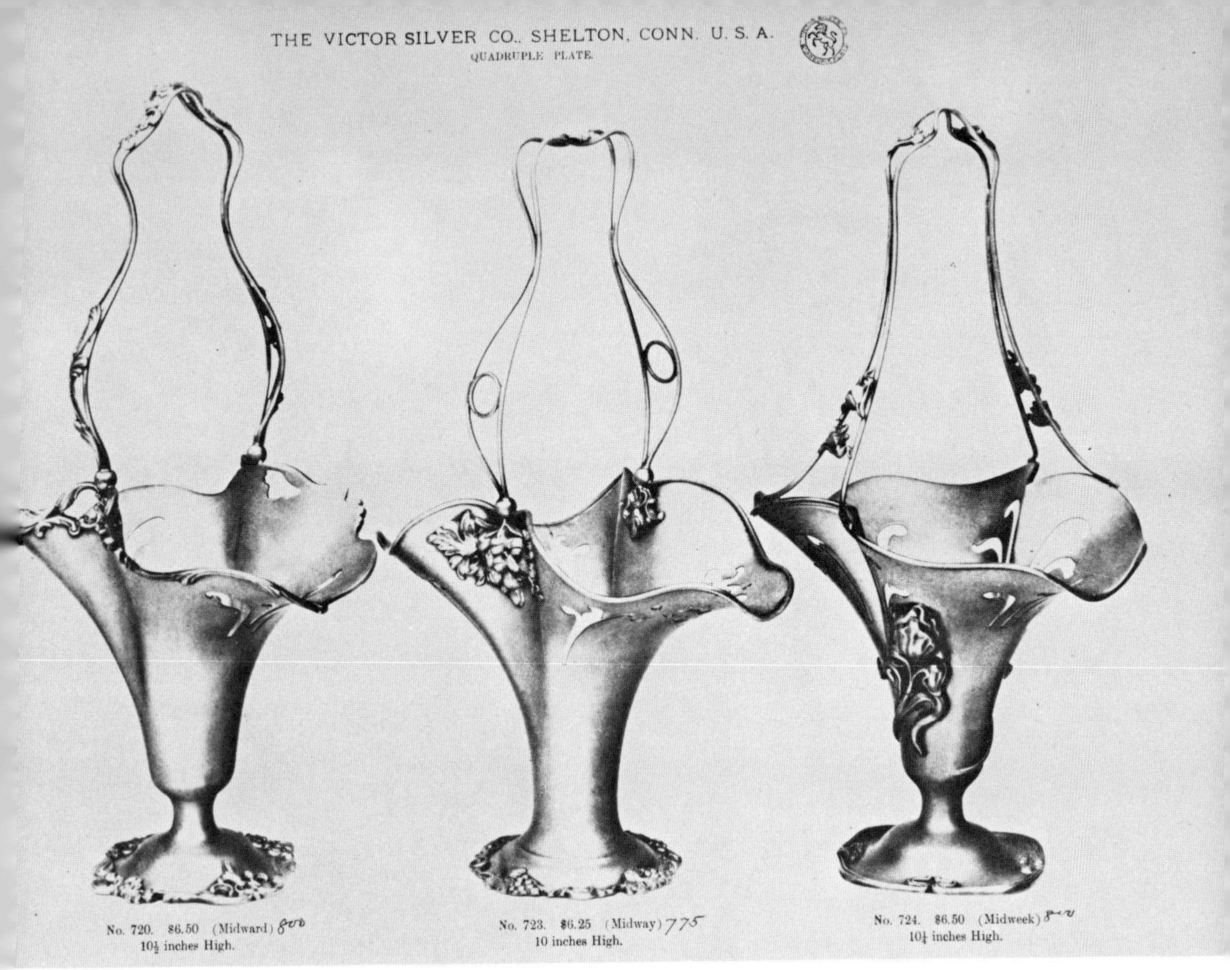

THE VICTOR SILVER CO., SHELTON, CONN. U.S.A.
QUADRUPLE PLATE.

No. 720. $6.50 (Midward)
10½ inches High.

No. 723. $6.25 (Midway)
10 inches High.

No. 724. $6.50 (Midweek)
10¼ inches High.

38. Art Nouveau vases made by Victor Silver Co. (a division of the Derby Silver Co., Derby, Conn.) and illustrated in their catalog about 1904.

'Tis an old adage that people judge you by your associates

It therefore behooves the enterprising jeweler who aspires to prestige and a reputation for business integrity to identify himself with those manufacturers whose productions have stood the test of years and have won general and enduring favor.

Homan Plate has been made since 1847

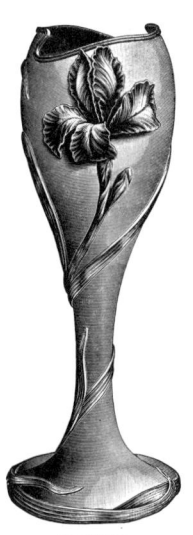

No. 2476 Vase
Manufactured in three sizes, 10, 15 and 20 inches

"A thing of beauty," executed in Combination French Gray-Burnished finish ornamented with twining iris leaf appliqué and flower in full relief.

39. Advertisement of Art Nouveau vase made by the Homan Mfg. Co. of Cincinnati, Ohio. *The Keystone*, August 1905.

39a. Ewer-vase in Art Nouveau style. Inscribed on front "Mr. & Mrs. J.C.B. Foster/From/Co. F. 2nd Reg't. F.I.T./Tampa, Fla." Pairpoint Mfg. Co., New Bedford, Mass. (circular mark). Designed and patented by Albert Steffin. Design Patent No. 37,008; Patented June 28, 1904.

40. "Fine Arts Line" of silverplated wares with cut and engraved glass inserts. Made by Wilcox Silver Plate Co. about 1938–42.

41. "Fine Arts Line" of silverplated wares with cut and engraved glass inserts. Made by Wilcox Silver Plate Co. about 1938–42.

42. "Fine Arts Line" of silverplated wares with cut and engraved glass inserts. Made by Wilcox Silver Plate Co. about 1938–42.

44. "Morgan" centerpiece and matching compotes. The copper-wheel crystal engraved pieces with bubble-ball stems were made by the Pairpoint Mfg. Co. before this line was purchased by the Wilcox Silver Plate Co. Silverplated holder and stands all marked with the Pairpoint "P in a diamond" trademark; holder marked "C 5500"; stands marked "C 1473."

43. Cut-glass plate with silverplated mounts. Made by Meriden Silver Plate Co. about 1900.

170 AMERICAN SILVERPLATE

World War II (Figs. 40–42). The line had been purchased from the Pairpoint Corporation of New Bedford, Massachusetts, about 1938 and was presented through a selected group of merchants. The glass inserts were from Sweden, from Mt. Washington Glass Company, and from the A. H. Heisey & Company glass companies. Difficulties in obtaining these glass inserts and wartime conditions caused the line to be discontinued.

Another beautiful line of silverplated articles with cut-glass inserts is represented here by the cut-glass plate made by the Meriden Cut Glass Company (Fig. 43). Actually housed in the same plant with Factory "N," the Wilcox Silver Plate Company, the Meriden Cut Glass Company was a part of the Meriden Silver Plate Company, organized in 1869 and later part of the International Silver Company.

1. Castor made by the Ames Mfg. Co., Chicopee, Mass. Exhibited at the New York Crystal Palace in 1854. *The World of Science, Art and Industry,* 1854.

CHAPTER VII

Silverplate for Table and Household Use

Castors

One of the most popular items made in silverplate, "dinner castors," as they were identified in old catalogs of silver manufacturers, most surely were derived from the cruet frames made for the reception of glass cruets for holding oil and vinegar and other condiments for use at the table. These date from the beginning of the eighteenth century in English silver.

Cruet frames were made in this country from about 1750. They were also made in England in "Old Sheffield Plate." In the 1830s the first castor frames were produced by britannia makers in this country but it was not until around the 1840s that they became an important article in the britannia trade. For example, the Taunton Britannia Manufacturing Company, now Reed & Barton, in 1834, shipped 410 castor frames, a total of 8.2 percent of their total shipments. In 1838, when the company had become Leonard, Reed & Barton, they sold 7,416 nickel-silver castor frames, or a total of 41.6 percent of their total shipments.

Early castors in silverplate were mainly set on low legs or on a relatively low center pedestal. A wide pierced band, or one embellished with ornate clusters of grapes and leaves, encircled the base of the container. A center handle was used for passing the castor at the table. Most castors provided space for six bottles.

A castor made by the Ames Manufacturing Company, Chicopee, Massachusetts, and exhibited at the New York Crystal Palace Exhibition in New York in 1854, is somewhat more elaborate than most of that period (Fig. 1).

During the 1850s "fancy castors" were developed, some of them patented. At the 1851 Crystal Palace Exhibition in London, Cartwright and Hirons, an English firm in Birmingham, exhibited a rotary castor. While this particular castor held wine glasses, the rotary principle was soon adapted to dinner castors.

A "cathedral type" castor in which the bottles are all enclosed was patented by Edward Gleason (Patent No. 18,740; December 1, 1857). This castor bears the trademark of R. Gleason & Sons of Dorchester, Massachusetts. Called a "magic castor," its revolving doors open to reveal six condiment bottles of Sandwich glass (Fig. 1a).

An earlier patent (October 21, 1856; Patent No. 15,946) had covered a bottle castor that was similar but did not revolve. It works on the same principle as "surprise" egg frames made by the English firm of Mappin & Webb.

Another castor bearing the trademark of R. Gleason & Sons accommodates six bottles and has a call bell in the center just below the handle (Fig. 1b).

Other castor designs patented by the versatile Gleason family were Design Patent No. 727, September 11, 1855, much like the magic castor, and a castor and egg-cup stand patented by R. Gleason, Jr., February 12, 1856 (Design Patent No. 763). Patent Office

171

copies of all these are too faded and battered to be reproduced.

A four-bottle castor, with bottles designed especially for the castor, was patented by William Parkin, October 25, 1870. The birds forming the four supports for the castor frame appear to be long-necked swans (Fig. 1c).

Green's Patent Vertically Revolving Castor (Fig. 2), made by the Meriden Britannia Company in 1860, operates on the principle later applied by G. W. Ferris to the "Ferris Wheel," one of the outstanding exhibits at the World's Columbian Exposition held in Chicago in 1893. This unusual castor was offered in the 1860 Meriden Britannia Company catalog (p. 23) but must not have been a commercial success because it was not shown in later catalogs.

Another impressive six-bottle dinner castor was made by the Meriden Britannia Company between 1855 and 1867 (Fig. 3). It had six deer-head ornaments, each placed directly in front of one of the bottles.

The more familiar revolving castors were offered by manufacturers in their catalogs at least as early as 1855 (Figs. 4, 5). Typical of these are the ones with pierced bands or ornate decorations of grape clusters. Entwined grapevines with applied decorations of grape clusters and leaves form the handles. The castors rest on low center pedestals or on short legs.

Dinner castors were made by all the better-known silver manufacturers from the very beginnings of the electroplating business. The Meriden Britannia Com-

1b. Castor with call bell. Made by R. Gleason & Sons, Dorchester, Mass. "PATENT REISSUED DEC. 27, 1859" on plate applied under the bell. This date probably refers to a patent on the bell.

1a. "Magic castor" patented by Edward Gleason, December 1, 1857; Patent No. 18,740. It bears the trademark of R. Gleason & Sons, Dorchester, Mass. *Left to right:* Doors closed; doors half open; doors fully open. *Insert:* Bottom of castor.

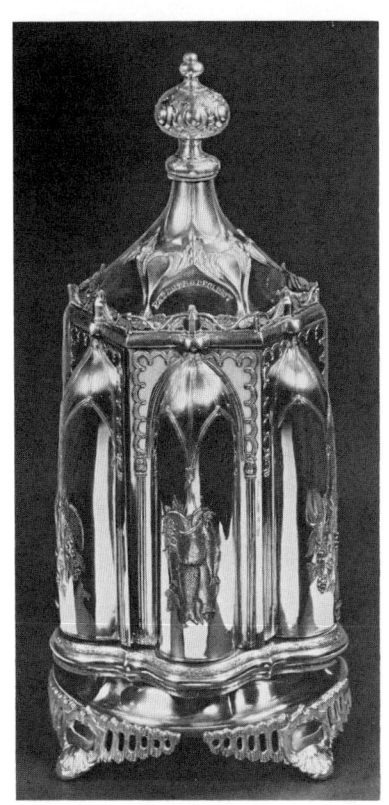

174 AMERICAN SILVERPLATE

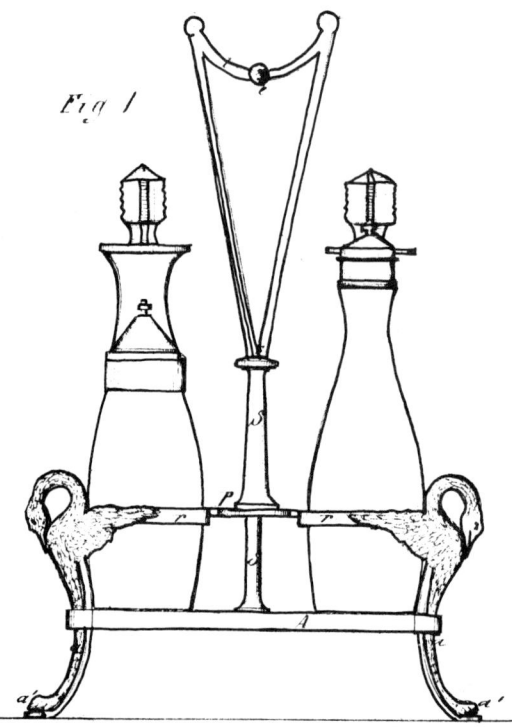

1c. Four-bottle castor patented by William Parkin. Design Patent No. 4,437; Patented October 25, 1870.

3. Dinner castor made by the Meriden Britannia Co. 1855–67.

pany was offering 75 different patterns in dinner castors in 1861. This number was increased to 122 by 1867. Among the dinner castors offered in the 1867

2. Green's Patent Vertically Revolving Castor made by the Meriden Britannia Co. in 1860.

VII. Silverplate for Table and Household Use 175

4–5. Revolving castors made about 1855 by Rogers Bros. Mfg. Co.

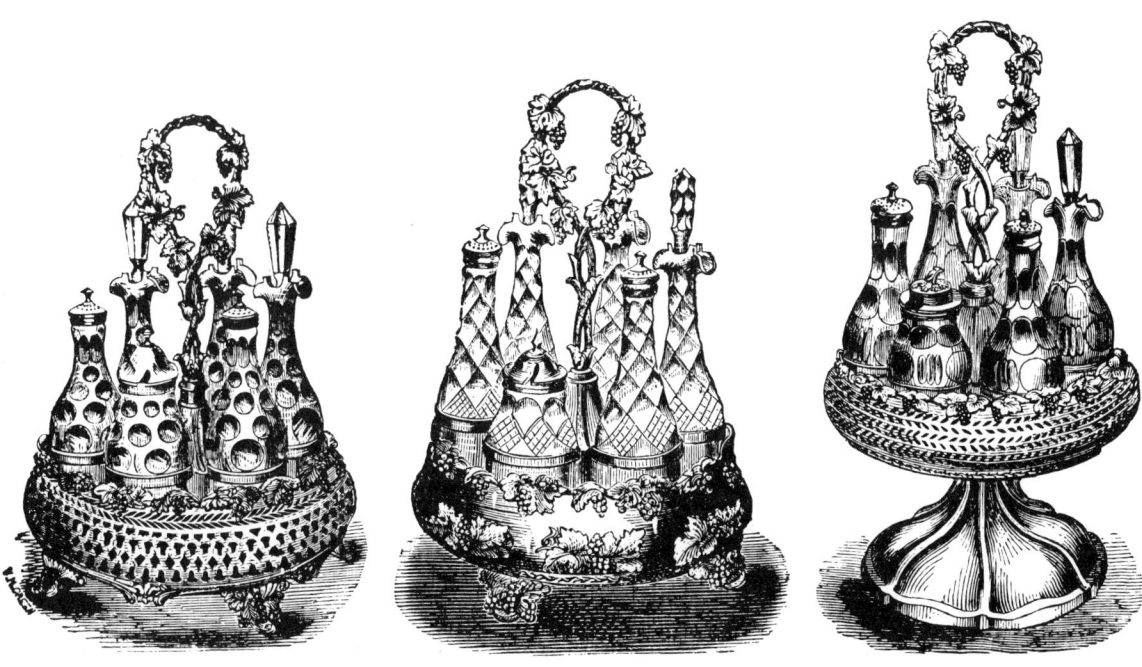

6–9. Meriden Britannia Co. catalog, 1867.

10. Meriden Britannia Co. catalog, 1867.

11. Dinner castor with medallion head decorations. Marketed by the San Francisco firm of Haynes & Lawton.

catalog, most contained receptacles for six bottles. Several were designed so that the bottles and bottle rack could be lifted out by the handle leaving a bottom part to be used as a fruit stand or nut bowl (Fig. 6).

Breakfast castors contained three or four bottles (Fig. 7). Some had egg cups and egg spoons (Fig. 7a); others included salt dishes and spoons (Fig. 8).

Closely related articles are the pickle or preserve stands and wine stands (Figs. 9, 10).

12–15. Reed & Barton catalog, 1877.

16–18. Reed & Barton catalog, 1877.   **19.** Reed & Barton catalog, 1885.

180 American Silverplate

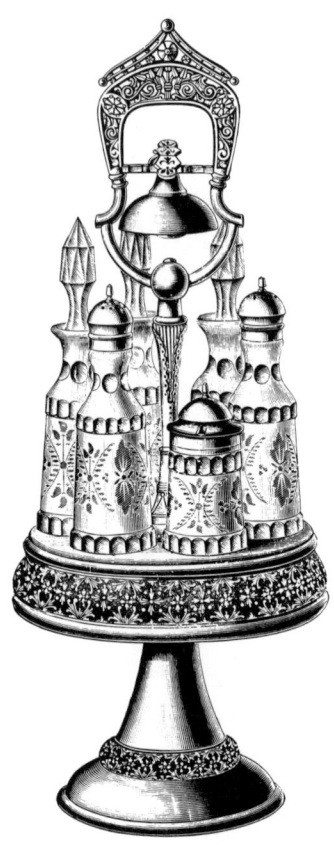

20. Meriden Britannia Co. catalog, 1886.

A castor with medallion head decorations was marketed by the San Francisco firm of Haynes & Lawton (Fig. 11). This castor is adorned with identical heads of the Athena type set in oval frames. It may be dated rather precisely as this partnership of Haynes & Lawton lasted only two or three years in the middle 1870s and advertised the manufacture of all sorts of electroplated tableware.

Revolving and fancy dinner castors offered by Reed & Barton in 1877 included a four-bottle castor in a cart drawn by a strutting peacock (Fig. 12). Others of the five- and six-bottle type rested on four legs or on rather tall pedestals, the earlier, more attractive basket types with wide pierced or decorated bands having disappeared from the market. Call bells were sometimes incorporated into the handles (Fig. 13).

The square castor frame patented by William Parkin was adapted for use as a pickle castor (Fig. 16).

Another illustration of the way a design motif could be utilized for more than one type of article is shown by the peacock on the pickle castor (Fig. 15). This same peacock was used on the dinner castor (*Fig. 12, above*) and also for two fruit stands shown in the same catalog.

Fancy designs in pickle castors were numerous (Figs. 14, 17). Some had very attractive engraved glass bottles. Quite a number were available in one-bottle or two-bottle styles.

In the 1880s the trend toward the tall, revolving castors was practically complete. This extreme height was further accentuated by taller handles, and in some cases, bells, egg cups or bouquet holders (Figs. 19, 20). The 1880s were the heyday of the castor. Reed & Barton offered a total of 160 different styles in their regular line. In addition, simpler styles were offered in hotel ware for use in hotels, restaurants, railroad dining cars, and ships' dining rooms.

Not only were castors offered in the numerous styles illustrated in the catalogs, other combinations could be made by selecting bottles of one's choice (Fig. 21). These bottles ranged from inexpensive engraved styles to the finest heavy cut glass. Most were clear glass but there were also cut-glass designs in amber, blue, and cranberry. An additional choice could be had in handles (Fig. 22). Four styles had flower vases and six others with call bells were offered.

A wide variety of styles in other types of castors were offered in the 1880s. Breakfast castors, individual castors,

21. Meriden Britannia Co. catalog, 1886.

No. 14½, $5.25.

No. 12, $4.50.

No. 14, $4.50.

No. 11, $5.75.

No. 13, $5.25.

No. 18, $7.00.

No. 19, $7.00.

No. 20, $9.00.

No. 21, $6.00.

No. 22, $5.75.

No. 23, $7.00.

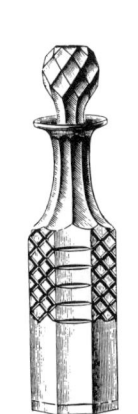
No. 102, $30.00.

No. 104, $30.00.

No. 95, $18.00.

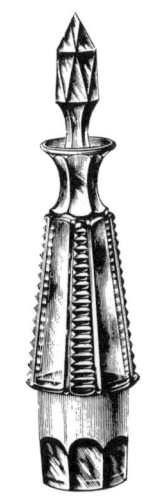
No. 97, $18.00.

No. 98, $18.00.

No. 99, $20.00.

182 AMERICAN SILVERPLATE

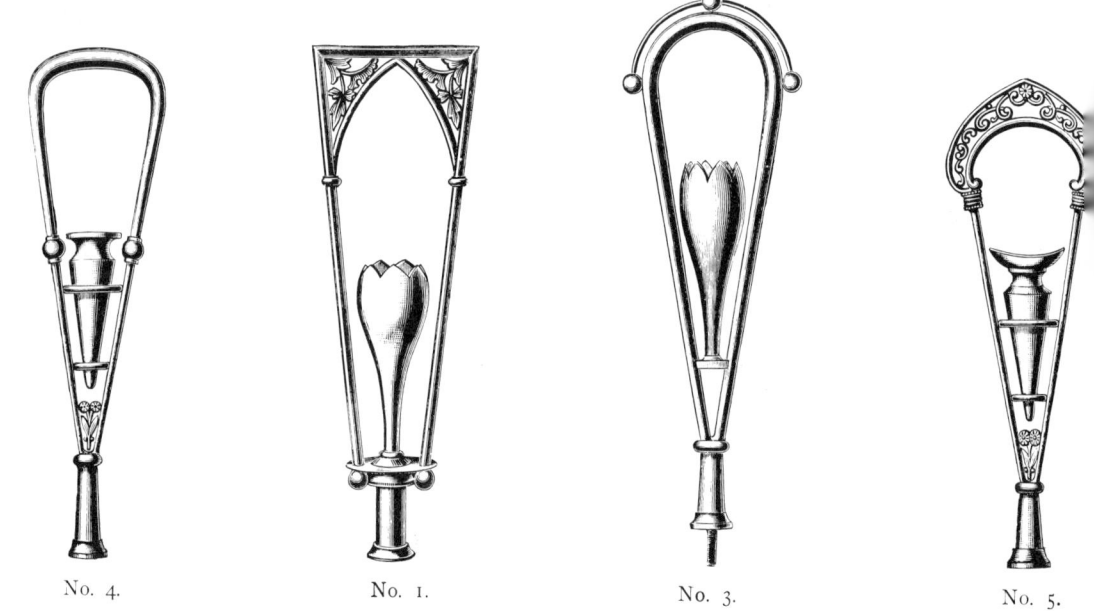

No. 4.   No. 1.   No. 3.   No. 5.

Vase, . $0.75 extra (ROCKSALT). Vase, . $1.50 extra (RIPRAP). Vase, . $1.50 extra (RISIBLE). Vase, . $0.75 extra

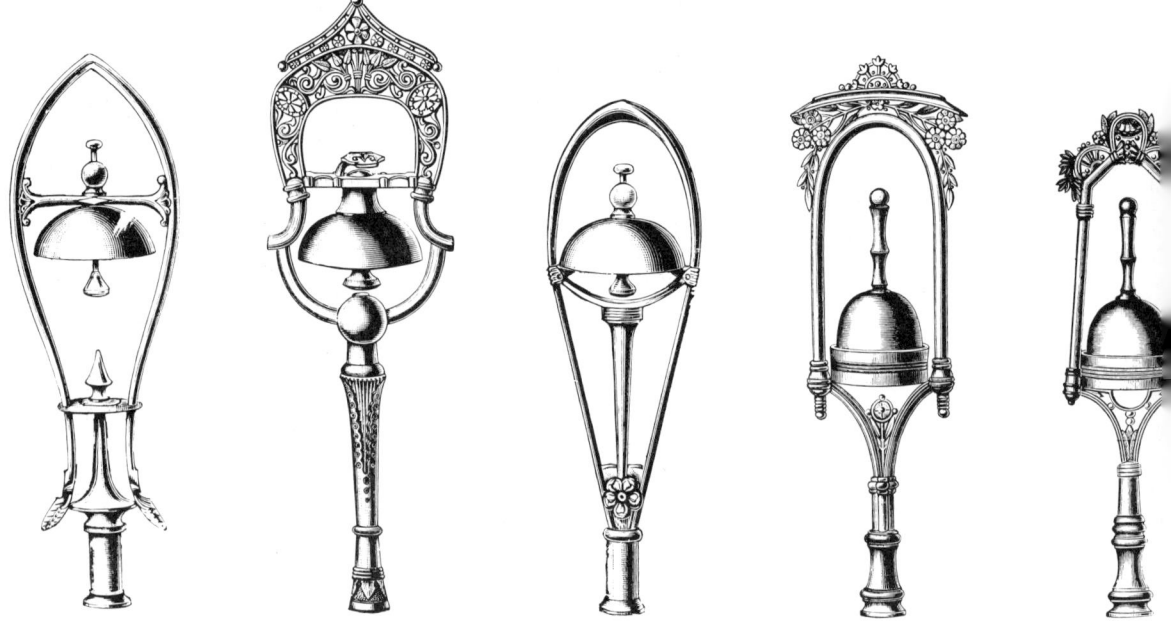

No. 3.   No. 5.   No. 4.   No. 7. Bell, or Toothpick   No. 6.

Bell, $2.00 extra (RIFLEMAN). Bell, $2.00 extra (RIDICULE). Bell, $2.00 extra (RIDGEPOLE). Holder, $1.50 extra (RIDDLE). Bell, $1.50 ex

22. Meriden Britannia Co. catalog, 1886.

VII. Silverplate for Table and Household Use   183

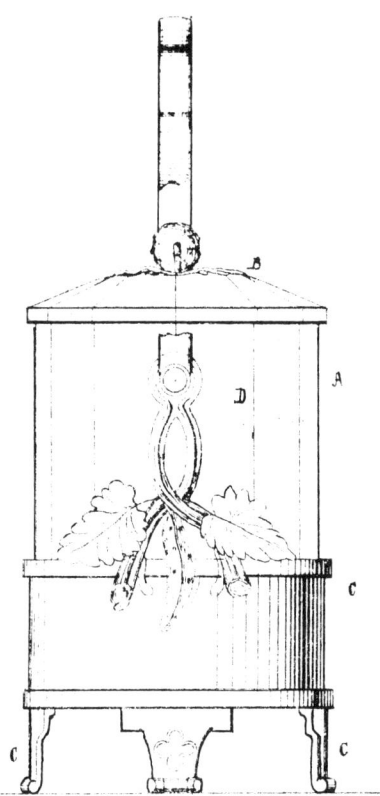

23. Pickle castor patented by George Gill. Design Patent No. 5,926; Patented June 11, 1872.

salad castors, pickle castors, and wine stands were all extremely popular.

Few of these designs were patented. An exception is the one patented by George Gill, June 11, 1872. The specifications claim that the oval shape and the cucumber decorations are new (Fig. 23).

It was in the 1880s that the pickle castor began to assume real importance. The glass containers, the main reason for their present popularity, were of clear or colored glass that was cut or engraved (Color Plate B; Fig. 24). In catalog pages, some were marked "Decorated" and "Assorted Colors" and appear to be enameled (Fig. 25). One is clearly labeled "Pomona Art Glass."

Much castor glassware was imported but it was also made by American firms. Two Meriden, Connecticut, firms supplied much of the glass for the Meriden Britannia Company and other silverware manufacturers who operated in that city. These were Bergen & Niland, a glass-cutting firm who, in the 1880s, had an extensive line of fine cut glass and also furnished cut and engraved castor bottles to the silver makers. Another firm in Meriden that made castor bottles was the Meriden Flint Glass Company. They were in business from 1876 to 1896, and made the bottles as well as cut them.

By the 1890s dinner castors were losing their place of prominence on the dining table and in the early 1900s they went out of style. As in the previous decade, emphasis was placed on the richly decorated glass rather than on the silverplated frames of pickle castors (Fig. 26). Individual castors, salad castors, breakfast castors, and wine stands were made, but in increasingly smaller numbers (Figs. 27–29).

Castors were such an important part of the silverplated-ware trade, that it may safely be assumed that they were made by every manufacturer. Their best quality castor frames were made of nickel silver and plated with a heavy, durable coating of silver. Others were made of white metal and, in old catalogs, it was frequently indicated that their second-quality goods did not carry their trademark.

Dinner castors and pickle castors have long been considered among the most desirable of collectibles. Dinner castors presently command prices several times more than they did originally, while pickle castors because of their richly decorated glass, are currently selling for even more. Because of this great demand, the collector should be aware that reproductions of all kinds of castors are being imported and are flooding the market.

24. Pickle castors of the 1880s. *Left to right:* Wilcox Silver Plate Co. (Meriden, Conn.); Rogers, Smith & Co. (Meriden, Conn.); Hartford Silver Plate Co. (Hartford, Conn.).

Centerpieces, Fruit Dishes, Berry Bowls, and Brides' Baskets

Centerpieces, fruit dishes, fruit stands, berry bowls, and brides' baskets whose richly decorated cut or engraved, clear or colored glass outweighed in importance the silverplated stands, began to dominate the center of the dining-room table about 1875, often relegating the ubiquitous castor to a position of lesser importance.

In the early 1860s the bowls, stands, and baskets of simpler design were of cut or engraved crystal or pressed glass. The Meriden Britannia Company's catalog of 1867 offered a line almost evenly divided between those entirely of silverplate and those with "Oval or round glass dishes, Assorted Colors," "White Ground Glass Lining," or "Fine Ruby or Green Dish," in a silverplated frame or a stand (Figs. 30–32). The glass in some appears to be engraved while in others it is plain. The metal frames and

25. Meriden Britannia Co. catalog, 1886.

VII. SILVERPLATE FOR TABLE AND HOUSEHOLD USE 185

. $5.00 (PARABLE).
ona Art Glass.

No. 223, . $5.00 (PARADISE).
Assorted Colors.

No. 156, . $5.00 (CROOKED).

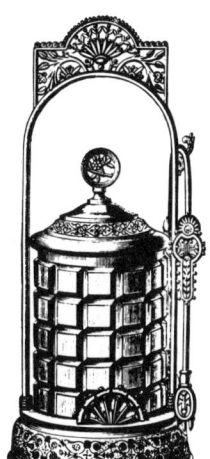

No. 212, . $3.75 (GRACEFUL).

No. 157½, . $5.00 (CRONY).

, $6.00 (CROCHET).

No. 221.
Crystal, . $4.00 (PARAFFINE).
Assorted Colors, 4.25 (PARALLEL).

No. 210, . $5.00 (PASTEL).

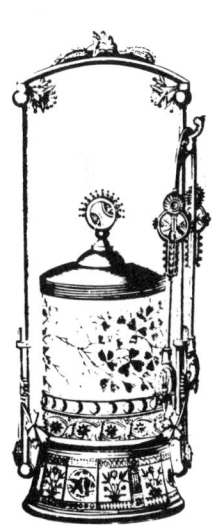

No. 206, . $3.75 (PARSON).

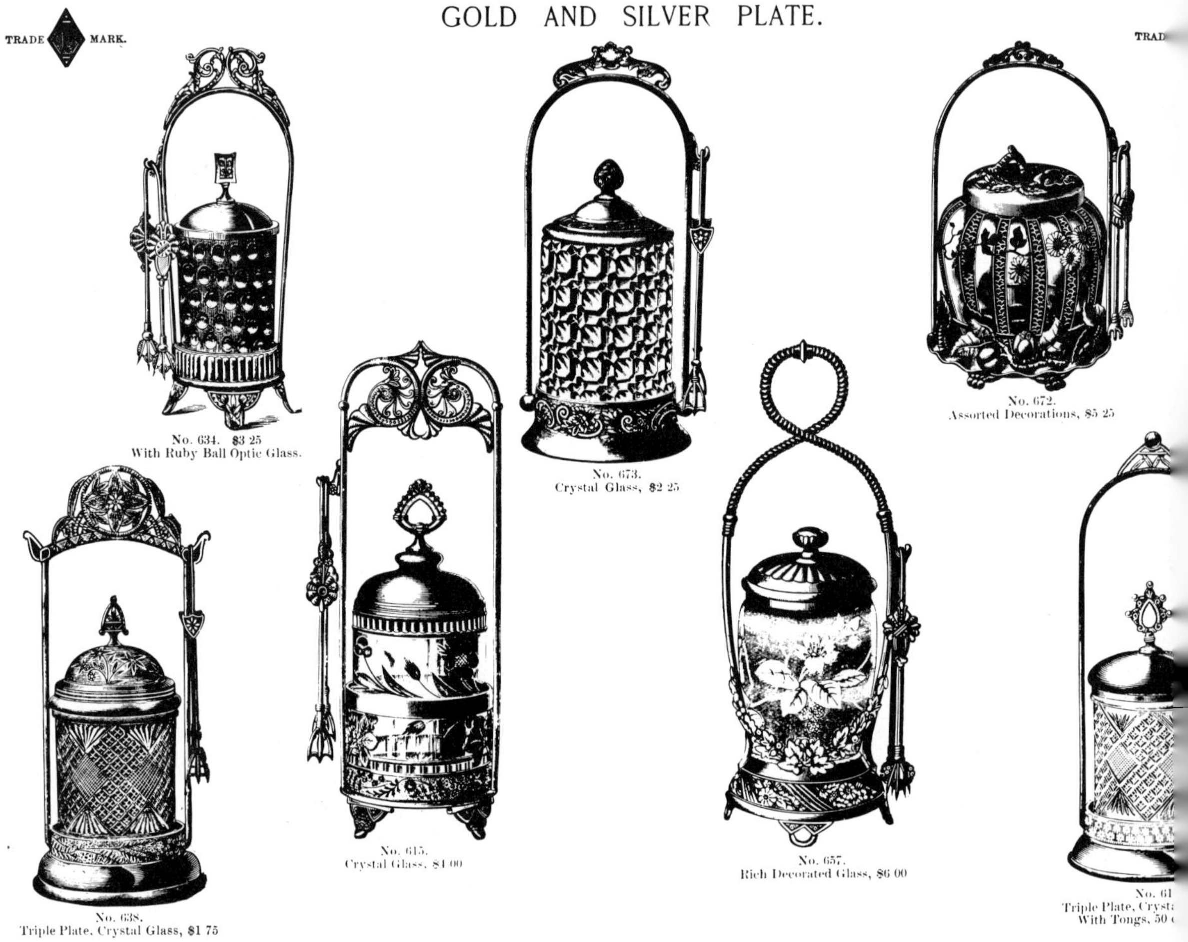

GOLD AND SILVER PLATE.

26. Pairpoint Mfg. Co. (New Bedford, Mass.) catalog, 1894.

stands had either a center pedestal or three or four low feet. Decorations were beading, gadrooning, applied continuous bands in Greek key, and other relatively plain designs. Three winged horses formed the feet and base of one. Sculptured heads and lion masks were featured on one stand while deer and grapevines on a rocky base formed the support for another. Rams' heads are noted on five of the 17 styles offered in 1867. But these are almost austere compared to the elaborate creations made a decade later.

Butterflies are perched on the column supporting the three-tier centerpiece with a vase in the center (Fig. 33).

27. Pickle or relish dish, Homan Silver Plate Co., Cincinnati, Ohio.

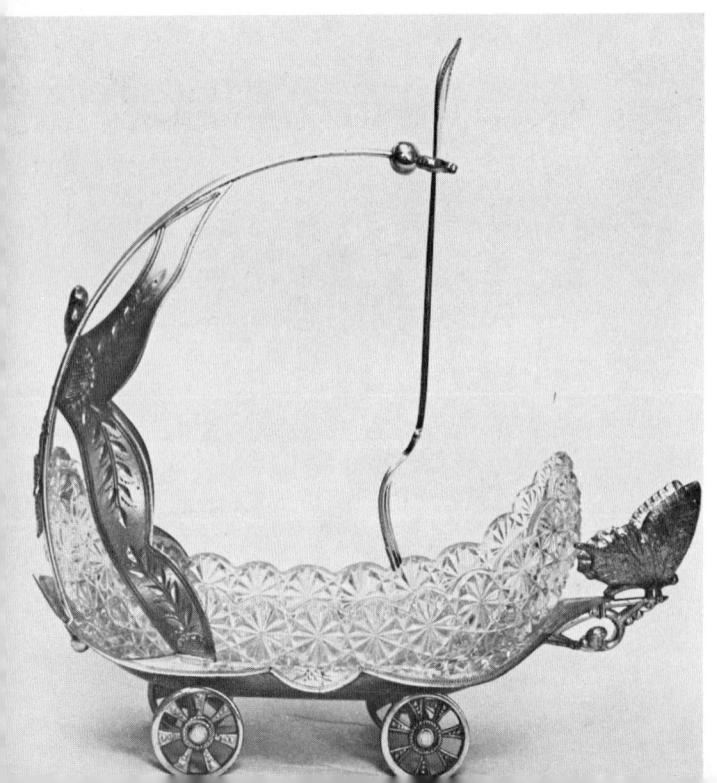

VII. Silverplate for Table and Household Use 187

28. Pickle castor.

29. Pickle castor made by the Pairpoint Mfg. Co. about 1894.

No. 0204.
Each, $40 00.

No. 0206.
Each, $36 00.

No. 03000.
Each, $14 00.

No. 01, Epergne.
Gilt Bottom. Each, $30 00.
No. 02, same as No. 01 only larger. Each, $33 00.

30. Meriden Britannia Co. catalog, 1867.

31–32. Meriden Britannia Co. catalog, 1867.

Made in 1872 by the Wilcox Silver Plate Company, this is an unusually large piece for its day. The decoration is applied bands of beading and engraved floral sprays.

A berry dish made by the Meriden Britannia Company in 1871 has a frosted-glass insert guarded by four Roman soldiers and two female heads mounted around the glass much in the same manner of ships' figureheads (Fig. 34). The frame rests on four hoof feet between which is an Egyptian sphinx made popular by Napoleon's Egyptian campaign.

An illustration of a Reed & Barton epergne in the September 1877 issue of the *Jeweler, Silversmith and Watchmaker* is of ". . . one of the most recent designs of Epergnes. There can hardly be a more beautiful or appropriate ornament for a dining table or buffet than this chariot of silver drawn by the proud peacock guided by Cupid." It was also featured in the Reed & Barton catalog of 1877 (Fig. 35). "Beautiful" and "appropriate" it must have been considered by the buying public as it was still being shown in their catalogs as late as 1885.

An early silverplated fruit stand made by the Meriden Britannia Company around 1879 has a pressed-glass crystal bowl in the "Tree of Life" pattern (Fig.

33. Three-tier centerpiece made by the Wilcox Silver Plate Co. in 1872. The vase may be removed and a flattened knob, usually stored beneath the base, may be screwed into its place.

34. Berry dish made by the Meriden Britannia Co. in 1871.

190   AMERICAN SILVERPLATE

35. From Reed & Barton catalog, 1877.

36). Half-caryatid figures form the support for one made by the Meriden Silver Plate Company before 1879.

Roman medallions, swans, cherubs playing harps, mythological birds and animals, storks, caryatids. floral swags, children playing with butterflies, winged cherubs, turtles, lions draped with floral swags, water lilies, and other floral motifs were among the decorations used in the mid-1870s on fruit stands, fruit dishes, and berry or preserve dishes, more than two-thirds of which had glass dishes (Fig. 37). This glass was mostly cut and engraved. Just as teapots and coffeepots of the 1870s had risen up on high supports, so did fruit stands. Center supports were caryatids or tall columns rising from domed bases dec-

36. Early silverplated fruit stands. *Left:* Pressed-crystal bowl in the "Tree of Life" pattern, Meriden Britannia Co. about 1879. *Right:* Cut and engraved crystal bowl atop a stand made by the Meriden Silver Plate Co. before 1879.

orated with continuous bands. Others were fanciful birds or animals. A few dishes stood on three or four tall legs. Some had two dishes and a few had a vase in the center for flowers.

Heads of fantastic birds support the cut and frosted glass insert of a fruit stand made by the Wilcox Silver Plate Company around 1880 (Fig. 38). Classical acanthus and laurel leaves form the decoration of the base.

As rapidly as craftsmen working with art glass created and patented new glass wares in the 1880s, silverplate manufacturers created a bewildering variety of mounts and stands to enhance them (Fig. 39).

Some of these stands were richly decorated with the Renaissance motifs which endured so many interpretations (Fig. 40).

Winged cherubs played with butterflies or birds, caryatids of classic Greek proportions and butterfly wings competed with other female forms "in the Egyptian manner" (Figs. 41–43). The stronger sex was ably represented by Poseidon, trident in hand and accompanied by miniature Tritons (Fig. 44).

Birds and animals of every kind abounded and animals-that-never-were scowled from their silverplated perches (Fig. 45). Flowers of all sorts bloomed profusely on glass as well as on the silverplated mounts.

Practically every manufacturer of silverplate and every glass house in the country combined their talents to produce what was surely the most unrestrained decorative table appointments ever created. Much glass was also imported from Europe. Because the manufacturers of silverplate were concerned mainly with the promotion of their sil-

37. From Reed & Barton catalog, 1877.

VII. Silverplate for Table and Household Use 193

No. 2980. $12.50.

No. 3210. $10.00.

No. 3190. $9.50.
" 3185. Size smaller, 8.50.

No. 3195.   Ruby Lining, $8.50.
" 03195. With Bail, "   9.50.

No. 2400. $20.00.

No. 3295. $18.00.

37 continued.

194 American Silverplate

No. 2730. $18.00.
Fancy Gilt, 21.00.

No. 3320. $15.00.
Fancy Gilt, 18.00.

No. 3120. $25.00.
Fancy Gilt, 28.00.

No. 3015. $25.00.
Fancy Gilt, 30.00.

37 continued.

VII. Silverplate for Table and Household Use 195

No. 03620. $25.00. Gold-lined, $30.00.
" 3260. Same, no Vase, 20.00. " 24.00.

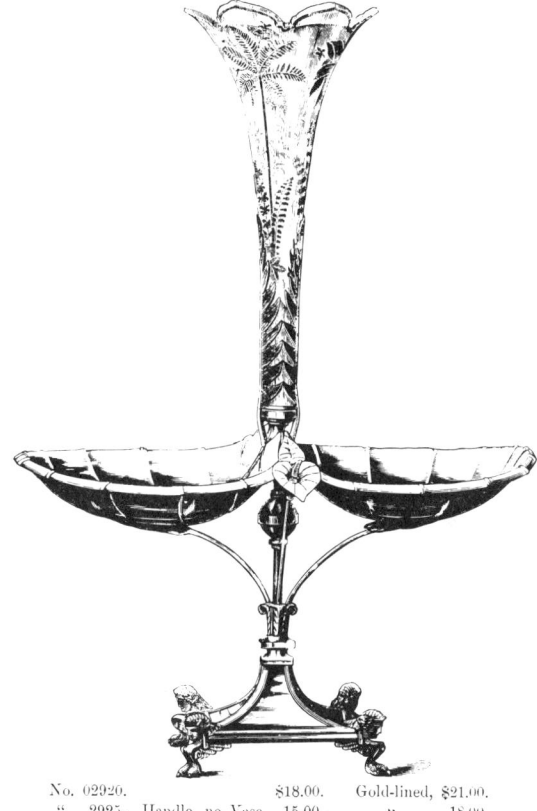

No. 02920. $18.00. Gold-lined, $21.00.
" 2925. Handle, no Vase, 15.00. " 18.00.

No. 3250. $20.00. Fancy Gilt, $25.00.

No. 3060. $55.00. Fancy Gilt, $65.00.

37 continued.

38. Fruit stand made by the Wilcox Silver Plate Co. about 1880.

39. Fruit dish made by the Wilcox Silver Plate Co. about 1880. The fluted dish has alternating bands of frosted and cut glass. A floral design is cut and engraved on the dish near the handle and another on the under side.

40. Reed & Barton catalog, 1885.

verplated mounts, the source of the glass was inadequately identified. Because of collectors' interest in nineteenth-century art glass many silverplated mounts have become separated from their glass containers.

Among the more restrained examples of fruit dishes and bowls were the colorless frosted ones with etched designs (Fig. 46). Agata, Amberina, Burmese, Peachblow, Pomona, and satin glass were used. Cut glass and pressed glass, both in many patterns, the latter in clear and in several colors, were popular. Decorated glass included the "Mary Gregory type." But in catalogs of silver manufac-

41. Reed & Barton catalog, 1885.

42. Meriden Britannia Co. catalog, 1886.

43. Meriden Britannia Co. catalog, 1886.

turers descriptions of glassware were limited to "Canary," "Ruby Lined," "Decorated Porcelain," "Crystal Engraved," "Assorted Colors," "Rich Cut Glass," "Malachite and Decorated Glass," "Colored Craquelle Glass," and "Rich Red or Blue Malachite Decorated Glass."

About the middle of the 1880s a limited number of the glass inserts with ruffled or fluted edges appeared in silver manufacturers' catalogs (Fig. 47). Greater numbers and varieties were produced in the 1890s and long after the turn of the century when their popularity as well as that of other elaborate "fancy wares" waned (Figs. 48, 49). Revival of interest in them has spurred the importation of reproductions. These reproductions are not made in the wide variety of styles once available but the collector would do well to buy only from reputable sources.

44. Meriden Britannia Co. catalog, 1886.

202 AMERICAN SILVERPLATE

ÉPERGNE.
No. 914. Gold-lined. $95.00. (WONDERFUL)
Gold-lined and Oxidized Finish, 110.00. (WOODEN)
With Vase, $10.00 extra.

No. 4235. Coral Rose and Decorated Glass, $14.75. (WOOD)
Gold and Oxidized Finish, 17.75. (WORDING)

No. 4020. Decorated Porcelain Bowl, $28.50. (WOODBINE)
Gold and Oxidized Finish. 33.50. (WOOL)

No. 04275. Colored and Decorated Glass, $16.25. (WOODL)
Gold and Oxidized Finish, 19.25. (WOOLLY)

45. Reed & Barton catalog, 1885.

VII. Silverplate for Table and Household Use

No. 3830. Fruit or Salad Bowl, Rich Malachite Glass,
Snow Flake and Appliqué Base, $28.00. (CASTAWAY)
Gold and Oxidized Finish, 33.00. (CASTIGATE)

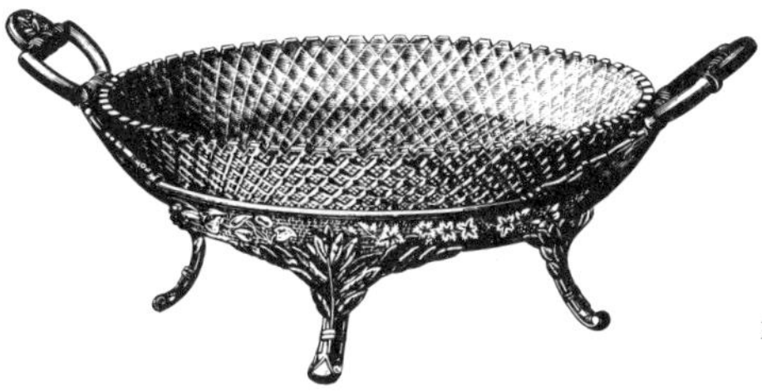

No. Colored and Decorated Glass, $16.50. (CASTILIAN)

No. 4030. Fruit or Berry Dish, Rich Cut Glass, $15.75. (CASUALTY)

No. 3640. Colored and Decorated Glass, $19.50. (CASUIST)

No. 3710. Fruit or Cake Basket, Sylvan Scene on Porcelain, $18.00. (CATALPA)

No. 3295. Cut and Engraved Glass, $18.00. (CATACOMB)

No. 3930. Colored and Decorated Glass, $19.50. (CATAMOUNT)

46. Reed & Barton catalog, 1885.

47. Meriden Silverplate Co. about 1896.

48. Silverplated basket marked "Rogers & Bro." Made about 1890; cased glass bowl with crystal edge, white, pink lined.

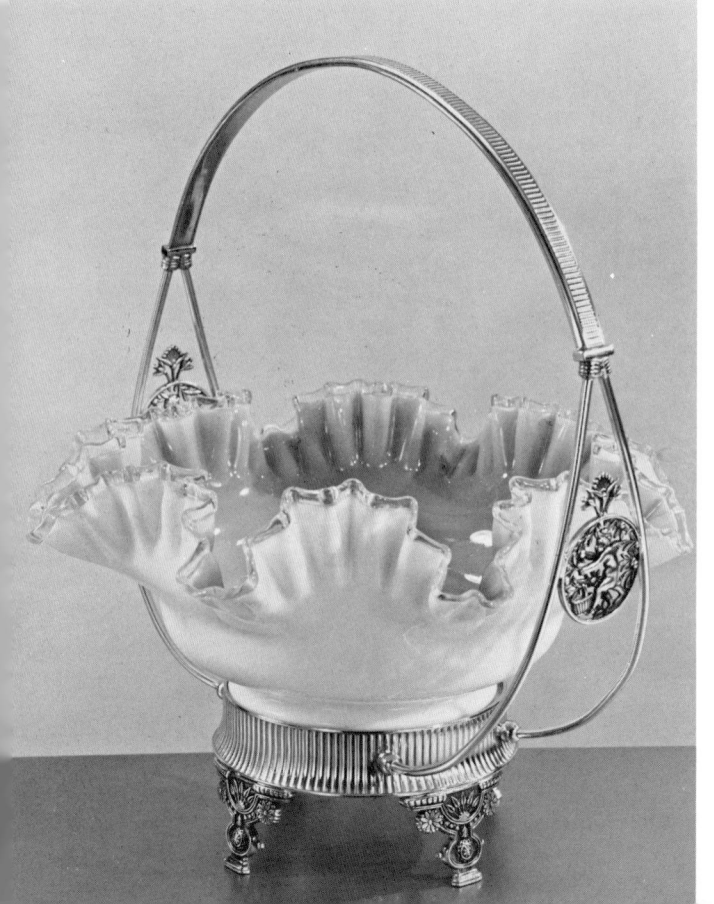

49. Wilcox Silver Plate Co. basket made about 1896, with cased pink over opal glass bowl decorated with gold leaves and flowers.

VII. Silverplate for Table and Household Use   205

52. Cased glass fruit bowl, lime green inside, plum outside, decorated with enameled flowers in high relief. The silverplated stand was made by the Meriden Britannia Co., in its Hamilton, Ontario, Canada plant, about 1895; 13 3/4 in. high.

Now called "brides' baskets" or "brides' bowls," because they were reputedly a favorite gift for the bride-to-be, they were at the time of their greatest popularity identified in catalogs and advertisements simply as "fruit baskets," "berry dishes," "fruit bowls," or "fruit stands," those with overhead handles being baskets; those on pedestals, bowls or stands (Color Plates A and D; Figs. 52–54).

53. Epergne or fruit stand made by the Taunton Silver Plate Co. before 1890.

Card Receivers

The custom of leaving calling or visiting cards is one that is about three centuries old. During Victorian days and until World War I the making of calls was bound with many rules. It was the duty of the women of each household to make "calls," such as calls of condolence or of congratulation, or calls on the sick. On making these calls they left their husbands' cards with their own.

Formal calls, involving the leaving of cards, on various members of the household and their house guests are seldom

THE VICTOR SILVER CO., SHELTON, CONN., U.S.A.
QUADRUPLE PLATE.

54. Art Nouveau confection epergne made by the Victor Silver Co. about 1900 to 1904.

made in these days of more informal living. Only in a few ultra-conservative communities are formal calls expected and few are the hostesses who, by having engraved a day of the week on the lower left of their cards, let it be known that they are "at home" to callers on a certain day.

The conventions followed for leaving cards were strict. Small white cards were used for formal calls though colored ones or those embellished with decalcomanias were utilized in less fastidious circles.

Handwritten cards, according to the late Carl Dreppard, were done by experts in the art of calligraphy who were lineal trade descendants of the old "letter writers" of the sixteenth century. Their work usually had the appearance of copperplate printing. When public education became widespread after the 1870s and the standards of penmanship less exacting, only professional penmen practiced the art. These chirographers pursued their trade in the streets, in parks, and at fairs. A package of visiting cards would quickly be ornamented with sweeping flourishes of elaborate birds and ribbons, swans, quill pens, and flowers.

There were handpainted cards done by professional artists and others commercially made by lithography. Still others were made by young ladies at home.

55. Meriden Britannia Co. catalog, 1867.

VII. Silverplate for Table and Household Use

No. 3.

Each, $4 50.

No. 5, with Nickel Dish.
Gilt Inside.
No. 5, 5¼ inch.   Each, $4 50.
No. 6, 6 inch.   Each, 5 00.

No. 7.
Gilt Inside
Each, $6 50.

No. 8.
Patent Polygon.

Engine Turned or Chased.
Each, $6 50.

No. 9, Grecian.
Plain Plated.
Plain Gilt.
Engine Gilt.
Grecian Gilt.

No. 9, Plain.
Each, $5 25.
Each,   6 00.
Each,   6 75.
Each,   7 25.

No. 12.
With Nickel Silver Handles.
Each. $6 75.

No. 10.
Plain Plated.   Each, $6 00.
Plain Gilt.   Each, 7 00.
Engine Gilt.   Each, 7 50.

No. 011. Three Medallions.
Each, $12 75.

No. 013.
Same as No. 011, but without Handles.
Each, $12 25.

208   AMERICAN SILVERPLATE

No. 1680. $5.50.
     Gold-lined,   6.50.

No. 2060. $11.00.
     Gold-lined, 12.50.

No. 1870. $6.00.   Gold-lined, $7.00.
 " 1860. 5.50.   "   6.50.

No. 1955. $6.50.
     Gold-lined,   7.50.

No. 190. $15.00.
     Fancy Gilt, 18.00.

No. 1998. $6.50.
     Gold-lined,   7.50.
 " 1990. Plain, 1.00 less.

No. 1590. $9.00.
     Gold-lined, 10.00.

No. 2044. $7.50.
     Gold-lined,   9.00.

56. Reed & Barton catalog, 1877.

VII. SILVERPLATE FOR TABLE AND HOUSEHOLD USE   209

No. 2125. $7.00.
Fancy Gilt,   8.50.

No. 02145. $8.50.
Fancy Gilt,   11.00.

No. 02135. $8.00.
Fancy Gilt,   9.50.

No. 1910. $5.00.
Gold-lined,   6.00.

No. 2105. $5.50.
Fancy Gilt,   7.00.

No. 1728. $6.00.
Gold-lined,   7.00.
" 1720. Plain,   5.00.
Gold-lined,   6.00.

No. 01874. $9.00.
Gold-lined,   10.00.

No. 1744. $5.50.
Gold-lined,   6.50.

No. 1958. $11.00.
Oxidized Figures,   12.00.

57. Reed & Barton catalog, 1885.

58. Reed & Barton catalog, 1885.

VII. SILVERPLATE FOR TABLE AND HOUSEHOLD USE 211

58 continued.

212 American Silverplate

58 continued.

59. Reed & Barton catalog, 1885.

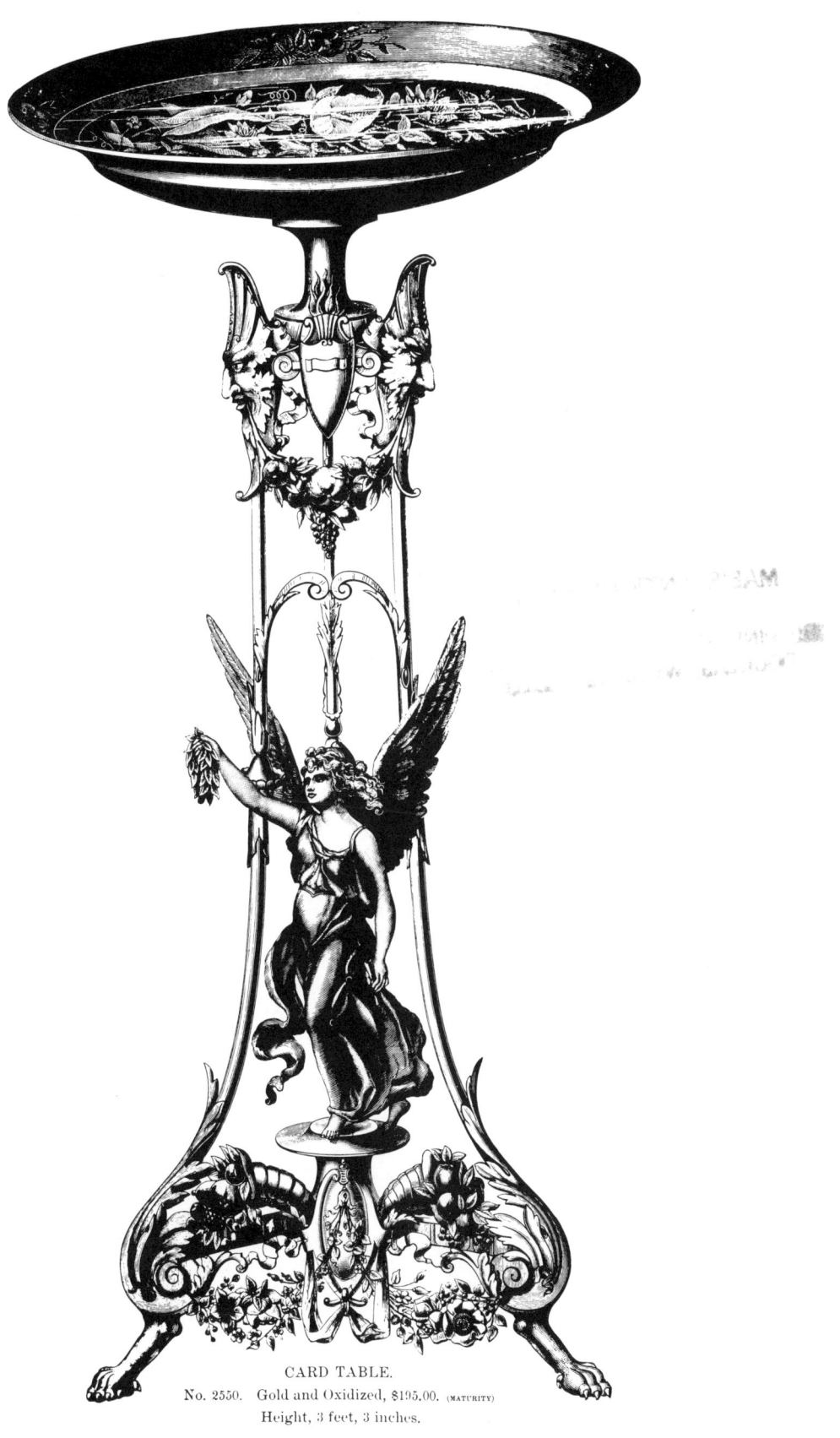

CARD TABLE.
No. 2550. Gold and Oxidized, $195.00. (MATURITY)
Height, 3 feet, 3 inches.

CARD TABLE.
No. 2560.   Gold and Oxidized, $275.00.   (MAUNDER)
Height, 3 feet. 3 inches.

59 continued.

VII. SILVERPLATE FOR TABLE AND HOUSEHOLD USE 215

No. 220.
Copper, Old Silver Standard, $6.50 (SURGICAL).
(Non-Tarnishable).

No. 211.
Chased, . . $6.00 (SURFEIT).
Chased, Gold Inlaid, 7.50 (SUPREME).

No. 221. MIRROR CENTRE.
Enameled Copper, Old Silver Standard, $7.50 (SUPINE).
(Non-Tarnishable).

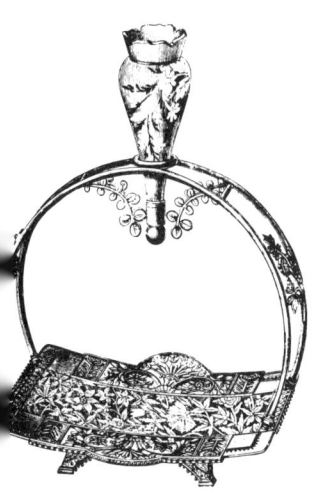

No. 215.
Silver, Brocade, Chased, . $7.50 (SUPERNAL).
de, Chased, X Gold Inlaid, 9.00 (SUPERBLY).
(Non-Tarnishable).

No 222.
Enameled Copper, Old Silver Mountings, $6.50 (SUNSHINE).
(Non-Tarnishable.)

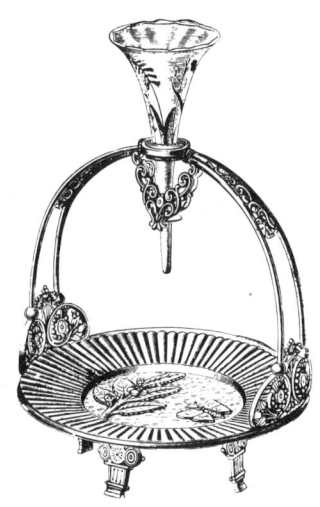

No. 207.
Hammered and Applied, . . $8.50 (MEDIUM).
Hammered and Applied, Gold Inlaid, 10.00 (MEDLEY).
(Non-Tarnishable.)

No. 224.
ased, Old Silver, . $8.50 (SURCINGLE).
ased, X Gold Inlaid, 10.50 (SUPERSEDE).
(Non-Tarnishable.)

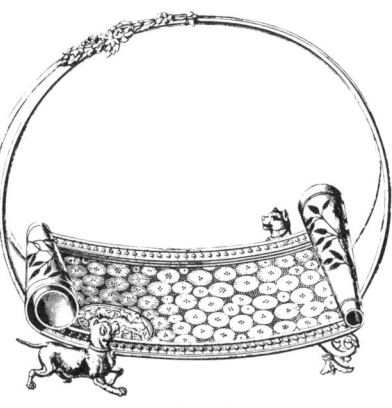

No. 218.
Moorish, Old Silver, . $12.00 (SUNLIGHT).
Moorish, Gold Inlaid, . 13.50 (SUNBEAM).
(Non-Tarnishable.)

No. 217.
Satin, . . $8.00 (SUPPORTER).
Satin, Gold Inlaid, . 10.00 (SUPERSCRIBE).
(Non-Tarnishable.)

60. Meriden Britannia Co. catalog, 1886.

216 AMERICAN SILVERPLATE

No. 219.
Hammered, Chased, . . $9.00 (SUMMIT).
Hammered, Chased, Gold Inlaid, 10.50 (SUMMARY).
(Non-Tarnishable.)

No. 194.
Satin, Engraved, . . $8.50 (HIRSUTE).
Satin, Engraved, Gold Inlaid, 10.50 (HIST).

No. 229.
Satin, ... $8.00 (PRAWN).
Satin, Gold Lined, . . 9.00 (PRACTICAL).
Satin, Gold Lined, Old Silver Border, 10.00 (POTENTATE).

No. 189.
Moorish, Old Silver, . $11.00 (HEXAGON).
Moorish, Gold, Inlaid, . 13.00 (HIATUS).
(Non-Tarnishable.)

No. 212.
Old Silver, . . $6.50 (SUFFUSE).
Old Silver, Gold Inlaid, 8.00 (SUITABLE).
(Non-Tarnishable.)

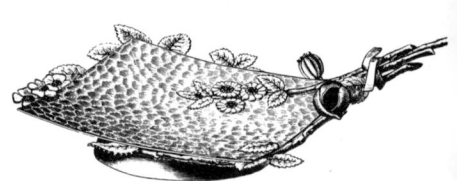

No. 188.
Hammered, Old Silver, . . $10.00 (HIBERNAL).
Hammered, Old Silver, Gold Inlaid, 12.00 (HICKORY).
(Non-Tarnishable.)

No. 182.
Chased, ... $7.00 (GROWTH).
Chased, Gold Lined, . . 8.00 (GRUDGE).
Chased, Gold Inlaid and Gold Lined, 8.50 (GRUFFLY).

No. 201.
Chased, . . $7.00 (MORALIST).
Chased, Gold Inlaid, 8.50 (MORDANT).

No. 199.
Old Silver, . . $8.50 (MEAL).
Old Silver, Gold Inlaid, 10.00 (MEANDER).
(Non-Tarnishable.)

61. Meriden Britannia Co. catalog, 1886.

62. Card receivers from The International Silver Co. Historical Collection. *Top:* Made by Rogers, Smith & Co., Hartford, Conn., between 1856 and 1862. *Middle, left to right:* Meriden Silver Plate Co., Meriden, Conn., about 1885; Hartford Silver Plate Co., Hartford, Conn., 1884. *Bottom, left to right:* Meriden Britannia Co., Meriden, Conn., 1873; Meriden Britannia Co., 1882; Derby Silver Co., Derby, Conn., 1883 (inscription on tray reads "Should Owl'd Acquaintance Be Forgot").

On leaving cards, bending of the corners had a special significance from which there developed a complicated "language of cards." In *Learning How to Behave,* Arthur M. Schlesinger wrote:

Quite apart from such details as the correct size and typography was the difficult symbolism involved in bending the edges. Turning down the upper right-hand corner signified a personal visit; the upper left corner, congratulations; the lower right-hand corner, adieu; the lower left corner, condolence; the entire left end, a call on the whole family. This practice, introduced from abroad shortly after the Civil War, commended itself to city dwellers who had little time or inclination for individual visits and yet did not wish to feel negligent to their duties. . . . Despite its conveniences, the custom was becoming passé by the 1890s. The sign language proved too great a tax on the human intelligence.

Such complicated proceedings naturally demanded special receptacles and so the card receiver came into being. Early ones were simple in design, consisting of a small tray about six inches in diameter mounted on a pedestal.

218 AMERICAN SILVERPLATE

No. 22.

No. 25.

No. 23.

63. Card stands in Meriden Britannia Co. catalog dated July 1, 1871.

In 1861, the Meriden Britannia Company offered four designs; in 1867 their catalog carried nine designs. By 1871 they offered 14 and in 1879 this number was increased to 31. Reed & Barton, in 1885, offered 38 different designs of card receivers and two elegant card tables on which to place them. The Meriden Britannia Company catalog of 1882 offered 53 different designs and the 1886 catalog 58 designs and six card tables. The peak of elaborate and unusual forms had been reached and their number declined sharply as did that of fancy napkin rings and other "fancy" pieces. By the 1900s only a few designs were offered, most of which were simple trays.

Ornaments on card receivers were numerous. They included butterflies and other insects, owls, elephants, children and cherubs, swans, frogs, peacocks, storks, fruit, squirrels, cats, dogs, flowers, foliage in fantastic arrangements, and other animals either *au naturel* or dressed in human garments. Colorful art-glass flower vases were included with some.

Even though card receivers were made for more than 40 years by every major silverplate manufacturer, and some small ones, and in a larger variety of styles than many other Victorian silver wares, they are scarce in antique shops today.

Card cases too were necessities for those ladies with any pretense of fashion. They were made in various materials, the first ones to reach this country being made of ivory or mother-of-pearl. Later imports from France and England were of gold, silver, papier-mâché and tortoiseshell. American silversmiths were making card cases of silver by the 1850s. Some of these were quite elaborate and had chains attached for easier carrying. They were often lined with silk and were sold in plush-lined boxes to pro-

64. Card receivers in Meriden Britannia Co. catalog, 1882.

220 AMERICAN SILVERPLATE

No. 2. Card Case.
Silver, . . . $3.50 (GROWN).
Old Silver, . . 4.00 (PRECISION).
Silver, Gold Inlaid, 5.00 (GRUB).

No. 4. Card Case.
Silver, . . . $3.50 (GRUEL).
Old Silver, . . 4.00 (PRECISELY).
Silver, Gold Inlaid, 5.00 (GRUFF).
Plush or Morocco Cases, $2.50 extra (GUARD).

No. 3. Card Case.
Silver, . . . $3.50 (GUESS).
Old Silver, . . 4.00 (PRECIPITATE).
Silver, Gold Inlaid, 5.00 (GUEST).

No. 030. Nickel Silver.
Satin, Engraved, . $7.25 (GROOM).
No. 030½. With Chain on side.
Satin, Engraved, . $7.25 (GROOVE).

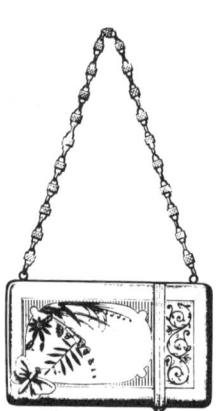

No. 031½. Nickel Silver.
Satin, Engraved, . $7.25 (GROPE).
Plush or Morocco Cases for above, $2.50 extra (GROUP).

No. 031. Nickel Silver.
Satin, Engraved, . $7.25 (GROT).

No. 032½. Nickel Silver.
Satin, Engraved, . $7.25 (GROW).
No. 032. With Chain on end.
Satin, Engraved, . $7.25 (GROWL).
Plush or Morocco Case, $2.75 extra (PRECINCT).

No. 050. Portemonnaie.
Satin, Engraved, . $9.50 (GRIND).
Silver, Gold Inlaid, 10.50 (GRIP).

No. 053. Portemonnaie.
Satin, Engraved, . $9.50 (GROCERY).
Silver, Gold Inlaid, 10.50 (GROCERY).

No. 051. Portemonnaie.
Satin, Engraved, . $9.50 (GRIT).
Silver, Gold Inlaid, 10.50 (GROAT).

No. 052. Portemonnaie.
Satin, Engraved, . $9.50 (GRIST).
Silver, Gold Inlaid, 10.50 (GRISTLE).

Plush or Morocco Cases for above, $3.00 each, extra (GROATS).

65. Card receivers of the elaborate type favored in the 1880s. Made by the Meriden Silver Plate Co. about 1884. The vase is of blue glass with enameled decoration in white and gold.

tect the fine finish. Until around 1900 cards were quite large and thin so that a protective carrying case was a necessity (Fig. 66).

66. Card cases made by the Meriden Britannia Co. about 1886.

Cake Baskets

Perhaps in no other articles in American silverplate have designers exhibited the restraint and good taste shown in the early cake baskets. Even during the years when card receivers, fruit baskets, and tea services reached the heights (or depths) of ostentation, cake baskets in simple, classic lines could be found.

The low, pedestaled cake baskets of the 1850s derived their shape and decoration largely from "Old Sheffield Plate" baskets of 20 to 30 years earlier

222 AMERICAN SILVERPLATE

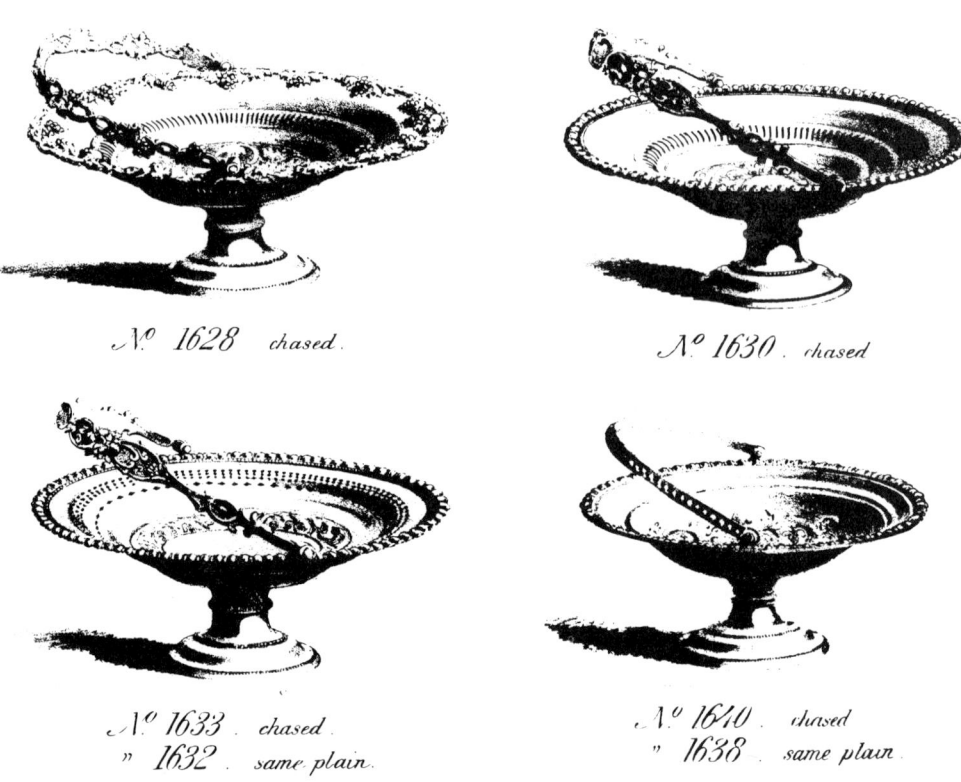

N° 1628 chased. N° 1630 chased

N° 1633 chased. N° 1640 chased
" 1632 same plain " 1638 same plain

67. Rogers Bros. Mfg. Co. catalog, 1857.   **68.** Rogers Bros. Mfg. Co. catalog, 1860.

(Fig. 67). They differ somewhat in that their pedestals are slightly taller and not of as great diameter. Handles tend to be a bit more ornamental than in the English versions. Clusters of grapes, similar to those used on tea and coffee services of the same period, were used on handles and borders. Other borders were rope or gadroon; beading ornamented the domed bases. Engraving and pierced designs decorated the bowls.

Shape and decoration of cake baskets through the 1860s remained basically the same though the proliferation of styles led to variations and to some new designs (Figs. 68, 69). While most cake baskets of the 1860s were round or oval on low pedestals, a few footed baskets were made (Fig. 70). Some baskets were made with fluted bodies and pedestals. Borders were rope, gadroon, egg-and-tongue, beading, or scrolls. Engraving and chasing in floral designs, Greek key, engine-turning, embossing, and pierced work were used (Fig. 71). The use of applied medallions made a simple and inexpensive way to create new designs using the same body. Various feet were applied to the same design body also to produce variations. Compare the cake basket marked "Springfield, Massachusetts" (Fig. 72) with the one by Parker & Casper Co. of Meriden, Connecticut (Fig. 73). The bodies are identical. Only the medallions, feet, and engraving are different.

A cake basket with mask decorations was made by Redfield & Rice of New York City between 1863, when the company name was changed from Bancroft, Redfield & Rice, and 1870 when the company failed (Fig. 74).

A cake basket made by the Meriden Britannia Company is illustrated in their 1867 catalog with different medallions and engraving (Fig. 75).

The design for a cake or fruit basket patented by William Parkin, Taunton, Massachusetts, March 1, 1870, and assigned to Reed & Barton, is one of the

69. Meriden Britannia Co. about 1862.
70. Rogers, Smith & Co., New Haven, Conn., about 1867.

224   American Silverplate

No. 1691.
Each, $8 50.

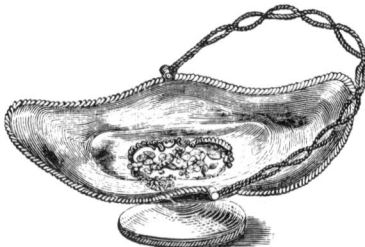

No. 1652.
Each, $9 00.

No. 1650.
Each, $9 00.

No. 1862, Plain.
Each, $9 50.

No. 1862, Grecian.
Each, $11 75.

No. 1862, Wreath.
Each, $11 75.

No. 1869.
Wreath Chased.   Each, $11 25.
Grecian Chased. Each, 11 75.

No 1868.
Open.   Each, $10 00.
Grecian Chased. Each, $12 00.

No. 1865.
Plain.   Each, $9 25.
Grecian Chased. Each, $12 00.
Damask Chased.   Each, 11 25.

No. 1678, Engine.
Grecian. Each, $11 25.
Engine.   Each,   9 25.
Plain.   Each,   8 50.

No. 1684, Open.
Open.   Each, $9 25.
Engine. Each, 10 00.
Damask Chased. Each, $11 25.
Grecian Chased. Each, 12 00.

No. 1686, Engine and Open.
Engine. Each, $8 50.
Open.   Each, 8 00.

72. Cake basket marked "Springfield, Massachusetts." Feet are identical to those on butter dish and on spooner made by the Meriden Britannia Co. (*See Figs. 109 and 198.*) Compare body of basket to the one made by Parker & Casper Co. (*Fig. 73*).

very few such patents (Fig. 76). From the lower part of each corner is a bracketed leg supporting the figure of a child, having one leg crossed on the other. The handle is surmounted by a bust. The angular body and handle are typical of the 1870s.

A cake basket made by the Wilcox Silver Plate Company of Meriden, Connecticut, in 1870 also reflects the straight lines of that decade (Fig. 77). Four warriors in full armor and helmets, carrying drawn swords guard the corners while a friendly looking dog romps atop the handle.

Another cake basket in the "squared-off" style introduced in the 70s was made by the Meriden Britannia Com-

71. Meriden Britannia Co. catalog, 1867.

73. Cake basket made by Parker & Casper Co. of Meriden, Conn. 1867–69. Compare body of basket with one marked "Springfield, Massachusetts" (*Fig. 72*).

74. Cake basket made by Redfield & Rice between 1863 and 1870.

pany in 1871 (Fig. 78). Four dogs act as guardians of the cake. Horsehead medallions are on each side of the basket just below the handle attachments.

The long legs and angular handles mark the cake basket made by the Meriden Britannia Company as a product of the 1870s (Fig. 79). This is further confirmed by the "Pat. 1874" stamped on the bottom. A wistful cherub perches

75. Cake basket made by the Meriden Britannia Co. about 1867.

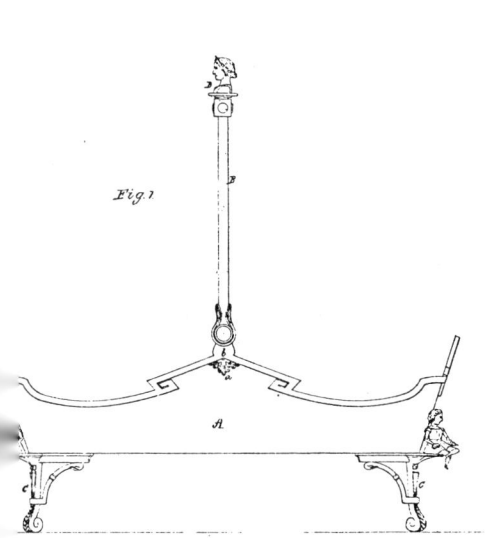

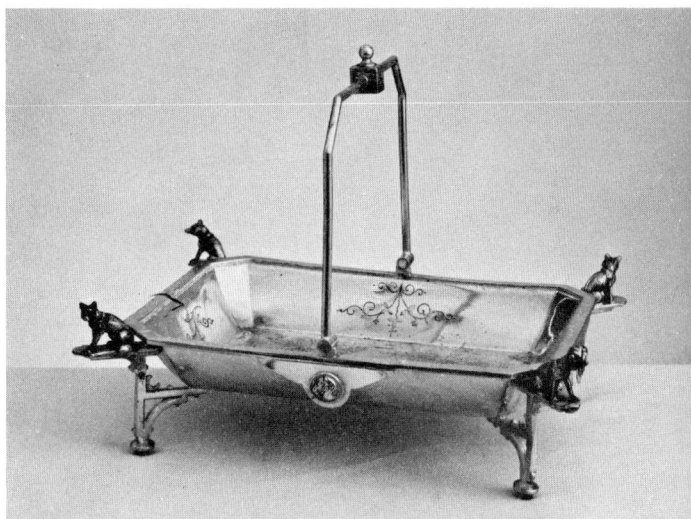

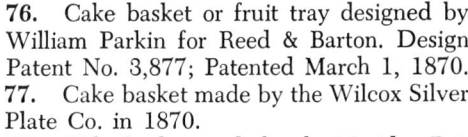

76. Cake basket or fruit tray designed by William Parkin for Reed & Barton. Design Patent No. 3,877; Patented March 1, 1870.
77. Cake basket made by the Wilcox Silver Plate Co. in 1870.
78. Cake basket made by the Meriden Britannia Co. in 1871.
79. Cake basket made by the Meriden Britannia Co. Stamped "Pat. 1874" though the patent could not be located in the Patent Office.

on a round ball placed between the tall supports.

Egyptian lotus blossoms are the theme of another Meriden Britannia Company cake basket made between 1873 and 1877 (Fig. 80).

Diversity of style marked the cake baskets of the 1880s. Some were heavily ornamented but by far the greater number were round baskets with overhead or bail-type handles whose decoration was usually formal Renaissance detail. Continuous applied borders were geometric, floral, or rarely scenes. These often flared out from the body of the piece. The most common support was a tall, slender pedestal with a flaring base for stability. Surface decoration was usually chased flowers, butterflies, birds, or cherubs, sometimes on matted ground. Niello, variegated gold, and

80. Egyptian motif is featured on this cake basket made by the Meriden Britannia Co. between 1873 and 1877.

81. Reed & Barton catalog, 1885.

VII. SILVERPLATE FOR TABLE AND HOUSEHOLD USE   229

gold inlaid (an electroplating process) often defined the designs in natural colors.

Some cake baskets of the 1880s stood on very tall legs or pedestals, many of which were heavily ornamented. The combination of decorative motifs used was often startling as in one made by Reed & Barton about 1885 (Fig. 81). Coroneted ladies' heads above acanthus-leaf scrolls support the bowl while a large beetle crawls down each of the four scroll legs.

Still others sat on low pedestals or legs such as the one made by the Meriden Britannia Company for Rogers & Bro. in 1886 (Fig. 82).

A cake basket made by the Derby Silver Company in 1883 rests on four bird-with-ball-and-claw feet (Figs. 83, 83a).

Reed & Barton devoted 16 pages of their 1885 catalog to the illustration of

82. Cake basket made by the Meriden Britannia Co. for Rogers & Bro. in 1886.

83. Round cake basket made by the Derby Silver Co. in 1883.

83a. Derby Silver Co., about 1885.

230 AMERICAN SILVERPLATE

No. 4113. $11.75. (CONCEDED)   Gold-lined, $13.75. (CONCLAVE)

No. 3958. $14.50. (CONCOCT)   Gold-lined, $17.50. (CONCURRED)
Gold-lined, Gold and Oxidized Finish, $19.50. (CONDIMENT)

No. 4135. $10.25. (CONDITION)   Gold-lined, $12.25.

No. 3700. $6.50. (CONDUIT)   Gold-lined, $8.50. (CONFERRED)

No. 3932. $11.50. (CONFESSOR)   Gold-lined, $13.50. (CONFIDANT)

No. 4105. $10.50. (CONFUSION)   Gold-lined, $12.50.

No. 4188. $13.75. (CONFLATE)   Gold-lined, $15.75. (CONFLUENT)
Chasing, Gold Variegated, and Oxidized Finish, $18.25. (CONFLUX)

84. Reed & Barton catalog, 1885.

118 different styles of cake baskets in their regular line (Fig. 84). Additional pages were devoted to about a dozen plain styles in hotel ware.

The Meriden Britannia Company catalog of 1886 illustrated 72 styles.

Cake baskets of the 1890s were mostly set on shorter legs and, while they were decorated, they did not reach the extremes of the 1880s (Figs. 85, 86).

A cake basket patented by Seth H. Leavenworth, Cincinnati, Ohio, April 18, 1893, and assigned to the Homan & Company, also of Cincinnati, is a typical 1890 style (Fig. 87).

85. Cake basket made by the Pairpoint Mfg. Co., New Bedford, Mass., about 1890–95.
86. Pairpoint Mfg. Co. catalog, 1894.

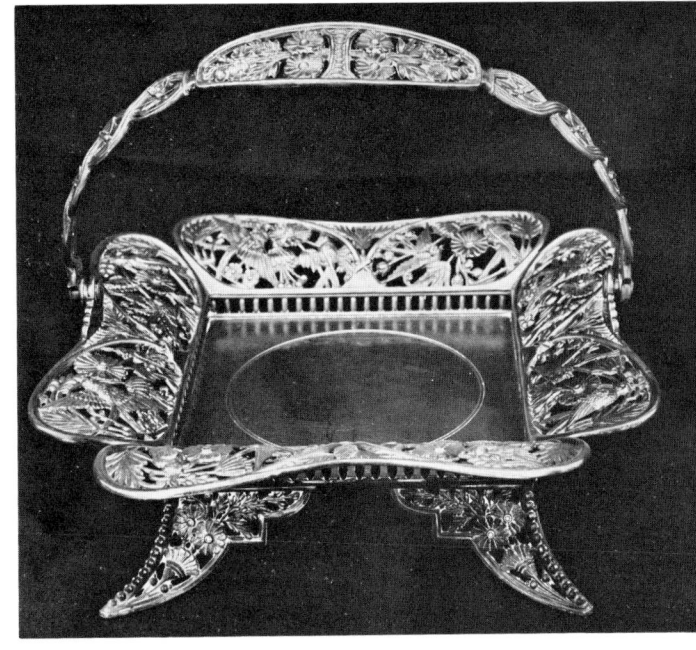

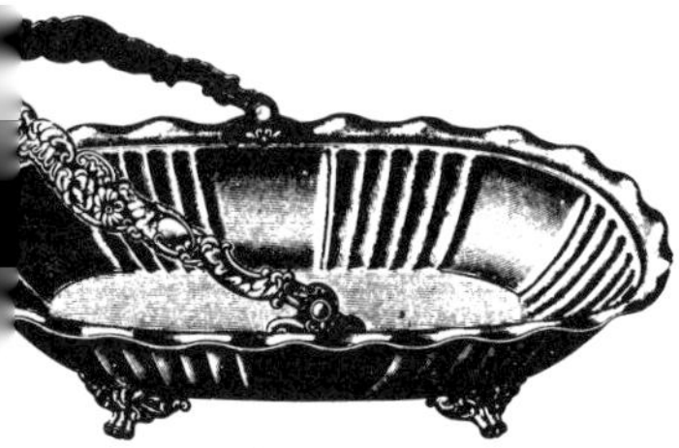

No. 1264.
Fluted, $7 25
" Gold Lined, 9 25

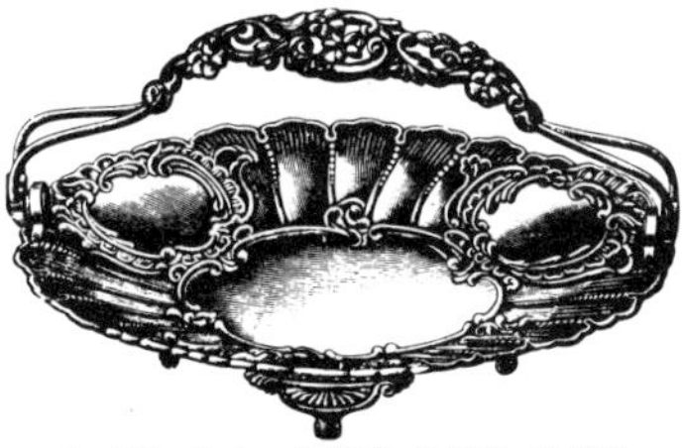

No. 1260. Embossed, $5 50. Gold Lined, $6 50
No. 1258. Same as above, less handle.
Embossed, $5 00. Gold Lined, $6 00

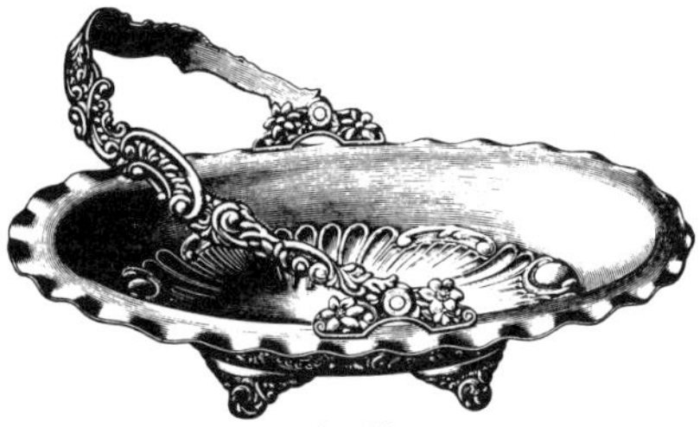

No. 1265.
Embossed, $7 50
" Gold Lined, 9 50
(Patented Nov. 28, 1893.)

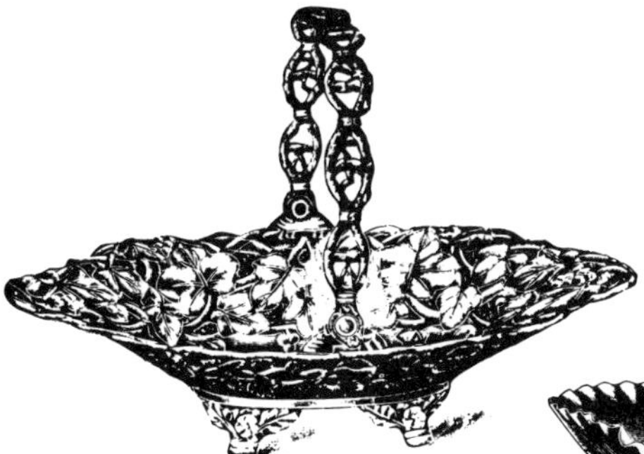

No. 1263. Embossed, $7 50. Gold Lined, $9 50
No. 1262. Same as above, less handle.
Embossed, $6 75. Gold Lined, $8 75

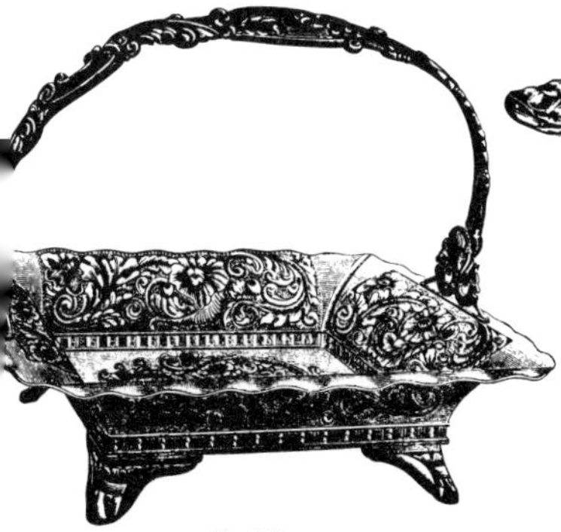

No. 1251.
Embossed, $10 00. Gold Lined, $12 00
(Patented Aug. 22, 1893.)

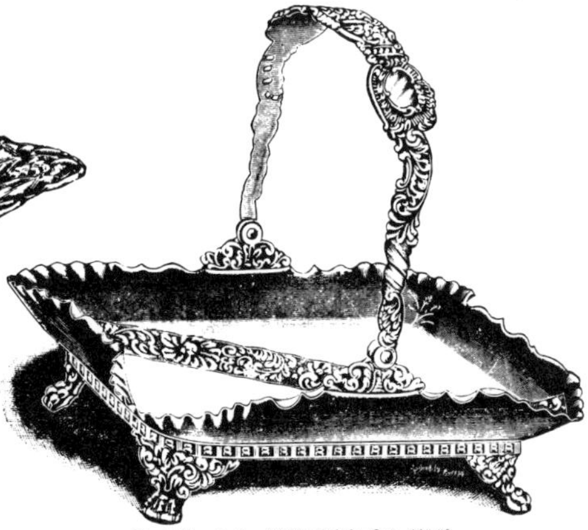

No. 1261. Satin, $9 50; Bright Cut, $10 00
Gold Lined, $2 00 extra.
(Patented Aug. 22, 1893.)

232 AMERICAN SILVERPLATE

A few styles of cake baskets were carried in catalogs after 1900, their styles similar to those of the 90s. These gradually gave way to small flat trays with simple bail-type handles. These were advertised as dual-purpose cake or sandwich trays (Fig. 88).

Never as numerous nor as diverse as fruit dishes and centerpieces, cake baskets, however, appear more frequently in antique shops.

Though cake baskets are similar in shape to fruit baskets, they have not been the objects of "collectors' mania" since they do not have the decorative art-glass inserts.

Waiters, Bread Trays, and Special Purpose Trays

Among the most useful pieces of silverplated hollow ware, waiters have always been a welcome addition to the housewife's cupboard.

Mostly oval or round in shape, early waiters varied in size from 10 to 30 inches. Nineteen styles are shown in the 1867 Meriden Britannia Company catalog (Fig. 89). This number does not take into account the great number of sizes, 11 in all. Applied borders were beaded, gadrooned, egg-and-tongue,

87. Cake basket designed by Seth Leavenworth, and assigned to Homan & Co., Cincinnati, Ohio. Design Patent No. 22,352; Patented April 18, 1893.
88. Dual purpose cake or sandwich trays which replaced the earlier cake baskets. Meriden Silver Plate Co. catalog, 1924.

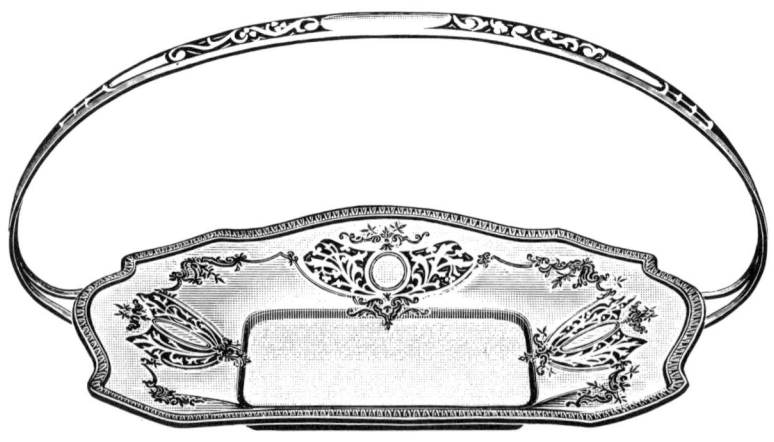

VII. Silverplate for Table and Household Use

89. Meriden Britannia Co. catalog, 1867.

90. Reed & Barton catalog, 1885.

and other geometric designs. Surface ornamentation was chased or engraved scrolls, floral designs, and, in a few instances, scenery.

Waiters were made to match tea services, coffee services, ice pitchers, and punch bowls (Fig. 90). Others were made in conservative designs to be used with everything.

Through the years, square, rectangular, oval, and round waiters have predominated (Figs. 91, 92). In the 1870s and early 1880s waiters shaped to fit the curve of the body as they were being carried, were in vogue (Fig. 93).

Special purpose trays and waiters include crumb trays, sandwich trays, and those with special appeal to children (Figs. 94, 95, 95a, 95b). Others were relish and aspic dishes, chop plates, meat dishes, and bread trays or baskets.

234 AMERICAN SILVERPLATE

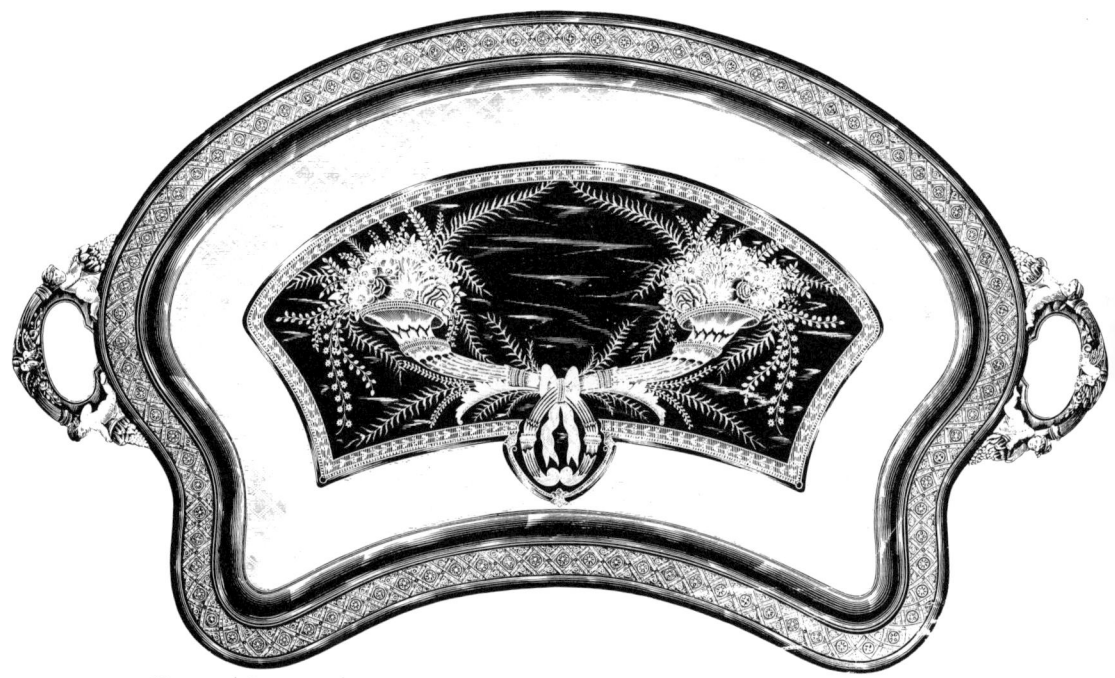

No. 2856. Patent Wire-strengthened Waiter (to match Nos. 2850 and 2856 Tea Sets), 26 inch, $65.00.
"   "   "   "   "   "   "   "   "   " 28 " 75.00.

91–92. Reed & Barton catalog, 1877.

No. 2149. Patent Wire-strengthened Waiter, to match Tea Set No. 2629, 22 inch, $48.00.
" "   "   "   "   "   "   "   "   " 24 " 56.00.
" "   "   "   "   "   "   "   "   " 26 " 66.00.

VII. SILVERPLATE FOR TABLE AND HOUSEHOLD USE 235

93. Meriden Britannia Co. catalog, 1877.
94. Reed & Barton catalog, 1885.

236 AMERICAN SILVERPLATE

No. 2. CRUMB TRAY.

No. 1. CRUMB BRUSH.

Some early bread baskets are almost indistinguishable from fruit baskets (Fig. 96).

The now more familiar oval bread tray was a development of the 1890s (Figs 97–100).

Mirror plateaus are popular for display of silver articles and cut glass (Fig. 101).

Butter Dishes

Though cows were imported to this country from England in 1624, there is little mention of them being used for any purposes except as beef and for milk until the eighteenth century when the dairy products, butter and cheese, began to appear as food. From that time until the rise of factory production about 1860, the making of butter and cheese was a household affair. In many households, especially on farms, this practice

95. Meriden Britannia Co. catalog, 1886.
95a. Wilcox Silver Plate Co. catalog, 1936.

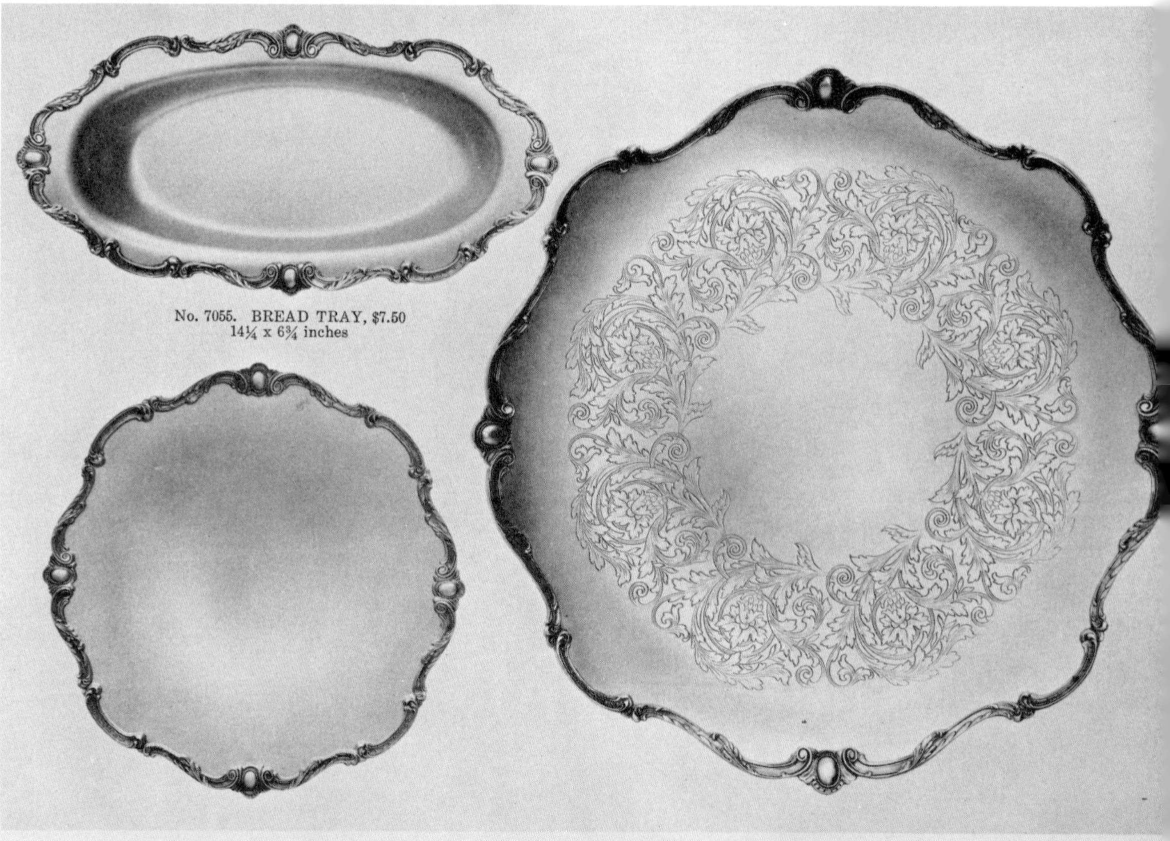

No. 7055. BREAD TRAY, $7.50
14¼ x 6¾ inches

No. 7055. SANDWICH PLATE, $7.50
Diameter 11 inches

No. 7055. ASPIC DISH, $17.50
Diameter 18 inches

VII. Silverplate for Table and Household Use 237

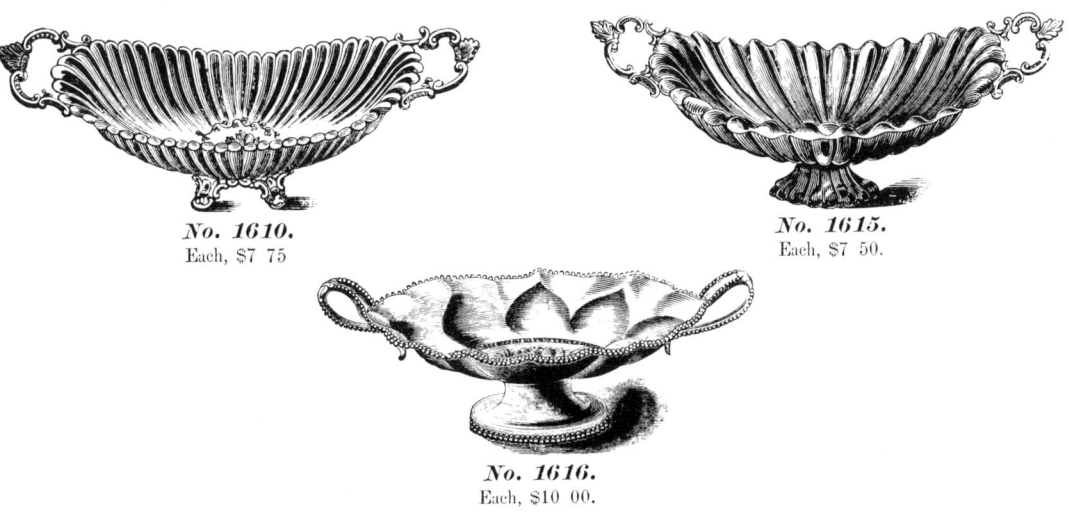

95b. Wilcox Silver Plate Co. catalog, 1936.

No. 1610.
Each, $7 75

No. 1615.
Each, $7 50

No. 1616.
Each, $10 00.

96. Meriden Britannia Co. catalog, 1867.

238 AMERICAN SILVERPLATE

97. Bread tray designed by Adolph Ludwig, Brooklyn, N.Y. Design Patent No. 21,621; Patented June 14, 1892.

98. Bread tray designed by Albert Steffin for the Pairpoint Corp., New Bedford, Mass. Design Patent No. 37,025; Patented July 5, 1904.

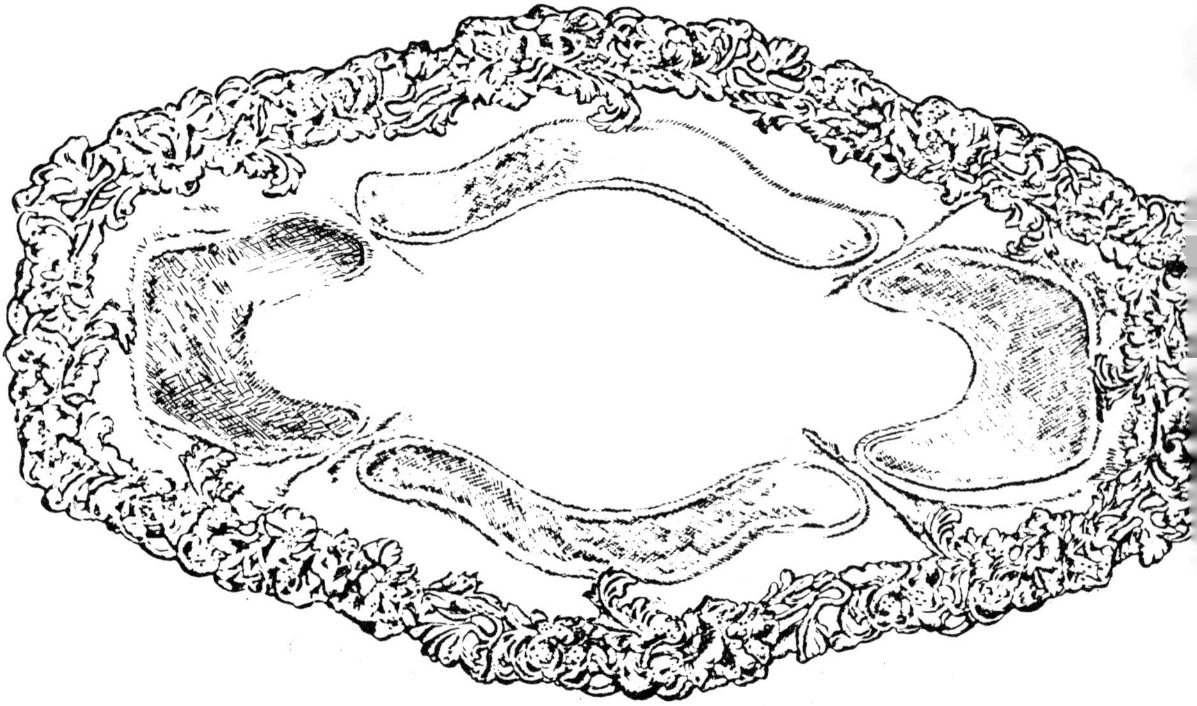

VII. Silverplate for Table and Household Use   239

99. Bread tray advertised by the Anchor Silver Plate Co. *The Keystone,* August 1905.

100. Bread tray designed by Paul R. Zinser for the Queen City Silver Co., Cincinnati, Ohio. Design Patent No. 39,401; Patented July 7, 1908.

240 AMERICAN SILVERPLATE

MIRROR PLATEAU

No. B—10 inch. Net Price, $4.50

Best French Plate Mirrors

Mounted on Quadruple-Plated Hard White Metal Frames

We are the **Originators** of this **Novelty**, and have the finest and most extensive line in the market. Prices and styles to meet all demands. Write for Catalogue No. 4.

The Biggins=Rodgers Co.

Main Office and Factory, **Wallingford, Connecticut**

Manufacturers of Medium-Priced Silver-Plated Hollowware

101. Mirror plateau advertised by Biggins-Rodgers Co., Wallingford, Conn. Note that they state that they are the originators. *The Keystone*, August 1905.
104. Meriden Britannia Co. catalog, 1867.

continued until long after World War I. Farm housewives, by custom, were entitled to "butter-and-egg" money which they accumulated by the sale of surplus to the nearest grocer. This was packed into wooden tubs or cut, wrapped in pound packages, and carried to market in wooden butter boxes. A bit later wooden butter molds or "prints," which usually held a pound of butter, were utilized to mold the butter. Butter prints were mostly round, cup-shaped, and had the print section with its long protruding handle separate from the cup. They varied in size from one inch in diameter to four inches, the latter size holding one pound of butter. The mold was dipped in cold water. The butter was then pressed in with a wooden paddle and forced out by pushing on the print handle. When finished, each pound of butter bore the pattern of the print. Fastidious housewives had individual patterns and many a pound of butter was chosen by the store's customer who was familiar with a particular "brand." It was to accommodate these round, one-pound prints of butter that the butter dish was made.

Since calorie-counting is in vogue and the high cholesterol content of butter fat is now constantly watched, the familiar

VII. SILVERPLATE FOR TABLE AND HOUSEHOLD USE 241

quarter-pound stick of butter is often replaced on modern tables by "soft-margarine" spreads made of corn oil or other vegetable oil. These spreads come packed in small, round plastic tubs whose contents fit nicely into old butter dishes. In numerous homes grandmother's old butter dish has come out of the attic, has been replated, and once again graces the table.

Britannia butter dishes were being made as early as 1855, before silverplated hollow wares had universal acceptance. A Meriden Britannia Company catalog of 1867 contains three pages of butter dishes, some of which were made to match tea services (Fig. 104). It was not until the 1880s that butter dishes were made in great number and variety.

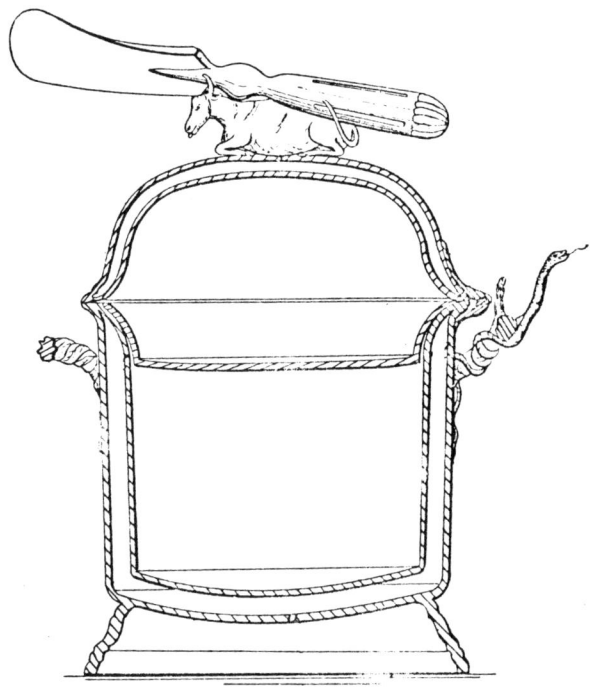

106. Butter-cooler patented by James H. Stimpson. The ice is suspended in a container above the butter dish. The theory being that cold air is of greater specific gravity than the surrounding atmosphere and will descend to the butter in the dish below. Patent No. 20,902; Patented July 13, 1858.

105. Double-walled butter-cooler patented by James H. Stimpson. Patent No. 12,876; Patented May 15, 1855.

An early britannia butter cooler was patented May 15, 1855, by James H. Stimpson, Baltimore, Maryland (Fig. 105). He was the son of the inventor of the double-wall ice-water pitcher. Earlier butter dishes had been made as Stimpson refers in the patent papers to "an Improvement in the Article Usually Called a Butter-Dish, which improvement I denominate a 'butter-cooler'. . . ." Specifications state:

An important advantage of my "butter-cooler" is, the keeping of the butter effectually cool and hard in hot weather, without putting ice on the butter. In the single-wall butter cooler the ice is laid on the butter, and the water from the ice falls into the dish below. This course is objectionable for several reasons. The butter is injured by the water, the ice is not always clean, and the ice is very much in the way, and very apt to be slipped or pushed out of its place. For these difficulties there is no remedy with the single-wall butter cooler, for if the ice should be placed in the dish below, it would melt away with great rapidity, and would fail to keep the butter cool and hard. In short, with the double-wall the ice may be placed below the diaphragm or butter shelf, with economy and effect, while with the single-wall the ice must be placed upon the butter. [And further] . . . making the support for the butter knife upon the cover or handle one or both, so that the knife cannot be put in place without closing the lid, thereby securing the economy of ice and the hardness of butter.

A second butter cooler patented by James H. Stimpson (Fig. 106), July 13, 1858, ". . . consists in having an ice receptacle supported over a butter dish as hereinafter shown, so that the butter will be cooled by the cool air which descends upon it in consequence of being of greater specific gravity than in the surrounding atmosphere." Additional advantages are outlined by the inventor in the patent papers,

It will of course appear evident to every one that this plan is far preferable to having a dish placed on a vessel containing ice or to laying ice on the butter in order to cool it, for in the former case all of the benefit of the ice is not obtained and in the latter case the ice in melting soon floods the butter and neither of the plans prevents flies and other insects from lighting on the butter. In my improvement the butter, in fact the whole implement, is surrounded in a cold atmosphere and insects will not penetrate it. In flying around in the warm atmosphere and reaching the cold, the transition from warm to cold is so sudden and the change so great, that they instantly shun the device. The butter therefore will not only be kept in a cool state, but also kept free from insects.

The principles of the double-wall butter dish and ice held in a container above the butter are both demonstrated in the acorn-shape butter dish illustrated (Figs. 107, 108). The two doors in the lower part swing out, one carrying the plate for the butter with it for easy access. The cover with cow finial lifts off and ice can be placed inside the dome which is sealed off from the butter compartment below. Though the butter cooler incorporates both principles, it is marked only with the date of the earlier Stimpson patent.

Most butter dishes had in common the two features of a high-domed cover to accommodate the high round "print" of butter and a pierced platform inside so that melted ice could drain into the container below (Fig. 109).

Removal of the butter dish cover while in use presented the problem of what to do with it. Some were merely removed and placed on the table. In the days of white damask cloths requiring much ironing this was not a happy solution because of the moisture. Several ingenious solutions to the problem were devised. Some were hinged; but hinges tended to break. The Reed & Barton catalog of 1885 shows one butter-dish cover which is balanced on edge in a rack designed for that purpose (Fig. 110). Some butter dishes had an

107–108. The principles of the double-wall butter dish and ice held in a container above the butter are both demonstrated in the acorn-shape butter dish. The two doors in the lower part swing out, one carrying the plate for the butter with it for easy access. Stamped "James H. Stimpson/Patented May 15, 1855/Baltimore, Md."

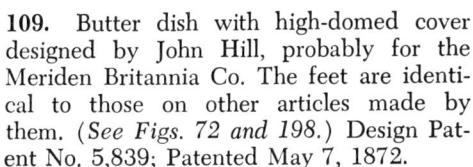

109. Butter dish with high-domed cover designed by John Hill, probably for the Meriden Britannia Co. The feet are identical to those on other articles made by them. (*See Figs. 72 and 198.*) Design Patent No. 5,839; Patented May 7, 1872.

244 AMERICAN SILVERPLATE

No. 4941.
Embossed, $8.00 (EMPERIL).

No. 4993.
With Patent Crystal Drainer.
Plain, $8.50 (IRRADIATE).
Embossed, Chased, 9.50 (ISINGLASS).

No. 4992.
With Patent Crystal Drainer
Plain, $8.50 (INVOL.
Embossed, Chased, 9.50 (IODIN

No. 4940.
With Patent Crystal Drainer.
Plain, $8.00 (EMPLOY).
Chased, 9.00 (EMPORIUM).

No. 4972.
With Patent Crystal Drainer.
Satin, $9.25 (SUBJUGATE).
Chased, 10.25 (EMIGRATE).

No. 4965.
With Patent Crystal Drainer.
Plain, $8.75 (EMOTION).
Chased, 9.50 (EMFALE).

VII. SILVERPLATE FOR TABLE AND HOUSEHOLD USE

112. *Left to right:* Butter dish with hanging cover, made by the Middletown Plate Co. about 1885; two butter dishes with revolving covers—shown open and partly closed—made by the Meriden Britannia Co. between 1882 and 1887.

arched handle from which the cover could be hung while butter was being removed (Fig. 111).

One popular style that is presently being widely reproduced is the "revolving butter dish" (Fig. 112). The cover is held by pins on either side. By turning a handle the cover rolls around under the base. Ernest Kaufmann of Philadelphia, Pennsylvania, patented a further improvement in which the inside bowl could be removed for cleaning (Fig. 113).

Patents concerning butter dishes are not numerous but one patented idea of the 1870s which received immediate acceptance was an insert of perforated

111. Butter dishes with sliding covers. Meriden Britannia Co. catalog, 1886.

113. Revolving butter dish with inside bowl which may be removed for cleaning. Patented by Ernest Kaufmann, Philadelphia, Pa. *The Watchmaker and Jeweler,* June 1870.

114. *Left to Right:* Butter dish matching tea service made by the Meriden Britannia Co. in 1896. Butter dish with hinged cover; marked "Wilcox Silver Plate Co.," about 1884. Butter dish with cow finial; made by Simpson, Hall, Miller & Co. of Wallingford, Conn.

115. Butter dish made by Pairpoint Corp. of New Bedford, Mass., about 1890.

116. Butter dish made by Sheffield Silver Co. of Brooklyn, N.Y., about 1900.

117. Butter dish made by Apollo Silver Co. of New York City, about 1900.

plate glass to fit over the metal butter shelf. This glass insert served the dual purpose of keeping the butter from contact with metal and of protecting the metal from knife scratches. It was carefully described in the 1886 catalog of the Wilcox Silver Plate Company as, "Composed of heavy beveled plate glass disk mounted in strong light frame or rim. This drainer is simple, sweet and clean, and cannot possibly give any metallic taste to butter." The Meriden Britannia catalog of the same year advised that, "Butter dishes not listed with the Patent Drainer can be furnished with them at 25 cents extra. . . ."

Generally, the styles of butter dishes followed those similar to teapots and coffeepots, some being made especially to match (Figs. 114, 115).

Butter dishes made around the turn

248   AMERICAN SILVERPLATE

118. Double-wall ice pitcher bearing name of James Stimpson, Baltimore, Md. Now in the Museum of History and Technology, Washington, D.C. (Collection of Dr. Joseph H. Kler.)

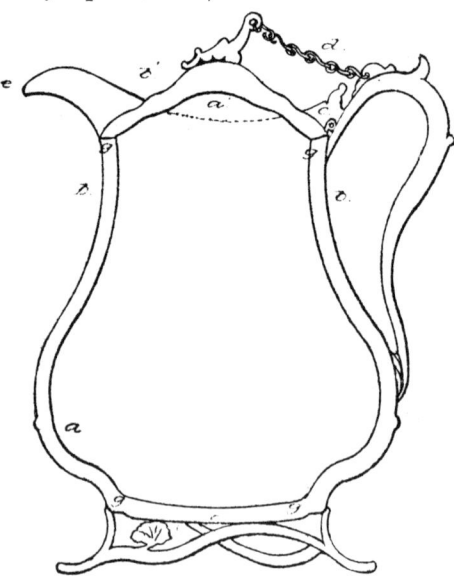

119. The first double-wall pitcher patented in the United States, Patent No. 11,819; October 17, 1854. Issued to James H. Stimpson, Executor (and son of) James Stimpson, Baltimore.

of the century and later were less complicated, usually consisting of a dish with cover and inside drainer (Figs. 116, 117).

Ice-Water Pitchers

Of the many ingenious ways to provide and maintain a supply of cool drinking water, one of the most popular and practical, before it was outmoded by mechanical refrigeration and its plentiful ice cubes, was the covered, multi-walled ice pitcher. The great number of patents and the space devoted to them in old catalogs testify to their popularity.

Ice pitchers turn up in attics or antique shops, their original purpose a mystery to the modern housewife. In their day they were hailed as a great improvement for keeping water cold.

There were many different styles; early ones had straight sloping sides—much like old-fashioned coffeepots (Fig. 118). Some came with a tray shaped to hold one goblet in front of the pitcher; later ones were mounted in elaborate tilting racks with one or more goblets. Matching waste bowls were often included.

A number of patents were issued for multi-walled ice pitchers. The first one was granted in the name of James Stimpson of Baltimore, Maryland (Fig. 119), which was actually issued to James H. Stimpson, executor and son. This was Patent No. 11,891, first issued October 17, 1854; extended seven years, reissued June 9, 1868, and still in possession of the Stimpson family in 1878. Stimpson did not claim the invention of a double-walled vessel except as applied to a pitcher. His patent was used on a royalty basis by manufacturers. These may often be identified by a metal disk soldered on the bottom of the vessel (Fig. 119a).

Early multi-walled pitchers have an inner lining of metal, with a space between the lining and the outer body

VII. Silverplate for Table and Household Use   249

October 5, 1858) was patented by James H. Stimpson, son and executor of James Stimpson (Fig. 120). While the inventor acknowledged that the treble wall added to the weight and expense of the pitcher, he stated that ". . . for very hot climates and damp atmosphere, it is of special use." And, "A blow upon a double wall pitcher may impair the non-conducting property of the air space between them, but in case of a third wall the blow will most likely cause only the contact of the two outer walls without affecting the integrity of the air space."

Still another ice pitcher was invented and patented by James H. Stimpson (No. 23,200, March 8, 1859). This improvement was for a double- or treble-wall pitcher, the inner wall of which consisted of a porcelain-coated metal shell that was soldered to the exterior (Fig. 121). This patent was used also on a

119a. Pencil rubbing of a disk on the bottom of an ice-water pitcher showing use of the Stimpson patent.

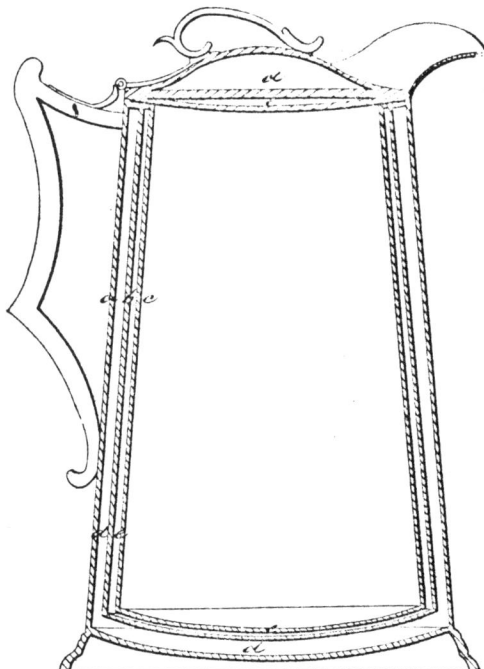

120. Treble-wall ice pitcher patented October 5, 1858, by James H. Stimpson. Patent No. 21,717.

for insulation. Later patents covered porcelain linings, some of them being detachable "to facilitate cleansing." One type was made whose lining was porcelain fused to sheet iron, this latter type lining being soldered to the outer body for durability.

A treble-wall ice pitcher (No. 21,717,

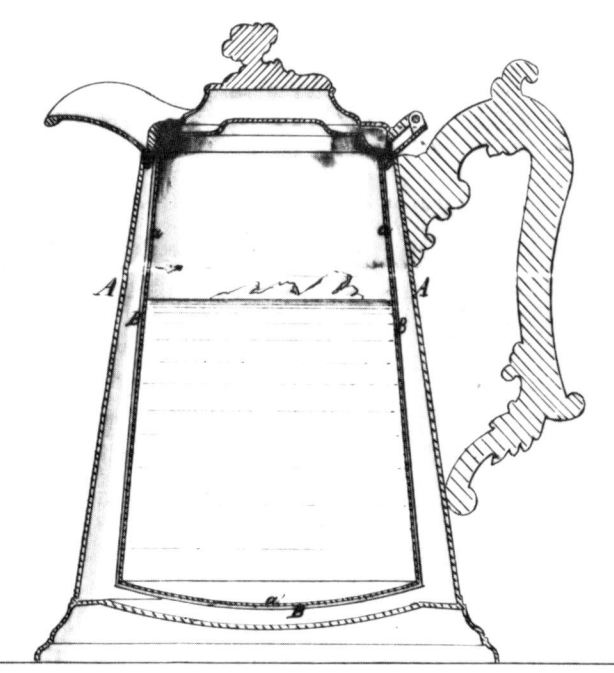

121. Double or treble-wall ice pitcher patented by James H. Stimpson, March 8, 1859. Patent No. 23,200.

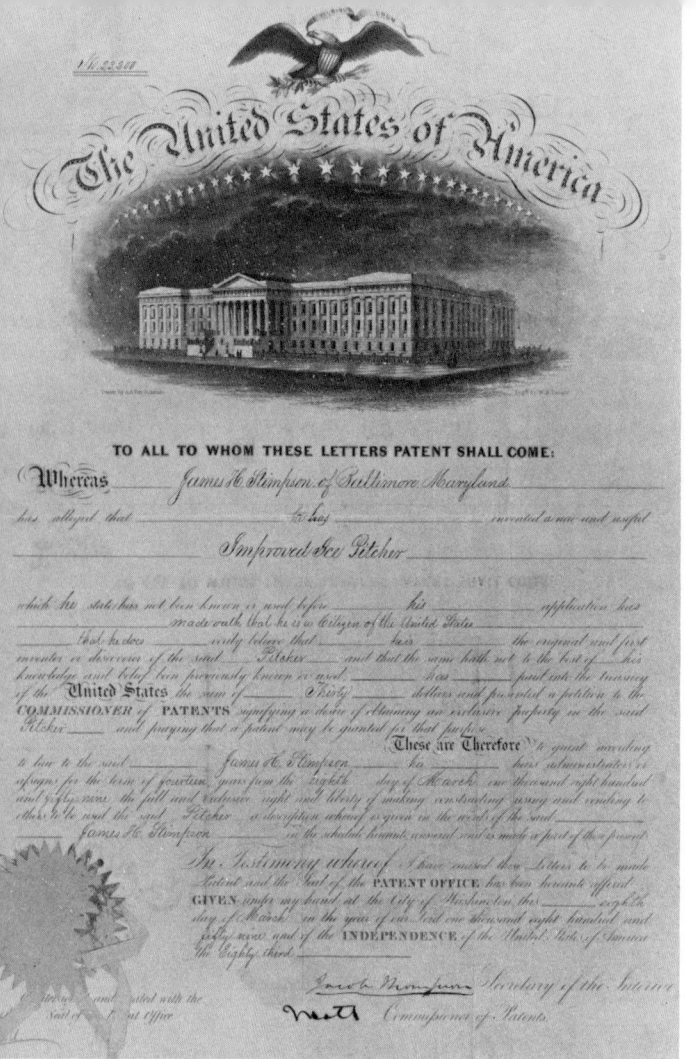

121a. Original Letters Patent for Stimpson's improved ice pitcher with porcelain lining were turned over to the Meriden Britannia Co. in 1868 when his widow sold the patent rights.

121b. Handwritten bill of sale for patent of ice pitcher with porcelain lining.

royalty basis. After James H. Stimpson's death in 1867, his widow sold the patent rights to Horace C. Wilcox, who was acting for the Meriden Britannia Company (Figs. 121a, 121b). The original patent papers were turned over to Wilcox and are still in the possession of the International Silver Company.

Other patents issued for improvements for ice pitchers were numerous. Among them were "Lyman's Patent Double Valve," issued June 8, 1858 (Fig. 122). This was a valve placed in the throat of the pitcher to keep out warm air. When the pitcher was tilted for pouring, the valve swung forward, permitting an easy flow of water.

N. Lawrence, Taunton, Massachusetts, patented for Reed & Barton, November 5, 1867, a small knob on the spout to be used as an aid in lifting the pitcher.

Ice pitchers are heavy—even medium-size ones weigh as much as ten pounds empty—so it is not surprising that there were several patents for stands with a tilting arrangement as an aid in pouring water from these large, heavy vessels (Figs. 123, 124).

A still later device was an ice pitcher with an outside shell of papier-mâché mounted in silverplate. These pitchers opened a field for decoration limited only by the artist's skill and imagination. They were somewhat lighter than those with metallic shells, but, being of a more fragile nature, fewer have survived.

Some of the tilting arrangements swung the pitchers from lugs on either side of the vessel. The first such arrangement was patented December 28, 1869, by John Gibson, Jr., Albany, New York. This ingenious inventor also patented a tilting device which did not require the pitcher to be made expressly for it and was consequently adapted for any pitcher already in use (Fig. 125). Instead of being supported by lugs on either side of the pitcher, a stand was provided on which the pitcher sat. These were manufactured by Reed & Barton.

VII. SILVERPLATE FOR TABLE AND HOUSEHOLD USE   251

No. 29, Engine Medallion.
Each, $13 00.

No. 28 Engine Medallion.
Each, $12 75.

No. 28, Medallion Engraved.
Each, $12 75.

No. 33, N, Engine.

No. 33, N, Engine, each,	$10 00.
No. 33, N, Plain, each,	9 00.
*No. 33, Engine, each,	10 00.
No. 33, Plain, each,	9 00.

LYMAN'S
PATENT
Double Valve.

Placed in the throat of the Nozzle to our Ice Pitchers.

Patented June 8th. 1858.

122. Meriden Britannia Co. catalog, 1867.

VII. SILVERPLATE FOR TABLE AND HOUSEHOLD USE 253

124. Patent tilting and revolving ice pitcher and stand, advertised by Adams, Chandler & Co. *The Watchmaker & Jeweler*, March 1870.

Only a few short years after ice pitchers were invented by the two Baltimore Stimpsons, father and son, designers and manufacturers seized upon them as a medium for presenting some rather fantastic ideas. Ernest Kaufmann's design for an ice pitcher, patented April 28, 1853, is a good illustration (Fig. 126). The spout appears to be an angry rooster, the finial a rather diffident baby walrus. The handle has a thumb rest which appears to be an angry feline and all these unrelated motifs are linked together with acanthus leaves and scrolls.

123. Tilting ice pitcher and goblet made by Barbour Bros. Co. before 1892.
125. Unlike most tilting arrangements, Gibson's did not require the pitcher to be made with lugs on either side. Any pitcher would sit on the stand. *The Watchmaker & Jeweler*, March 1870.

We call the attention of the Trade to our
PATENT TILTING AND REVOLVING
ICE PITCHER AND STAND,
With SLOP BOWL Combined,
The greatest improvement yet made in Ice Pitchers. We also manufacture a full line o
Table and Communion Plated Ware,
And Guarantee every Article.
ADAMS, CHANDLER & CO.,
SALESROOM—20 JOHN STREET, NEW YORK,
FACTORY—36, 38 & 40 COLUMBIA ST., BROOKLYN, L. I
Send for Illustrated Circular and Price Lists.

REED & BARTON,
Manufacturers of the Finest Quality of
Electro-Plated Table Ware,
OF EVERY DESCRIPTION,

Patentees and Manufacturers of the
Seamless Lined Ice Pitcher,
which, after a very careful test by Dr. S. Dana Hayes, State Assayer of Massachussetts, was approved by him as preserving water perfectly pure, and the lining being made from one piece, *without seam* or *joint*, will never be *liable to leak*.

Also Manufacturers of
Gibson's Patent Tilting Stand for Ice Pitchers,
which enables the person using to pour water from the Pitcher without being compelled to lift it, and which is so constructed that the base forms a tray, or salver, for holding the goblet and for catching the water that may condense and drip from outside of Pitcher.

This Tilting Stand (differing in this respect from all others), does not require the Pitcher to be made expressly for it, and is consequently adapted for any Pitcher now in use.

With the Pitcher, it forms a complete and very ornamental Water Set.

Factories Established at Taunton, 1824.
Salesroom at Factory and No. 2 Maiden Lane, New York.

254 AMERICAN SILVERPLATE

126. Unrelated motifs are combined to create this unusual ice pitcher designed by Ernest Kaufmann, Philadelphia, Pa. Design Patent No. 1,751; Patented April 28, 1863.

127. Placement of the helmeted man below the pitcher's spout is unusual. Designed and patented by Ernest Kaufmann, Philadelphia, Pa. Design Patent No. 2,327; Patented May 29, 1866.

The motifs on Kaufmann's later ice-pitcher design of 1866 may not be as unrelated but their placement is strange (Fig. 127). The finial consists of an eagle with his wings partially spread and his head bent down towards the head of a serpent which he has grasped in his talons. A border is applied to the lower edge of the lid. The spout is ornamented with suitable arabesques and it extends in a graceful curve which is surmounted by a curved architrave. Below the spout projects the head of a helmeted man. A border of arabesques ornaments the bottom edge of the body of the pitcher. The thumb rest on a gracefully curved handle is in the shape of a helmeted man.

128. Meriden Britannia Co. catalog, 1867.

No. 3, XX, Paneled Chased.
Each, $17 00.

No. 3, Scenery Chased, (B).
Each, $18 00.

No. 3, Wreath Chased.
Each, $16 00.

No. 3, N, Grape Chased.
Each, $14 25.

No. 3, Plain.
Each, $13 00.

No. 3, N, Plain.
Each, $13 00.

No. 2, Wreath Chased.
Each, $14 25.

No. 2 Engine.
Each, $12 75.

No. 2, Plain.
Each, $11 25.

129. Meriden Britannia Co. catalog, 1867.

PATENT FOUNTAIN PITCHER.

Patented April 28, 1885.

New, durable, simple in construction, works easily, will not get out of order, and keep ice longer than any other Ice Pitcher manufactured.

No. 241. FOUNTAIN PITCHER.
Porcelain Lined.
Satin, Engraved, $30.00 (POLAR). Hammered, $30.00 (POLE).
Metal Lined, $3.00 less.

No. 240. FOUNTAIN PITCHER.
Porcelain Lined.
Satin, $28.00 (GENESIS). Chased, $30.00.
Metal Lined, $3.00 less.

Ice-water pitchers were always a relatively expensive article but their great popularity is indicated by the variety of styles advertised.

The Meriden Britannia Company catalog for 1861–62 showed 14 different styles. In 1867, 36 styles were offered (Figs. 128, 129); for 1879, 45 styles; and in 1886 no less than 57 varieties were offered (Fig. 130).

In 1885 Reed & Barton illustrated 51 styles in their catalog (Fig. 131). By 1896 the number had dwindled to 14 and by 1900 the demand had practically disappeared.

In their heyday, ice-water pitcher sets were considered appropriate and impressive for presentation as awards and to honor famous personages.

These old ice-water pitchers are characteristic of American Victorian silverplate as well as being exemplary of the

130. Meriden Britannia Co. catalog, 1886.

258   American Silverplate

ARCTIC CHASED ICE WATER SET.
No. 36.   Set complete, Five Pieces, Goblets and Bowl gold-lined, $55.50. (CUTLET)

| No. 1974. | Ice Pitcher, | $19.00. (CUTTER) | No. 1974. | Goblets, gold-lined, each, $4.75. (CUTTING) |
| No. 1974. | Bowl, gold-lined, | 9.00. (CYCLE) | No. 05114. | Waiter, 16 inch, 18.00. (CYCLOID) |

130 continued.

Cover Detached from China-Lined Pitcher.

VENETIAN CHASED AND EMBOSSED ICE WATER SET.
No. 515.   Set complete, Three Pieces, Goblet gold-lined, $42.25. (CRACKING)

No. 2099. Ice Pitcher, $25.00. (CRADLING)   No. 2099. Goblet, gold-lined, $5.25. (CRANNIED)   No. 41. Waiter, 13 inch, $12.00. (CRASHING)

131.   Reed & Barton catalog, 1885.

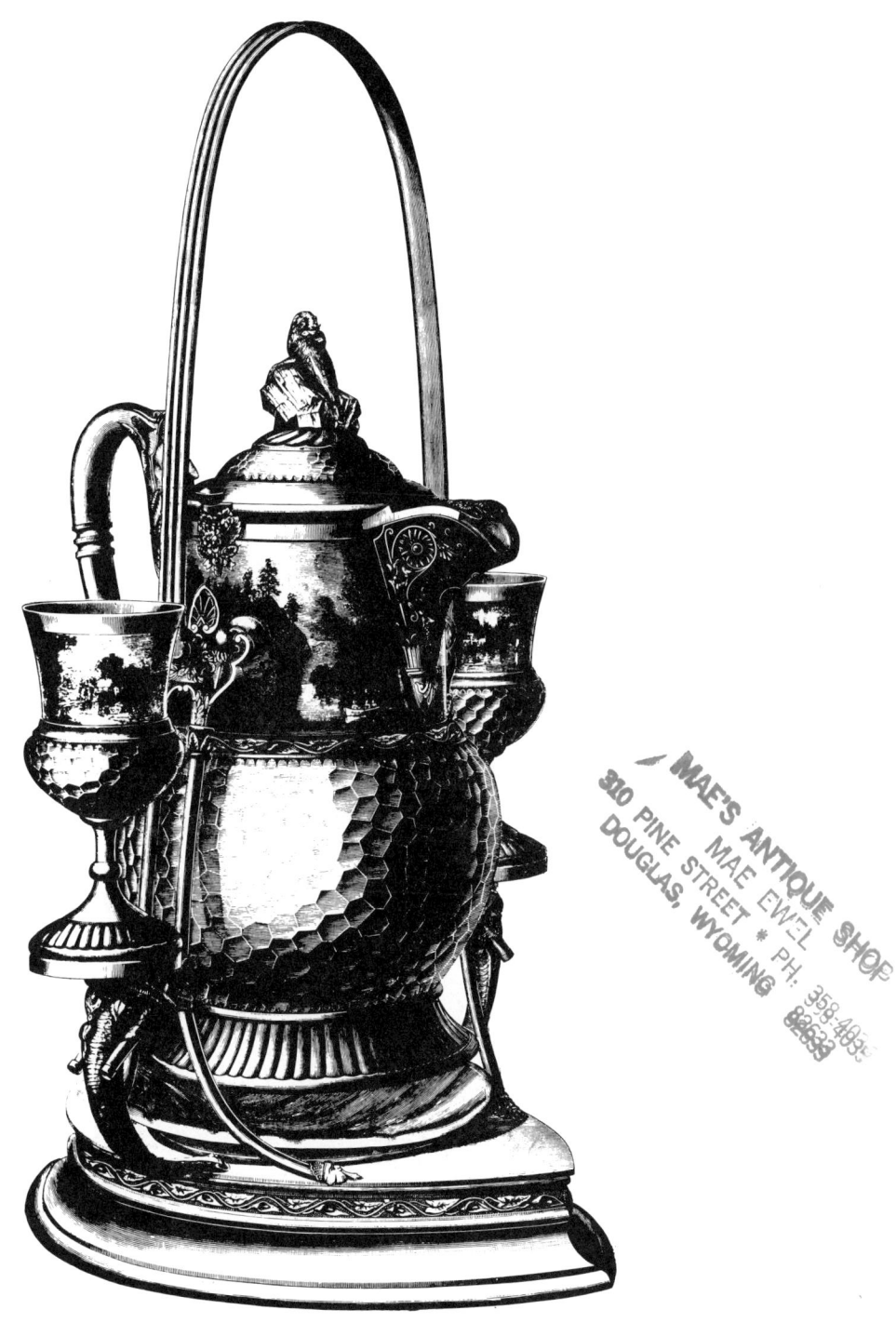

No. 64. Set complete. Four Pieces, Goblets and Tilter gold-lined, $72.50. (PROLIX)
Old Silver and Gold Finish. 85.00. (RIDDLE)

No. 2175. Ice Pitcher, $26.50. (PROMOTE)   No. 2175. Goblets, gold-lined, each, $5.50. (PROLONG)
Old Silver and Gold Finish, 32.50. (RIDE)   Old Silver and Gold Finish, 7.50. (RIDGE)

No. 350. Tilter, gold-lined. $35.00. (PROMISE)
Old Silver and Gold Finish. 37.50. (RIFT)

131 continued.

260 American Silverplate

FINE HAMMERED AND ENGRAVED TILTING ICE WATER SET.
No. 38. Set complete, Four Pieces, Goblets and Tilter gold-lined, $115.00. (CURATOR)
  With Gold Ornamentation, 144.00. (CURATIVE)
No. 1938. Ice Pitcher, $25.00. (CURB) No. 1938. Goblets, gold-lined, each, $5.50. (CURDLE)
  No. 200. Tilter, gold-lined, $79.00. (CURE)

131 continued.

FINE HAMMERED AND MOSS ROSE CHASED ICE WATER SET.

No. 508. Set complete, Five Pieces, Goblets and Bowl gold-lined, $64.50. (CRUSADER) Chasing, Gold Variegated, $92.50. (CRUSING)

No. 1988. Ice Pitcher, Chasing, Gold Variegated, $32.00. (CUBE) No. 1988. Goblets, gold-lined, each, $4.75. (CRYER) Chasing, Gold Variegated, 7.75. (CUBED) No. 1988. Bowl, gold-lined, $9.00. Chasing, Gold Variegated, 13.00. (CUBICAL)

No. 65308. Waiter, 18 inch, $22.00. (CUCUMBER) 16 inch, $19.00. (CUD) Chasing, Gold Variegated, 32.00. (CUDGELED) 27.00. (CUDGEL)

ICE WATER SETS.

SNOW FLAKE TILTING ICE WATER SET.
No. 26. Set complete, Four Pieces, Goblets and Drawer gold-lined, $50.00. (CRUCIFORM)
No. 1894. Ice Pitcher, $20.00. (CRUDELY)   No. 1894. Goblets, gold-lined, each, $4.00. (CRUELTY)
No. 195. Tilter, gold-lined Drawer, $22.00. (CRUET)

131 continued.

SNOW FLAKE AND ENGRAVED TILTING ICE WATER SET.
No. 25. Set complete, Three Pieces, Goblet and Drawer gold-lined, $49.00. (CROTCH)
No. 1933. Ice Pitcher, $23.00. (CROTCHED)   No. 1933. Goblet, gold-lined, $5.00. (CRUE)
No. 205. Tilter, gold-lined Drawer, $21.00. (CRUCIFY)

epitome of the era of "good living" (Fig. 132). Not many are now used for their original purpose, but they are in demand for buffet suppers and other occasions when guests may serve themselves either hot or cold drinks.

As ice became more plentiful the double-wall ice pitchers were replaced in more and more homes by single-wall pitchers, often with matching goblets and trays. As with the earlier multi-wall pitchers, the newer ones were made in many styles (Figs. 134–137).

Porcelain-lined ice-water urns may be considered closely related to the double-wall ice pitcher as their function is that of providing easily available cold water. Those intended for domestic use were often decorated with polar bears, icebergs, and other Arctic motifs (Fig. 138).

Very elaborate ice-water urns intended for hotel use and for Mississippi River steamers were truly formidable in size and decoration (Fig. 139). A

134. Small water pitcher made by Reed & Barton.
132. Two silver-plated ice-water pitchers made by the Meriden Britannia Co.

264 American Silverplate

135. "The Marguerite" water set in Art Nouveau style, made by the Derby Silver Co. about 1904.

136. "Fern" design water pitcher made by Meriden Britannia Co. about 1905.

137. "Crocus" design water pitcher made by the Derby Silver Co. about 1904.

138. Reed & Barton catalog, 1885.

139. Reed & Barton catalog, 1877.

140. Meriden Britannia Co. catalog, 1886.

"double-walled, seamless, lined Ice-Water Urn, manufactured for the Mississippi River Steamer 'R. E. Lee,'" was made by Reed & Barton about 1875. Priced then at $1,500 it stood 60 inches tall and had a capacity of 22 gallons. A graceful water nymph, holding an ewer and offering a bowl of water, surmounted the top, while children, whose goblets had been filled, perched on a platform just below the dome.

An ice-water urn of more modest proportions was made by the Meriden Britannia Company (Fig. 140). Its capacity was five gallons. The butterfly-winged ladies who adorn it are similar to those used on trophies and other Meriden Britannia Company articles.

Pitchers

Early syrup cups or pitchers followed the general styles of English milk pots from which they may have been derived (Fig. 141). However, most early ones may be easily distinguished from milk pots by a small drip plate. The invention of a patent cut-off inside the pitcher obviated the need for the drip plate (Figs. 142, 143).

Syrup pitchers were sometimes made as an adjunct to complete a tea service (Fig. 144).

Designed in a great number of styles until after the turn of the century, syrup pitchers declined in popularity and have

141. Meriden Britannia Co. catalog, 1867.

No. 198.

Porcelain, . $5.00 (PUNK).

No. 180.

Plain,	.	$4.50	(FABRICATION).
Engine,		5.50	(FABRICATE).
Chased,		5.50	(FABULIST).

No. 1.

Satin, $5.00 (FACETIOUS).

No. 187.

Plain, . $4.50 (FACE).

No. 193.

Decorated Porcelain, . $5.00 (LASCAR).

No 184.

Plain, . $5.00 (FACILE).
Silver Chased, 6.00 (FACING).

No. 186.

Plain, . $5.00 (FACTOR).
Chased, . 6.00 (FACTORY).

No. 2½.

Plain, . $5.00 (FACT).
Chased, . 6.00 (FACTION).

No. 1.

Chased . $6.00 (FACTOTUM).

142. Meriden Britannia Co. catalog, 1886.

143. Syrup cup made by the Pairpoint Mfg. Co. New Bedford, Mass., about 1894.

272   AMERICAN SILVERPLATE

No. 2962. Butter Dish, $9.50. (ARSENAL)

No. 2962. Spoon Holder, gold-lined, $8.50. (ARTERY)

No. 2962. Sirup Pitcher, $9.50. (ARTESIAN)

No. 2962.   SNOW FLAKE AND CHASED TEA SET.

| No. 2962. Set of Six Pieces. $64.00. (ARTIFIED) | Coffee. $13.00. | Tea, 6 half-pints. $12.00. | Water, 5 half-pints. $11.50. | Sugar. $9.00. | Cream, gold-lined. $9.50. | Bowl, gold-lined. $9.00. | Set. without gold lining $1.00 less. |

No. 2962. Urn, 12 half-pints, $37.00. (ARTISAN)   Spoon Holder, gold-lined, $8.50. (ARTERY)   Butter Dish, $9.50. (ARSENAL)
No. 4262. Patent Wire-Strengthened Waiter, 24 inch, $58.00. (ASBESTOS)   26 inch, $64.00. (ASCEND)

144. Reed & Barton catalog, 1885.

virtually disappeared from current catalogs (Figs. 145–148).

Smaller pitchers, made for specialized purposes, such as the serving of milk and cream usually matched tea services.

Dessert Services

Fancy dessert services consisting of sugar bowl and creamer did not necessarily match the tea service (Figs. 149, 150, 150a).

Larger dessert services often included a spoon holder and later ones sometimes

included a bowl for the dessert (Fig. 151).

Linings were made of clear, cranberry, ruby, and blue glass.

Punch Bowls, Wine Coolers, Wine-Bottle Cases, Liquor Labels

Elaborate punch sets were made in the 1860s through the 1880s consisting of large punch bowls, a tray, and matching goblets (Fig. 152). Probably few of

145. Syrup pitcher, marked "Kann & Sons Mfg. Co., Baltimore, Md." Made about 1895.

146. Syrup pitcher and drip plate. Pitcher marked "Hartford Silver Plate Co.,"; plate marked "Barbour Silver Co." Both made about 1895.

147. Syrup pitcher made by Webster Co. of North Attleboro, Mass., about 1895.

274 AMERICAN SILVERPLATE

No. 2670. Butler Finish, $6.00 (Incurring)

148. Syrup pitchers and plates made by the Victor Silver Co. (a division of the Derby Silver Co.) Shelton (now Derby), Conn., about 1900–05.

149. Sugar bowls and cream pitcher made by Simpson, Hall, Miller & Co. of Wallingford, Conn. Identical to those illustrated in their catalogs of 1868 and 1871.

VII. Silverplate for Table and Household Use

Spoon Holder.

Sugar Bowl.

Cream Pitcher.

No. 50. Dessert Set. Ruby Glass Lining.

	Height.	Plain Cover.	Chased Cover.
Sugar Bowl, ...	6 inches	$4.50 (Patroness)	$5.25 (Paul)
Cream Pitcher, ...	4½ "	4.00 (Paulus)	. . . .
Spoon Holder, ...	4½ "	4.00 (Pauline)	. . . .
Set of Three Pieces, ...		$12.00 (Pauper)	$13.25 (Pavilion)

150. Simpson, Hall, Miller & Co. catalog, 1868.

150a. Sugar basket with ruby glass lining. Marked "Hall, Elton & Co./Wallingford, Conn./Triple Plate/8."

276 AMERICAN SILVERPLATE

151. Meriden Britannia Co. catalog, 1886. 152. Meriden Britannia Co. catalog, 1886.

No. 1 Repousse. Capacity, 1½ Gallons.
Six Gold Lined Goblets, Complete, . . $96.00

No. 2. Punch Ladle.
Silver, Gold Inlaid and
Gold Lined. . . $20.00

No. 3. Punch Bowl. Capacity, 4 Gallons.
Engraved, Silver, Gold Inlaid and Gold Lined, . . $150.00

these were ever made. Even the later punch sets of the 1890s are not plentiful (Fig. 153). They usually consist of punch bowl, tray, cups, and ladle.

An unusual punch bowl and wine cooler would have set off any gentlemen's party with great elegance (Fig. 154).

Ice tubs and wine coolers of simpler form could be had for less important occasions (Fig. 155).

Wine-bottle cases were made in both pint and quart sizes (Fig. 156). According to the catalog, "Wine taken from the ice and placed in these felt-lined bottle holders will retain its temperature and the cases present an elegant appearance."

Liquor labels and other bar goods were made in great quantity (Fig. 157).

Cups and Goblets

Through long tradition, silversmithing has been associated with vessels for drinking liquids, whether potent or mild. Indeed, the earliest example of

153. Punch bowl, cups, and ladle made by the Meriden Britannia Co. about 1895.

American silver is a tiny dram cup made by John Hull and Robert Sanderson, Boston, Massachusetts, about 1651. Other very early American silver, much of it preserved because of its ecclesiastical use, consists of standing cups, beakers, tankards, small cups, mugs, and canns (similar to mugs, but a trifle larger). Few of these forms were carried unchanged into the mid-nineteenth century when silverplating began. Standing cups became goblets and small cups may be considered the ancestors of the cups so universally presented to babies and small children.

Goblets and cups were both made in many styles and were decorated with engraving, engine-turning, applied medallions, and chasing (Figs. 158–160). Goblets of the 1880s usually matched ice-water pitchers.

Children's cups were chased, engraved, embossed, or had applied dec-

VII. Silverplate for Table and Household Use 279

No. 6. Punch Bowl and Wine Cooler Combined.
Engraved, Gold Inlaid and Gold Lined,   .   .   . $275.00 (Ottoman).
Capacity, 4 Gallons.

154. Meriden Britannia Co. catalog, 1886.

280   American Silverplate

Ice Tub.

No. 21, ... $8.00 (PADDOCK).
No. 20, with Bail (see No. 23), 7.50 (PAGE).

Ice Tub.

No. 23, ... $15.00 (PAGEANT).
No. 24, with Handles (see No. 21), 16.00 (PAGODA).

No. 5.   Ice Tub.

Plain, ... $6.75 (PACKET).
Satin, ... 6.75 (PADDLE).

No. 29.

Silver, . . . $7.50 (WINTERGREEN).

No. 28.

Silver, ... $9.00 (WINDFALL).
Old Silver, . . 10.00 (WHOOPS).
XX Old Silver, . 13.00 (WIMBLE).
Gold Lined, $2.00 Extra.

No. 3.   Ice Tub.

Plain, . . . $16.50 (PADLOCK).

No. 30.

Silver, . . . $8.50 (WINDROW).

No. 27.

Silver, ... $9.50 (WILLOWY).
Old Silver, . . 11.00 (WILDFIRE).
XX Old Silver, . 14.50 (WHOLESOME).
Gold Lined, $2.00 Extra.

155. Meriden Britannia Co. catalog, 1886.

VII. Silverplate for Table and Household Use 281

No. 8.

Satin C,	$15.00	(WHERRY).
Satin C, Old Silver,	17.50	(WHEREVER).
Satin C, XX Gold Inlaid,	24.00	(WHERETO).

No. 6.

Engraved, . . . $16.50 (OUTWEIGH).

No. 2.

Plain, . . . $12.50 (OUTRUN).
Satin Shield, . . 12.50 (OUTSIDE).

No. 1.
Same as No. 2, only Plain Ring Handles.
Plain, . . . $11.00 (OUTSPREAD).

No. 10.

Chased,	$27.50	(WHITENESS).
Moorish, Old Silver,	30.50	(WHITEBAIT).
Moorish, Gold Inlaid,	35.00	(WHIRLBONE).

No. 9.
Same as No. 10, Without Inside Lining.

Chased,	$18.00	(WHIPSTOCK).
Moorish, Old Silver,	21.00	(WHIPSAW).
Moorish, Gold Inlaid,	25.50	(WHIPCORD).

No. 11.

Satin, . . . $15.00 (WHIFFLE).
Satin, Engraved, . . 17.00 (WHETHER).

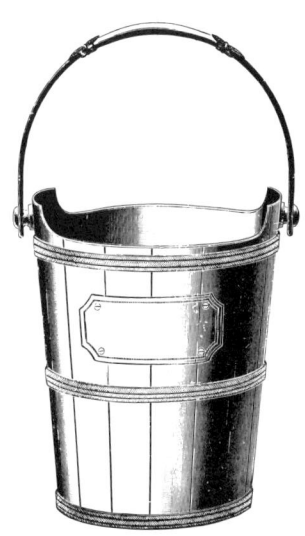

No. 5.

Plain, . . . $16.75 (OUTPOST).

155 continued.

282 AMERICAN SILVERPLATE

156. Meriden Britannia Co. catalog, 1886.
157. Reed & Barton catalog, 1885.

No. 100. Spice Dish, gold-lined, $18.00. (KNAG)

No. 135. Spice Dish, gold-lined, $49.50. (KNAPPING)
Gold-lined, and Oxidized Figure, 54.50. (KNAPSACK)

No. 120. Spice Dish, $19.50.
Gold-lined, and Oxidized Figure, 24.50.

No. 50. Soda Tumbler Holder, $2.25. (KNAB)

No. 55. Soda Tumbler Holder, $2.75. (KITCHEN)

No. 100. Tom and Jerry, $3.75. (KIDS)

BAR URN.
No. 7 half-pints, $25.00. (LOCATE)
10 half-pints, 30.00. (LOCATION)

CRACKER BOWL.
No. 59. $22.50. (MASON)
No. 54. Chased Body, 30.00. (MANTLE)

SPICE DISH.
No. 150. Gold-lined, $30.00. (MANTLING) Bouquet, $1.75 extra.

TODDY KETTLE.
No. 20. 4 half-pints, $21.00. (LOCKAGE)

No. 45. Bar Strainer, $4.25. (KINGDOM)

(CUT ONE-THIRD SIZE.)
BEER PITCHER.
With draught from bottom.
No. 210. 10 half-pints, $12.50. (KINDRED)
12 half-pints, 13.50. (LOCKER)

No. 1. Bombilla, $4.75. (LOCUST)

No. 20. Muddler, $2.75. (KINDLING)

No. 30. Bar Strainer, $3.75. (KINSFOLK)

No. 40. Bar Strainer, $4.75. (KINSHIP)

Hot Whiskey Pitcher, $4.75. (KINSMAN)

Hot Whiskey Pitcher, $5.50. (KISSING)

NICKEL SILVER LIQUOR LABELS.
Assorted, per dozen, $12.00. (KEDGE)
Lettered to order.

No. 145. Hot Whiskey Pitcher, $6.75. (LODGING)

157 continued.

284   AMERICAN SILVERPLATE

No. 386. $2.75.
      Gold-lined, 3.50.

No. 510. $2.50.
      Gold-lined, 3.25.

No. 895. $3.00.   Gold-lined, $3.
 "   890. Plain, 2.50.   "   3.

No. 1010. $2.50.   Gold-lined, $3.25.
 "   1015. Chased, 3.25.   "   4.00.

No. 609. $2.50. Gold-lined, $3.25.
 "   600. 1.75.   "   2.50.

No. 530. $2.25. Gold-lined, $3.00.

No. 570. $2.50. Gold-lined, $3.25.

No. 110. Child's Bowl, $6.00. Gold-lined, $7.50.
 "   "   "   Plate, 5.00.

No. 460. $2.75. Gold-lined, $3.50.

No. 215. Child's Tray, 16 inch, $18.00.
 "   210.   "   "   plain,   15.00.

158. Reed & Barton catalog, 1877.

VII. SILVERPLATE FOR TABLE AND HOUSEHOLD USE

No. 1378, Medallion.	No. 1378, Chased.	No. 1378, Plain.	No. 1378, Engine.	No. 1380, Chased.	No. 1380, Plain.	No. 12, Plain.	No. 12, Medallion.
Plain Plated. Each, $2 25.	Plain Plated. Each, $2 25.	Plain Plated. Each, $2 25.		Plain Plated. Each, $2 50.	Plain Plated. Each, $2 50.	Plain Plated. Each, $2 25.	Plain Plated. Each, $2 25.
Plain Gilt. Each, 3 00.	Plain Gilt. Each, 3 00.	Plain Gilt. Each, 3 00.		Plain Gilt. Each, 3 25.	Plain Gilt. Each, 3 25.	Plain Gilt. Each, 3 00	Plain Gilt. Each, 3 00
Engine Plated. Each, 2 50.	Engine Plated. Each, 2 50.	Engine Plated. Each, 2 50.		Engine Plated. Each, 3 00.	Engine Plated. Each, 3 00.	Engine Plated. Each, 2 50.	Engine Plated. Each, 2 50.
Engine Gilt. Each, 3 25.	Engine Gilt. Each, 3 25.	Engine Gilt. Each, 3 25.		Engine Gilt. Each, 3 25.	Engine Gilt. Each, 3 25.	Engine Gilt. Each, 3 25.	Engine Gilt. Each, 3 25.
Grecian or Damask Chased Plated. Each, $3 00.				Grecian or Damask Chased Plated. Each, $3 25.		Grecian or Damask Chased Plated. Each, $3 00.	
Grecian or Damask Chased Gilt. Each, $3 75.				Grecian or Damask Chased Gilt. Each, $4 00.		Grecian or Damask Chased Gilt. Each, $3 75.	
						Medallion Plated. Each, $3 00.	
						Medallion Gilt. Each, 3 75.	

No. 95, Plain.	No. 95, Medallion.	No. 95, Medallion.	No. 1377, Wreath Chased.	No. 1377, Grecian Chased.	No. 1377, Straight Line Engine.
Plain Plated. Each, $2 50.			Plain Plated. Each, $2 50.		
Plain Gilt. Each, 3 25.			Plain Gilt. Each, 3 25.		
Engine Plated. Each, 2 75.			Engine Plated. Each, 2 75.		
Engine Gilt. Each, 3 50.			Engine Gilt. Each, 3 50.		
Grecian or Damask Chased Plated. Each, $3 25.			Grecian or Wreath Chased, or Straight Line Engine Plated. Each, $3 25.		
Grecian or Damask Chased Gilt. Each, 4 00.			Grecian or Wreath Chased, or Straight Line Engine Gilt. Each, $4 00.		
Medallion Plated. Each, 3 25.					
Medallion Gilt. Each, 4 00.					

No. 1500, Engraved.	No. 1376, Wreath Chased.	No. 1379, Engine.	No. 1379, Chased.
Plain Plated. Each, $2 75.	Plain Plated. Each, $1 50.	Plain Plated. Each, $2 00.	
Plain Gilt. Each, 3 50.	Plain Gilt. Each, 2 25.	Plain Gilt. Each, 2 75.	
Engine Plated. Each, 3 00.	Engine Plated. Each, 2 00.	Engine Plated. Each, 2 25.	
Engine Gilt. Each, 3 75.	Engine Gilt. Each, 2 75.	Engine Gilt. Each, 3 00.	
Grecian Chased Plain. Each, 3 50.	Wreath or Grecian Chased Plated. Each, $2 25.	Grecian or Damask Chased Plated. Each, $2 50.	
Grecian Chased Gilt. Each, 4 25.	Wreath or Grecian Chased Gilt. Each, $3 00.	Grecian or Damask Chased Gilt. Each, 3 25.	
Medallion Plain. Each, 3 50.			
Medallion Gilt. Each, 4 25.			
Engraved Plain. Each, 3 50.			
Engraved Gilt. Each, 4 25.			

159. Meriden Britannia Co. catalog, 1877.

286 AMERICAN SILVERPLATE

  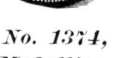  

No. 1375,   *No. 1375,*   *No. 1374,*   *No. 1374,*   *No. 1374,*
Scenery Chased.   *Plain.*   *Medallion.*   *Engine.*   *Plain.*

Plain Plated.	Each, $2 25.		Plain Plated.	Each, $2 00.
Plain Gilt.	Each, 3 00.		Plain Gilt.	Each, 2 75.
Engine Plated.	, 2 50.		Engine Plated.	Each, 2 25.
Engine Gilt.	Each, 3 25.		Engine Gilt.	Each, 3 00.
Grecian or Damask Chased Plated.	Each, $3 00.		Grecian or Damask Chased Plated.	Each, $2 50.
Grecian or Damask Chased Gilt.	Each, 3 75.		Grecian or Damask Chased Gilt.	Each, 3 25.
Scenery Gilt.	Each, $5 25.		Medallion Plated.	Each, 2 50.
			Medallion Gilt.	Each, 3 25.

No. 1373,   *No. 1373,*   *No. 1371,*   *No. 1370.*   *No. 1370,*   *No. 1370,*
Plain.   *Engine.*   *Engraved.*   *Grecian Chased.*   *Engine.*   *Plain.*

Plain Plated. Each, $1 75.	Plain Plated. Each, $1 60.	Plain Plated. Each, $1 65.
Plain Gilt. Each, 2 50.	Plain Gilt. Each, 2 25.	Plain Gilt. Each, 2 25.
Engine Plated. Each, 2 00.	Engraved Plated. Each, 2 25.	Engine Plated. Each, 2 00.
Engine Gilt. Each, 2 75.	Engraved Gilt. Each, 3 00.	Engine Gilt. Each, 2 60.
Grecian or Damask Chased Plated. Each, $2 50.		Grecian or Damask Chased Plated. Each, $2 25.
Grecian or Damask Chased Gilt. Each, $3 25.		Grecian or Damask Chased Gilt. Each, 3 00.

No. 33,   *No. 36,*   *No. 33,*   *No. 3*   *No. 34,*   *No. 34,*   *No. 37,*   *No. 39,*
Chased.   *Plain.*   *Plain.*   *Wreath Chased.*   *Grecian Chased.*   *Medallion.*   *Engraved.*   *Engraved.*

No.	Plain Plated.	Plain Gilt.	Engine Plated.	Engine Gilt.	Grecian or Damask Chased Plated.	Grecian or Damask Chased Gilt.	Medallion Plated.	Medallion Gilt.
33	$1 75	$2 25	$2 00	$2 50	$2 25	$2 75	$2 25	$2 75
34	1 65	2 15	1 90	2 40	2 15	2 65	2 15	2 65
36	2 00	2 50	2 25	2 75	2 50	3 00	2 50	3 00
37	1 75	2 25	2 00	2 50	2 25	2 75	2 25	2 75
*38	1 90	2 40	2 15	2 65	2 40	2 90	2 40	2 90
39	2 25	2 75	2 50	3 00	2 75	3 25	2 75	3 25

* No. 38 in size is between Nos. 37 and 39, but same style.

160. Meriden Britannia Co. catalog, 1877.

VII. Silverplate for Table and Household Use

No. 141.

ain, . . $2.25 (FLUME).
ain, Gold Lined, 2.75 (FLUNG).
hased, . . 2.75 (FLURRY).
hased, Gold Lined, 3.25 (PERSPIRE).

No. 142.

Plain, . . $2.50 (FLUTE).
Plain, Gold Lined, 3.00 (FLUTING).
Chased, . . 3.00 (FLYER).
Chased, Gold Lined, 3.50 (FOAM).

No. 132.

Plain, . . $2.00 (FEBRUARY).
Chased, . . 2.50 (FEED).
Chased, Gold Lined, 3.00 (FEELING).

161. Meriden Britannia Co. catalog, 1886.

orations of animals, birds, flowers, and other subjects with special appeal to children (Figs. 161, 162, 162a, 163).

Other cups were made for special purposes such as shaving and "Collapsion Cups" for the traveler (Figs. 164, 165). Moustache cups were almost a necessity for the protection of hirsute adornments favored in the 1880s (Figs. 166, 167).

Another special-purpose cup was the invalid cup, part of a "Sick Call" outfit, used by the clergy in visiting the sick (Fig. 168).

Cups as "badges of travel" or souvenirs have had a long popularity which continues to the present time (Fig. 169).

Chafing Dishes, Baking Dishes, and Other Serving Containers

The chafing dish consists of one dish within another, the outer vessel being filled with hot water and in direct contact with the heat source and the inner a container for food (Fig. 170). The chafing dish operates on the same principle as a double boiler.

162. Child's cup made by Hall, Elton & Co., Wallingford, Conn.

162a. Child's cup marked "Columbia Silver Co./Quadruple Plate/Portland, Me./ 1183."

163. Child's cup made by Reed & Barton about 1885.

No. 3. Open.
Plain, . $1.50 (FLEW)

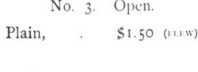

No. 3. Closed.

No. 4. Closed.

No. 2. Open.
Plain. . $1.55 (FLECE)

View showing Cup only.
No. 5. SILVER EGG COLLAPSION CUP, FULL SIZE.
Satin, Gold Lined, . . $3.00 (LITIMUS)

View showing Cup complete, balanced to stand on end.

No. 4. Open.
Plain, . $2.00 (F

No. 1. Open.
Plain, . $1.30 (
Engine, . 1.65 (

164. Meriden Britannia Co. catalog, 1886.

No. 143.
Plain, ... $4.00 (FLOW).
Chased, . . . 4 50 (FLOWER).
Chased, Gold Lined, 5.00 (PHYSICAL).

No. 143.
Hammered, ... $4.50 (PHILANDER).
Hammered, Old Silver, . . 5.00 (PHILIPPIC).
Hammered, Old Silver, Gold Lined, 5.50 (PIANIST).

165. Meriden Britannia Co. catalog, 1886.

VII. Silverplate for Table and Household Use 289

No. 128.
rcelain, with Plated Mountings, $3.75 (FLOWS).

165 continued.

View showing Soap Box or top of No. 175 Cup.

No. 175. Moorish, Old Silver.
Combination Cup and Soap Box.

Satin,	. . . .	$5.50 (PIANO).
Satin, Engraved,	. .	7.00 (PICAYUNE).
Moorish, Old Silver,	.	7.50 (PICKEREL).

No. 7. Moustache.

Plain,	. . . .	$6.50 (FOLIAGE).
Plain, Gold Lined Cup,		7.25 (FOLIO).
Chased,	. . .	9.00 (FOLK).
Chased, Gold Lined Cup,		9.75 (FOLLOW).

No. 8. Moustache.
Satin, Gold Lined Cup, . . $6.50 (PIGMENT).
Brocade Chased, Gold Lined Cup, 8.00 (PIGEON).

166. Supplement to Meriden Britannia Co. catalog, 1882.

No. 9. Moustache.
Satin, Gold Lined Cup, . $7.00 (PILGRIM).
Satin Engraved, Gold Lined Cup, 8.50 (PILASTER).

167. Moustache cup made by Wilcox Silver Plate Co. about 1895.

168. "Sick Call" invalid cup, part of an outfit used by the clergy in visiting the sick. Marked "Homan Silver Plate Co./ Pat'd. April '97."

While the chafing dish may be associated in the minds of some with midnight dormitory parties, "bachelor girl" affairs, Sunday night suppers, or after-ski parties, it can claim a place in history at least as far back as the sixteenth century. Ancient English spellings were "chaffyndyche," 1538; "chafindish," 1580; "chaffendish," 1612; and "chafen-dish," 1692. The present form, "chafing dish," dates to 1843.

Chafing dishes began as portable grates and charcoal was used in the under pan. Chafing dishes of the late 1880s and 1890s employed an alcohol burner. More recently, the less dangerous solid fuels, such as Sterno, were used. Even more modern are those with electric burners.

One article associated with the chafing dish and often mistaken for a cigar lighter is the alcohol flagon (Figs. 170a, 170b). This is a small flagon with a long spout. Most are shaped something like a small teapot but may be readily distinguished by the very long spout and spout cover which is attached by a chain and also by the knob near the handle which pumps alcohol into the "Asbestos Lamp" or burner.

College-dormitory cooking, usually after "lights out" during the Gibson Girl period, demanded a chafing dish. Countless recipes were invented, "Welsh rarebit" being a favorite. The Gorham Company and the Meridan Britannia Company both issued cook booklets of recipes for chafing-dish cookery in order to promote the sales of their silverplated chafing dishes and related table kettles and other accessories for the Sunday night tea table.

Chafing dishes were a "must" for every college girl and for every young housewife from the 1890s until World War I. While they may have lacked something in popularity between the

169. Souvenir cup from St. Louis, made by Apollo Silver Co., New York City.

VII. Silverplate for Table and Household Use   291

170. Smith, Patterson & Co. (Boston, Mass.) catalog, 1900.

No. 25.   Alcohol Flagon, $4.90
Nickel Plated.   Capacity, ¾ pint.
Airtight, pours when you press the knob on the handle.

170a. Alcohol flagon used to fill burners used with chafing dish. Smith Patterson & Co. (Boston, Mass.) catalog, 1900.

170b. Patent drawing of alcohol flagon patented by Sigmund Sternau, Lionel Strassburger, and John P. Steppe and assigned to S. Sternau & Co., Brooklyn, N.Y. Design Patent No. 37,211; Patented November 8, 1904.

171. Modern food warmer and chafing dish. Sheridan Silver Co., Taunton, Mass.

172. Meriden Britannia Co. catalog, 1867.

VII. Silverplate for Table and Household Use

173. Entree dish with heater. Sheridan Silver Co., Taunton, Mass.

174. Meriden Britannia Co. catalog, 1886.

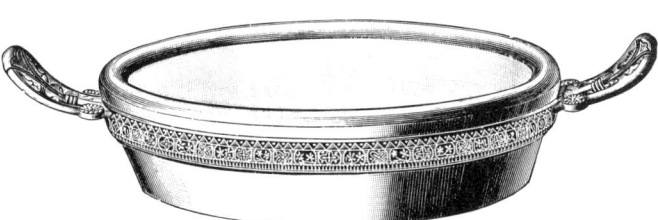

No. 84½. 9 inch, Six Half Pints, . $7.50 (METAPHOR).
No. 84.   9½ inch, Eight Half Pints, . 8.00 (MESSAGE).

No. 117.
 inch, Eight Half Pints, . . $16.00 (WITTINGLY).
 inch, Eight Half Pints, Old Silver, 17.00 (WHIRLPOOL).

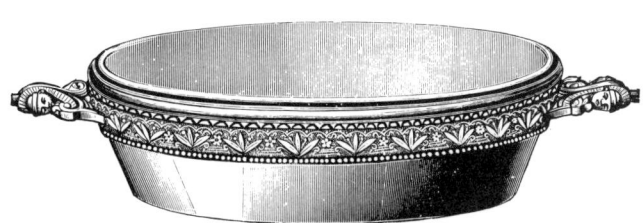

No. 82½. 9 inch, Six Half Pints, . $6.75 (MEND).
No. 82.   9½ inch, Eight Half Pints, . 7.50 (MENTAL).

175. Baking dish with porcelain liner. Made by Homan Silver Plate Co., Cincinnati, Ohio, about 1885–1890.

two World Wars, the servant shortage, which led to buffet service and a more relaxed way of entertaining, has led to new usages. The ubiquitous outdoor barbecue and a recent interest in cheese fondue have made the chafing dish once more a household necessity (Fig. 171).

Closely related to the chafing dish, and antedating it in American silverplate by at least 30 years, is the entree dish with heat lamp (Fig. 172). The Rogers Bros. Mfg. Co. catalog of 1860 carries an illustration of three different designs. Two of these were made in both 11- and 12-inch sizes and with or without hot-water dishes.

Later catalogs, with greater numbers of entree dishes, give mute testimony to the popularity of these heated dishes (Fig. 173). They are still found to be especially useful in serving buffet suppers.

Baking dishes with porcelain linings and silverplated receptacles were made with or without covers (Fig. 174). These porcelain linings are held in place by a silverplated metal rim. Only the porcelain lining goes into the oven. This is then fitted into the silverplated receptacle for serving at the table (Figs. 175, 176).

What to do with the cover at the table was neatly solved by a baking dish with a cover which slides up and is held in place on an overhead rack (Fig. 177).

Modern baking dishes have ovenproof liners of Pyrex glass or of "pyro-ceramics." Some have covers of the same material rather than the more elegant silverplated ones.

Covered vegetable dishes, some with dual-purpose covers which could double as separate dishes, date back at least as far as 1594 but those which have lock handles which may be removed from the covers to form two dishes were not made until shortly before the nineteenth century. Made originally in solid silver and in "Old Sheffield Plate," the form was readily copied by manufacturers of American silverplate and were illustrated in early catalogs (Figs. 178–180). Styles have changed very little (Fig. 181).

Some say that "tureen" was named

VII. Silverplate for Table and Household Use   295

No. 2403. Baking Dish.

176. Baking dish advertised by Rockford Silver Plate Co., Rockford, Ill. *The Keystone*, May 1903.

for Marshal Tureene of France who once used his helmet to hold soup, but a more logical derivation is from the Latin root, *terrena lanx*, "earthenware dish," for tureens were originally pottery vessels. The French *terrine*, "earthenware pot," shows more clearly the relationship to the original Latin than does our Anglicized "tureen."

When silver serving dishes with covers and handles were first made in the early part of the eighteenth century the name "tureen" was applied with no thought to its original meaning.

Tureens of the nineteenth century were measured by their capacity and varied from two "half-pints" to eight quarts (Fig. 182). Small tureens were made for oysters, gravy, and terrapin; larger ones for soup.

The long-legged look, used for tea and coffee services of the 1870s, was also applied to tureens (Fig. 183).

Later tureens were often made with low bases and had matching trays (Fig. 184).

The animal figures, used for finials, handles, and feet, may have been intended as clues to the contents of the tureens (Figs. 185–186).

No. 0368.   Patent Cover, without Spoon, $25.00.   (WHEATEN)
Capacity of China Dish, 8 half-pints.

177. Reed & Barton catalog, 1885.

No. 010.

	Plain.	Chased.
11 inch,	$30 75.	$34 50.
12 inch,	34 00.	38 25.

No. 04400.

	Plain.	Chased.
11 inch,	$29 75.	$33 50
12 inch,	33 00.	37 25.

No. 04434, Elizabethan.

	Plain.	Chased.
11 inch,	$26 75.	$31 00.
12 inch,	29 50.	33 75.

No. 1.

Plain.	Each, $18 50.
Chased.	Each, 21 75.

Same with Hot Water Dish.

Plain.	Each, $22 50.
Chased.	Each, 25 75.

178. Meriden Britannia Co. catalog, 1867.

VII. Silverplate for Table and Household Use 297

SILVER EMBOSSED VEGETABLE DISH, LOCK HANDLE.
No. 1544. 12 inch, $50.00. (LENTEN)   Oxidized, $55.00. (LEONINE)
            11 inch, 45.00. (LENS)   Oxidized, 50.00. (LENTIL)

179. Reed & Barton catalog, 1885.

OVAL VEGETABLE DISH, LOCK HANDLE.
No. 1225. 13 inch, $35.00. (LEPROUS)

180. Reed & Barton catalog, 1885.

181. Covered vegetable dish with lock handle cover. The handle may be removed and the cover used as a separate dish. Made by F. B. Rogers Silver Co., Taunton, Mass.

182. Meriden Britannia Co. catalog, 1867.

No. 1970. Embossed Old Silver.

184. Meriden Britannia Co. catalog, 1886.

185. Reed & Barton catalog, 1885.

183. Tureen made by the Meriden Britannia Co. about 1878.

300   AMERICAN SILVERPLATE

186. Reed & Barton catalog, 1885.

187. Nut bowls of the 1880s frequently had squirrels as decoration.

VII. Silverplate for Table and Household Use 301

188. Reed & Barton catalog, 1885.

189. Meriden Britannia Co. catalog, 1886.

302   AMERICAN SILVERPLATE

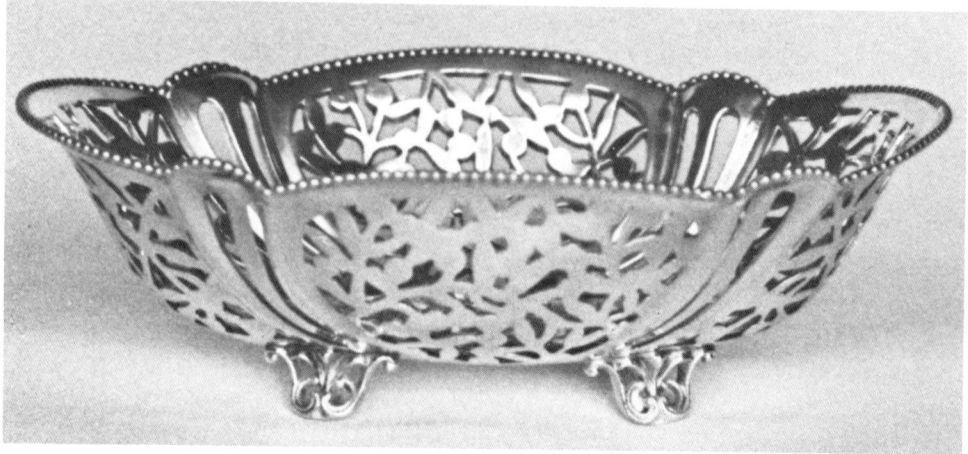

190. Bonbon dish made by Pairpoint Mfg. Co., New Bedford, Mass., about 1890.

Other vessels whose decoration definitely gives a clue to their use are the ornate nut bowls which were often made in the shape of a large coconut or acorn and frequently had a perky squirrel perched on top (Figs. 187–189).

Bonbon dishes were a form which developed in the 1890s in American silverplate. Pierced work, such as in this Pairpoint dish with its simple beaded border, were popular as were the type with bail handles (Fig. 190).

Spoon Holders

Spoon holders of the two handled "vase" type were called spoon goblets in an early Rogers Bros. Mfg. Co. catalog and may be considered an exclusively American form. While spoon trays, spoon racks, and combination sugar bowls and spoon racks and egg cups and spoon racks are found elsewhere, the vase-shaped spoon holder is an American invention. Possible confusion may arise with some English sugar basins which also have two handles and are mostly without covers. These, however, are usually more squat in shape.

One of the earliest styles found was illustrated in an 1857 Rogers Bros. Mfg. Co. catalog (Fig. 191).

A Meriden Britannia Company catalog published 10 years later offered 15 different styles of spoon holders (Fig. 192). Some of these were made to match tea services; others did not (Figs. 193, 194).

Spoon holders of the 1850s and 1860s were usually vase shaped and with two handles. Most rested on a pedestal while a few had four feet (Figs. 195–198).

While spoon holders of this type are relatively plentiful, less commonly found is the spoon rack with slots for a dozen spoons (Fig. 199).

In the 1870s fancy types of spoon holders made their appearance. Some had bells incorporated into their design (Fig. 200). Spoon racks which revolved in much the same manner as dinner castors were made but are relatively hard to find (Fig. 201).

191. Early style spoon holder. Rogers Bros. Mfg. Co. catalog, 1857.

VII. Silverplate for Table and Household Use

192. Meriden Britannia Co. catalog, 1867.

193. Spoon holders made to match tea services. *Left to right:* Meriden Silver Plate Co., about 1886; Middletown Plate Co., 1867; Meriden Britannia Co., 1867; Simpson, Hall, Miller & Co., 1878.

194. Spoon holders which were not part of tea sets. *Left to right:* Middletown Plate Co., about 1888; Rogers, Smith & Co., New Haven, Conn., between 1867 and 1871; Barbour Silver Plate Co., early 1900's; Wilcox Silver Plate Co., 1880.

195. Spoon holder made by Redfield & Rice, New York City, between 1863 and 1870.

196. Spoon holder with soldered-on disk marked "Lucius Hart Mfg. Co./Triple Plate,/New York." Lucius Hart is known to have purchased pieces "in the metal" and to have done his own plating. Pieces handled in this way are often marked with the soldered-on disks.

197. Spoon holder marked "Rogers, Smith & Co., New Haven, Conn., #1859." Identical to one illustrated in the Meriden Britannia Co. catalog, 1867.

198. Spoon holder marked "Meriden B. Company/#1879." Note the feet which are identical to cake basket (*Fig. 72, above*) and to butter dish (*Fig. 109, above*), the latter patented by John Hill.

306 AMERICAN SILVERPLATE

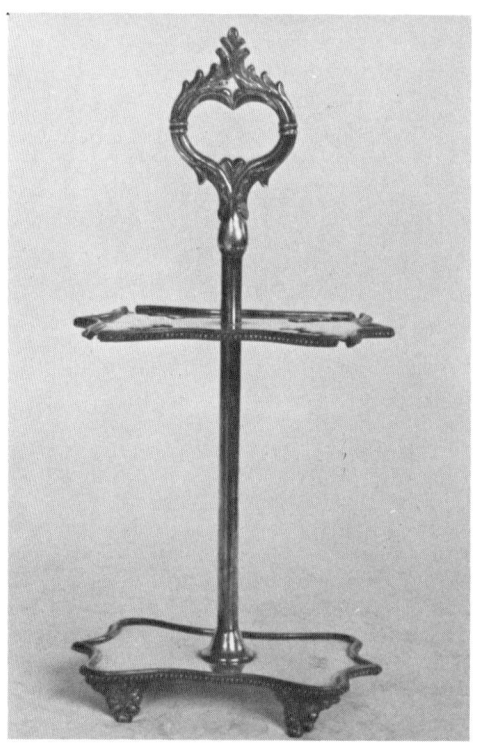

199. Spoon rack for twelve spoons. Unmarked, but it is identical to one illustrated in the Meriden Britannia Co. catalog, 1867. Goods plated on white metal were often sold without their trademark.

No. 0195. With Bell, $8.50.
           Gold-lined,   9.50.

No. 0186. With Bell, $8.50.
           Gold-lined,   9.50.

200. Reed & Barton catalog, 1877.

VII. Silverplate for Table and Household Use 307

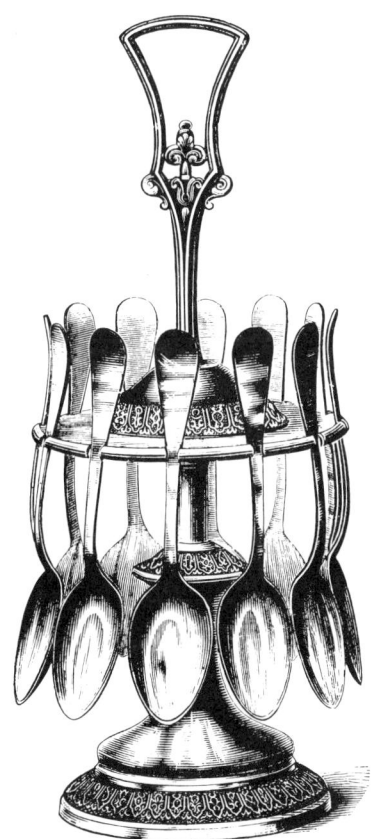

SPOON RACK.
Revolving.
No. 50. Without Spoons, $8.50.

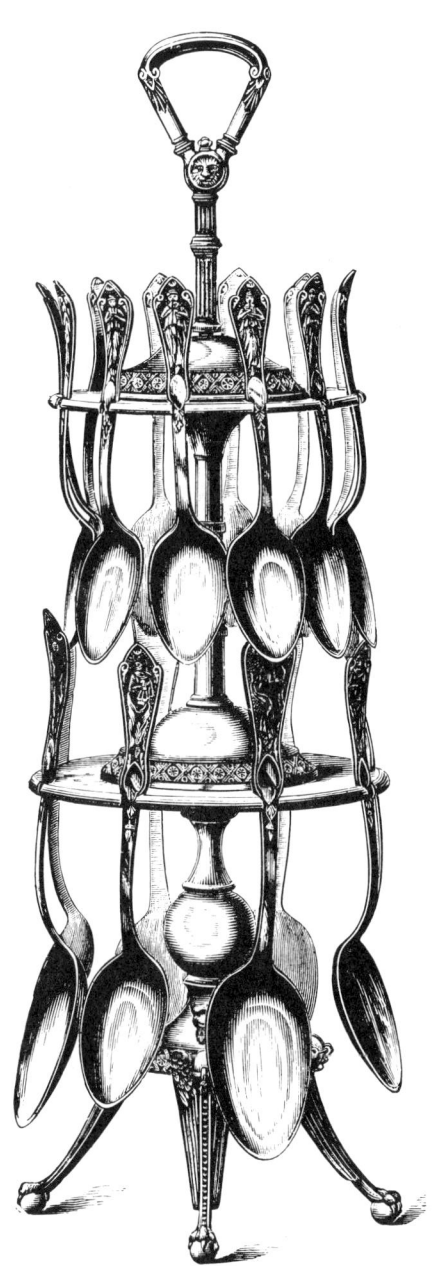

DOUBLE SPOON RACK.
Revolving.
No. 70. Without Spoons, $15.00.

201. Reed & Barton catalog, 1877.

308 AMERICAN SILVERPLATE

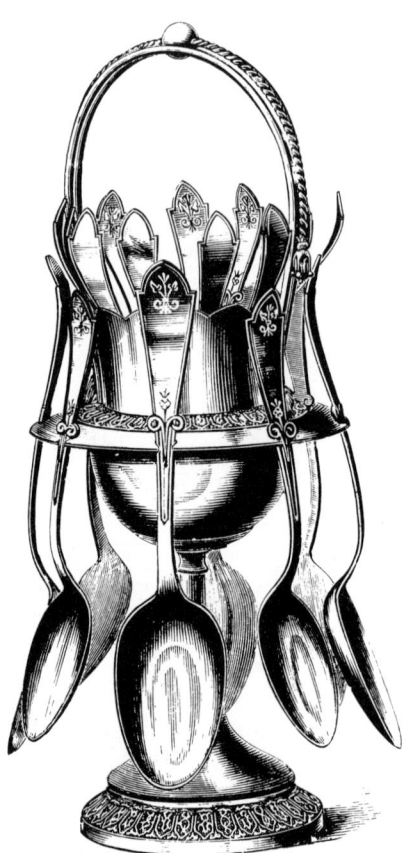

COMBINATION RACK AND SPOON CUP.
No. 60. $11.00.
Gold-lined, 12.00.

202. Reed & Barton catalog, 1877.

An unusual spoon rack is a combination rack and spoon cup with bail handle (Fig. 202). Slots on an outside rim hold eight spoons while a center cup accommodates others.

In the 1870s spoon holders were sometimes illustrated on the same page with tea services and considered parts of a complete service. Spoon holders of this type may usually be distinguished from the waste bowls, which were considered an essential part of every tea service, by their handles and by being slightly taller and more slender. There are exceptions which may be taken for sugar bowls though ordinarily American sugar bowls have covers. Even in the case of lost covers, a rim indicates where a cover once rested.

One unusual and quite rare type of spoon holder was made with a glass bowl insert in the "Tree of Life" pattern (Fig. 203).

In the 1879 catalog of the Meriden Silver Plate Company there are other unusual spoon holders, one of which is shaped like a cart (Fig. 204). Another is a tray with bail handle.

Among the double spoon holders made by the Wilcox Silver Plate Company in the 1880s, one has cups in the form of acorns (Fig. 205). The ornament

203. Rare and unusual spoon holder with glass bowl in the "Tree of Life" pattern. Made by the Meriden Britannia Co. and shown in their catalogs as early as 1879.

VII. Silverplate for Table and Household Use

204. Meriden Silver Plate Co. catalog, 1879.

205. Examples of double spoon holders: *Left:* Cups in the form of acorns. Ornament at base of handles is two squirrels. Made by Wilcox Silver Plate Co. about 1884. *Right:* Made by Wilcox Silver Plate Co. about 1880.

BELL SPOON HOLDER.
No. 287.   Gold-lined, $12.75.   (BRAIDING)

BELL SPOON HOLDER.
No. 284.   Gold-lined, $11.50.   (BRANCH)

206. Reed & Barton catalog, 1885.

VII. Silverplate for Table and Household Use   311

SPOON BOAT.

No. 1. $8.25. (BRAZE)

Gold-lined, 9.75. (BREADTH)

207. Reed & Barton catalog, 1885.

at the base of the handle is in the form of two squirrels. Oak leaves and acorns form the feet and arm supports.

The 1885 Reed & Barton catalog illustrates 45 styles of spoon holders in their regular line. Some of these match tea services. Still others intended to match tea services are not shown on these pages but are illustrated or listed with the tea sets themselves.

"Bell Spoon Holders" are among the unusual ones illustrated (Fig. 206). Another one is called a "Spoon Boat" and is shaped like a canoe (Fig. 207).

Their hotel-ware section contains spoon holders in very plain style.

The Meriden Britannia Company also made spoon holders in their regular line of silverplate in addition to those of their hotel ware. Forty-two designs were illustrated separately in their 1886 catalog while additional ones were made to match tea sets (Fig. 208). Some of the unusual designs included double ones. One spoon rack featured a call bell while another had a flower vase in the center (Figs. 209, 210).

Some spoon holders of the late 1880s reflect the more restrained type of decoration of that period (Fig. 211).

Combination sugar bowls and spoon racks first made their appearance about 1874. Five styles were illustrated by photographs in an 1874 Middletown Plate Company catalog. Two of these held only six teaspoons while the others held twelve. An especially attractive one was made by this same company (Fig. 212). The finial is a butterfly—a motif which found great favor in the 1880s and 1890s. Those with the bird finial are more common (Fig. 213).

These combination sugar bowls and spoon racks are favorites among spoon collectors who use them to display favorite spoons. They continued to be made well into the twentieth century.

Another unusual spoon holder made by the Middletown Plate Company about 1892 was in the form of an open flower blossom (Fig. 214).

Small, shallow trays for holding spoons used at the tea table date back to the time of George I. In an English painting of about 1725, which now hangs in Colonial Williamsburg, Virginia, there is such a spoon boat or tray with scalloped edges. These small trays continued to be made from time to time and in other

312 American Silverplate

208. Meriden Britannia Co. catalog, 1886.

VII. Silverplate for Table and Household Use 313

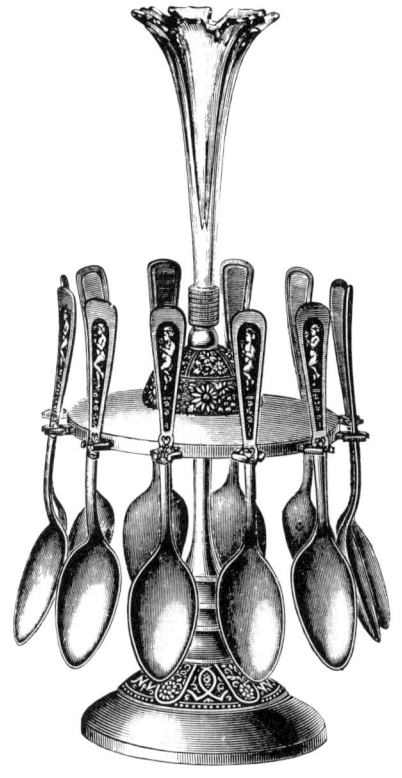

209. Meriden Britannia Co. catalog, 1886.

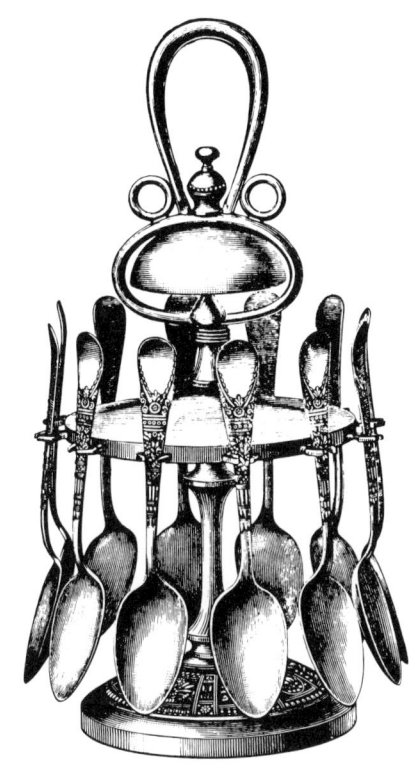

210. Meriden Britannia Co. catalog, 1886.

211. Spoon holder marked: "J. A. Eisenhardt/Balto./Md." Made about 1887–88.

212. Combination sugar bowls and spoon racks. *Left:* Middletown Plate Co., 1879; *right:* Meriden Britannia Co. (in a circle), 1896.

213. Sugar bowl and spoon holder combination made in the early twentieth century by J. Rogers Silver Co., New York City.

materials, such as porcelain and glass. Both of these materials were especially favored in the 1890s. Except when they can be identified through old catalogs, it is often difficult to be sure of their intended use.

A spoon tray made by the Meriden Britannia Company (Fig. 215) and a spoon boat made by Reed & Barton (Fig. 207), both around 1885, might not be readily identified without the catalog reference.

Spoon trays, such as the one made by E. G. Webster & Son of Brooklyn, New York, around 1895–1900, are popular with spoon collectors for the display of

214. Middletown Plate Co. catalog, 1892–93.

VII. Silverplate for Table and Household Use

215. Meriden Britannia Co. catalog, 1886.

spoons (Fig. 217). A somewhat later type was made by the Homan Silver Plate Company of Cincinnati, Ohio (Fig. 218).

In the 1880s and 1890s almost all tea services could be obtained with matching spoon holders. Soon after 1900 these spoon holders went out of style though the combination bowls and spoon holders were carried in catalogs into the 1930s.

217. Spoon tray made by E. G. Webster & Son, Brooklyn, N.Y.

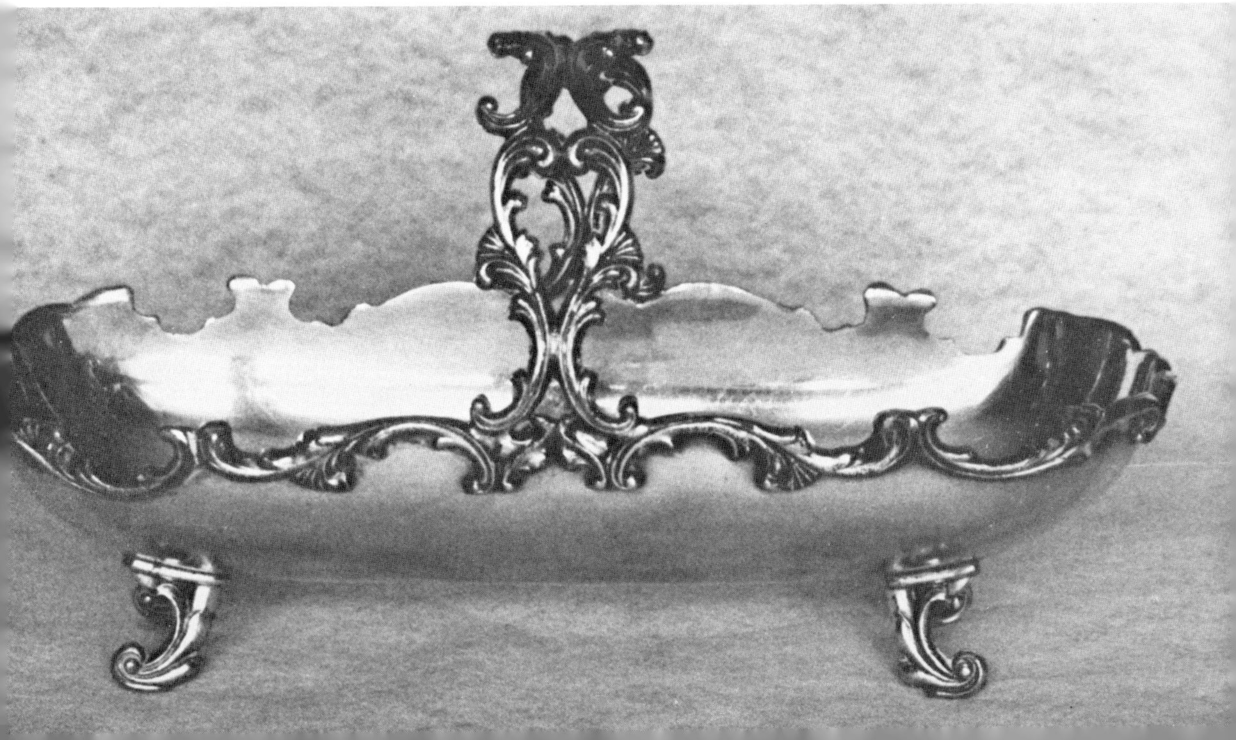

Celery Stands

The word "celery" comes from the French *céleri*, which is derived from the Greek Celery (*Apium graveolens*) is a native of Europe, Asia, and Africa, in the older parts of which it was cultivated prior to the Christian era. Believed to be the same plant as *selinon*, which is mentioned in Homer's *Odyssey*, written about 850 B.C., it is also known by many names in modern languages. These are all derived from the same root word and sound remarkably similar. The similarity of names indicates a comparatively recent and wide distribution and use of the plant.

The first recorded use of the word *céleri* is in a ninth-century poem written in France or Italy in which the medicinal uses and merits of the plant are given. In the sixteenth century, when its culture was begun in Italy and northern Europe, it was still a primitive plant and was used for medicinal purposes only.

Its first recorded use as a food was in France in 1623 where for about a hundred years it was used only as flavoring. By the middle of the seventeenth century, in France and Italy, the stalks and

218. Spoon tray marked "SHEFFIELD DESIGN/Made in U.S.A./H.M.C. EPNS WMMTS/0235/Homan Silver Plate Co."

219. Meriden Britannia Co. catalog, 1867.

VII. Silverplate for Table and Household Use

No. 60.
Decorated, $10.50 (REPLENISH).

No. 63.
Venetian Thread Glass, $8.50 (PAYABLE).
Assorted Colors.

No. 59.
Decorated, $9.50 (REFINE).
Assorted Colors.

No. 55, $8.50 (DAMSON).

No. 53, $11.00 (DANCE).
Crystal Cut.

No. 61.
Decorated, $12.50 (REFFED).
Assorted Colors.

No. 57.
al, Cut, $10.50 (REPEATER).

No. 62.
Crystal, Engraved, $11.00 (REFLAT).

No. 58.
Decorated, $10.50 (REPLACE).
Assorted Colors.

220. Meriden Britannia Co. catalog, 1880s.

318 AMERICAN SILVERPLATE

No. 225. $9.25. (ESCAPADE)

No. 215. Amberina Glass, $13.50. (ESCHEAT)

No. 200. $12.50. (ESSENTIAL)

No. 190. $10.00. (ESPECIAL)

No. 150. $16.00. (LIMITED)
Gold and Oxidized, 19.00. (LIMNER)

No. 290. $12.50. (LIMP)

No. 140. $14.00. (LIMPID)

No. 280. $13.50. (LINDEN)

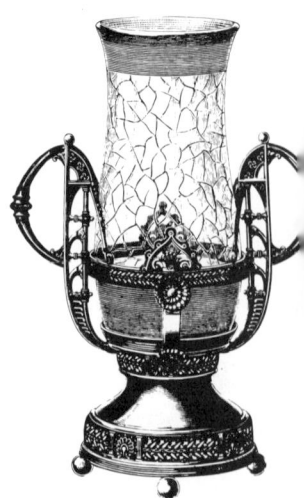

No. 195. $12.75. (ESSAY)

221. Reed & Barton catalog, 1885.

VII. SILVERPLATE FOR TABLE AND HOUSEHOLD USE 319

$6.50. (LIKENESS)
Engraved Glass. 7.00. (LILAC)

CELERY BASKET.
No. 230. $12.75. (ESPOUSAL)

No. 270. $7.50. (LILY)
Gold Finish, 8.50. (LIMB)

No. 240. $7.75. (LIMBER)

No. 250. $13.00. (LIME)

No. 260. $9.75. (LIMIT)

No. 220. $9.00. (ESCHEW)

No. 210. $16.00. (ESSENCE)

No. 175. $12.00. (ESQUIRE)

221 continued.

leaves were sometimes eaten with an oil dressing.

Improvement of the wild type began in the late seventeenth and early eighteenth centuries in Italy, France, and England. In the mid-eighteenth century in Sweden, wealthy families enjoyed the luxury of celery that had been stored in cellars. From that time on, its use spread rapidly. Though it is not known which group of colonists brought it to this country, four cultivated varieties were being grown here in 1806.

Prior to the early 1940s it was thought necessary to blanch celery to remove the green color and bitter taste. Consumer acceptance of the Pascal and Utah types, which remain green when ready for eating, has permitted producers to discontinue blanching.

Commercial production of celery in the United States began in the valley of the Kalamazoo River, near Kalamazoo, Michigan, in the 1880s. Because it is a highly perishable product, celery growing is a specialized operation.

It is appropriate that a vegetable with such an historic past should have had special containers designed for its service.

Celery stands appeared in catalogs of the silverplate manufacturers in the 1860s (Fig. 219). By the 1880s the number of styles presented was considerably greater (Fig. 220); they assumed lesser importance in the 1890s. By 1900 very few were illustrated.

Celery stands and baskets are of two general types—the tall stands and low rectangular trays of cut glass set in footed silverplated frames (Fig. 221). The tall stands outnumber the low trays by about seventeen to one in the early catalogs consulted. In later ones the ratio was five to three. At the present time, celery is most often served in low oval or rectangular dishes.

Celery stands are sought especially by glass collectors for the variety of glassware used. Glass in the earliest ones seems to have been plain, cut, and engraved clear glass. "Ruby, Decorated," "Venetian Thread, Assorted Colors," "Crystal Cut," "Crystal Engraved," and "Decorated, Assorted Colors," are the designations mentioned in catalogs of the 1880s.

CHAPTER VIII

Small Silverwares and Novelties

Self-Pouring Teapots and Coffeepots

Self-pouring teapots and coffeepots, or pump pots as they are now sometimes called, were marketed by Paine, Diehl & Company, commission merchants in Philadelphia (Fig. 1). Paine, Diehl & Company were not manufacturers, but had the pots made by manufacturers of silverplate under Royle's Patent of 1888 (Fig. 2). They were not listed in Philadelphia city directories after 1895, so the pots in existence presumably were made between 1888 and 1895.

The term "pump pot" is apt. According to their advertisements, "By simply lifting the lid and shutting it down, the coffee or tea runs out of the spout at will. It is a neat adaptation of pneumatics. . . ."

These self-pouring pots were made by various manufacturers, in several styles, and in three materials—white metal, silverite (a composite of tin, nickel, platinum, etc., according to the advertisements), and silverplate, with the latter being the most expensive.

The example illustrated is one of several styles made by the Meriden Britannia Company. It is now displayed in the offices of the International Silver Company.

Dainty Devices for the Proper Eating of the Orange

A patented orange peeler, complete with illustrations for its proper use was shown in the 1879 catalog of Holmes, Booth & Haydens of Waterbury, Connecticut (Figs. 3, 4). With its strange, curved blade, it would almost defy identification without the catalog pages for reference.

George Clark Edwards of the Holmes & Edwards Silver Company of Bridgeport, Connecticut, on April 22, 1890, patented a new design for an orange spoon (Fig. 5). The leading feature of the design was the shape of the bowl which was described as being a triangle. There was the additional notation that any suitable handle may be used in connection with the bowl.

Rogers & Bro. made a new type of orange peeler in table and pocket sizes and assorted patterns and finishes (Fig. 6). The table size was put up six in a plush-lined paper box while the pocket size was packaged separately in a leather sheath in a paper box. These were patented January 5, 1893. Advertisements carried directions for use, including an illustration of the proper method of holding in the hand.

Whether it was the bumper crop of oranges produced in 1894 or the "orange cure" which necessitated the consumption by the patient of anywhere from one to three dozen oranges daily, we do not know, but something inspired several silver manufacturers all in the same year to produce a number of "dainty devices for the proper eating of this delicious and seasonable fruit."

In 1894 the Wilcox Silver Plate Company of Meriden, Connecticut, introduced two new orange cups, "differing in many particulars from any others so

1. Self-pouring or pump pot marketed by Paine, Diehl & Co., Philadelphia. The example illustrated is one of several styles made by the Meriden Britannia Co. from 1888 to 1895.

2. Paine, Diehl & Co. "flyer" explaining the operation of their self-pouring teapots and coffeepots.

Illustrating the flow from a Self-Pouring Pot.

P. D. & CO.

SELF-POURING
TEA AND COFFEE POTS.

NO BURNT HANDS,
    LIFTING POT,
        ACHING ARMS,
            SOILED CLOTHES.
SAVES 25% OF TEA.
    THE SPOUT CAN'T STOP UP.

"TURNS DRUDGERY INTO PLEASURE."

To be seen at

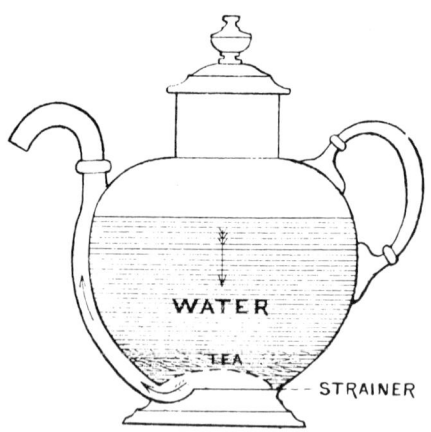

Every lady knows that the best tea is amongst the leaves.

The Self-Pouring Pot pours from the bottom beneath the leaves, consequently every drop of water has to pass through the leaves. The tea leaf is porous like a sponge and lying as it does directly over the strainer, the water passes not only around but **through** the leaf, extracting them to the utmost, making a saving of from 25 to 50 per cent. **The spout can't stop up.**

Read Tea Merchant's Opinion—An Expert.

3. Holmes, Booth & Haydens catalog, 1879.

HOLMES, BOOTH & HAYDENS, 21

ORANGE PEELER.

PATENTED AUGUST, 1879.

In offering the above ingenious device to the Trade, it being the only one ever invented, warrants the manufacturer in believing it will fill a want the Orange-loving public have long felt. Who has not experienced the necessity for something of the kind, when compelled to peel this luscious fruit (for want of a better means) with thumb and fingers?

IT CERTAINLY IS AN ARTICLE that, soon as known, will be recognized as a necessity in every first-class Hotel, Restaurant and Private Family, consequently must have a large and ready sale, especially in all orange-growing countries.

It is made of Nickel Silver, extra heavily plated, and warranted in every respect. Price, $12.00 per dozen.

Discount to the Trade.

4. Holmes, Booth & Haydens catalog, 1879.

22 HOLMES, BOOTH & HAYDENS

FIRST OPERATION.

HOLMES, BOOTH & HAYDENS. 23

SECOND OPERATION.

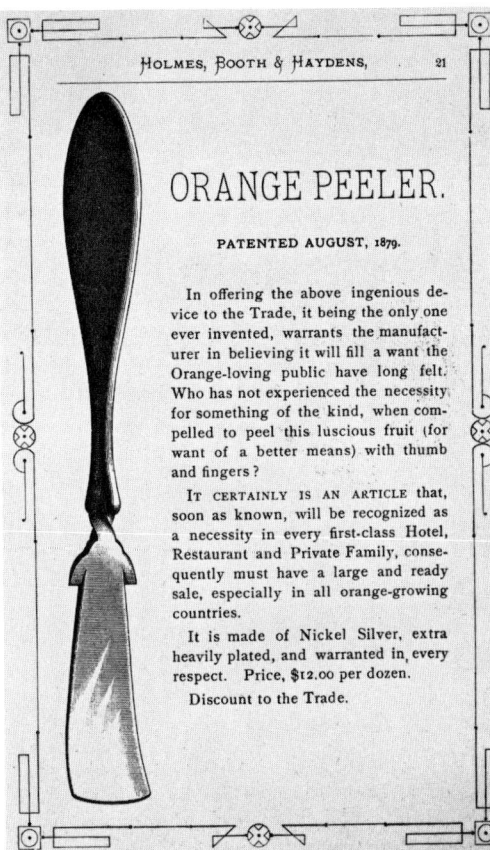

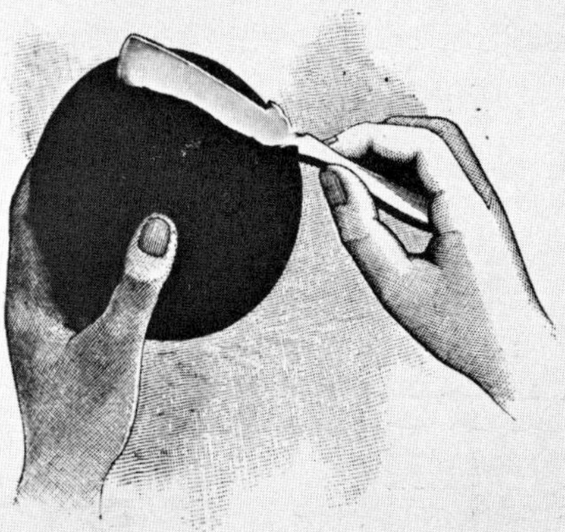

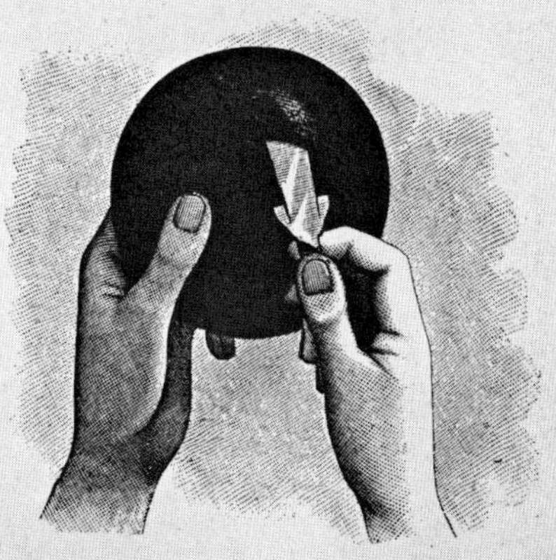

324 American Silverplate

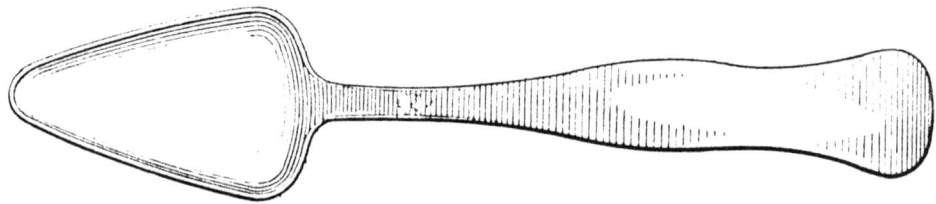

5. Orange spoon with triangle-shaped bowls, designed by George Clark Edwards, Holmes & Edwards Silver Co. Design Patent No. 16,770; Patented April 22, 1890.

6. Rogers & Bro. advertisement of their new practical novelty, an orange peeler. Patented January 5, 1893.

A Practical Novelty.

·The <u>Orange Peeler</u> hereon illustrated is conceded by all who have used it to be perfect in its operation, neatly removing the peel without soiling the fingers.

Made in table and pocket sizes, assorted patterns and finishes. Table size put up six in plush lined paper box; pocket size each in leather sheath in paper box.

PRICE FOR EACH SIZE $6.00 PER DOZEN.

Special Discount to the Trade.

Directions for Using.

Hold the Peeler in the right hand, Orange in left, with thumb of right hand on orange as shown in cut; with flat face of hook placed square on orange, draw with pressure enough to insert hook in and under peel, revolve orange in left hand, drawing peeler in opposite direction until peel is cut into as many sections as desired, when it may be easily removed by inserting back of peeler under loose point of section. The blade on back of peeler is useful for removing the soft white under skin.

Rogers & Brother,
16 Cortlandt Street,

New York.

VIII. Small Silverware and Novelties

Two New Orange Cups.

The Wilcox Silver Plate Company, of Meriden, Conn., has produced two new orange cups, differing in many particulars from any others so far shown. Both are mounted on stands, and one is plain, re-

taining the half orange simply by the suction created by pressing the fruit into the cup. The other has a peculiarly formed

prong for the purpose of engaging the rind of the fruit and retaining it in position. The accompanying illustrations disclose the characteristics of the two pieces. They are made in silver plate.

7. Two cups designed to hold oranges; made by Wilcox Silver Plate Co., 1894. *Jewelers' Weekly*, January 31, 1894.
8. Orange knife with saw back, introduced by Rogers & Bro. *The Jewelers' Circular*, December 12, 1894.

far shown." Both were mounted on stands (Fig. 7). One was plain, retaining the half orange simply by the suction created by pressing the fruit into the cup. The other had a peculiarly formed prong for the purpose of engaging the rind of the fruit and retaining it in position.

According to a contemporary account,

> Among the most practical and desirable articles produced for the proper eating of the orange is the orange knife illustrated here [Fig. 8], and first introduced by Rogers & Brother, the makers of the celebrated (Star) Rogers & Bro. A1. brand of electro silver plated flatware. The essential feature of the device is the saw back; the cutting edge is retained, making the knife adapted to the requirements of an all round fruit knife. The handles come either in pearl, ivoride or plated silver. The firm having made a great sale of this knife as well as of their orange sets, comprising 1 knife and 1 spoon, or 6 knives and 6 spoons, put up in plush lined boxes.

Rogers & Hamilton Company of Waterbury, Connecticut, also produced their version of the orange spoon (Fig. 9). They advertised that the peculiar construction of the bowl yields a shape which fits the carpel of the orange perfectly, remove cleanly and deftly every particle of pulp and gives great strength to that portion of the spoon at the junction of the bowl and handle where this is most desirable. They were made in the "Majestic" (illustrated), "Monarch," "Shell," and "Cardinal" flatware patterns.

A dainty set put out by the Meriden Britannia Company with the "1847 Rogers Bros." trademark was the "Savoy" orange spoon and knife (Fig. 10). The serrated knife blade was designed to be "useful for dividing oranges into sections

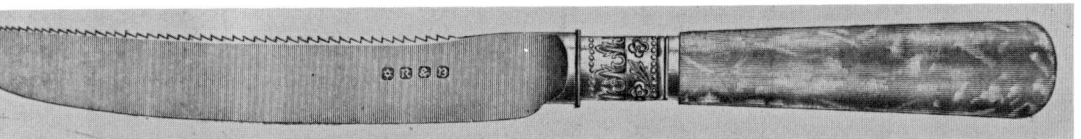

9. Orange spoon made by Rogers & Hamilton Co. *The Jewelers' Circular,* December 12, 1894.

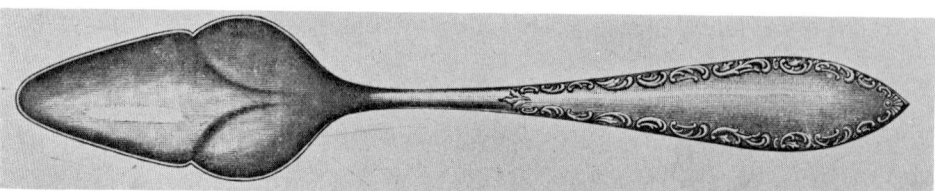

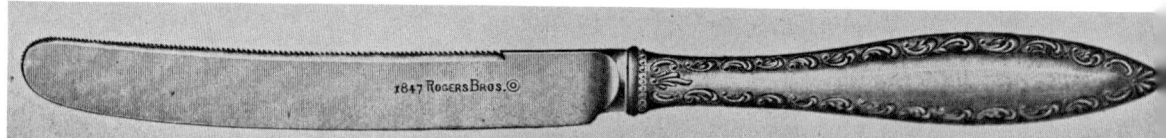

10. Orange spoon and knife with serrated back blade, made by the Meriden Britannia Co. *The Jewelers' Circular,* December 12, 1894.

and the artistic shape of the spoon's bowl is excellently adapted to the purpose for which intended."

The orange holder made by the Pairpoint Manufacturing Company of New Bedford, Massachusetts, had two spear-like attachments on the sides of the bowl (Fig. 11). These were designed to penetrate the skin and hold the orange in place. They were attached to the orange cup by chains in order that they might not be lost when not in use.

Salts

The term "saltcellar," applied to a small container for holding salt at the table, was derived from the term "salte-seller," an erroneous spelling of the name by which the vessel was known in the latter part of the fifteenth century. "Seller" is a variant of the earlier

ORANGE CUP.   PAIRPOINT MFG. CO.

11. Orange holder made by the Pairpoint Mfg. Co. *The Jewelers' Circular,* December 12, 1894.

VIII. Small Silverware and Novelties 327

salsar, salare, and *salere* or *selere,* all derived from the Latin *salarius,* through the old French *salière,* or "salt-holder." Our word "salary" was derived from the Latin *salarium,* or money which was allowed to soldiers for the purchase of salt.

Salt is an essential part of man's diet, not only for the added flavor to foods, but also so that the loss through perspiration may be replaced in order to maintain the proper body chemical balance.

Formerly obtained principally through the evaporation of sea water, salt was an expensive commodity. Because of its essential nature and its scarcity, salt was held in high esteem and figured in sacred rites along with bread. Therefore, the container for salt at the table was fittingly an object of considerable importance.

The great or standing salt was the most important single article of domestic plate in the Middle Ages. During the Elizabethan times smaller versions were used. By the close of the seventeenth century the standing salt had passed out of fashion. The small "trencher salts," so named from being set near individual trenchers or plates, became the style as salt became more easily procurable. The tendency away from common eating vessels also aided this shift. Salt spoons seem to have been introduced about this time. Salts of this period were often fitted with blue glass liners.

12. Meriden Britannia Co. catalog, 1867.

In early American silverplate, salts were usually round, varying in diameter from about two and a half inches to three inches (Fig. 12). Low pedestal bases or three short legs were the usual supports. Decoration was usually in the form of a gadroon edge, beading, engine turning, engraving, chasing, and, of course, the lion mask applied just above each foot. Most were available with gilt linings or ruby glass.

One magnificent salt made by the Gorham Company bears three applied medallion heads (Fig. 13). This piece was obviously treasured since it was handed down twice. The inscription reads, "C. T. G. 1906 from J. G. from C. T. G. 1866."

13. Large silverplated salt dish bearing three applied medallion heads; made by the Gorham Mfg. Co. Diameter 2 7/8 in.

328 AMERICAN SILVERPLATE

No. 39, . . . $3.75

No. 41, . . . $3.00

No. 40, . . . $3.50

No. 8, . . . $2.75
Gilt, . . . 3.00

No. 14, . . . $3.00

No. 36, . . . $4.50

No. 15, . . . $4.00

No. 12. Gilt, . . $3.00

No. 9, . . . $2.25

No. 10, . . . $3.00

No. 11. Ruby Lining, Gilt, $3.00

14. Meriden Britannia Co. catalog, 1877.

Collectors and antique dealers alike have shown a tendency to use the term "master salt" to apply to large salt dishes and to large size salt spoons. This is incorrect. These large salt dishes and spoons are just that—large size as opposed to individual salts and spoons, and are intended for use at the table by more than one person.

Containers with pierced lids for casting pepper were found forming the upper parts of bell-shaped salts of the Elizabethan and Jacobean periods. Casters as separate articles in English silver appear not to have been generally made before the latter part of the seventeenth century. The first American examples were made about the beginning of the eighteenth century.

Early casters, or shakers as they are sometimes called, were often made in sets of two or three, for the service of mustard, pepper, and other spices. In sets of three, one was larger and intended for sugar. These containers for "casting" condiments on food were often combined with cruets for oil and vinegar and fitted into caster or cruet frames. During the middle of the eighteenth century the two casters were used for Jamaica and Cayenne pepper, some sets also containing an additional caster for sugar or salt.

American silverplate catalogs of the 1860s show only pepper casters, or pepper boxes, as they are called, and sugar sifters.

Catalogs of the 1870s contain salt dishes of glass set in silverplated frames. These are made in diverse shapes, some of the fluted shell shapes being especially attractive (Fig. 14). Others, entirely of silverplate and gold lined, were in the shape of broken egg shells, small tubs, and round bowls, the latter being decorated with cast and applied animals (Fig. 15). These could be purchased in pairs in "Fine Morocco Case" with spoons.

The development of salt shakers, as distinguished from salt cellars or open salts, was dependent on several other developments. One of the first of these was the invention of threads in the glass of screw-neck bottles. The greater number of salt shakers were made of glass and had metal tops. This innovation was patented by John Mason, best known for fruit jars, on November 30, 1858. The earliest recorded salt shaker with molded screw threads in the glass has "Pat'd Sept. 15, 1863" molded in the glass near the base.

The name "Shaker salt" was used in magazines and by glass manufacturers as early as 1884 to differentiate between shakers and open salt dishes. And, in 1890 the term "salt shaker" was first used in a description of a patent. "Shaker" had been commonly used to apply to a vessel in which drinks were mixed so the shift in names required several years in order to come into common use.

In the 1885 Reed & Barton catalog the term "salt shaker" is used in the Index, but on the pages where these articles are illustrated they are called "Salts and Peppers." It was not until the mid-1890s that the term came into general use. While the name "saltceller" is usually applied to open salt dishes, it was still frequently applied to salt shakers until after the turn of the century.

Other inventions and improvements which aided the development of salt shakers were the many devices to prevent the caking of salt; the invention of the American lever-press for making pressed glass in about the 1820s and the improvements in lime glass in the 1860s, both of which helped to lower the cost of glassmaking; finding of corrosion resistant materials for containers and tops; and improvements in the salt itself.

One of the many inventions to prevent caking of salt was the "salt dredge" patented in April 1885. A combined agitator and clearer, it consisted of a spindle with breaking heads. An extension from the upper head kept that head from entering the neck of the bottle and causing clogging.

Two "Pepper Boxes" which are actually shakers, are illustrated in the Meriden Britannia Company catalog for August 1, 1867.

By the 1880s, individual shakers for pepper and salt were made in the shape of animals, birds, thimbles, "Kate Greenaway type" of children, and other whimsical figures. The Meriden Britannia Company advertised an owl pepper box in 1871. In the 1882 catalog of the Wm. Rogers Mfg. Co. an owl pepper box was shown also. The Meriden Silver Plate Company catalog of 1884 carried a number of whimsical pepper and salt shakers (Fig. 16). The Meriden Britannia Company, in their 1886 catalog, illustrated peppers in the shape of animals, birds, an acorn, and "Kate Greenaway type" children (Fig. 17).

Others were made in more conventional shapes such as baluster, inverted pear, and truncated cones. Table salts of heavy plain or cut glass were set in

330 AMERICAN SILVERPLATE

No. 28.
Gold Lined, ... per pair, $6.00
With Fine Morocco Case and Spoons, per pair, 10.50

No. 29.
Gold Lined, ... per pair, $6.50
With Fine Morocco Case and Spoons, per pair, 10.75

No. 34. SALT AND MUSTARD SET.
Gold Lined, ... $9.00
With Fine Morocco Case and Spoons, . . 14.75

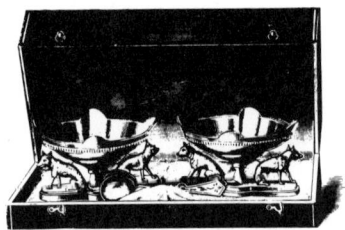

No. 27.
Gold Lined, ... per pair, $6.00
With Fine Morocco Case and Spoons, per pair, 10.60

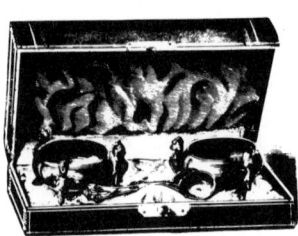

No. 18.
Gold Lined, ... per pair, $4.50
With Fine Morocco Case and Spoons, per pair, 8.50

15. Meriden Britannia Co. catalog, 1877.

VIII. SMALL SILVERWARE AND NOVELTIES 331

No. 784.	No. 779.	No. 765.	No. 781.	No. 778.	No. 780.
$2.00. (STRIDE)	Silver, $1.75. (HOUND)	Silver, $2.25. (HOOD)	Silver, $2.00. (HUCKSTER)	Silver, $1.50. (HOSTILE)	Silver, $1.00. (HOWITZER)
2.50. (STRIFT)	Old Silver, 2.00. (HOUR)	Oxidized, 2.50. (HOOK)	Gilt, 2.25. (HUDDLE)	Gilt, 1.75. (HOSTLER)	Gilt, 1.25. (HOWL)
3.00. (STRING)	Old Sil. & Sil., 2.25. (HOUSE)	Gilt, 2.75. (HOOF)		Old Silver, 1.75. (HOTEL)	
	Old Sil. & Gilt, 2.50. (HOVEL)			Old Sil. & Gilt, 2.00. (HOTSPUR)	

 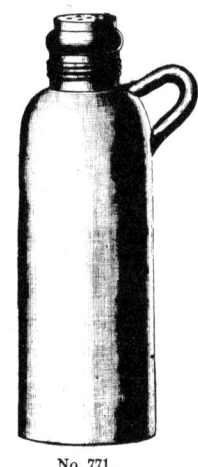   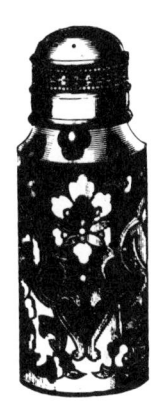 

No. 773.	No. 771.	No. 774.	No. 772.	No. 762.	No. 785.
$1.50. (HORRID)	Gilt Top, $2.25. (HORNET)	Silver, $1.50. (HORSE)	Gilt Top, $2.50. (HORRIBLE)	Longwy, $1.00. (HONEST)	Silver, $2.50. (STROKE)
Top, 1.75. (HORRIFY)	Hammered, 2.50. (SPARK)	Gilt, 1.75. (HOSE)	XX Gilt, 3.25. (TOKEN)		Gilt, 3.00. (STROLL)
	Hammered, Applied and Gilt, 3.00. (SPARROW)				XX Gilt, 3.50. (STRONG)

16. Meriden Silver Plate Co. catalog, 1884.

silverplated frames. Bail handles had an attachment for hanging a small salt spoon (Fig. 18).

Salts, peppers, and sugar sifters were illustrated in Reed & Barton's 1885 catalog. Conventional shapes as well as whimsical animals are found there. Especially interesting are the patented "Self-righting" sets made in the shapes of dogs and cats or acorns (Fig. 19). Their presumably weighted, rounded bases would keep them upright.

Open salt dishes were made of clear, frosted, or ruby glass set in silverplated frames (Fig. 20). An unusual one was a "China-lined" salt on a turtle base (Fig. 21).

Salt and pepper shakers of the 1880s were of plain, cut, engraved, or enameled glass. Decoration on the enameled shakers was in floral designs, birds, scenery, or geometric figures. Others that are quite appealing have "Mary Gregory type" decoration (Fig. 22). Pronged agitators inside are to keep the salt free-flowing.

These decorated glass salt and pepper shakers are eagerly sought by collectors.

332 AMERICAN SILVERPLATE

No. 70.
Silver, . . $1.00 (CURE).
X Gilt, . . 1.25 (CURDLE).

No. 67.
Silver, . . $1.00 (COUNTERPLOT).
Silver, Gilt Cap, 1.25 (COUNTERSIGN).

No. 68.
Silver, . . $1.00 (COUN
Oxidized and Gilt, 1.25 (COUN
Gilt, . . 1.50 (COUN

No. 71.
Silver, . . $2.00 (CURBY).
X Gilt, . . 2.25 (CURTAIL).

No. 69.
Silver, . . $2.00 (CURRICLE).
X Gilt, . . 2.50 (CURRIER).

No. 04. Pepper or Salt.
Nickel Silver.
Silver Top, . . $1.25 (COU
Gilt Top, . . 1.50 (COU

No. 72.
Old Silver, . . $2.25 (CURE).
X Gilt, . . 2.75 (CURFEW).
X Gilt, Oxidized, 3.00 (CURIOUS).

No. 65.
Silver, . . $2.00 (COUNTERPOISE).
Gilt, . . 2.50 (COUNTERPART).

No. 66.
Silver, . . $2.00 (COUNSEL).
Gilt, . . 2.50 (COUNTENANCE).

No. 73.
Old Silver, . . $2.25 (CURL).
X Gilt, . . 2.75 (CURLEW).
X Gilt, Oxidized, 3.00 (CURRANT).

17. Meriden Britannia Co. catalog, 1886.

VIII. Small Silverware and Novelties 333

18. Meriden Britannia Co. catalog, 1886.

21. Reed & Barton catalog, 1885.

19. Reed & Barton catalog, 1885.

20. Reed & Barton catalog, 1885.

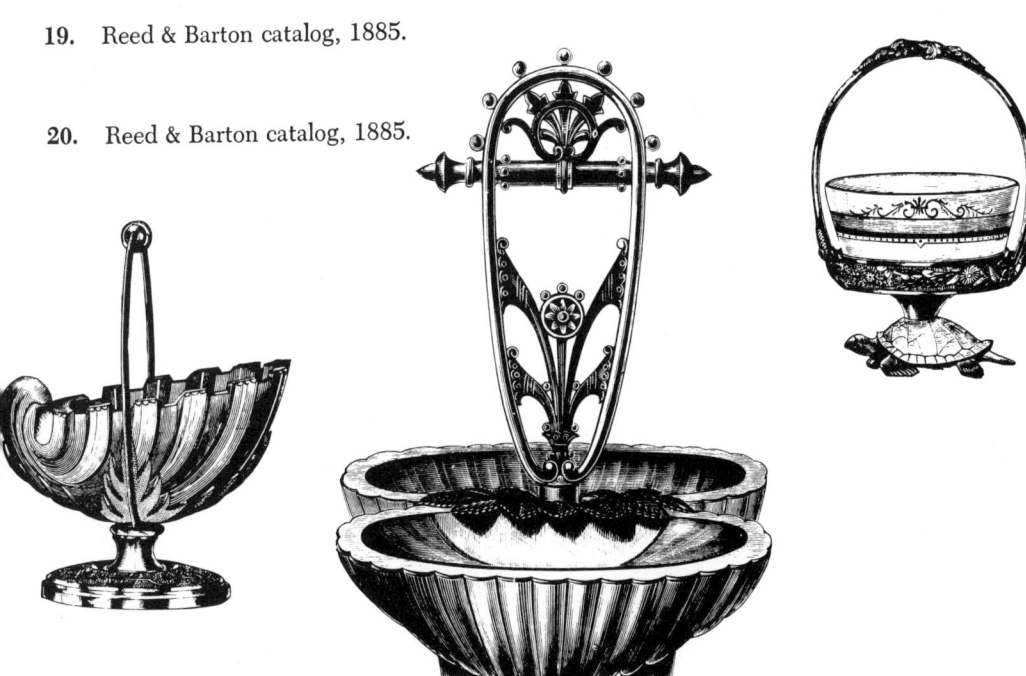

22. Reed & Barton catalog, 1885.

Spoon Warmers

Spoon warmers are a form that developed in English silverplate during the Victorian era. Fairly numerous there, they were made in the shape of nautilus shells, clam shells, buoys, sauce boats, helmets, hunting horns, coconuts, pumpkins, eggs set on rock-like bases, and in more conventional shapes such as oval boxes.

Spoon warmers were filled with hot water and placed on the table to warm the spoons to be used for porridge and also to warm gravy ladles.

They have often been mistaken for sugar bowls or jam containers. Most have a hinged lid with a cut-out portion to accommodate one or more spoons. Others have a fixed cover with an opening cut out in a double cyma curve.

Extremely rare in American silverplate, the spoon warmer illustrated was made by Reed & Barton about 1910 (Fig. 23). It differs from English examples examined in having scroll feet in place of the more usual rock-like base.

Napkin Rings

Napkin rings, an essential feature of every Victorian dining room, are said to have been derived from "nefs," which go back to the fourteenth century. These vessels, made in the form of sailing ships, were of silver or silver-gilt and were where the napkins of royalty or of the lord and lady of the manor were kept. Knives and other table utensils, the goblet and the salt used by the master of the house were kept there also, but chiefly it was an ornament which reflected the affluence of its owner. Nefs were of Continental, not English, origin.

Until the introduction of forks for table use by individuals in the seventeenth century there would have been little use for napkin rings. Food was eaten with the fingers which were washed frequently during meals. Servants brought ewers of water and basins for washing. Napkins, considerably

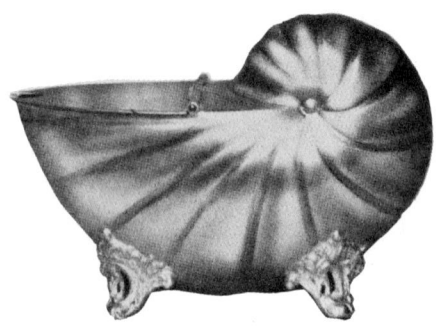

23. Spoon warmer made by Reed & Barton about 1910–11. Extremely rare in American silverplate. Advertised in Reed & Barton catalogs about 1911.

VIII. Small Silverware and Novelties 335

No. 1005.   Per dozen, $6.00.
" 1000. Plain. "   " 4.50.

No. 410.   Per dozen, $9.00.

No. 1025.   Per dozen, $7.00.
Gold-lined,   "   " 10.00.

No. 966.   Per dozen, $9.00.
Gold-lined,   "   " 12.00.

No. 1126.   Per dozen, $18.00.
Fancy Gilt,   "   " 24.00.

No. 1088.   Per dozen, $10.00.
Gold-lined,   "   " 13.00.

No. 386.   Per dozen, $10.50.
Gold-lined,   "   " 13.50.

No. 1194.   Per dozen, $27.00.
Gilt or Oxidized Figure,   "   " 33.00.

24-25. Reed & Barton catalog, 1877.

336 AMERICAN SILVERPLATE

No. 945.   Per dozen, $14.00.
Fancy Gilt, "   "   19.00.

No. 625.   Per dozen, $12.00.
Gold-lined, "   "   16.00.

No. 650.   Per dozen, $10.00.
Gold-lined, "   "   15.00.

No. 1100.   Per dozen, $12.00.
Gold-lined, "   "   15.00.

No. 1185.   Per dozen, $30.00.
Oxidized or Fancy Gilt Figure, "   "   36.00.

No. 1175.   Per dozen, $27.00.
Oxidized or Fancy Gilt Figure, "   "   33.00.

26–27. Reed & Barton catalog, 1877.

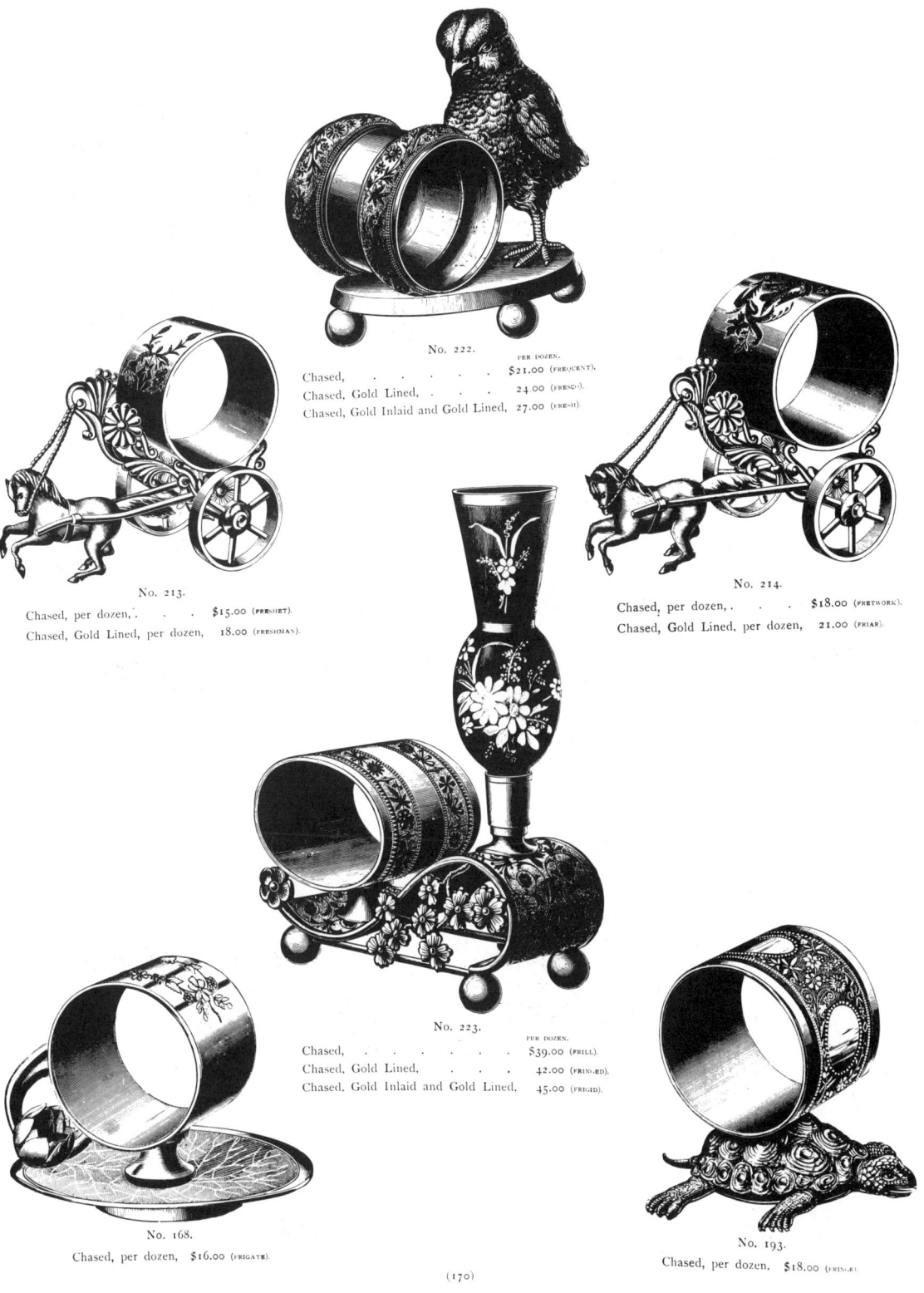

28. Meriden Britannia Co. catalog, 1882.

338   AMERICAN SILVERPLATE

No. 211.
Chased, per dozen, $18.00 (FRISK).

No. 212.
Chased, per dozen, $18.00 (FRISKY).

No. 194.
Chased, per dozen, $21.00 (FROCK).

No. 195.
Chased, per dozen, $21.00 (FROG).

No. 219.
Chased, per dozen, $33.00 (FRONTAL).

No. 159.
Silver Satin, per dozen, $24.00 (FROLIC).

No. 200.
Chased, per dozen, $21.00 (FROND).

29. Meriden Britannia Co. catalog, 1882.

larger than we now use, ordinarily were treated as towels and were removed after use.

Paintings through the centuries show napkins in use but napkin rings made their first appearance in literature in 1838 in *Work-woman's Guide*, a magazine devoted to needlework. Here directions were given for knitted "checked napkin rings" to be stiffened with wire or buckram. Therefore napkin rings may be considered a product of the Victorian age.

The Meriden Britannia Company catalog of 1860 first listed three styles of napkin rings but did not illustrate them. The August 1, 1867, issue of that company's catalog illustrates 15 designs. These were rings whose decoration consisted of beading, engine-turning, engraving, and applied medallions.

The first patent for napkin rings was issued in 1869.

By 1877 the Meriden Britannia Company illustrated 40 different styles on six pages. Of these, 19 had figures or raised ornaments, these being shown for the first time. The Reed & Barton catalog for 1877 devoted four pages to illustrations of 51 different designs of napkin rings, 18 of which might be classified as figurals.

The Meriden Britannia Company catalog for 1886 assigned seven pages to napkin rings, 35 of which were figurals and 51 were round, rectangular, or triangular bands. The 1885 Reed & Barton catalog devoted ten and a half pages to its 43 figural napkin rings and 86 round, square, or triangular bands.

The numbers in succeeding catalogs fell off sharply near the turn of the century and disappeared almost entirely when they were supplanted by celluloid ones in the early 1900s.

While plain, round napkin rings would undoubtedly hold a napkin efficiently, it is the figural ones which appeal to today's collectors. They were first designed for the children of Victorian days who were taught to roll up their

30. Simpson, Hall, Miller & Co. (Wallingford, Conn.) catalog, 1878.

napkins properly and put them in their napkin holders. Few of the figurals now serve that purpose but they do bring delight to adult collectors.

Figural napkin rings are strictly American in origin. Animals, such as cats, dogs, chickens, rabbits, squirrels, goats, birds, turtles, butterflies, ponies, and dolphins are just a few of the motifs used. Children at play comprised another favorite motif, especially those seemingly inspired by the figures created by Kate Greenaway and illustrated in her books, *Kate Greenaway Birthday Book* and *Under the Window*.

Napkin rings with small glass bud vases attached are quite rare today. They are often sought for the glass vase, which is usually hand enamelled.

Most large manufacturers of silver-

VIII. SMALL SILVERWARE AND NOVELTIES 341

32. "Boy on a Dolphin" napkin ring made by the Meriden Britannia Co.

31. A group of figural napkin rings by various makers.

plated wares featured figural napkin rings in their catalogs. The Meriden Britannia Company, Meriden Silver Plate Company, Wilcox Silver Plate Company, Middletown Plate Company, and Simpson, Hall, Miller & Company, all of which later became part of the International Silver Company, made them in the Meriden, Connecticut, area.

In addition to Reed & Barton, already mentioned, napkin rings were made by James W. Tufts, Boston, Massachusetts; Homan Manufacturing Company, Cincinnati, Ohio; Pairpoint Manufacturing Company, New Bedford, Massachusetts; Derby Silver Company, Derby, Connecticut; Rockford Silver Plate Company, Rockford, Illinois; Aurora Silver Plate Company, Aurora, Illinois; and Acme Silver Company, Boston, Massachusetts.

There was an exchange of the various parts of articles of silverplate among

33. Children's napkin rings made by Simpson, Hall, Miller & Co. in 1886 and illustrated in their catalog that year. Note that the same little girl was used on nos. 030, 031, 032, and 036.

34. Simpson, Hall, Miller & Co. catalog, 1886.

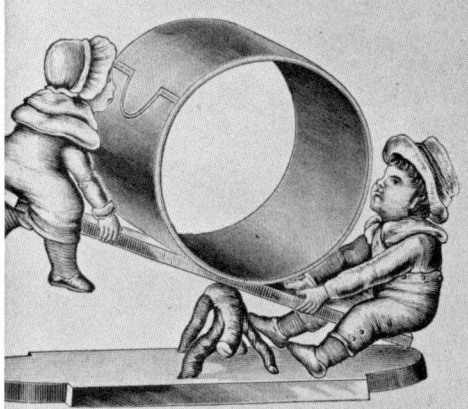

No. 029.
Gold Lined . . . . . Each, $2.00 (*Gamester*)
Fancy Gilt . . . . . " 2.50 (*Gammon*)
Full Size.

No. 026.
Chased and Gold Lined . . Each, $2.25 (*Gamut*)
Fancy Gilt . . . . . " 2.75 (*Gander*)
Full Size.

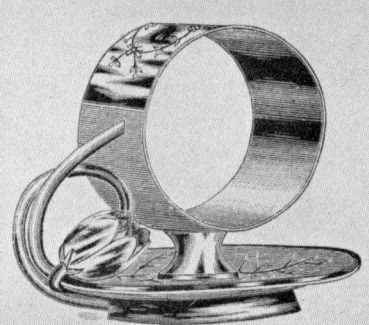

No. 04.
Chased . . . . . Each, $1.35 (*Cabin*)
Chased and Gold Lined . . " 1.58 (*Cactus*)
Full Size.

No. 010.
Chased . . . . . Each, $1.50 (*Canopy*)
Chased and Gold Lined . . " 1.75 (*Canter*)
Full Size.

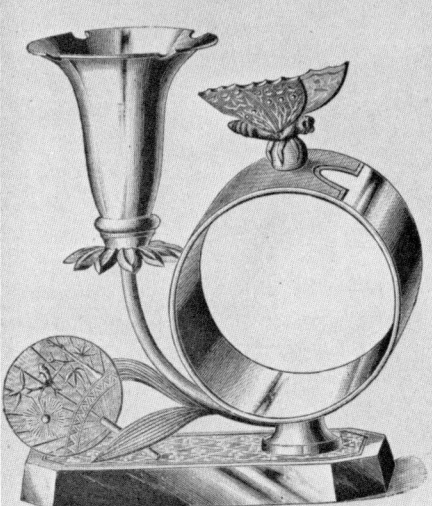

No. 024.
Chased . . . . . Each, $2.00 (*Cajole*)
Chased and Gold Lined . . " 2.25 (*Caldron*)
Fancy Gilt . . . . . " 2.50 (*Calf*)
Full Size.

No. 021.
Chased . . . . . Each, $1.75 (*Carriage*)
Chased and Gold Lined . . " 2.00 (*Cartoon*)
Full Size.

35. Napkin ring made by the Meriden Britannia Co. around the turn of the century for presentation to a retiring railroad tycoon.

36. Napkin clip made by E. & J. Bass, New York City.

37. A representative group of figural napkin rings. *Top row, left to right:* The first three were made by the Meriden Britannia Co. in 1877, 1888, and 1878; the last made by Rogers, Smith & Co. in 1878. *Center, left to right:* The Kate Greenaway girl, Meriden Britannia Co. in 1886; Meriden Britannia Co. in 1878; Wilcox Silver Plate Co. in 1884 (the dog has glass eyes); Barbour Silver Plate Co. in 1895. *Bottom:* Wm. Rogers Mfg. Co. in 1889; E. G. Webster & Bro. in 1873; Derby Silver Co. in about 1886, Meriden Silver Plate Co. in 1879.

346   AMERICAN SILVERPLATE

No. 250.
Chased,   per dozen, $30.00 (LOBBY).

No. 235.
Chased,   per dozen, $24.00 (APPEAL).

No. 251.
Chased,   per dozen, $30.0

38. Meriden Britannia Co. catalog, 1886.

39. Representative figural napkin rings.

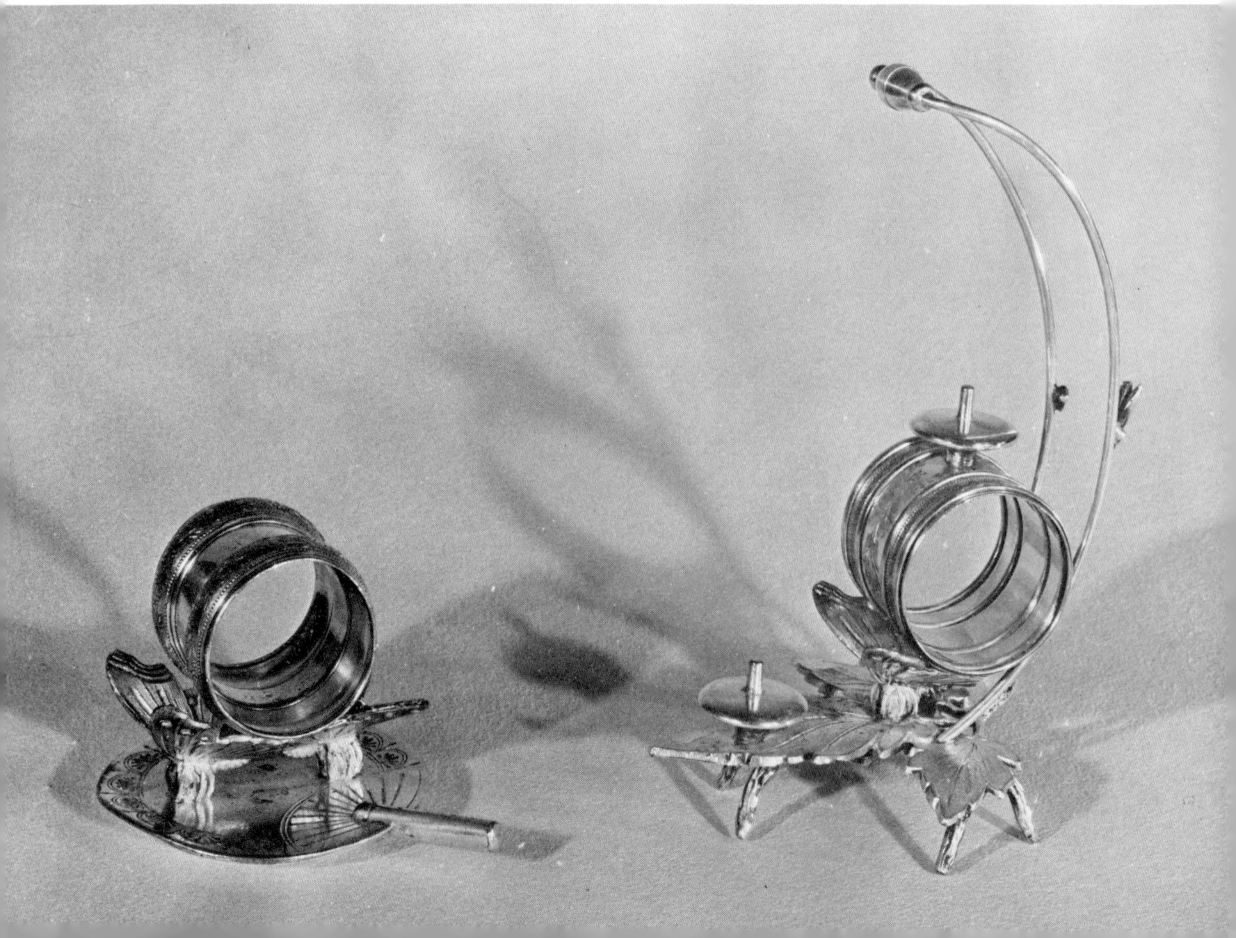

40. Representative figural napkin rings.
41. Individual castors. *Left to right:* Wilcox Silver Plate Co., about 1873; ring is ornamented with bird and nest with three eggs. Meriden Britannia Co., 1873; the little plate on rack in back is for butter. Simpson, Hall, Miller & Co. 1879.

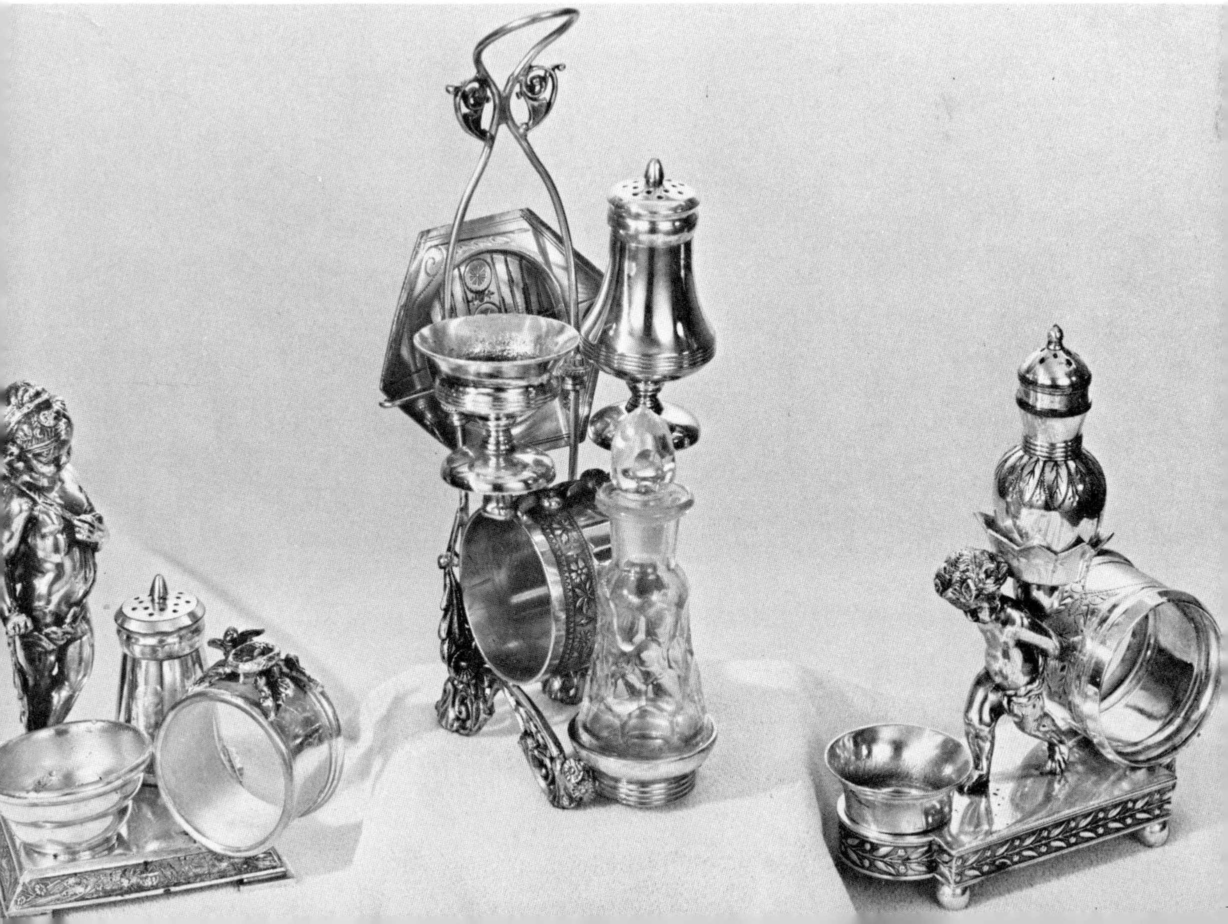

348 American Silverplate

competitors in silver manufacturing so that it is not unusual to find identical napkin rings, or sometimes only the same ornaments, bearing two different trademarks. Some are unmarked.

Combination napkin rings and individual casters were a related item. Simple styles included a salt dish and pepper shaker in addition to the napkin ring. More elaborate ones included a small condiment bottle for vinegar and a small butter plate.

While tastes have changed and paper napkins are in vogue, figural napkin rings are a favorite collector choice.

A note of caution should be added—reproduction napkin rings from Japan are currently being advertised.

Knife Rests

Knife rests were used to support carving knives and keep the tablecloth clean. Smaller versions for individual use were sometimes placed at each table cover.

42. A representative group of knife rests.

Most knife rests consisted of a metal bar supported by birds, animals, flowers, or human figures (Fig. 42). They were made in sufficient variety to afford the collector ample choice for an interesting collection.

Sardine Boxes

Sardine boxes were designed with glass inserts or were glass boxes with silverplated lids and set in silverplated frames (Figs. 43, 44). The glass was decorative and served the added purpose of eliminating odor which tends to cling to silver.

Miscellaneous Small Tablewares

Some small tablewares, such as muffineers, tea balls, tea strainers, and butter plates are not to be found in large quantities (Fig. 45). Condensed-milk-can holders are little enough known to make their identification difficult. They might easily be thought to be oversize mustard containers.

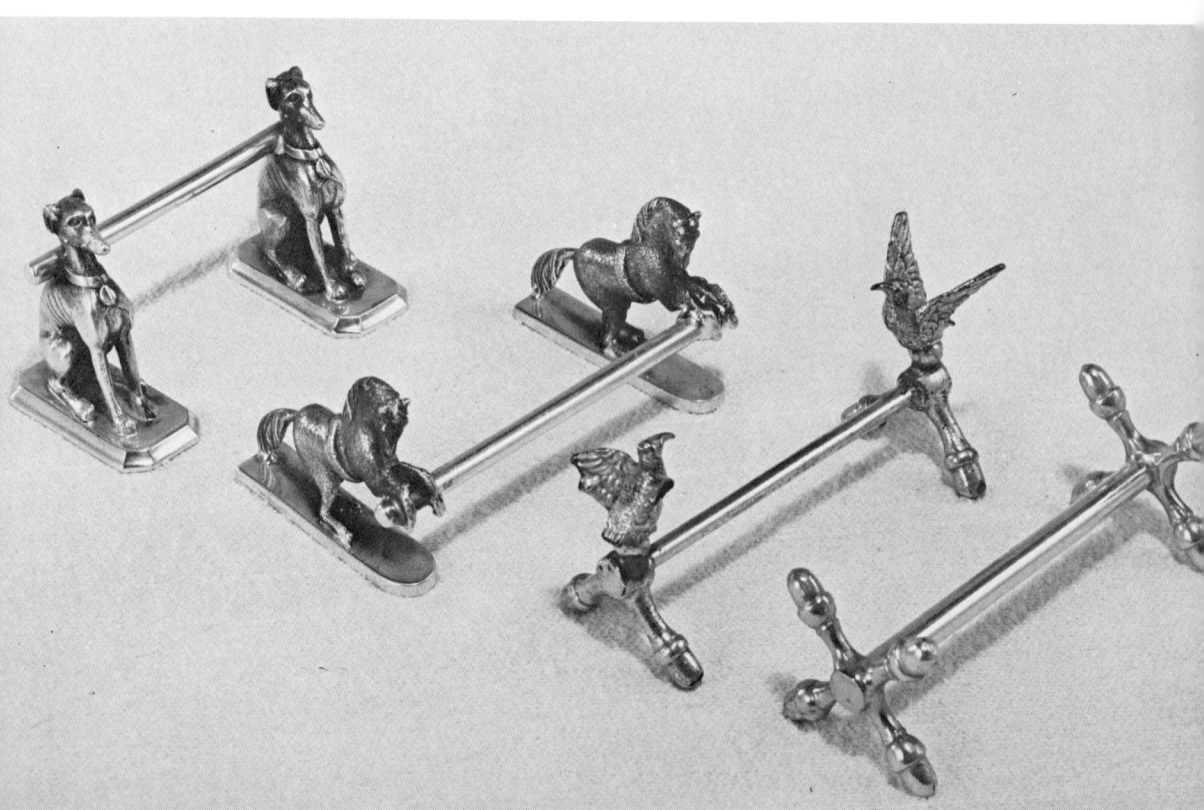

VIII. SMALL SILVERWARE AND NOVELTIES 349

Fine Cut Glass.
No. 35. Sardine Box.
$7.50.

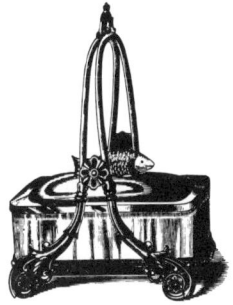

Fine Cut Glass.
No. 40. Sardine Box.
$6.50.

Fine Cut Glass.
No. 30. Sardine Box.
$6.00.

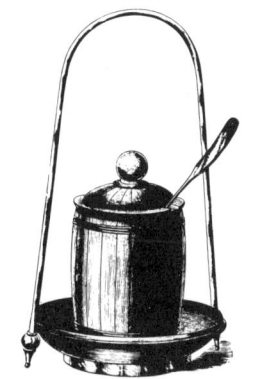

No. 10. Mustard Pot.
$3.50.

No. 70. Cheese Dish.
Fine Cut Glass Cover.
$8.00.

No. 25. Sardine Box. Ivy Chased.
Plain, ... $4.25.
Chased, ... 5.00.

No. 10. Gravy Boat.
$7.00.

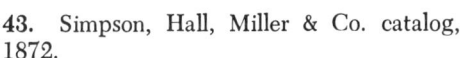

43. Simpson, Hall, Miller & Co. catalog, 1872.

350 AMERICAN SILVERPLATE

No. 05.
Nickel Silver, Silver Soldered, $13.50 (PHANTOM).

No. 1876, . . $10.00 (PHENIX).

No. 1867.

Satin,	$5.00
Engraved,	6.00
Hammered,	6.00
Hammered, and Applied,	6.50

No. 1878, . . $10.00 (PERTAIN).

No. 1880, . . $10.50 (PERTINENT).

No. 1881, . . $11.50 (PERUN

No. 1874, Satin, Engraved, $10.50 (PICA).

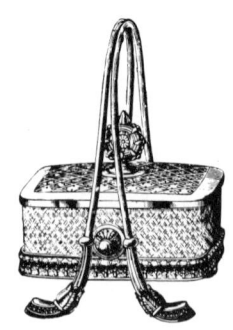

No. 1877, . . $12.00 (PICTURE).

No. 1875, . . $10.50 (PICKET).

SARDINE TONGS, $1.50 each (see Flat Ware) (PICNIC).

44. Meriden Britannia Co. catalog, 1877. **45.** Small tablewares. 13th Annual Illustrated Catalogue and Price List of A. C. Beckman.

VIII. SMALL SILVERWARE AND NOVELTIES 351

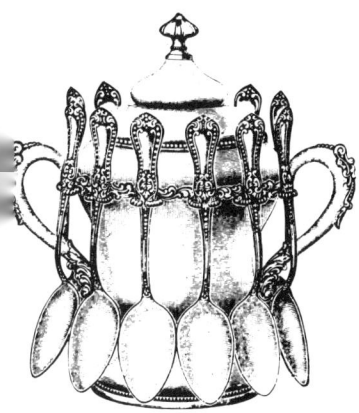

Combination Sugar Bowl, with spoon rack.
No. F-543 Satin, without spoons............$4 50
No. F-543 With spoons................. 6 50
Height, 8¼ inches. (Forbes Silver Co.)

No. X-018 Combination Sugar Bowl, with spoon rack............$2 00
Satin, burnished cover. Height, 7 inches. Triple plated, stamped quadruple plate. (Manhattan Silver Plate Co.)

No. B-1910 Sugar Sifter............$4 05
Satin, B. C. Height, 5 inches. (Barbour Silver Co.)

Condensed Milk Can Holder.
No. M-11 Satin $4 86
No. M-11 Satin, engraved 5 94
Cut ½ size. (Meriden B. Co.)

No. W-20 Sugar $2 50
Cut glass effect bowl.
Height, 4¾ inches. (E. G. Webster & Son.)

No. X-2900 Sugar Sifter............$2 00
Satin, engraved, triple plate, stamped quadruple plate; height, 5 inches. (Manhattan Silver Plate Co.)

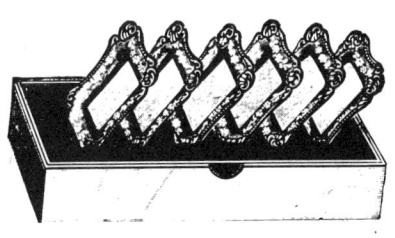

No. M-07 Individual Butter Plates. Per set of six..$6 48
Burnished, chased border. Cut ½ size.
Put up in satin lined box. (Meriden B. Co.)

No. M-0108 Tea Ball only............$3 24
No. M-25 Tea Ball Holder............ 1 94
Burnished. Cut ½ size. (Meriden B. Co.)

No. M-20 Muffineer, satin............$3 24
No. M-20 "   satin, engraved......... 4 32
Cut ½ size. (Meriden B. Co.)

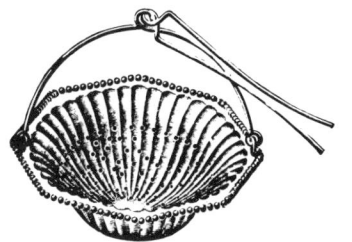

No. M-120 Tea Strainer................$1 35
Burnished. Cut ½ size. (Meriden B. Co.)

No. M-0100 Tea Ball............$3 50
Burnished, chased center. Cut ½ size. (Meriden B. Co.)

No. M-46 Corn Holder, each 54c
Burnished. Cut ½ size. (Meriden B. Co.)

No. M-35 Knife Rest, length 3½ inches..........72c
Burnished. (Meriden B. Co.)

SOLID NICKEL AND SILVER-PLATED MATCH SAFES

In this line we illustrate only a few of our Best Selling and Most Serviceable Styles.

No. 300—Price per doz., **$1.50**
Mascot Ornamented, Solid Nickel

No. 301—Price per doz., **$1.50**
Mascot Plain, Solid Nickel

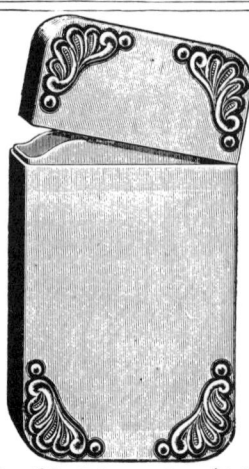

No. 400—Price per doz., **$1.50**
Solid Nickel, Ornamented

No. 303—Silver-plated
Price per doz., **$1.75**

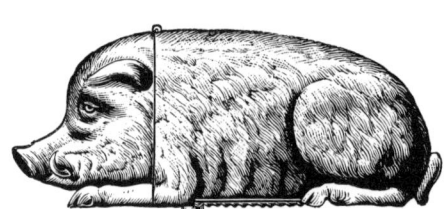

No. 302—Price per dozen, **$1.25**
Zulu, Solid Nickel

No. 304—Silver-plated
Price per doz., **$1.50**

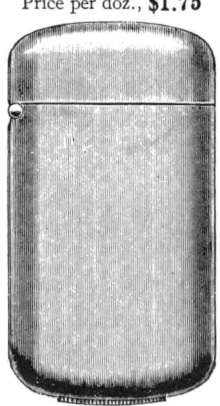

No. 840—Plain Nickel
Price per doz., **$0.75**

No. 305
Price per doz.,
$0.85
Charm

No. 307
Price per doz.,
$1.25
Automatic, Nickel

No. 306
Price per doz.,
$0.75
Excelsior, Hammered

No. 308—Silver-plated
Price per doz., **$1.50**

46. Elgin-American Mfg. Co., Elgin, Illinois, catalog, about 1895.

47. Illustrated Price List of Otto Young & Co. Chicago, Ill., 1895.

SILVER-PLATED MATCH BOXES.

CUTS ARE EXACT SIZE. PRICES EACH.

No. 2907. $3.00
Satin Engraved.
Gold Lined.
Quadruple Plated.

No. 2908. $3.00
Satin Engraved.
Gold Lined.
Quadruple Plated.

No. 2909. $2.40
Satin Engraved.
Gold Lined.
Quadruple Plated.

No. 2910. $2.40
Chased.
Gold Lined.
Quadruple Plated.

No. 2911. $2.40
Chased.
Gold Lined.
Quadruple Plated.

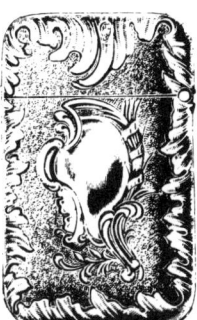

No. 2912. $2.40
Fancy Chased.
Gold Lined.
Quadruple Plated.

No. 2913. $2.00
Chased.
Silver Lined.
Quadruple Plated.

No. 2914. $1.80
Satin.
Gold Lined.
Quadruple Plated.

No. 2915. $1.50
Satin Chased.
German Silver.
Quadruple Plated.

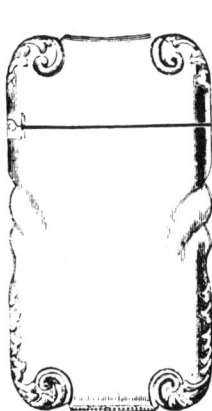

No. 2916. $1.25
Satin.
German Silver.
Quadruple Plated.

No. 2917. 60c.
Chased.
Old Silver.
Double Plated.

No. 2918. 50c.
Satin Chased.
Aluminum.

Match Safes, Pocket Match Boxes, and Toothpick Holders

From man's first discovery of the usefulness of fire, he has attempted to find a convenient means of starting it. "Banking the furnace" for the night can still be remembered by our elders. Our word "curfew" comes from the Old French *cuevrefu* or *couvrefeu*, a regulation directing that fires be covered at a fixed time—a signal for children to retire from the streets and also a means of conserving fuel. Fires were so difficult to rekindle that fires were covered to keep live coals through the night. It was partially for convenience and partially to conserve fuel that led to the invention of matches.

Rubbing dry sticks together to create friction and cause a spark or striking a flint and steel over dry tinder were early methods used to start a fire.

In 1669 the Hamburg alchemist, Hennig Brand (Brandt) discovered phosphorus which was soon used in fire-producing forms but it was not adapted to the manufacture of matches until 160 years later.

In 1680 both Godfrey Haukwitz and Robert Boyle produced a primitive form of matches which were coarse sheets of paper coated with phosphorus in com-

49. Toothpick holder or match safe made by the Meriden Britannia Co. *Jewelers' Weekly*, March 14, 1894.

bination with splinters of wood tipped with sulphur. Phosphorus was priced at the equivalent of $250 an ounce so that these early matches were used only by the extremely wealthy.

It was not until 1781 that further inventions led to the production of modern matches. The Phosphoric Candle or Ethereal Match, made in France, was comprised of paper tipped with phosphorus and sealed in a glass tube. When the tube was broken, admission of air set the paper on fire. The Pocket Luminary, made in Italy in 1786, was a small bottle lined with oxide of phosphorus. Sulphur-tipped wood splints ignited when rubbed on this coating and then withdrawn from the bottle.

The first really practical friction matches were made in Stockton-on-Tees, England, in 1827 by an apothecary, John Walker. Wooden or cardboard sticks were coated with antimony sulphide, potassium chlorate, gum, and starch. Three inches long, they were ignited by being drawn through a pleat of glass paper.

In 1830, phosphorus was substituted for antimony sulphide as an ingredient for match heads. These phosphorus matches were deadly poisonous. It was not until 1911, when William A. Fairburn of the Diamond Match Company substituted harmless sesquisulphide of phosphorus that this dreadful occupation hazard was removed. This new nonpoisonous formula was presented to

48. Silverplated match box made by William A. Rogers to commemorate the sinking of the *Maine*. *Jewelers' Weekly*, April 27, 1898.

QUADRUPLE SILVER-PLATED SMOKERS' ARTICLES.

No. 2929. Etched Cigar Lamp. $2 40.

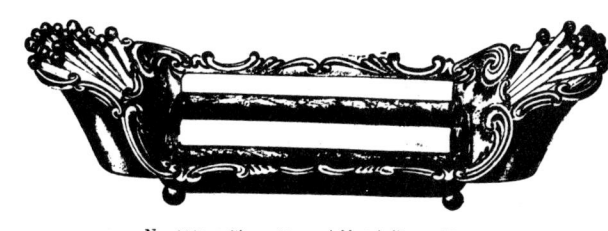

No. 2930. Cigarette and Match Tray, $5 40.

No. 2931. Chased Ash Tray. $1 00.

No. 2932. Chased Ash Tray and Match Holder. $3 00. Match Holder Gold Lined.

No. 2933. Chased Cigar Holder and Ash Tray. $1 75.

No. 2935. Chased Ash Tray. $1 25.

No. 2934. Chased Double Cigar Holder and Tray. $3 50.

No. 2936. Chased Smoking Set. $3 50.

No. 2937. Satin Bright Cut, Gold Lined, Smoking Set Complete, $6 50.

No. 2938. Fine Chased Cigar Box for 50 Cigars. $18 50.

50. Illustrated Price List of Otto Young & Co., 1895.

51. Representative group of toothpick holders or match safes.

52. Meriden Britannia Co. catalog, 1886.

VIII. SMALL SILVERWARE AND NOVELTIES 357

No. 28.

Silver, Gold Lined, . . $3.00 (POTTER).
Gold Inlaid and Gold Lined, 3.50 (POUND).

No. 33.

Silver, . . $2.50 (FUNDAMENT).
Old, Silver, . . 3.00 (FOREVER).

No. 23.

er and Gold, . $3.25 (POSTURE).

No. 1. PORCUPINE.
Silver, . . $1.12 (POSTAL).

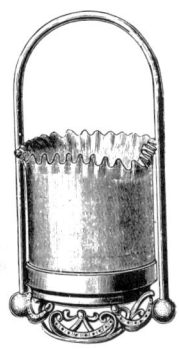

No. 32.

Silver, . . $2.75

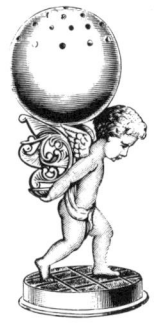

No. 24.

er and Gold, . $3.50 (POTASH).

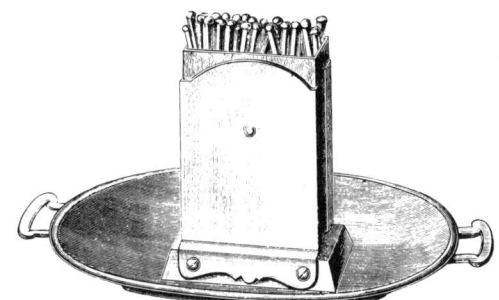

No. 34. SAFETY MATCH BOX HOLDER.
Enameled Copper, . . $4.50 (FURBISH).

No. 22.

Gold Lined, . $3.00

No. 25.

l Silver, Gold Lined, $3.75 (POSITIVE).

No. 26, $3.00 (POTENT).

No. 29.

Silver, Gold Lined, . $5.00
Gold Inlaid and Gold Lined, 6.00

No. 020.
Old Silver, $2.00 (DOOR).

No. 021.
Old Silver, $2.50 (DORIC).

No. 022.
Old Silver, $1.75 (DOT

No. 016.
Plain or Satin, $1.50 (PRACTICE).
Engraved,   2.00 (PRAISE).
Hammered, Old Silver,   2.50 (PRANCE).

No. 019. MOORISH.
Hammered, Old Silver, $3.00 (DOUBTFUL).
Moorish, Old Silver,   3.25 (DRAGOMAN).
Moorish, Gold Inlaid.   3.75 (DOZE).

No. 019.
Plain or Satin, $1.75 (PRA
Satin, Engraved,   2.25 (PRA

No. 12.
Old Silver, $3.00 (PRECLUDE).

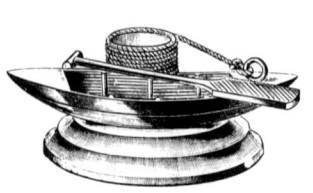

No. 11.
Old Silver and Gold, $2.75 (PRECIPICE).

No. 13.
Old Silver, $2.50 (PRECEDE).
Old Silver and Gold, 3.00 (HAILSTONE).

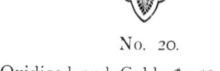

No. 21.
Oxidized and Gilt, $5.00 (PRECISE).

52 continued.

No. 20.
Oxidized and Gold, $4.50 (P

VIII. Small Silverware and Novelties   359

53. Reed & Barton catalog, 1885.

360 American Silverplate

HAMMERED AND APPLIQUÉ.
No. 017. Copper Match Safe,
$2.25. (PRETEXT)
(FULL SIZE.)

NICKEL SILVER.
No. 115. Tobacco Box, $3.25. (PRETOR)
Gold-lined, 4.00. (PRETORIAN)
(FULL SIZE.)

NICKEL SILVER.
No. 105. Tobacco Box, $3.50. (PREVAIL)
Gold-lined, 4.25. (PREVALENT)
No. 107. Engraved same as No. 115, same price.
(FULL SIZE.)

PERSIAN CHASED.
No. 122. Nickel Silver Match Safe
Old Silver, $2.75. (PR
No. 022. Copper, 2.75. (PR
(FULL SIZE.)

PERSIAN CHASED CIGARETTE CASE.
No. 124. Old Silver and Gold, $6.50. (PREVISION)
No. 0124. Copper, 6.50. (PREWARN)
(FULL SIZE.)

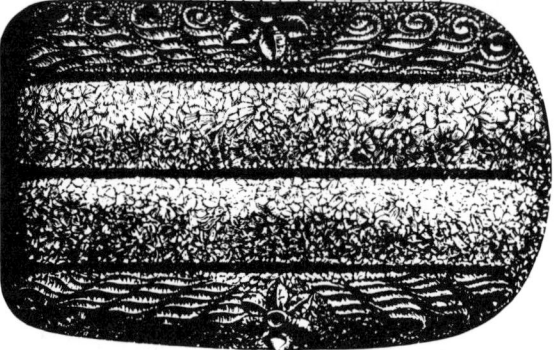

INDIA CHASED CIGAR CASE.
No. 0105. Copper, $11.50. (PREY)
No. 105. Old Silver, 11.50. (PREKING)
Old Silver and Gold, 11.50. (PRID
(FULL SIZE.)

ENGRAVED CIGARETTE CASE.
No. 122. Old Silver and Gold, $5.75. (PRIM
No. 0122. Copper, 5.75. (PRIM
(FULL SIZE.)

SMOKER'S SET, WITH CIGAR LIGHTER.
No. 0157. Copper, $48.50. (PRIMEVAL)
No. 157. Old Silver, 48.50. (PRIMING)
(ONE-HALF SIZE.)

POCKET MATCH SAFE.
No. 02. Copper and Appliqué, $1.75. (PRIMAGE)
(FULL SIZE.)

CIGAR LIGHTER AND ASH RECEIVER.
No. 0130. Copper, $11.75. (PRIMARY)
No. 130. Old Silver, 11.75. (PRIMATE)
(ONE-HALF SIZE.)

CIGARETTE HOLDER.
No. 0142. Copper, Gold-lined, $10.00. (PRIME)
(ONE-HALF SIZE.)

VENETIAN CHASED AND APPLIQUÉ SMOKER'S SET, WITH CIGAR LIGHTER.
No. 0152. Copper, $42.00. (PRIMITIVE)
No. 152. Old Silver, 42.00. (PRIMLY)

53 continued.

VIII. SMALL SILVERWARE AND NOVELTIES 361

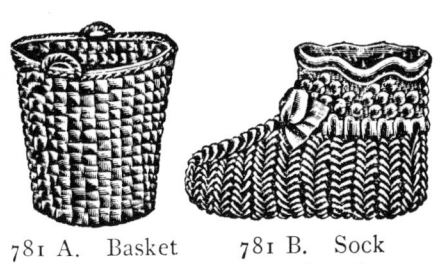

781 A. Basket Match Safe.   781 B. Sock Match Safe.

781 C. Match Safe.   781 D. Match Safe. All the above are also made as Pin Cushion.

E. Match Safe.   781 F. Match Safe

54. Kelley & McBean (Niagara Falls, N.Y.) catalog, about 1894.

the government for use of all rival companies, a humanitarian gesture which won public commendation from President William Howard Taft. These new matches accomplished other things. The new formula raised the point of ignition more than 100 degrees, a considerable safety factor. Also, experiments proved that rats would gnaw on the phosphorus match heads and ignite them, but would not touch the new ones even when starving.

With the invention of the phosphorus friction match, a means of storing and carrying them was a logical development. Early catalogs show small containers to be used in the home, some of which were designated as toothpick holders or match safes. The two- to three-inch-long match boxes, now called match safes by most collectors, did not appear in catalogs in great numbers until the 1890s. Both types of containers were made in various materials and in many styles. Whimsical ones, such as boots, shoes, baskets, hats, hearts, owls, coiled snakes, dogs, monkeys, pigs, and roosters appear to have been made between the 1890s and about 1910 when pocket lighters began to replace them.

At the time when these match safes were new, ladies did not smoke at all and gentlemen smoked cigars. Some of the smoking accessories were cigar holders, cigar boxes, cigar lamps, and cigar-ash receivers.

Sewing Birds

Sewing birds were patented by Charles Waterman, Meriden, Connecticut, on February 15, 1853. This patent led to the production of a whole new aviary of birds for American "bird watchers" and provided needleworkers with a decorative as well as useful work clamp (Fig. 55).

Clamps for holding needlework were made of metal as early as the eighteenth century and of wood at least a century earlier. Not all of these clamps were made in the form of birds, some being butterflies, dogs, cats, and mice. By far the greater number made since Waterman's patent have been in the form of birds, some with one or two pincushions.

Sewing birds are fastened to the edge of a table by a clamp. The beak of the bird is opened by pressing the tail feathers together, the material to be sewed is inserted, and the beak closed by a spring when the tail feathers are released.

In the first price list of the Meriden

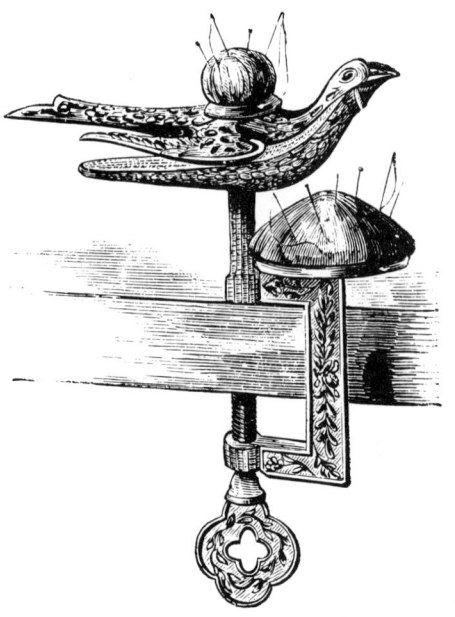

Britannia Company, issued in January 1853, there were sewing birds listed. Ledgers of the company, starting that same month, show that sewing birds were an important item. The company's total sales for that year were close to $300,000; of that total, $25,000 was received for the sale of 52,000 sewing birds.

Though Waterman's first patent was dated February 15, 1853, he must have made them earlier because they were advertised in the *Hartford Times* by Elihu Geer, a dealer, in the latter part of 1852 (Fig. 56). This same dealer was one of the principal customers of the Meriden Britannia Company for sewing birds early in 1853 and continued buying for a long time.

One style of silverplated sewing bird was illustrated in the 1867 Meriden Britannia Company catalog.

55. Meriden Britannia Co. catalog, 1867.

56. *Hartford Times,* June 5, 1852.

After the patent expired, many manufacturers made them. They continued to be illustrated in catalogs of the Meriden Britannia Company of 1867 and 1871.

57. Toilet sets. *Left:* Meriden Britannia Co., made in the 1870s. *Right:* Toilet stand with ring drawer made by the Meriden Silver Plate Co., 1879.

No. 200. TOILET.

Silver, $60.00 (INCOGNITO).
Silver, Gold Inlaid, 75.00 (INCOME).

No. 152. With Jewel Drawer.

Silver, $20.00 (HOUND).
Silver, Gold Inlaid, 22.00 (HOUSE).

No. 211.

Silver, $30.00 (MORTISE).
Silver, Gold Inlaid, 35.00 (MOSLEM).

58. Meriden Britannia Co. catalog supplement, 1882.

VIII. Small Silverware and Novelties 365

No. 152. With Jewel Drawer.
Silver, . . . $20.00 (HOUND).
Silver, Gold Inlaid, 22.00 (HOUSE).

No. 151.
Silver, . . $17.00 (HOVER).
Silver, Gold Inlaid, 19.00 (HUB).

No. 178.
Silver, . . $26.50 (HUDDLE).
Silver, Gold Inlaid, 29.00 (HUB).

No. 124.
X X Coral Rose, . . $33.00 (HOVERING).
Gold and Steel Finish, 36.00 (HUFF).

59. Meriden Britannia Co. catalog, 1882.

366 AMERICAN SILVERPLATE

No. 172. With Jewel Drawer.
Silver, . . $31.50 (HORNPIPE)
Silver, Gold Inlaid, 34.50 (HORSE).

No. 174. With Jewel Drawer.
Silver, . . $27.50 (HOSE).
Silver, Gold Inlaid, 30.00 (HOSIER).

No. 173.
Silver, . . $35.00 (HOST).
Silver, Gold Inlaid, 37.50 (HOSTAGE).

60. Meriden Britannia Co. catalog, 1882.

VIII. SMALL SILVERWARE AND NOVELTIES 367

No. 940, $15.00.
Pink, Blue or White.

No. 941, $25.00.
Malachite. Blue, Pink, White or Canary.

61. Middletown Plate Co. catalog supplement, 1879.

After that date it would appear that they were not. Another Meriden firm, Bradley & Hubbard Manufacturing Company, continued to make them until around 1930.

Following World War II, sewing birds were advertised and sold from about 1947 to about 1953.

Collectors have found sewing birds fascinating because of the wide varieties made. Dr. Manton Copeland, naturalist, wrote an essay that is a sort of tongue-in-cheek classification into types. (*See Bibliography.*)

Boudoir Accessories

Accessories for milady's boudoir have always been the most fascinating as well as the most numerous small items available to collectors. From small beginnings in the late 1860s, by the mid-1870s all sorts of accessories to delight the feminine eye were made by the manufacturers of silverplate (Figs. 57–61).

Toilet Stands

Highly popular from the middle of the 1870s through the 1890s were the toilet stands with one or more bottles and jars for cologne, toilet water, and puffs. Some included a vase for flowers and a drawer for jewelry. Though these appear to be among the scarcest of items in today's antique market, the great numbers that appear in old catalogs attest to their former popularity.

Styles varied from simple, one-bottle silverplated stands holding a two-ounce bottle to elaborate ones with bottles for

62. Reed & Barton catalog, 1885.

63. Reed & Barton catalog, 1885.

VIII. Small Silverware and Novelties   369

64. Reed & Barton catalog, 1885.

cologne, puff box, mirror, and caryatid candelabra holding six candles. Stands were often decorated in gold.

Other silverplated stands, also decorated with gold, were designed to accommodate three bottles with a vase to match (Fig. 62). The rings holding the bottles in place are supported by caryatid figures.

In old catalogs little mention is made of the glass. In one, the bottles are called, "Malachite blue, pink, white or canary." In another, they are called, "Crystal Rose Glass," and in another "Aqua Marine decorated."

Decorative motifs on the glass are as varied as the design of the silverplated stands. Floral designs are perhaps the most numerous but children at play, butterflies, birds, and animals are also found (Fig. 63). Among the most charming are those with children in white enamel decorations in the so-called "Mary Gregory style."

Great numbers of these delightful accessories were illustrated in catalogs from about 1877 until 1890. Fewer styles appeared during the 1890s and by 1900 toilet stands had virtually disappeared from the market.

Mirrors

Equally charming and equally as scarce as the elaborate toilet sets are the plate-glass mirrors and sconces that were designed to appeal to feminine taste (Fig. 64). Decorations were cherubs, flowers, and birds.

Boxes

Victorians loved boxes (Fig. 65). They were favorites for gifts and were made to hold gloves, handkerchiefs, jewelry, "beauty patches," cards, stamps, pins, sweets, and many other things, as well as music boxes. All well-appointed ladies' dressers held at least a glove box, handkerchief box, and jewel box, often in matching sets. Some of those most often sought by today's collectors are the ones with glass inserts which are described in old catalogs as "Rich Decorated Malachite Glass" (Fig. 66).

Victorian jewelry was plentiful, which meant that the ladies required jewelry boxes in which to store all the little treasures so dear to feminine hearts. Many of these boxes were square or rectangular ones with embossed and richly decorated tops. The most fascinating of all, however, are those ingenious delights made in novelty designs. Illustrated is one in the form of a hollow sphere on which Cupid raises and lowers the lid by means of a weight attached to a silverplated chain (Fig. 67).

Others might easily be mistaken for butter dishes as their covers are hung overhead when not in use, much like the butter dishes from which their design may have been derived (Fig. 68).

One jewel casket is combined with a watch stand in an ingenious arrangement of drawers (Fig. 70).

Other jewel caskets were made of glass with silverplated mounts. Though no mention is made of the types of glass in the catalogs, much of it is richly decorated (Fig. 71).

Miscellaneous Dresser Appointments

Hairpin boxes, watch stands, picture frames, thimble holders, curling sets, puff boxes, and hat-pin stands were among the other dressing-table appointments (Figs. 72–74).

Silverplated dresser sets of comb, brushes, hand mirror, and related pieces do not appear in the earliest catalogs. Combs and brushes with silverplated handles and backs appeared in the 1880s in a limited number of designs (Fig. 75). During the 1890s matching sets were made which included whisk brooms, mirror, military brush, hairbrush, combs, cloth brush, and hat brush (Fig. 76).

Dresser sets in Art Nouveau styles were especially plentiful. The female

HIGH GRADE QUADRUPLE PLATE TOILET ARTICLES.

Manufactured by E. C. Webster & Son.

No. W 393. Hairpin or pin box.
ousse, silver..$1.75
d enamel...2.50

No. W 338. Jewel box.
Repousse, bright silver, satin lining................$6.50
Length, 6⅜ inches; width, 3½ inches; height, 2¾ inches.

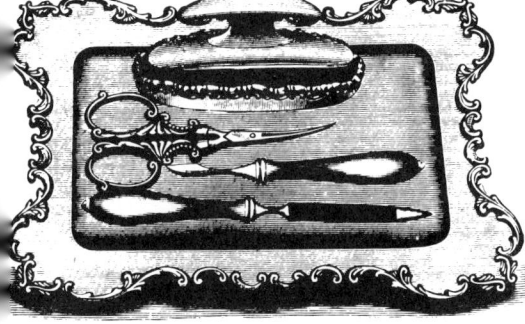

No. W 86. Manicure set.
atin finish, Rococo border.........................$8.50
Length of tray, 7½ inches.

No. W 314. Glove box.
Repousse, bright silver, satin lining...............$12.00
Length, 10⅜ inches; width, 3⅜ inches; height, 3 inches.

No. W 105. Curling set.
Repousse, bright silver, with folding irons, ebony handles..........$9.50
Length of irons, 10 inches.
Length of box, 6½ inches; width, 3½ inches; height, 2¾ inches.

No. W 101. Curling set.
Repousse, bright silver...............................$5.50
Length, 7⅜ inches.

65. Carson, Pirie, Scott & Co. (Chicago, Ill.) catalog, 1898–99.

372 AMERICAN SILVERPLATE

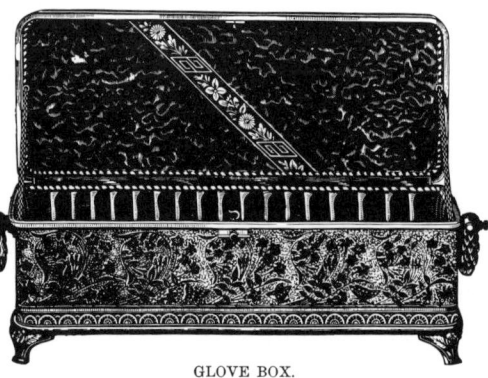

GLOVE BOX.
No. 210. Satin-lined, $32.50. (GRATITUDE)
Gold and Oxidized, 42.50. (GRAVE)

BOUDOIR SET.
THREE PIECES TO MATCH.

HANDKERCHIEF BOX.
No. 70. Satin-lined, $30.00. (GRATIS)
Gold and Oxidized, 40.00. (GRATUITY)

JEWEL BOX.
No. 530. Satin-lined, $22.50. (GRAVEL)
Gold and Oxidized, 30.00. (GRAVELLY)

GLOVE BOX.
Rich Decorated Malachite Glass.
No. 200. Satin-lined, $37.00. (GRAZE)
Gold Finish, 43.00. (GRAZIER)
No. 65. Handkerchief Box to match, $35.00. (GRAZING)
Gold Finish, 41.00. (GREASE)

HANDKERCHIEF BOX.
Rich Decorated Malachite Glass.
No. 50. Satin-lined, $37.00. (GRAVITY) Gold Finish, $45.00. (GRAY)
No. 205. Glove Box to match, $39.00. (GRAYISH) Gold Finish, $47.00. (GRAYNESS)

HANDKERCHIEF BOX.
Rich Decorated Glass.
No. 60. Satin-lined, $25.00. (GREAT)
Gold Finish, 28.00. (GREATNESS)

66. Reed & Barton catalog, 1885.

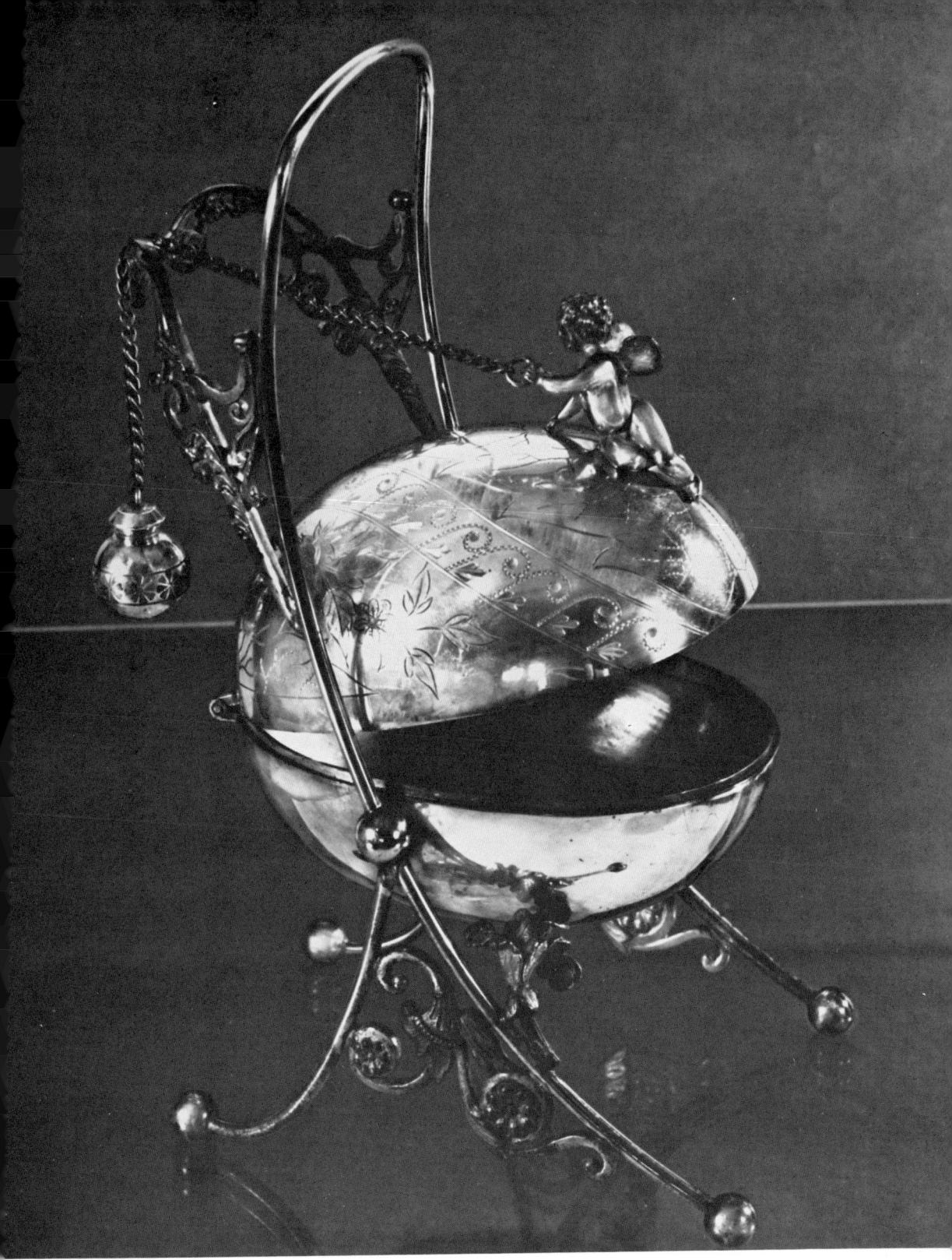

67. Novelty jewel box made by Wilcox Silver Plate Co. about 1884.

374 AMERICAN SILVERPLATE

68. Reed & Barton catalog, 1885.

70. Reed & Barton catalog, 1885.

No. 103. BONBON BOX.
Satin, Engraved, . . . $11.50 (CHARTISM).
Satin, Engraved, XX Gold Inlaid, 13.50 (CHARY).

No. 72.
Old Silver, . $7.50 (GRATER).

No. 101. BONBON BOX.
Satin, Old Silver, . $10.50 (CHEAPLY).
Satin, Gold Inlaid, 12.00 (CHARMING).

No. 106.
Old Silver, . $10.50 (CHALDRON).
Gold Inlaid, . 12.00 (CHALICE).
(PATENTED.)

No. 99. BONBON BOX.
Silver, . . $10.50 (CEREMENT).
Silver, Gold Inlaid, 11.50 (CERAMIC).

No. 100. BONBON BOX.
Old Silver, $15.00 (CEREMONY).
Gold Inlaid, 16.50 (CERTIFY).

No. 102. BONBON BOX.
Silver, . $12.00 (CENTRAL).
Silver, Gold Inlaid, 13.50 (CHARACTER).

No. 92.
Old Silver, . $12.50 (CHERRY).
Gold Inlaid, . 15.00 (CHECKER).

No. 43.
Chased, . $9.00 (GOVERN).
With Mirror, 10.50 (GOVERNOR).
(PATENTED.)

No. 53.
Chased, . $12.50 (GOAT).
(PATENTED.)

No. 93.
Silver, . $15.00 (CHEERFUL).
XX Gold Inlaid, 18.00 (CHEROOT).

No. 34.
Gold and Steel Finish, $13.50 (GNARL).

No. 48. GLOVE BOX.
Silver, Satin Lined, Crystal Cover, . $13.50 (GOAD).
Silver, Gold Inlaid, Satin Lined, Crystal Cover, 15.00 (GOAL).

No. 35.
Gold and Steel Finish, $15.00 (GNARLED).

71. Meriden Britannia Co. catalog, 1886.

376   American Silverplate

No. 50, $7.50 (GRAND).

No. 40.
Old Silver, $10.50 (GOTHIC).

No. 1¼.
Porcelain, $3.00 (GOTH).

No. 59.
Old Silver, $10.50 (GLEN).
Silver, Gold Inlaid,   12.00 (GLIB).

No. 36, $8.50 (GRAFT).

No. 65.
Silver, $11.50 (GLEAM).

No. 71.
Silver, $15.00 (GREATLY).
Silver, Gold Inlaid,   17.50 (GRECIAN).

No. 64.
Silver, $23.00 (GLISTEN).
Silver, Gold Inlaid,   25.00 (GLITTER).

No. 67.

71 continued.

VIII. SMALL SILVERWARE AND NOVELTIES 377

No. 88. HANDKERCHIEF BOX.
Silver, ... $24.00 (LOGIC).
Silver, Gold Inlaid, . 26.00 (LOGMAN).

No. 84.
Silver, . . . $11.00 (MATURE).
Silver, Gold Inlaid, 12.50 (MAXIM).
Crystal, Plated Mountings.

No. 55. HANDKERCHIEF BOX.
Silver, Crystal Cover, . . $15.00 (GNASH).
Silver, Gold Inlaid, Crystal Cover, 16.50 (GNAT).

No. 85.
Old Silver, . . . $9.00 (MATIN).
Gold Inlaid, . 11.00 (MATINEE).
XX Gold Inlaid, . 13.00 (MATRON).

No. 81.
Silver, . . . $30.00 (LOUNGE).
Silver, Gold Inlaid, . 35.00 (LOUVRE).

No. 87.
Silver, . . . $15.00 (MATTING).

No. 63.
Silver, . . . $19.00 (GLOBE).
Silver, Gold Inlaid, . 20.50 (GLOSS).

No. 68.
Silver, . . . $20.00 (GRITTY).
Silver, Gold Inlaid, . 22.00 (GRIZZLE).

No. 61.
Silver, . . . $15.50 (GLEBE).
Silver, Gold Inlaid, . 17.00 (GLEE).

71 continued.

378 American Silverplate

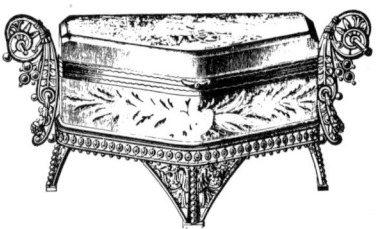

No. 73.
Silver, . . . $20.50 (GRANTEE).
Silver, Gold Inlaid, 22.50 (GRANULATE).

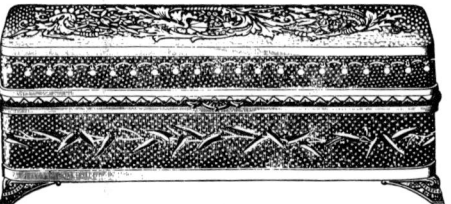

No. 89. Handkerchief Box.
Silver, . . . $24.00 (LOGWOOD).
Silver, Gold Inlaid, . 26.00 (LOITER).

No. 86.
Silver, . . . $15.00 (LONEL*)

No. 95.
Enameled Copper Base, Silver Mountings, $21.00 (EYESTONE).

No. 91.
Old Silver, . . . $12.00 (EYEBROW).
Gold Inlaid, . . 14.00 (EYEBALL).

No. 96.
Enameled Copper Base, Silver Mountings, $15.50 (

No. 82.
Silver, . . . $25.00 (LOTION).
Silver, Gold Inlaid, 30.00 (LOTUS).

No. 62.
Silver, . . . $15.50 (GLIDE).
Silver, Gold Lined, 17.00 (GLIMPSE).

No. 83.
Silver, . . . $25.00 (LOOT).
Silver, Gold Inlaid, 30.00 (LOOSER).

71 continued.

VIII. SMALL SILVERWARE AND NOVELTIES 379

THIMBLE HOLDER.
No. 25. $3.00 (GRANDLY)
Gold or Oxidized, 3.50 (GRANDEUR)

WATCH STAND.
No. 50. $7.50 (GRANTED)
Gold Finish, 8.50 (GRANTING)

WATCH STAND.
No. 45. $6.50 (GRANULE)
Gold Finish, 7.50 (GRAPE)

WATCH STAND.
No. 35. $5.00 (GRAPPLE)
Gold or Oxidized, 6.00 (GRASS)

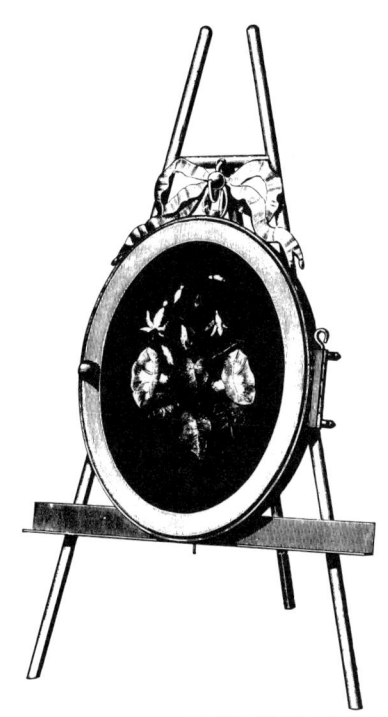

STAND FOR TWO CABINET PHOTOGRAPHS. With Florentine Mosaic Panel.
Illustration shows Stand when Closed.
No. 25. $30.00 (GRASSY)
Gold and Steel Finish, 35.00 (GRATEFUL)

STAND FOR TWO CABINET PHOTOGRAPHS. With Florentine Mosaic Panel.
Illustration shows Stand when Open.
No. 30. $32.50 (GRATIFY)
Gold and Oxidized Finish, 37.50 (GRATING)

THIMBLE HOLDER.
No. 20. $2.50 (GRANDSIRE)
Gold or Oxidized, 3.00 (GRANDSON)

PUFF BOX.
No. 25. $4.50 (GRANITIC)
Gold-lined, 5.50 (GRANNY)
(ONE-THIRD SIZE.)

WATCH STAND.
No. 40. $5.75 (GRAPHIC)
Gold Finish, 6.75 (GRAPNEL)

WATCH STAND.
No. 55. $9.00 (GRASP)
Gold and Oxidized, 10.50 (GRASPING)

72. Reed & Barton catalog, 1885.

380 AMERICAN SILVERPLATE

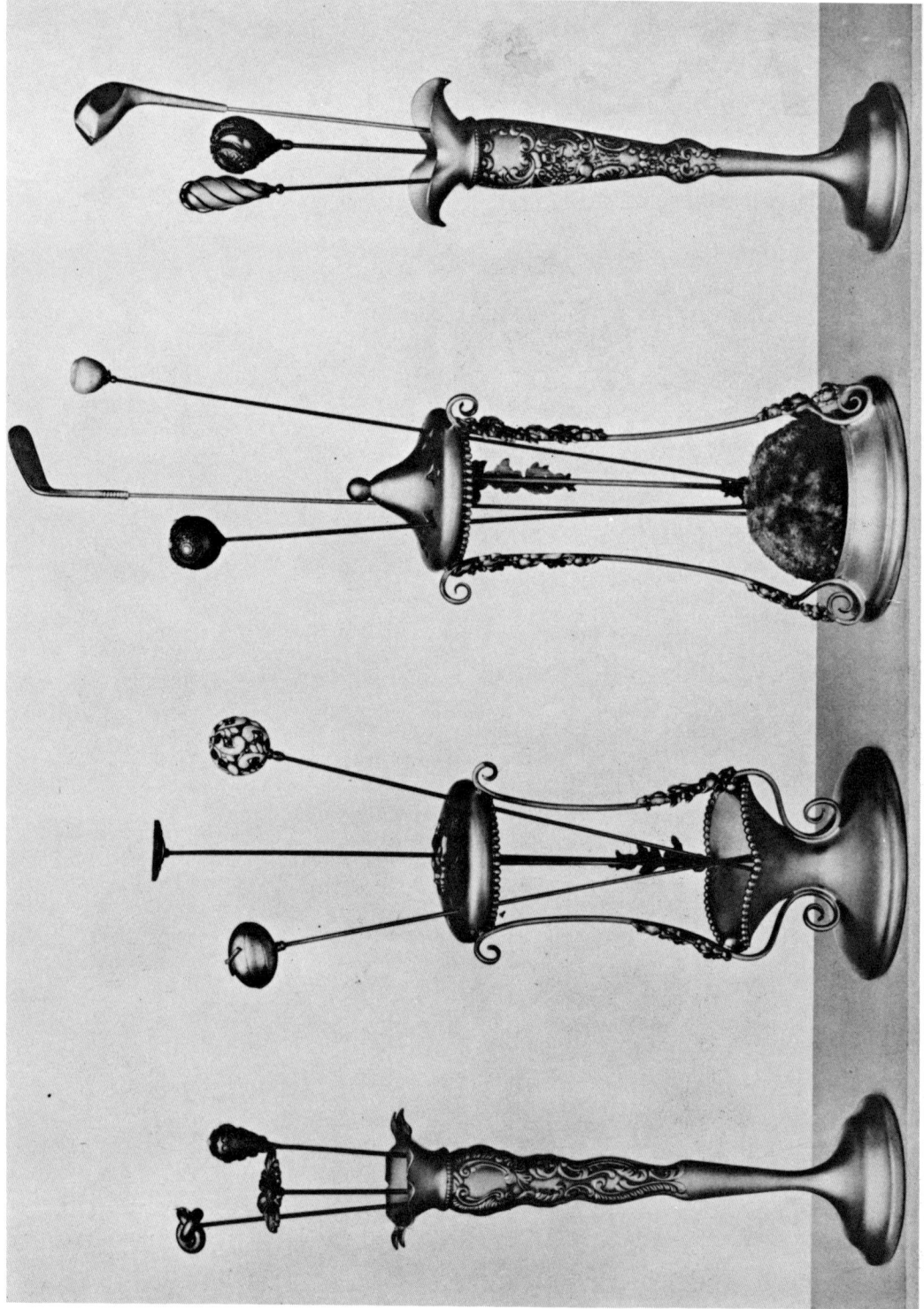

73. Victor Silver Co. (Shelton, Conn.) catalog, about 1890–1900.

74. Victor Silver Co. (Shelton, Conn.) catalog, about 1900–1905.

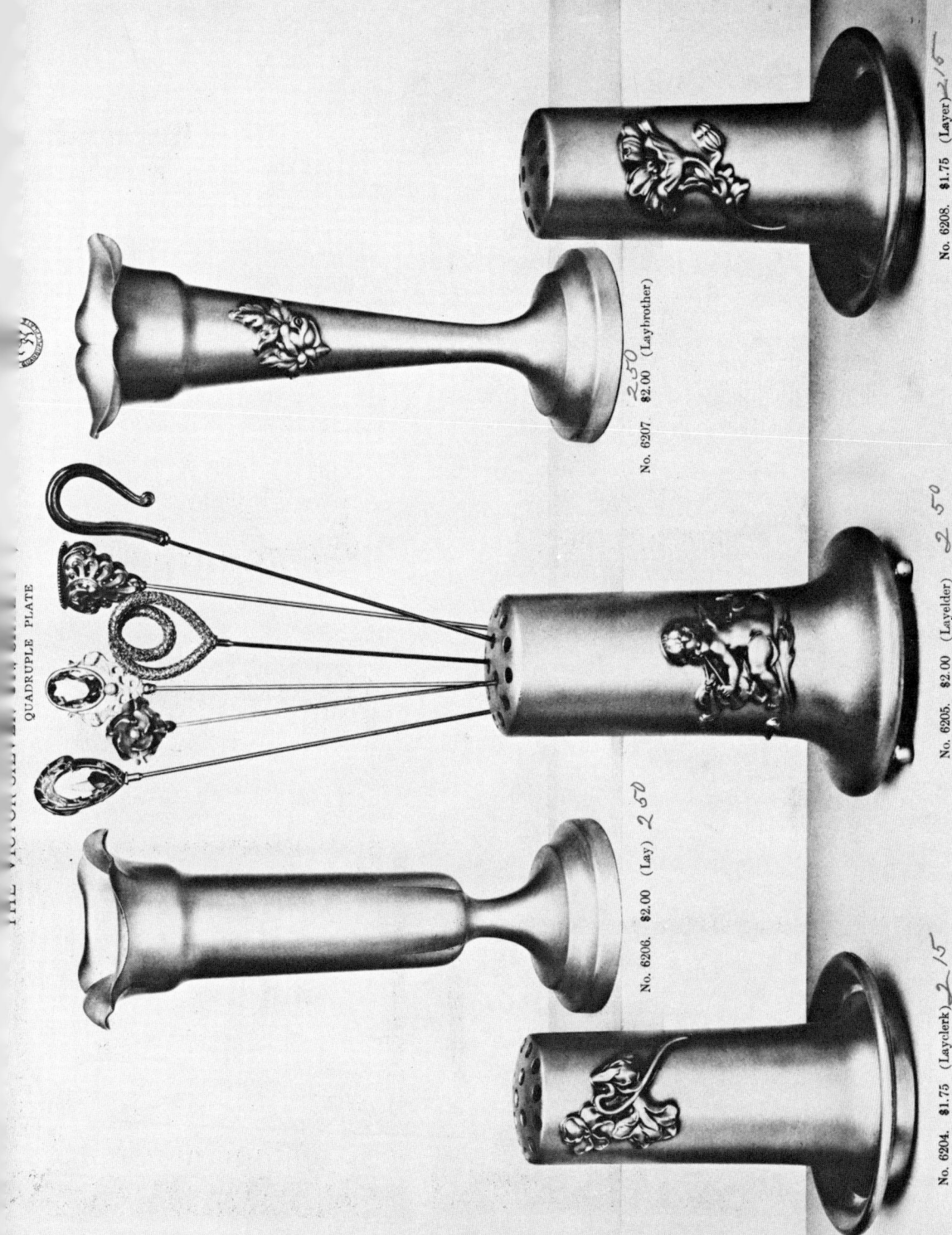

No. 010. Back Comb.
Silver, . . $2.50 (GARMENT).
Silver, Gold Inlaid, 3.00 (GARNER.)

No. 011. Back Comb.
Satin, Engraved, . . $2.50 (GARNET).
Satin, Engraved, Gold Inlaid, 3.00 (GARNISH).

No. 012. Back Comb.
Silver, . . $1.75 (GARB).
Gilt, . . 2.00 (GARDEN).

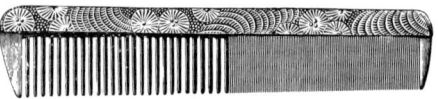

No. 40. Moorish, Old Silver Comb.
Satin, . . $3.25 (REALIZE). Hammered, Old Silver, $3.50 (RAWHIDE).
Arabesque, Old Silver, 3.50 (RECITAL). Moorish, Old Silver, . 3.75 (REACTION).
Embossed, . . $4.00 (RECAPTURE).

No 20. Hammered Comb.
Satin, . . $3.00 (PROVIDENT). Hammered, Old Silver, $3.25 (PR
Arabesque, Old Silver, 3.25 (PRELATE). Moorish, Old Silver, . 3.50 (PB
Embossed, . . $3.75 (PROGNOSTIC).

No. 300. Embossed Hair Brush.
Satin, . . $5.50 (PRIMARY). Arabesque, Old Silver, $6.00 (PRESUMER).
Satin, Engraved, 6.00 (PREFECT). Hammered, Old Silver, 6.00 (PROFUSELY).
Embossed, . . 8.00 (PRODUCT). Moorish, Old Silver, . 6.50 (PRINCELY).

No. 500. Hammered Military Hair Brush.
Satin, . . $6.50 (REALITY). Hammered, Old Silver, $7.00 (READI
Satin, Engraved, 7.00 (REASONER). Moorish, Old Silver, . 7.50 (RAVEN

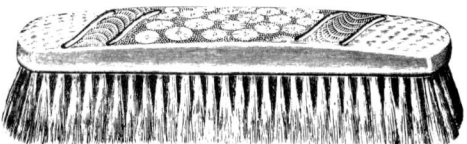
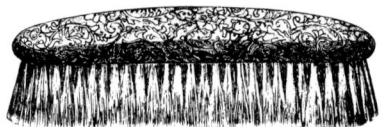

No. 200. Moorish, Old Silver Clothes Brush.
Satin, . . $5.50 (PRESSURE). Hammered, Old Silver, $6.00 (RAVAGE).
Satin, Engraved, . 6.00 (PRELUDE). Moorish, Old Silver, . 6.50 (RAVELIN).
Arabesque, Old Silver, 6.00 (PRESAGE). Embossed, . . 8.00 (RAWNESS).

No. 100. Arabesque, Old Silver Hat Brush.
Satin, . . $4.75 (PRESENCE). Hammered, Old Silver, $5.25 (PR
Satin, Engraved, . 5.25 (PREPENSE). Moorish, Old Silver, . 5.75 (PR
Arabesque, Old Silver, 5.25 (PREMIER). Embossed, . . 7.00 (PR

Hair Brush and Comb in Plush Case, complete, $14.75 (RATHER).
No. 300 Moorish, Old Silver Hair Brush, . 6.50 (RATTLE).
No. 40 Moorish, Old Silver Comb, . . 3.75 (RATIO).
Plush Case, ... 4.50 (RASH).

Hat and Clothes Brush in Plush Case, complete, $15.75 (QUIVER).
No. 100 Satin, Engraved Hat Brush, . . 5.25 (QUOTA).
No. 200 Satin, Engraved Clothes Brush, . . 6.00 (QUONDAM).
Plush Case, ... 4.50 (QUICKSTEP)

75. Meriden Britannia Co. catalog, 1886.

VIII. SMALL SILVERWARE AND NOVELTIES 383

76. Pairpoint Mfg. Co. (New Bedford, Mass.) catalog, 1894.

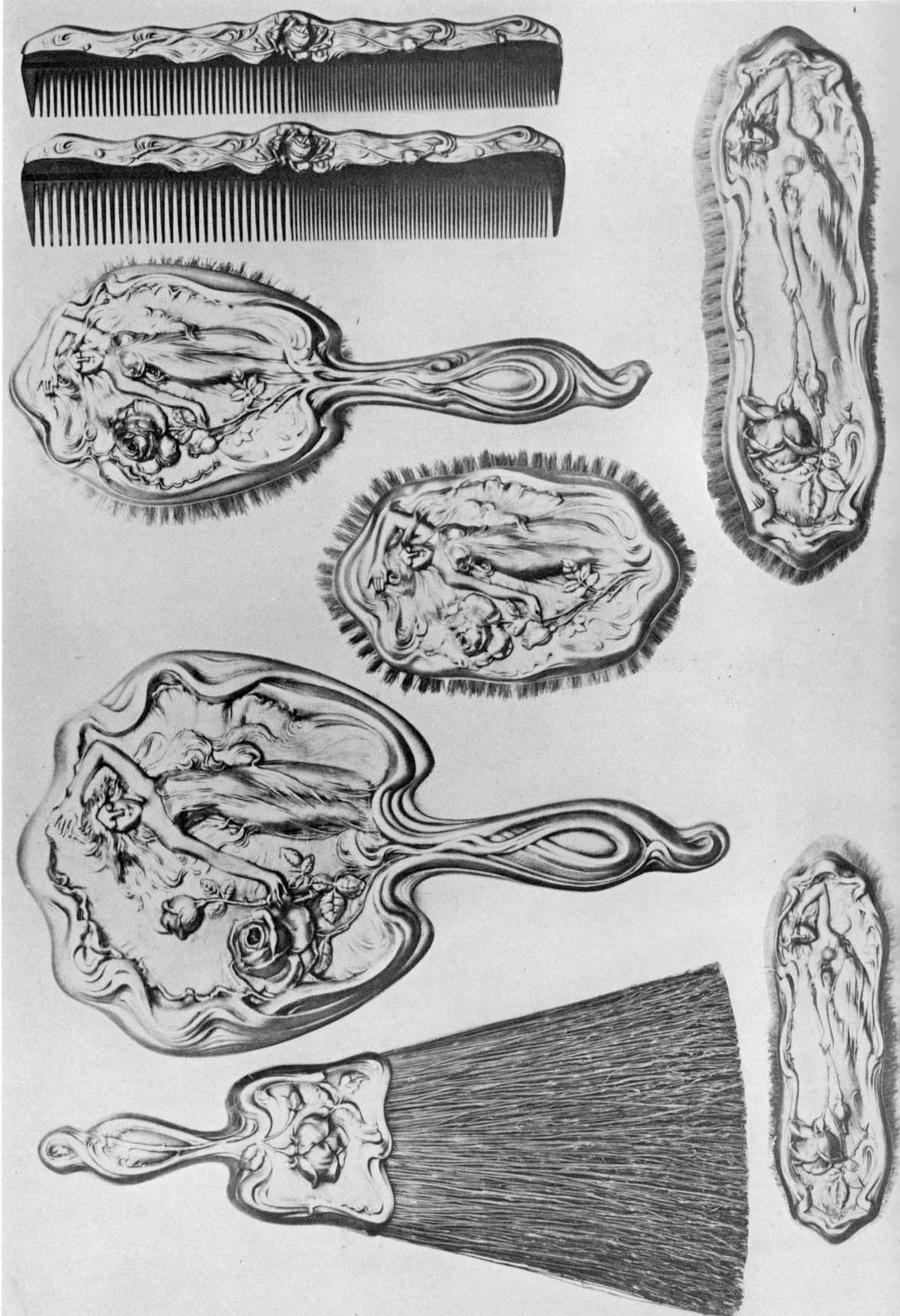

form with swirling draperies and flowing hair was one of the dominant motifs. Dresser sets of this period often bore "flowery," names such as "The Birth of the Rose" (Fig. 77). This flower, which is difficult to adapt to the requirements of the Art Nouveau style because of its stiff stem, has been successfully incorporated into the design by use of asymmetrical and vigorous curves which create the feeling of constant movement.

More often than not, the pieces of dresser sets have become separated. Combs and brushes, whose teeth and bristles are so subject to attrition, are seldom found in good condition. Often only the mirror remains (Fig. 78).

Pin trays in Art Nouveau style were made in numerous designs and appear to be plentiful in today's antique market (Fig. 79).

A few manicure sets were available in the 1880s but they reached a greater popularity around the turn of the century (Fig. 80). These sets included such pieces as nail file, polisher, cuticle knife, corn knife, scissors, and cream boxes.

While the slide fasterner, forerunner of the modern zipper, was invented by Whitcomb L. Judson and patented by him August 29, 1892, it was 20 years before the idea was developed into a marketable product and another 10 years before it was readily accepted by the public. Many folks were still "buttoning up," and even bending over to button their shoes and boots throughout the first quarter of the twentieth century. Buttoned shoes were first popular about 1860 but it was not until about seven years later that some inventive genius got around to devising the buttonhook (Fig. 81).

The earliest hooks were made with horn or tortoiseshell handles. Later ones were made of many other materials including bone, sterling, silverplate, ivory, and wood. Sterling ones were often

77. Derby Silver Co. catalog, about 1904.

78. Art Nouveau hand mirror. No marks.

made in flatware patterns to match table services and were included in the set. Some of these sterling buttonhooks were made as advertising for shoe stores. Probably even more of those for advertising

79. Pin tray made by the Queen City Silver Co. (Cincinnati, Ohio), about 1900–05.

80. Meriden Britannia Co. catalog, 1886.

No. 50. Hammered Old Silver Manicure Set, Seven Pieces in Plush Case, $21.50 (REFUTE).
    Cream Boxes, . each, $2.00 (REGALIA).   Polisher, . . 4.00 (REFUSAL).
    Nail File, . . . 2.75 (REGALE).   Scissors, . each, 1.75 (REFUGE).
    Cuticle Knife, . . 2.75 (REGAIN).   Plush Case, . 4.50 (REDTOP).

VIII. SMALL SILVERWARE AND NOVELTIES 387

No. 51. Satin Engraved Manicure Set, Ten Pieces in Plush Case, . . $28.75 (RAPPER).

ream Boxes, . each, $2.00 (REFRESH).	Polisher, . $4.00 (REDNESS).	No. 2 Glove Button Hook, $1.50 (REFEREE).
cissors, . . each, 1.75 (REFRACT).	Cuticle Knife, 2.75 (REENACT).	No. 3 Button Hook, . 2.00 (RECOGNIZE).
ail File, . . . 2.75 (REFORM).	Corn Knife, 2 75 (REFINERY).	Plush Case, . . . 5.50 (REFLEX).

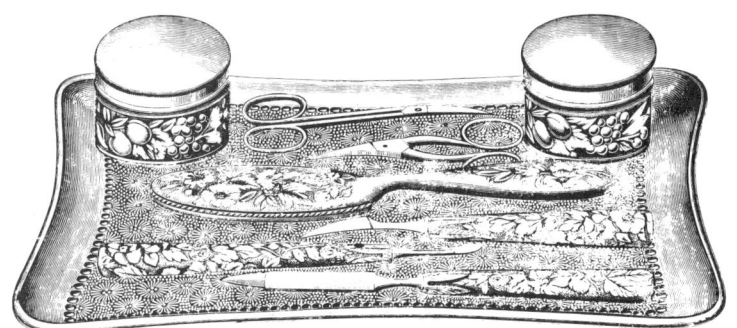

No. 52. MANICURE SET. Embossed, Old Silver.
Nine Pieces with Tray, . . . $25 50 (THIRSTY).

il File, . . $2.25 (THINLY).	Cuticle Knife, . . $2.25 (THEREON).	Scissors, . . each, $1.75 (THICKNESS).
lisher, . . 3.75 (THEREAT).	Corn Knife, . . . 2.25 (THANKLESS).	Cream Boxes, . " 2.00 (TEUTONIC).

. 115—9 inch Tray. Moorish, Old Silver, $7.50 (TERRIFY).

80 continued.

Silver Glove-Buttoner, No. 1

Sent, postpaid, as a Premium for a Club of 3 Three months' Subscribers and 5 cents extra to pay postage.

This dainty little article will be appreciated by all the ladies. It can be worn as a chatelaine or watch-chain charm, or carried in the purse.

Price, 50 cents, postpaid.

Gold-Plate or Silver Glove-Buttoner, No. 2

Either one sent, postpaid, as a Premium for a Club of 5 Three months' Subscribers and 5 cents additional to pay the postage

We have a large variety of Glove-buttoners in fancy patterns, both in the best rolled Gold-plate and in Silver.

In ordering No. 2, state whether Gold-plate or Silver is desired.

Price of No. 2, 70 cents, postpaid.

purposes were made of tin or other base metals, some being silverplated (Fig. 82).

Glove hooks look much like, but are smaller than, buttonhooks.

Hair Receivers

One essential to ladies' good grooming equipment which often stumps today's collectors is the hair receiver (Fig. 83). Almost always consisting of a bowl with a cover with a hole in the center, it differs in this latter respect from butter dishes with which it might be confused.

Probably by far the greater number were made in hand-painted porcelain or in the newly invented celluloid; many were made of silverplate to match dresser sets of combs and brushes. Hair receivers were in great demand during the 1890s and until after World War I when ladies began to wear their hair short.

Because of the cover with the large opening, they are in demand today for floral arrangements for such short-stemmed flowers as pansies and violets.

A Beautiful Oxidized Silver-Plated Button-Hook
IN A SATIN-LINED CASE

Sent, postpaid, as a Premium for a Club of Three 3 months' Subscribers at 25 cents each; or, for 2 Subscribers and 15 cents extra. Price, 35 cents, postpaid.

This Button-Hook is 7½ inches long, and beautifully chased. It is Triple-plated and of the best quality. It is, on account of its length, not only extremely convenient, but will be found to be an ornament for any lady's dressing-table.

Price, 35 cents, postpaid.

81. *Ladies' Home Journal* Supplement, May 1891.

VIII. SMALL SILVERWARE AND NOVELTIES 389

83. Hair receiver. Marked "Wilcox Silver Plate Co./Quadruple Plate/5 Gilt." Diameter 4 5/8 in.

82. Meriden Britannia Co. catalog, 1886.

Vinaigrettes and Chatelaines

Because of poor sanitation and the foul odors which confronted sensitive noses, an aromatic orange carried in the hand was for centuries the only safeguard against disease. During his reign Henry VIII banished the aromatic orange in favor of a jeweled pouncet box enclosing a tiny sponge soaked in aromatic vinegar. The correct procedure of inhaling the pouncet box was one of the social graces. These boxes were widely used in the seventeenth century by doctors, clergymen, and merchants whose occupations took them into disease-ridden areas. Later the name was changed to sponge box and silversmiths' tradecards of the mid-eighteenth century frequently mention them. They continued to be made into the early part of the nineteenth century when, under the influence of the novels of Sir Walter Scott, they were known again as pouncet boxes.

Georgian chemists of the 1770s improved aromatic vinegars with a strong

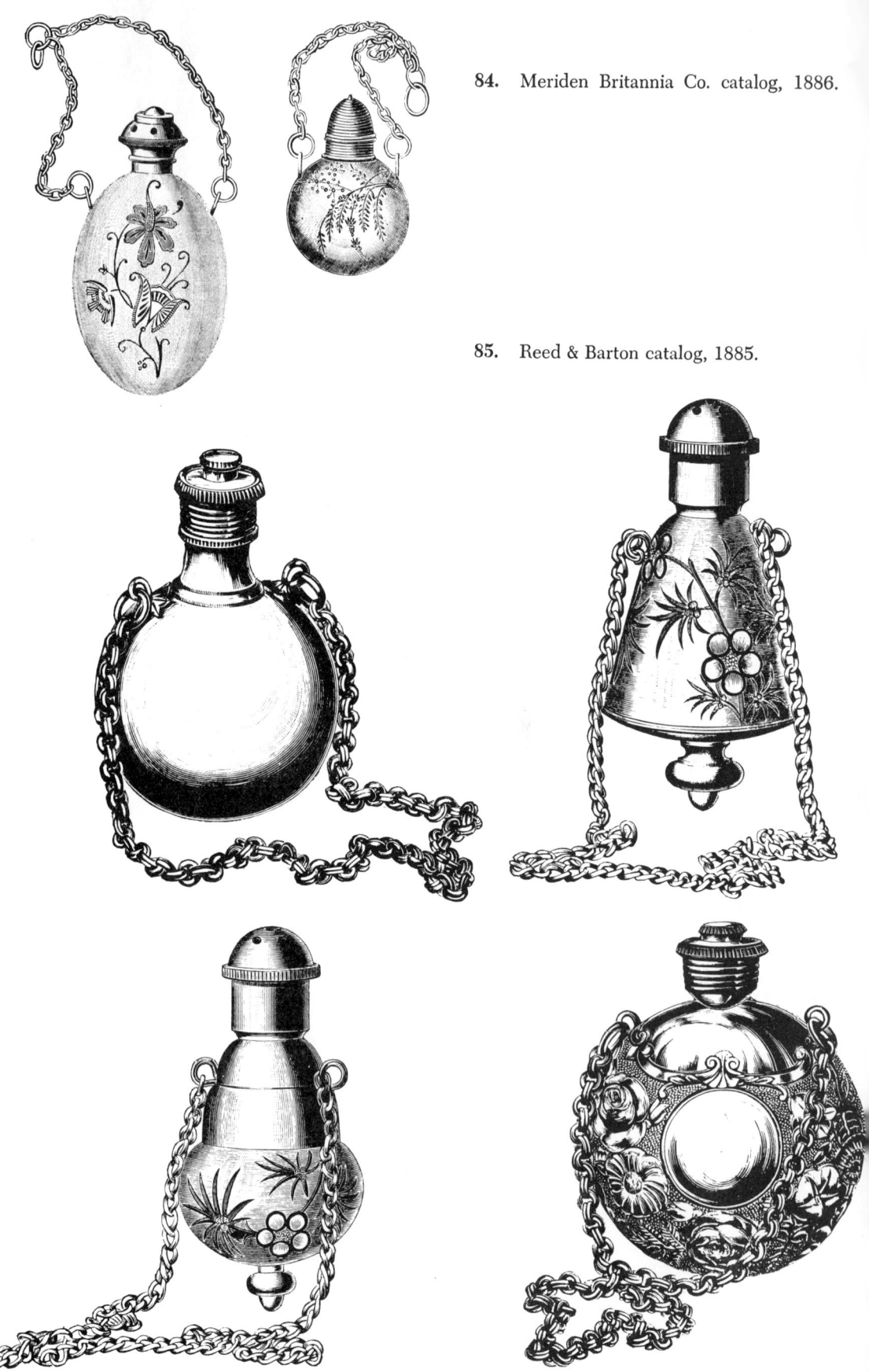

84. Meriden Britannia Co. catalog, 1886.

85. Reed & Barton catalog, 1885.

VIII. Small Silverware and Novelties 391

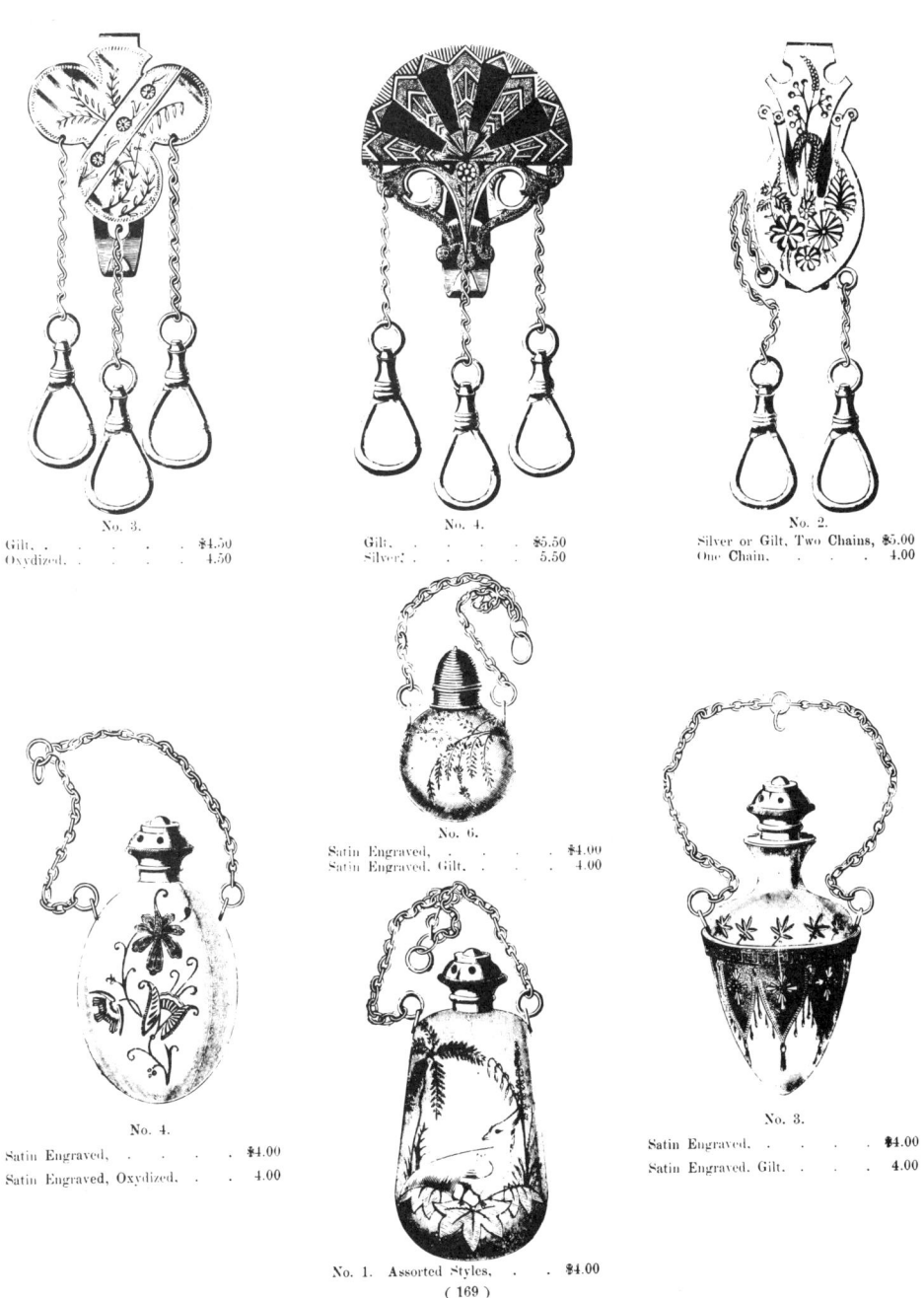

86. Meriden Britannia Co. catalog, 1877.

No. 20. Ash Holder, $4.25. (HUMIDITY)
Gold-lined, 4.75. (HUMILIATE)
Gold-lined and Oxidized, 5.25. (HUMMING)

87. Meriden Britannia Co. catalog, 1886.

No. 10. Shaving Cup, $5.25. (LOADING)

acetic acid base enriched with concentrated perfumed oils. For this, silversmiths designed a new container which was first listed as an aromatic vinegar box. The name vinaigrette was first used about 1801. Further improvement was made in commercial aromatic vinegars in the 1820s. While early vinaigrettes were carried loose in the pocket or bag, by 1830 they were provided with a tiny eye to which a chain was attached.

After the invention of smelling salts, about 1900, the fashion of carrying vinaigrettes fell into disfavor (Figs. 84, 85).

Chatelaines originated in medieval times and consisted of a long waist chain and pendant clasp from which were hung the keys, purse, and other trinkets. In Victorian times the waist chain had been replaced by a deep hook which was attached over the waist band (Figs. 86, 87). A shaped plate from which chains with swivel ends dangled were used for suspending scissors,

88. Reed & Barton catalog, 1885.

thimble cases, small scent bottles, and other trifles. The fashion of wearing chatelaines subsided in the 1850s but was revived in 1871 by Princess Alexandra of Wales. They remained in vogue for another 20 years.

Personal Accessories for Gentlemen

Personal accessories for gentlemen were not made in as many styles as those for ladies, nor were there as many articles made. However, the gentlemen were not neglected. Shaving cups and soap boxes, buttonhooks, shoe horns, and shaving brushes were made for use at home or for travel. Whisk brooms and holders, collar-button boxes, horsehide razor strops with silverplated mountings, pocket fruit knives, and

89. Meriden Britannia Co. catalog, 1886.

BUTTON HOOKS, SHAVING BRUSHES, ETC.

WHITE METAL.   NICKEL SILVER.

No. 3. Button Hook.

Satin, $1.75 (REMAND).   Satin, Engraved, $2.00 (REMAIN).   Hammered, Old Silver, $2.00 (REMEDY).

No. 2. Glove.
Satin, Engraved,   . $1.50 (REMARK).
Hammered, Old Silver,   1.50 (REMIND).

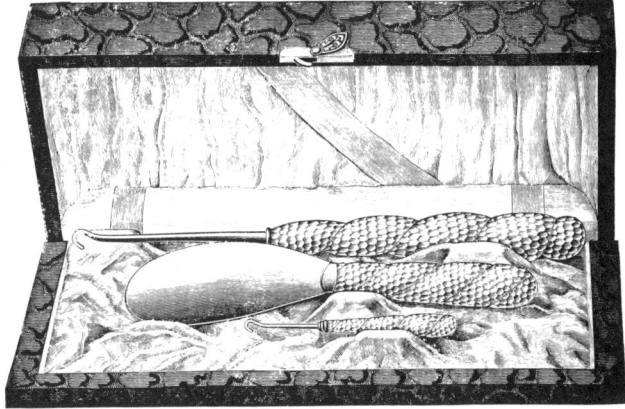

Plush Case, containing one each:

No. 5 Hammered, Old Silver Button Hook,   . $3.00 (RELIANCE).
No. 5 Hammered, Old Silver Shoe Horn,   .   3.00 (REGISTRY).
No. 1 Hammered, Old Silver Glove Buttoner,   1.50 (REGATTA).
Complete, in Case, ...   11.50 (REGULATION).

 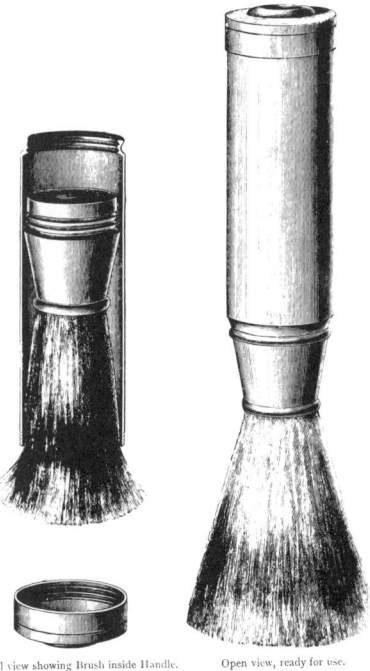  

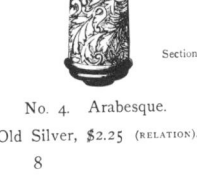

Sectional view showing Brush inside Handle.   Open view, ready for use.

No. 4. Arabesque.
Old Silver, $2.25 (RELATION).
8

No. 4. Traveling Shaving Brush.
Satin,   .   . $3.75 (REINSURE).
Hammered, Old Silver, 4.25 (RELEVANT).

No. 2. Shaving Brush.
Satin,   .   . $3.50 (RELENT).
Hammered, Old Silver, 4.00 (RELAPSE).

No. 6. Moorish.
Hammered, Old Silver, $3.00 (REGARD).
Moorish, Old Silver,   .   3.50 (REISSUE).
No. 6. Shoe Horn to match.
Hammered, Old Silver, $3.00 (RELIC).
Moorish, Old Silver,   .   3.50 (RELISH).

394 American Silverplate

No. 6. Moorish, Old Silver Whisk Broom.
Satin, ... $2.75 (rabble).
Arabesque, Old Silver, . 3.00 (remiss).
Hammered, Old Silver, . 3.00 (remnant).
Moorish, Old Silver, . 3.25 (remodel).

Plush Case, containing Infant Hair Brush and Puff Box.
Complete, ... $14.25 (repast)
No. 400 Brush—Moorish, Old Silver, 3.75 (repay).
No. 9 Puff Box—Old Silver, . . 6.00 (rental).
Plush Case, ... 4.50 (remount).

No. 5. Hammered Whisk Broom.
Satin, ... $2.75 (repairer).
Arabesque, Old Silver, . 3.00 (rentroll).
Hammered, Old Silver, . 3.00 (renewal).
Moorish, Old Silver, . 3.25 (rendition).

No. 45. Whisk Broom Holder.
Enameled Copper, Old Silver Pockets, $9.00 (remorse).
(Price does not include Broom.)

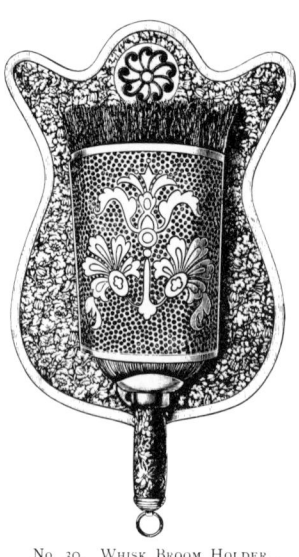

No. 30. Whisk Broom Holder.
Old Silver, . . . $9.75 (remote).
Old Silver, Gold Inlaid, . 10.75 (remove).
(Price does not include Broom.)

90–91. Meriden Britannia Co. catalog, 1886.

VIII. SMALL SILVERWARE AND NOVELTIES 395

92. Collar-button box. St. Louis Silver Co., St. Louis, Mo. Made between 1904 and 1912.

JOY & SELIGER'S COLLAR BUTTON BOX.

92a. *Jewelers' Weekly,* November 16, 1892.

92b. *Jewelers' Weekly,* January 1, 1896.

Long Enough when in use.
Short Enough when not in use.
Fine Enough for a king and
Good Enough for any gentleman.

If you haven't this in stock, order **at once.**

Best Horse Hide Strop. Coils automatically in holder.

PAIRPOINT MFG. CO.,
NEW BEDFORD, MASS.

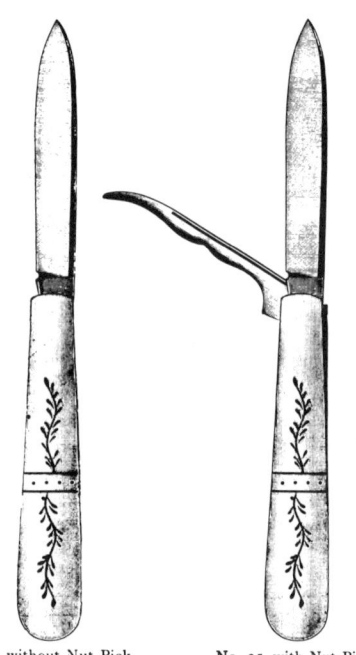
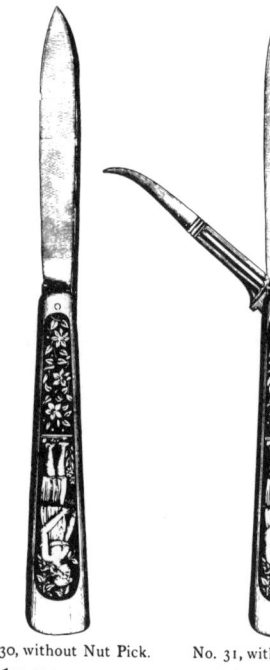
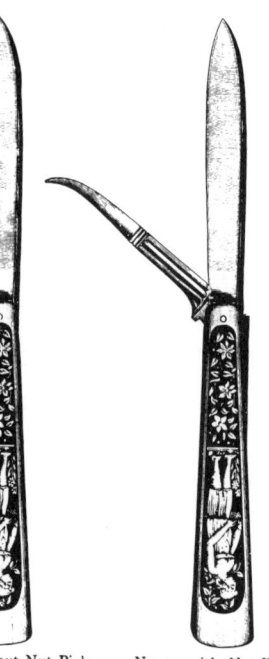
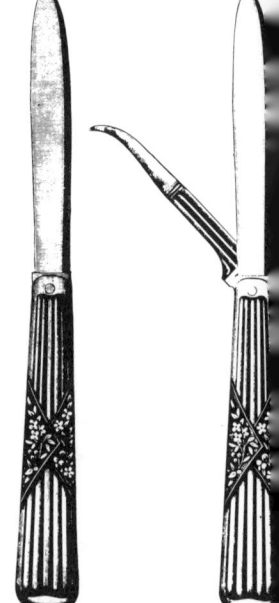

No. 34, without Nut Pick.
Satin, . . $7.50 (GUNBOAT).
Satin, Engraved, 9.00 (GYPSUM).

No. 35, with Nut Pick.
Satin, . . $9.00 (HEADLONG).
Satin, Engraved, 10.50 (HEADWIND).

No. 30, without Nut Pick.
$13.50 (HARMLESS).

No. 31, with Nut Pick.
$16.25 (HAREBELL).

No. 28, without Nut Pick.
$13.50 (HARDSHIP).

No. 29, with Nut Pick.
$16.25 (HABITAT).

SOLID STEEL PLATED FRUIT KNIVES. (Prices per Dozen.)

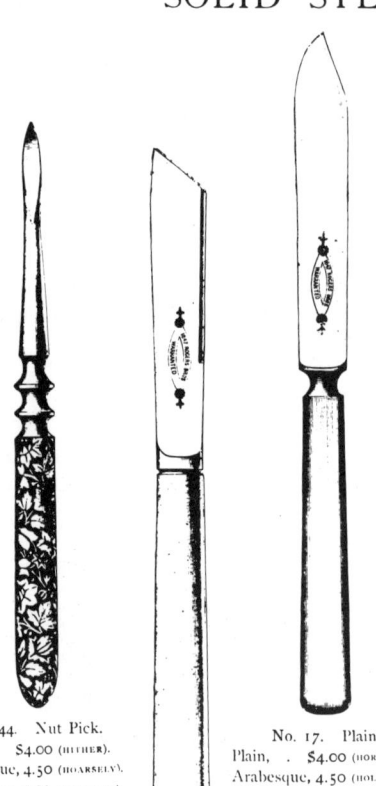

No. 44. Nut Pick.
Plain, . $4.00 (HITHER).
Arabesque, 4.50 (HOARSELY).
Old Silver, 5.00 (GUNSMITH).

No. 25. Satin.
Satin, $4.00 (HORSEBACK).
Plain, 4.00 (GUILELESS).

No. 17. Plain.
Plain, . $4.00 (HORNBILL).
Arabesque, 4.50 (HOLDBACK).
Old Silver, 5.00 (GUIDANCE).

No. 32. Arabesque.
Arabesque, $6.00 (HELPMATE).
Old Silver, 6.50 (GUERILLA).

No. 32. Satin.
Plain, $5.50 (HEREWITH).
Satin, 5.50 (HEARTILY).

No. 26. Plain.
Plain, $4.00 (HOT-BED).
Satin, 4.00 (HELIX).

No 26. Arabesque.
Arabesque, $4.50 (HISTORIAN).
Old Silver, 5.00 (HOLLYHOCK).

No. 32. Nut Pick.
Satin, . $5.50 (HUB).
Arabesque, 6.00 (HORS).
Old Silver, 6.50 (HOR).

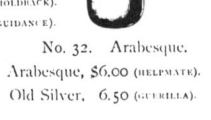

93. Meriden Britannia Co. catalog, 1886.

VIII. SMALL SILVERWARE AND NOVELTIES 397

Coaster, 5½ inch, Wood Bottom, $7.00. (JUPITER)
Coaster, 4½ inch, Wood Bottom, 6.00. (JURAT)

No. 20. Coaster, 4½ inch, $4.00. (JURIST)
No. 40. Coaster, 5½ inch, 5.00. (JUSTIFY)

For Nickel Silver Coasters, see page 361.

No. 12. Coaster, 5 inch, $4.50. (JUTLAND)
No. 12. Coaster, 6 inch, 5.50. (JUSTLY)

No. 52. Flask, $12.00. (KALE)

No. 63. Flask, $15.00. (KANGAROO)

No. 720. 2 No. 90 Bottles and 4 Goblets, $44.50. (KANSAS)

No. 700. 3 No. 110 Bottles and 6 Goblets, $85.00. (KANT)
Gold and Silver Finish, 95.00. (KANTISM)

NICKEL SILVER LIQUOR LABELS.
Assorted, per dozen, $12.00. (KEDGE)
Lettered to order.

No. 710. 3 No. 90 Bottles and 9 Goblets, $62.50. (KEELHAUL)

94. Reed & Barton catalog, 1885.

398   AMERICAN SILVERPLATE

95. Silverplated flask commemorating the sinking of the *Maine*. *Jewelers' Weekly & Horological Review*, June 15, 1898.

pocket flasks were among the silverplated articles made for gentlemen (Figs. 88–92, 92a, 92b, 93, 94).

Silverplated flasks were sometimes made as mementoes of such events as the sinking of the battleship *Maine*, whose destruction by explosion in Havana Harbor, Cuba, February 15, 1898, is considered the direct cause of the Spanish-American War. The one illustrated was made by Simpson, Hall, Miller & Company with an embossed picture of the ill-fated man-o'-war under full sail in the open sea (Fig. 95). Beneath the picture is the sentiment, "Remember the *Maine*."

Desk Accessories

Desk accessories for both men and women include stamp boxes, ink stands, paper knives, letter openers, thermometers, calendars, erasers, knife sharpeners, and plain ink wells (Figs. 96–103).

96. Stamp box made by the Meriden Silver Plate Co.

97. Desk set made by Reed & Barton; with "World" trademark.

VIII. Small Silverware and Novelties 399

400 AMERICAN SILVERPLATE

98. *The Manufacturing Jeweler,* October 25, 1894.

99. Illustrated wholesale catalog and price list of the Fort Dearborn Watch & Clock Co., 1904.

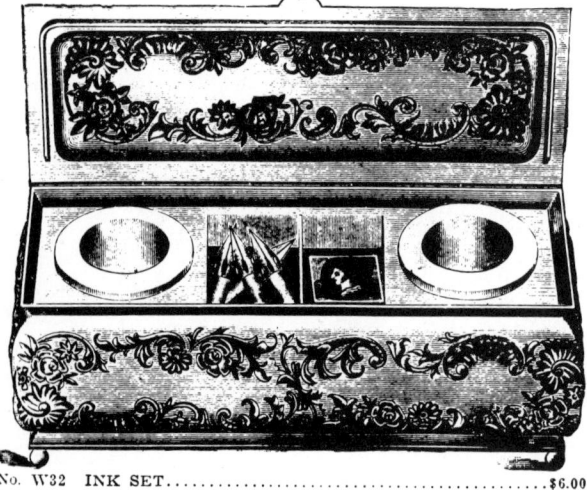

No. W32 INK SET..................................$6.00

Two Ink Wells, Stamp and Pen Point Boxes. Dimensions, 6x2¼ inches. Height, 2 inches.

No. W8 CALENDAR..................................

Perpetual. Etched Gray, Silver or Old Brass. Height, 5¼ inches.

No. W38 INK SET, SILVER..................................$6.70

Cut Glass Bottle, Pen Rack, Wiper and Stamp Box. Height, 4½ inches; Length, 7⅝ inches.

No. W331 PERPETUAL CALENDAR..................................$3

Etched, French Gray. Length, 5½ inches. Height, 4¼ inches.

No. 200. Stamp Box.
Old Silver, Gold Lined, . $4.75 (QUIETLY).

No. 201. Stamp Box.
Satin, . . $3.75 (QUIETUS).

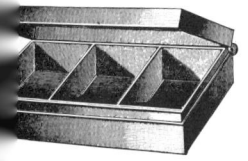

No. 202. Stamp Box.
. . . $3.00 (QUICKSET).
red, Old Silver, 3.75 (QUIESCENT).

No. 106. Shaving-Stick Box.
Satin, . $2.25 (QUINTAL).
Satin, Engraved, 2.75 (QUITTANCE).

No. 106. Shaving-Stick Box.
Hammered, Old Silver, $3.00 (QUITE).
Moorish, Old Silver, . 3.50 (RAIL).

No. 46. Cigar Lamp.
Old Copper, . $5.00 (PROMOTE).
Old Silver, . 5.50 (PROMOTER).

No. 15. Cigar Lamp.
mered, Old Copper, . $4.50 (PRONE).
mered, Old Silver, . 5.00 (PRONOUN).

No. 2. Shaving Set.
With Drawer for Razor, . $13.50 (INCLUDE).

No. 01. Liquor Label.
er dozen, . . $6.00 (PEDIGREE).

No. 02. Liquor Label.
Per dozen, . . $12.00 (PEDIMENT).

Nos. 01 and 02 Labels furnished with Assorted Names if desired.

100. Meriden Britannia Co. catalog, 1886.

	No. 41.	No. 29.	No. 30.	
	Hammered, $5.50 (ASCRIBE).	Gold and Silver, $3.50 (PITCH).	Gold and Silver, $4.50 (PISTOL).	
No. 40.	Hammered, Gold Inlaid, 6.50 (ASPEN).			No. 45.
Silver, $4.50 (ASTUTE).				Old Copper and Gold, $8.50
Gold Inlaid, 5.00 (ATHLETE).				Old Silver and Gold, 9.00

No. 32.	No. 38. OLD SILVER.	No. 39.
Silver, $8.00 (PLASTER).	Hammered, $9.00 (ASSUME).	Silver, $8.00 (ASPHALT).
Gilt, 9.00 (PLASTIC).	Hammered, Gold Inlaid, 10.50 (ASTONISH).	Gold Lined, 9.00 (ASSEMBLY).

No. 46. WITH LETTER SCALE.	No. 42. WITH LETTER SCALE.	No. 48.
Hammered, Old Copper and Gold, $9.50 (CAPACITY).	Silver, $10.00 (PETITION).	Enameled Copper, Old Silver Mountings, $7.50
Hammered, Old Silver and Gold, 10.00 (CALIPERS).	Old Silver, 11.00 (PETREL).	

No. 28.	No. 51.	No. 18.
Silver, $9.00 (PLANET).	Old Silver, $18.00 (CASTE).	Old Silver, $9.00 (PLAC)
Gold and Steel, 10.50 (PLANK).	Gold Inlaid, 20.00 (CHOICELY).	Gold Inlaid, 10.00 (PLAID)

101. Meriden Britannia Co. catalog, 1886.

No. 43.
Old Copper, . $3.50 (CASEMATE).
Old Silver, . 4.00 (CASESHOT).

No. 31.
Silver, Gold Inlaid, . $6.25 (PISTON).

No. 44.
Old Copper, . $4.50 (CASTAWAY).
Old Silver, . 5.00 (CASTIGATE).

No. 47.
Enameled Copper, Old Silver Mountings, $4.75 (CHEST).

No. 49.
Old Silver, . $8.50 (CASSIMERE).
Gold Inlaid, . 10.00 (CASSINO).

No. 37.
Old Silver, $6.00 (PLATONIC).

No. 36.
Old Silver, . . $5.50 (PLATINA).
Old Silver, Gold Inlaid, 6.50 (PLATING).

No. 50.
Old Silver, . $10.50 (CASHBOOK).

No. 35.
Old Silver, . . $4.50 (PLAT).
Old Silver, Gold Inlaid, 5.50 (PLATE).

101 continued.

404 AMERICAN SILVERPLATE

102. Reed & Barton catalog, 1885.

VIII. Small Silverware and Novelties 405

| No. 156. | $13.00 (HOPE) |
| Gold and Oxidized, | 16.50. (HOPPER) |

No. 160. $13.50 (HONORABLE)
Gold and Oxidized, 16.50. (HONORARY)

No. 145. $8.00 (HOODWINK)
Gold and Oxidized, 9.50. (HOPEFUL)

No. 170. $18.00 (HOOD)
Gold and Oxidized, 21.50. (HOODLESS)

No. 90. $9.50 (HOPING)
Oxidized, 11.50. (HOPKINS)

No. 165. $14.75 (HORDE)
Gold and Oxidized, 17.75. (HORNET)

No. 135. $7.25 (HOREHOUND)
Gold or Oxidized, 8.75. (HORIZON)

No. 125. With gold-lined Drawer, $28.50. (HORNY)
Gold and Oxidized, 32.50. (HORNISH)

No. 120. With gold-lined Drawer, $24.00. (HORN)
Gold and Oxidized, 28.00. (HOROLOGE)

102 continued.

Stamp boxes may usually be distinguished from hairpin boxes, which are often about the same size, by having a half-cylinder or rounded bottom rather than being flat.

Ink erasers with steel blades were often made with handles which matched dresser sets and were even illustrated in old catalogs along with these rather than with desk accessories. For this reason they have sometimes been assumed to be part of manicure sets. One article of pedicure sets does bear a superficial resemblance. The corn or cuticle knife, however, usually has a blade with a straight cutting edge, while the ink eraser blade almost always had a curved cutting edge. A few have a double curved edge cutting blade.

No. 7. Shoe Horn.
Silver, . . $2.00 (SUBLIME).
Etched, Old Silver, 2.50 (SUBSALT).

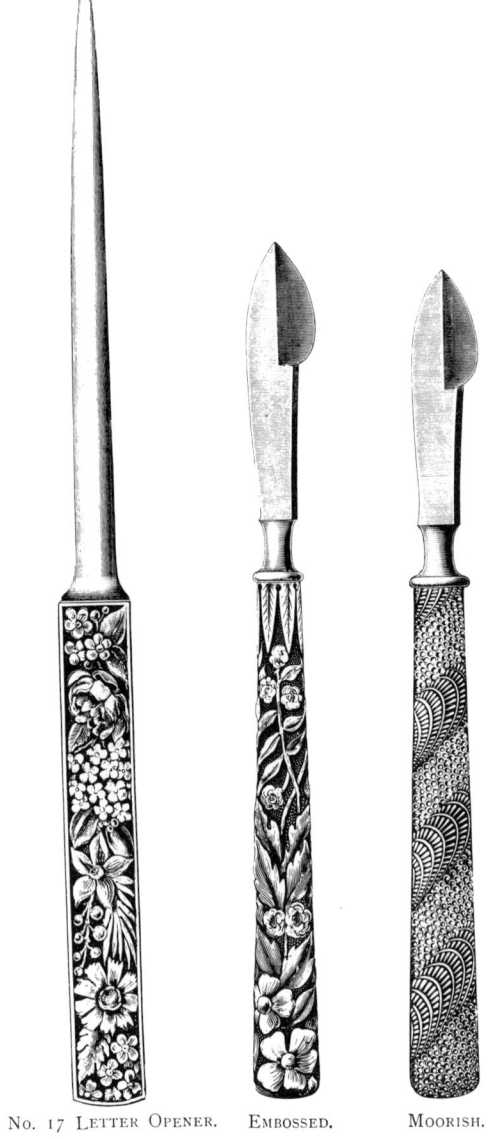

No. 17 Paper Knife. No. 17 Letter Opener. Embossed. Moorish.
No. 17 Ink Erasers.
Embossed, Old Silver, . $2.75
Moorish, Old Silver, . 3.00

103. Meriden Britannia Co. catalog, 1886.

CHAPTER IX

Lighting Devices

From the days that primitive man huddled in dark caves, illuminated only by the light of his campfire or by burning faggots, there has been a constant search for better ways to sweep away the dark and bring light into the home. Crude pottery and hollowed-out stone held burning oil or animal fat, in which moss, or later a rag or stringlike cotton wick was placed. A comparison of these with the iron, tin, and pewter lamps of early Colonial days shows how little progress had been made in artificial lighting in thousands of years.

Being abundant, fish oil was most in use for early lamps. Its unpleasant odor did not increase its desirability. When it was discovered that whale oil was a superior illuminating fluid, many lamps with closed fuel container were designed for its use. Other lamps were designed to burn grease or lard oil or for the explosive camphene discovered in the 1830s. The latter was made from a combination of distilled turpentine and alcohol.

The invention of the Argand lamp in 1780 with its various improvements was really the beginning of better lighting. A hollow tube, rather than a thin round or flat wick, allowed a current of air to come up through the center of the burning wick as well as on the outside. By this means an abundant supply of oxygen was constantly renewed as the heat of the lamp created a draft. Therefore the carbon was entirely consumed and a strong bright light without smoke resulted. A later development was the glass chimney to direct the draft against the flame. This principle of Argand's is the one upon which all later oil-burning lamps were constructed. Argand lamps were considered a great luxury, and except in homes of wealth were not generally adopted.

Various improvements were devised for grease or lard-oil lamps. One was the introduction of a third tube of copper used between the two brass wick tubes. Being a good conductor of heat, the copper conveyed hot air from the flame down to the bottom of the oil font and prevented the congealing of the oil—a severe problem in winter.

Lard oil was commonly used as the illuminant in the great lighthouses of the world until as late as 1880, at which time a satisfactory burner using kerosene was constructed and adopted.

Whale oil, however, remained the American favorite for domestic lighting and between 1800 and 1845 more than 500 patents for whale-oil lamps were granted in this country. While gas was the illuminant of city mansions it was not in general use except where a gas plant and pipe system were available.

At the dawn of history petroleum was already a useful commodity. In the building of Babylon and in the pyramids of Egypt it was used. Early Egyptians used it in embalming; it was used as axle grease on Hittite chariots. The Old Testament contains references to the occurrence and use of petroleum. Our word "naphtha" is derived from the old Hebrew word *nephthar,* the oil used to light the altar fire.

In the literature of ancient Greece

408 AMERICAN SILVERPLATE

No. 115.

No. 128.

No. 127.

No. 126.

1. Britannia metal lamps for "burning fluid" or oil. Two wicks, side by side, create a stronger current of air so that more oxygen comes in contact with the wicks, insuring freer burning and more and stronger light. Oddly, three wicks do not work as well as two. This invention is attributed to Benjamin Franklin. Meriden Britannia Co. catalog, 1855.

No. 150.

No. 155.

No. 420.

No. 415.

No. 410.

No. 405.

2. Britannia metal lamps for burning lard oil, a fuel used extensively in New England about 1800. Meriden Britannia Co. catalog, 1855.

IX. Lighting Devices 409

No. 480.

Old or Bright Copper,	$48.00 (ABANDON).
Old Silver,	52.00 (ABASH).
Old Silver, X Gold Inlaid,	57.00 (ABBESS).
Old Silver, X X Gold Inlaid,	62.00 (ABDICATE).

No. 490.

Old or Bright Copper,	$43.00 (ABDUCTION).
Old Silver,	48.00 (ABJECTLY).
Old Silver, X Gold Inlaid,	52.00 (ABOLITION).
Old Silver, X X Gold Inlaid,	57.00 (ABSORBENT).

3. Kerosene-burning lamps. Meriden Britannia Co. catalog, 1882.

4. Kerosene lamps with ball-type glass shades. Meriden Britannia Co. catalog, 1882.

No. 615.
d Copper, . . . $15.00 (STREAMLET).
d Copper and Old Silver, 17.00 (STRETCHER).

No. 610.
Enameled Copper, Old Silver Mountings, . $27.50
Globe Extra.

No. 655.
Old Copper, Old Silver Mountings, $100.00 (STRICTLY).
Height, when extended, 68 inches.

5. Meriden Britannia Co. catalog, 1886.

No. 25. Rochester Burner.
Bright Cut Copper Finish, $9.50

No. 20. Rochester Burner.
Old Silver Finish, $9.50   Copper Finish, $8.50

These prices are Net, and do not include Shade.

6. Kerosene-burning table lamps. Note that the Rochester burners are mentioned. Wilcox Silver Plate Co. catalog, 1886.

and Rome are many references to the use of oil. Pits were dug as early as 400 B.C. to mine oil in what is now Albania, where primitive refining methods were used. The Chinese were drilling wells as deep as 2,000 feet about the time of Christ. They used primitive equipment to tap deposits of natural gas, which they used for heat and illumination. At the time of Columbus rock oil recovered from natural seepages was used for medicinal purposes. And in North America natives used asphalt and crude oil for religious and medicinal purposes and for waterproofing before the fifteenth century. Early explorers found natives on this continent using oil in some form in whatever areas it occurred.

Petroleum from brine wells was transported in wooden barrels from Tarentum, Pennsylvania, to New York City and Baltimore, Maryland. This oil went to market by canal, river, and railroad, for the production and distribution of coal oil distilled from coal was a thriving business around Pittsburgh, until ruined by the advent of the cheaper kerosene distilled from crude oil.

John D. Rockefeller accumulated his fortune by selling Perfection Kerosene, Polarine Machine Oil, and Mica Axle

IX. LIGHTING DEVICES 413

Grease. Standard Oil horse-drawn wagons peddled kerosene, Rayo lamps, and Perfection coal oil stoves from 1880 to 1920.

As early as 1850 lamps for burning kerosene were advertised and sold. Wherever the lamps were bought, one could also buy the oil. A man by the name of Kier, in Pittsburgh, distilled kerosene from surface petroleum. Though it was planned originally to be sold as a medicinal oil, its use as a lamp oil was soon discovered. So rapidly was it adopted that the price rose. It was the invention of the process for making coal oil from coal and the contemporary invention of the coal-oil lamp which provided the impetus which led to the drilling of the first well for the express purpose of finding oil. Edwin L. Drake, supervisor of the Seneca Oil Company, drilled near Titusville, Pennsylvania. Their first well came in at 69 1/2 feet on August 27, 1859, and ushered in the oil age.

Kerosene, which had been selling up

No. 24. Rochester Burner.
Cushioned Old Silver.
With Handles, . . . $12.50

No. 19. Rochester Burner.
Oxidized Finish, $13.00   Bright Copper Finish, $9.50

No. 21. Rochester Burner.
Old Silver Finish, $10.50   Copper Finish, $9.00

These prices are Net, and do not include Shade.

7. Wilcox Silver Plate Co. catalog, 1886.

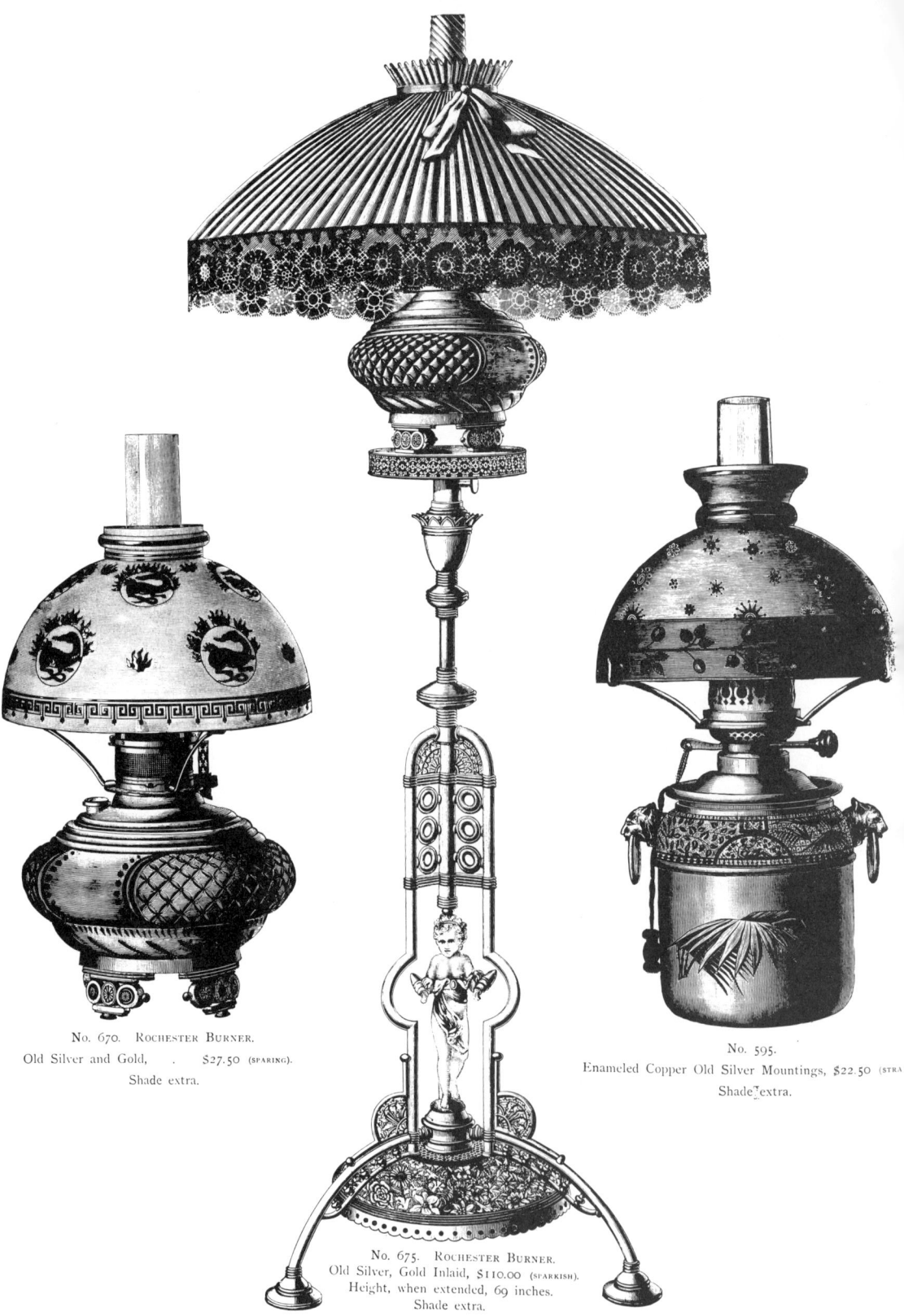

8. A Rochester burner was incorporated into these lamps, including the "floor model." Meriden Britannia Co. catalog, 1886.

IX. Lighting Devices 415

No. 660. Rochester Burner.
Old Copper, . . $25.00 (strangely).
Old Silver, . . 27.50 (stratify).
Shade extra.

No. 685. Extension Lamp.
Complete with No. 680 Lamp.
Old Silver, Gold Inlaid, . $125.00 (stratum).
Height, when extended, 75 inches.

No. 680. Rochester Burner.
Old Silver, . . $27.50 (streamer).
Shade extra.

9. Extension lamp table on which one of the regular table models could be placed. Meriden Britannia Co. catalog, 1886.

10. Oil lamps. *Left to right:* Rogers, Smith & Co., 1882; Meriden Britannia Co., 1882; boudoir lamp by Meriden Silver Plate Co., about 1896. The shades on the first two are reproductions. The boudoir lamp originally had a fancy shade of cloth, lace, and ribbons.

to a dollar and a half a gallon, soon became cheap enough for universal use. The price dropped to two cents a gallon.

The first mineral oil used as a lighting fluid, kerosene had many advantages. It was abundant and it was cheap; it was light and could climb a relatively long wick by capillary action, which made it possible to keep the oil container well below the burner and out of the way of the light. Kerosene was far less explosive and gave as brilliant illumination as the more dangerous camphene. And its mass production led to the similar mass production of relatively inexpensive lamps to burn "coal oil" as it was then called.

The first patent for American kerosene lamps was issued in 1859, along with 40 others that same year. During the next 20 years others were patented at the rate of about 80 new ones a year. Outstanding among the improvements in kerosene lamps was the well-known "Rochester Burner," which employed a circular wick and a central draft principle, operating very much like the earlier Argand lamps.

As early as 1855 the Meriden Britannia Company produced whale-oil and grease lamps and in 1882, in response to the demands of the large market for kerosene lamps, they offered 22 lamp designs in a variety of plated finishes.

IX. LIGHTING DEVICES   417

Shades and globes were not included in the catalog list price but could be purchased at an average price of $1.25 to $2.50 apiece. The number of styles offered by the Meriden Britannia Company in 1886 was 29, including six styles of extension lamps. The latter consisted of regular lamps placed on a silverplated platform which could be raised or lowered. The tallest could be extended to 75 inches.

The Meriden Britannia Company and other silver manufacturers did not manufacture the lamp burners. They used the Rochester burners or others. Two types of burners which were sold all over the world and spread the name of Meriden, were this Rochester burner introduced by Edward Miller & Company in 1884 and the B & H burner made by Bradley & Hubbard Mfg. Company, founded in 1854. A great many of the lamps illustrated in Meriden Britannia Company catalogs specifically mention the Rochester burners.

Other companies also made numerous styles of silverplated kerosene lamps. Among them, Reed & Barton was outstanding with 32 designs which they offered in 1885. All of these were table

No. 2660.
Old Silver, $20.50 (HARMOST).

No. 2658.
Old Silver, $18.25 (HARMEL).

11. Meriden Silver Plate Co. catalog, 1888.

| *No. 8.* | *No. 5.* | *No. 4.* | *No. 3.* | *No. 2.* | *No. 45.* |
| Per pair, $8 00. | Per pair, $5 75. | Per pair, $5 25. | Per pair, $5 00. | Per pair, $4 50. | Per pair, $4 25. |

| *No. 55.* | *No. 93.* | *No. 92.* | *No. 90.* | *No. 91.* | *No. 91.* |
| Per pair, $5 75. | With Extinguisher. Per pair, $6 00. With Extinguisher and Snuffer. Per pair, $7 00. | With Extinguisher. Per pair, $5 00. Without Extinguisher. Per pair, $4 50. | Per pair, $5 75. | With Extinguisher. Per pair, $5 25. | Per pair, $4 75. |

13. Meriden Britannia Co. catalog, 1867.

models; none of them were the extension type. No mention is made of the type of burners used. The Wilcox Silver Plate Company offered five designs in their 1886 catalog and the Meriden Silver Plate Company showed four in their 1888 catalog.

Manufacturers of silverplated wares dropped out of the lamp business even before the turn of the century though kerosene lamps continued to be carried in mail-order catalogs of general merchandise for many years. Electrified candlesticks with shades, sometimes called "Electroliers," were carried as late as the 1920s, but most lamp production was left to those who specialized.

Candles are of two basic types—either dipped or made in molds—and have undergone little change through the centuries. The materials from which they are made depends mainly on availability. For instance, in this country cattle were not common until about 1655–60 so that there was little tallow for making candles. But large numbers of deer and bear roamed the woods and their fat was used. Beeswax, from the honeycombs of the swarms of wild bees, bayberries growing near the salt water of sand dunes, and spermaceti, a fatty substance from the head of the sperm whale, all made excellent candles. Candles have always been expensive and have been used more for special occasion lighting than everyday use.

Candlesticks also are of two basic types, pricket and socket. Pricket candlesticks have a spike or pricket for holding the candle in place while the socket candlesticks have a hole or socket into which the candle fits.

Candlesticks have been made of iron, tin, pewter, wood, glass, brass, silver, "Old Sheffield Plate," pottery, and

14. Reed & Barton catalog, 1885.

  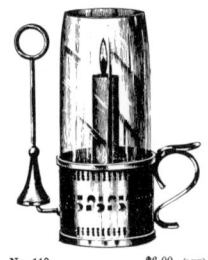

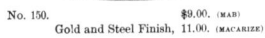

15. Reed & Barton catalog, 1885.
16. Candlestick marked: "Charles W. Hamill & Co.,/Triple Plate/Baltimore, Md." Made between 1877 and 1884.

other earthernware and in a variety of styles. Manufacturers of silverplated wares lost no time in making their own interpretations of current styles.

An early Meriden Britannia Company catalog (Fig. 13) illustrates six tall candlesticks whose turnings are remarkably like those of the britannia ones being made 30 years earlier. (Few candlesticks were made in this country prior to 1830, most of those in use being imported.) These designs were not unique in this country. A catalog of T. Bradbury & Sons, Sheffield, England, about 1844, illustrated three similar designs which were late transitional from copper to German silver, fused plate to electroplate.

The six chamber sticks illustrated in the 1867 Meriden Britannia Company catalog were also based on much earlier designs which were popular in the eighteenth century.

Candlesticks and candelabra of the 1880s were more elaborate in design than many earlier ones (Figs. 14, 15). Candlesticks, especially, were often whimsical in nature (Figs. 16, 17).

17. Lighting device marked: "MF'D & PLATED BY/REED & BARTON/1520."

422 AMERICAN SILVERPLATE

One Pair, Closed.   No. 130. TRAVELING CANDLESTICKS.   Single, Open.
(Full Size.)

Silver,   .   .   per pair, $4.00 (MARVEL).
Hammered,   .   per pair, 5.00 (TANNERY).

18. Meriden Britannia Co. catalog, 1886.

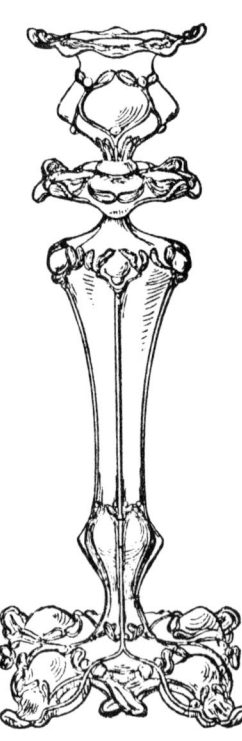 

19. Candlestick designed by Emile Bächle, Meriden, Conn., for International Silver Co. Design Patent No. 36,231; Patented February 17, 1903.

20. Candlestick designed by Ellerson L. Brainard, Danbury, Conn. Design Patent No. 36,751; Patented January 26, 1904.

21. Five-light water-lily candelabrum, Meriden Britannia Co., about 1900–05.

IX. LIGHTING DEVICES 425

Candelabra No. 602

The Secret of Success

in handling Silverware is to secure, first of all, such salable goods as assure the most substantial profit to you and maximum satisfaction to your customer—goods that combine finest quality in their grade with beauty of style and popular price.

Our new line is a triumph of economy and excellence

POOLE SILVER CO., Taunton, Mass.

Manufacturers of

FINEST QUALITY of ELECTRO PLATE

23. Advertisement of Poole Silver Co., Taunton, Mass. *The Keystone,* August 1906.

22. Art Nouveau candelabrum, Pairpoint Mfg. Co., New Bedford, Mass., patented April 12, 1904.

A traveling candlestick which came apart and formed its own carrying case provided an ingenious solution to provide light away from home (Fig. 18).

Candlesticks were especially adaptable to the interpretation of Art Nouveau styles (Figs. 19–22). The curves of the female figure, swirling draperies, and long flowing hair were a dominant motif in Art Nouveau. Another recurring motif is the tall climbing stalk with interlaced and undulating stems and flowers. These were all incorporated into Art Nouveau candlesticks.

It is generally recognized that single candlesticks, used perhaps in pairs, are suitable for informal occasions and are adaptable for placement in a variety of ways while candelabra are usually reserved for more formal use (Fig. 23). Purchase of a variety of such pieces has always been a major expenditure to

24–25. All-purpose multiple candelabra. Webster-Wilcox, a division of International Silver Co.

All this from One Pair of Candelabra

If you find the full 19½ inch height is a shade too tall, just remove one section and your candelabra are now 17½ inches tall. All parts are connected with a simple friction fit. A twist of the wrist removes them or fastens them securely.

If you would like a single 5-light candelabrum as a beautiful centerpiece on your table, separate 5-light arms are available. By adding these to the #706/3 candlestick parts, you have a candelabrum 19½ inches tall; 17½ inches tall; or 14 inches tall.

No. 705 5-Light Candelabrum Arms only
Each, $75.00

For small parties or when dining alone, you have a choice of candelabra 14 inches tall or 12 inches tall by removing the central post sections and assembling as shown.

Then, when you wish, lay aside the candelabra arms and you have a pair of low, medium, tall or taller candlesticks.

Left to Right: Height 2½ inches, 4½ inches, 8½ inches, 10½ inches.

Truly Webster-Wilcox silverware is versatile.

which a solution is found in the all-purpose multiple candelabra illustrated. The parts are connected with a simple friction fit. The complete candelabra are 19 1/2 inches tall; this height may be reduced by two inches on removing one section. Either three-light or five-light arms are available, depending on whether two are to be used, one on either end of a dining table, or one to be used as a centerpiece. The center post may be reduced still further in height by removing additional sections. All the arms may be laid aside to form a pair of low, medium, tall, or taller candlesticks (Figs. 24, 25).

CHAPTER X

Flatware

The earliest silverplated flatware patterns sold in this country were modeled after coin-silver spoons. The Rogers brothers who did most of the early manufacturing of silverplated flatware were all makers of coin-silver spoons, so it was natural that their first silverplated products should follow the designs with which they were familiar (Figs. 1, 1a).

Beginning in 1820 William Rogers was apprenticed to Joseph Church and learned the silversmith's trade. In 1825 he was admitted to partnership. Coin-silver spoons made by them were marked "CHURCH & ROGERS."

Early in 1830 Asa Rogers, brother of William, formed a partnership with John A. Cole in Berlin, Connecticut, and made coin-silver spoons bearing the mark "ROGERS & COLE." This partnership was dissolved in 1832.

William Rogers, while continuing his own business in Hartford, took an interest in his brother Asa's business in Berlin and produced spoons marked "A. ROGERS JR. & CO."

In 1836 the partnership of Church & Rogers was dissolved and William opened his own store at 6 State Street, Hartford. His coin-silver spoons were then marked "(EAGLE) WM. ROGERS (STAR)."

Simeon, another brother, learned the trade in William's business and in 1841 William took him into partnership. Their coin-silver spoons were marked ("EAGLE) WM. ROGERS & CO. (STAR)."

William's son, William Rogers, Jr., also learned the trade and in 1844 was admitted to his father's business (Simeon retiring). The coin-silver spoons were then marked "(EAGLE) WM. ROGERS & SON (STAR)."

In 1861 to 1865, William Rogers, Jr., continued alone and produced coin-silver spoons under his own mark "(EAGLE) WM. ROGERS, JR. (STAR)."

Beginning in 1862 the "1847 ROGERS BROS." trademark was used on the Rogers brothers silverplated spoons. Before that time pieces were marked "ROGERS BROS." or "ROGERS BROS. MFG. CO."

The "1846 (ANCHOR) ROGERS (ANCHOR)" trademark was used only about two years when William Rogers formed the Wm. Rogers Mfg. Co. in 1865. At that time he was apparently in disagreement with the Meriden Britannia Company which was making the "1847 ROGERS BROS." line, and William decided to go them one better and stamp his 1846. However, this was stopped by a suit and he changed the mark to "1865 WM. ROGERS MFG. CO."

The Rogers brothers had built a solid reputation based on their care and skill as silversmiths. This same care and skill was behind the first production of Rogers brothers silverplate in 1847. They used only German silver as a base, which through years of experimentation had convinced them was best adapted for the new silverplated spoons. William was a stickler for details; not only must the base metal be exactly the right mix-

430 AMERICAN SILVERPLATE

1. *Above:* Coin-silver spoons made by the Rogers brothers from 1825 to 1861. *Below:* One of the first silverplated spoons made by the Rogers brothers in 1847.

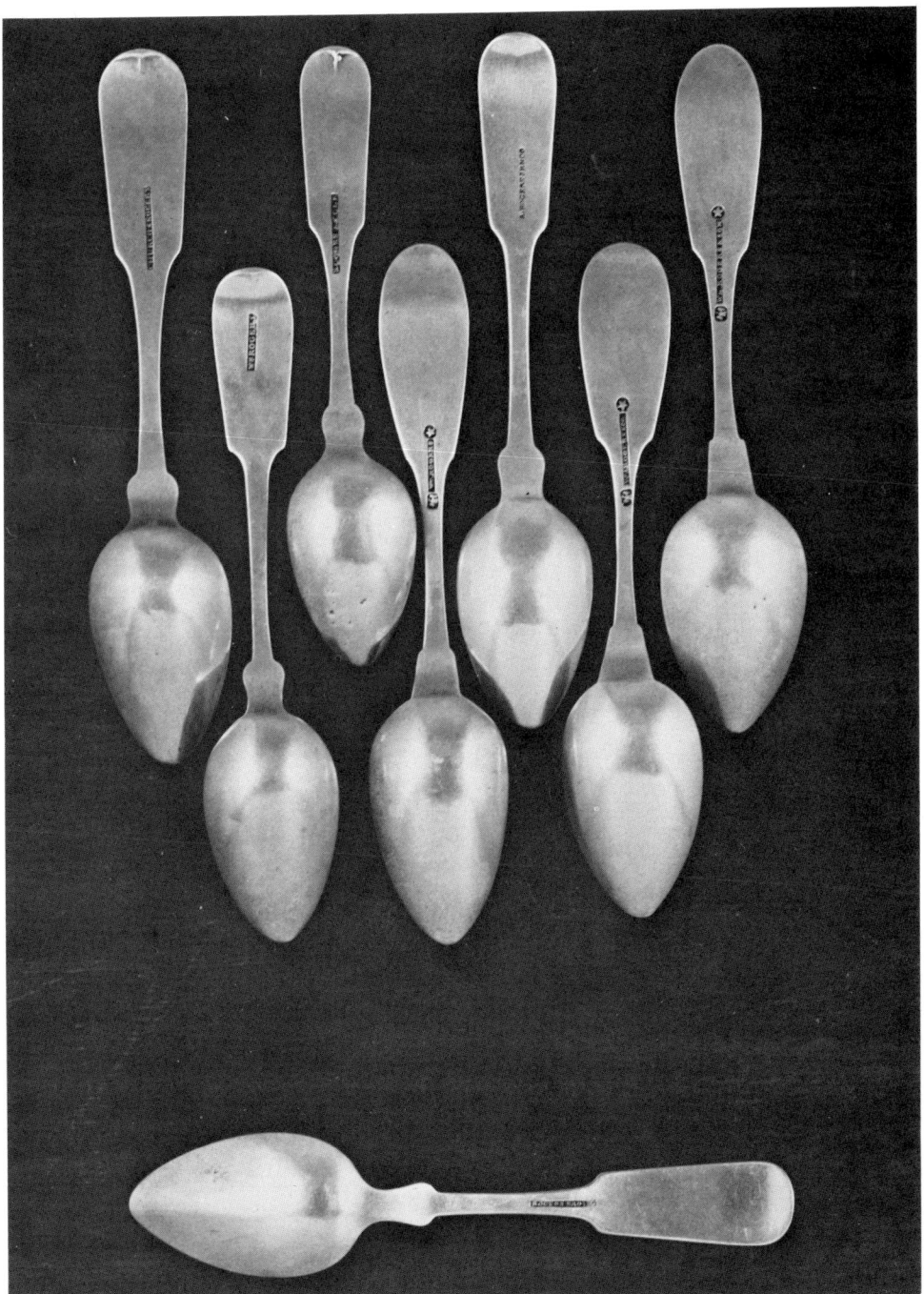

1a. Reverse sides of spoons and their marks. *Above, left to right:* "CHURCH & ROGERS," 1825; "WM. ROGERS," 1830; "ROGERS & COLE," 1830–32; "(EAGLE) WM. ROGERS (STAR)," 1836; "A. ROGERS JR. & CO.," 1832; "(EAGLE) WM. ROGERS & CO. (STAR)," 1841–55; "(EAGLE) WM. ROGERS & SON (STAR)," 1844–61. *Below:* "ROGERS & BRO.4."

ture and shape and thickness to make a durable and practical article but the dies also had to be perfect.

To insure that a sufficient amount of silver was deposited on each piece it was his rule that all pieces, whether spoons, forks, butter knives, or sugar spoons, should be weighed in the blank before plating. After careful calculation he decided how much silver should be deposited. He established a standard in pennyweights or ounces which they should carry. They were weighed before and after plating to insure that the proper amount of silver had been deposited. William also considered the burnishing and finishing of equal importance.

At first, only "Plain," "Threaded," and "Tipped" patterns were sold. Then, in 1848, "Olive," which is believed to be the first fancy pattern made in this country was made by Rogers & Bro., Waterbury, Connecticut. Though earlier the pattern had been sold here, the blanks had been imported from England and only the plating was done in this country.

Rogers & Bro. was exclusively a flatware plant, producing the German silver blanks for the trade. By 1869 they were also supplying blanks for many other concerns to plate and finish after stamping them with their own trademark. Their line of flatware was stamped "(STAR) ROGERS & BRO. A1."

The Gorham Company also marketed its first plated flatware pattern in a design which had been made earlier in coin silver. Their "Roman" pattern was patented in 1861 and made in coin silver (Fig. 2). John Gorham, son of the founder, Jabez Gorham, took into partnership his cousin, Gorham Thurber and changed the name of the firm to Gorham & Thurber, February 1, 1850. At this time silver electroplated wares made by the firms of Elkington & Co. of Birmingham, and Dixon & Sons of Sheffield, England, had attracted much attention in this country. Substantial amounts of their products had been purchased by American retailers. John Gorham considered this a challenge and decided to meet the competition. He further strengthened his organization by taking into the firm another cousin, Lewis Dexter, and again in 1852 changed the firm name—this time to Gorham and Company.

On May 1 of that same year John Gorham sailed to England to visit factories in Birmingham and Sheffield, the Mint in London, and the Woolwick Arsenal. In England he hired skilled arti-

2. "Roman" pattern teaspoons made by the Gorham Co. *Left:* Coin-silver, patented 1861. *Right:* Silverplate—Gorham's first plated pattern.

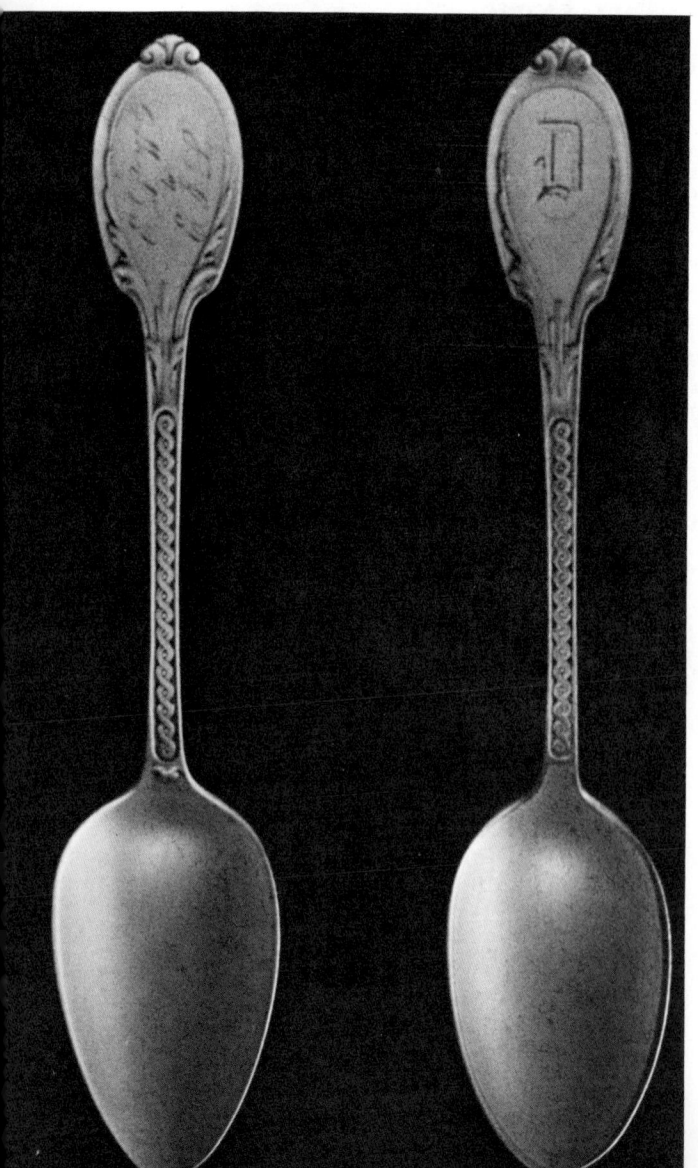

X. FLATWARE 433

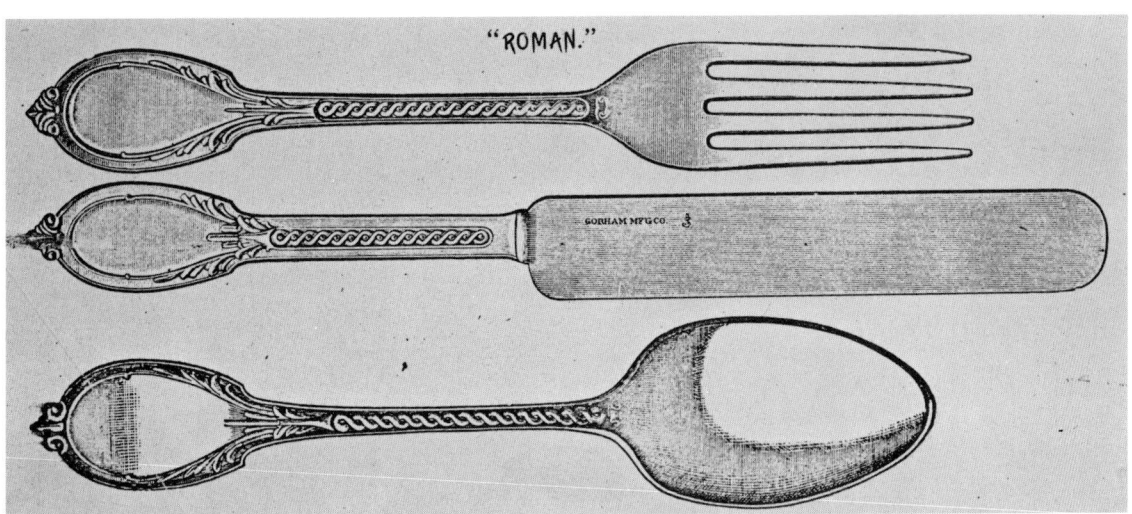

3. First made as a silverplate pattern in 1865, "Roman" was still featured in Gorham catalogs as late as 1884.

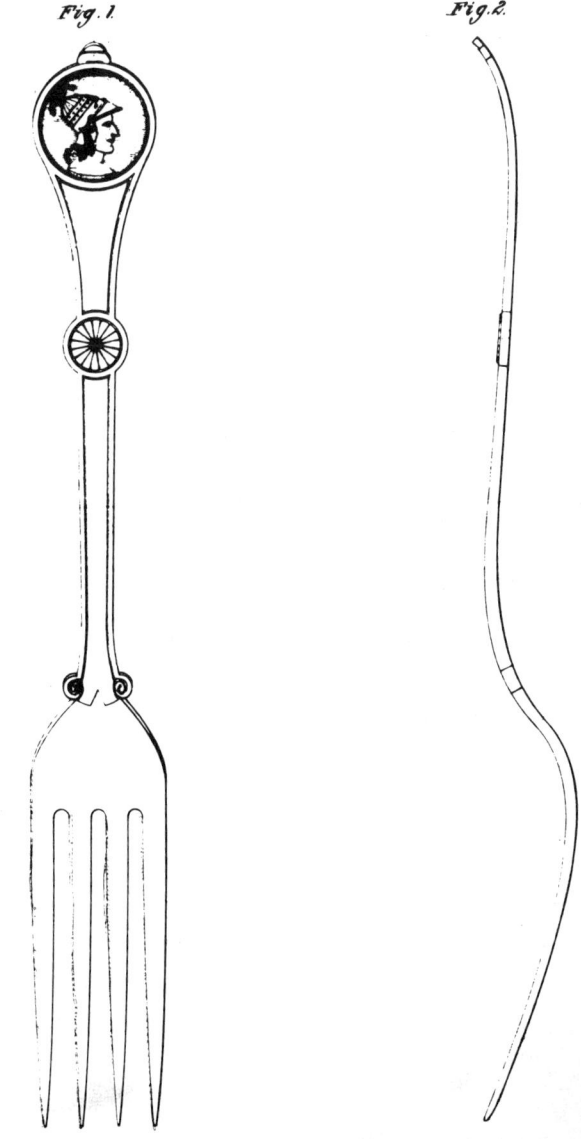

sans in various branches of metal working. Until the outbreak of the Civil War in 1861 the firm made steady progress in the manufacturing of silver hollow ware on a quantity basis for the trade, instead of receiving small commissions from retail jewelers for special orders, which had been the general practice among silversmiths. The advent of the Civil War made necessary the temporary abandonment of silver as a basic material. By 1863 the decision was made to use the factory facilities for the production of electro-silverplated wares using nickel silver as the base. The retooling and die work occupied almost two years and in 1865 the first of these wares were marketed. The "Roman" flatware, previously made only in coin silver, became their first silverplated pattern. It obviously was well received as it was still being carried in 1884 and illustrated in their catalogs (Fig. 3).

4. "Roman Medallion," designed by Henry G. Reed and patented by him December 29, 1868. Design Patent No. 3,302.

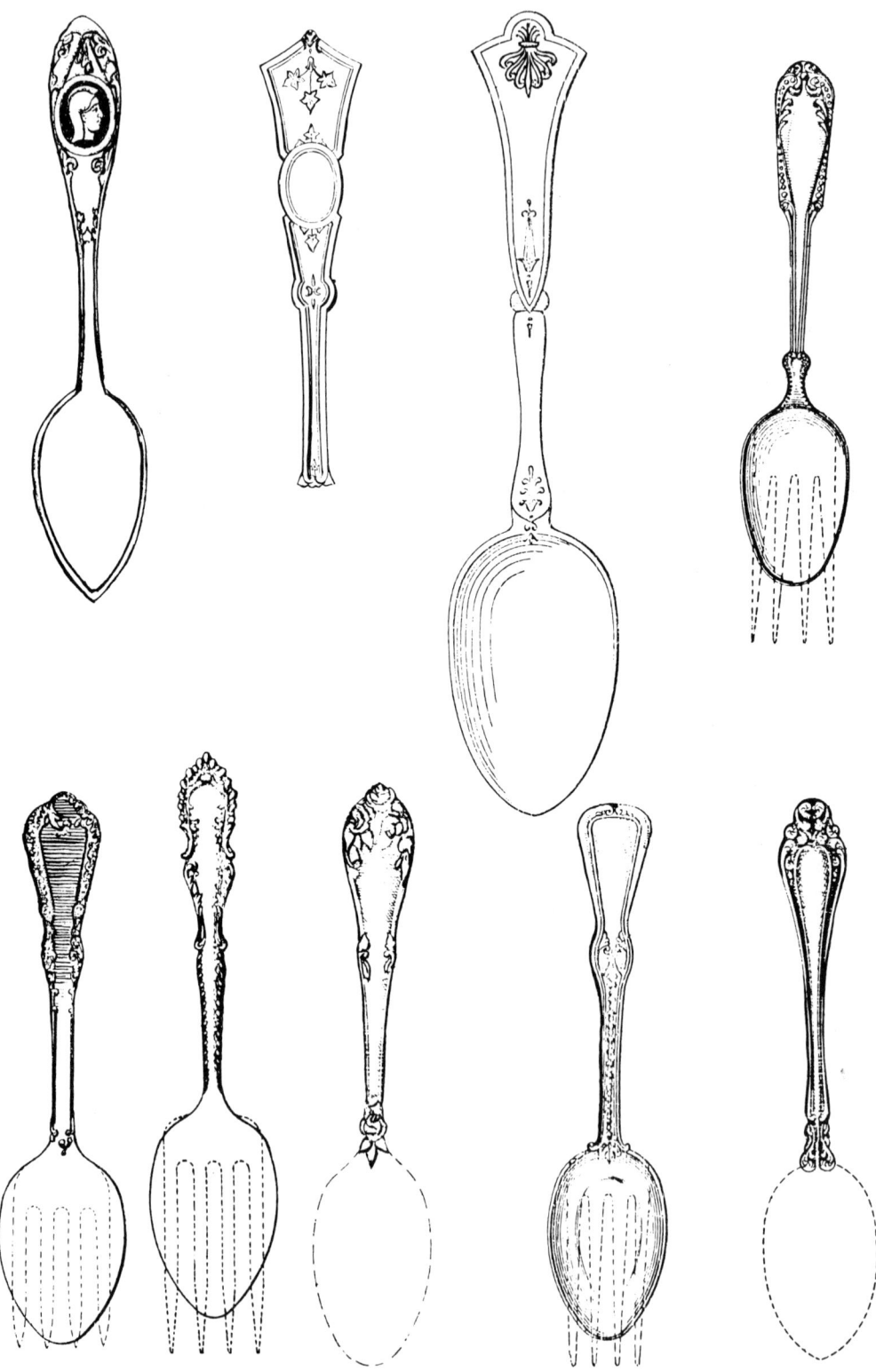

The Gorham Company ceased production of silverplated flatware May 1, 1962.

While the Rogers brothers produced great quantities of spoon blanks and supplied them to other manufacturers for plating and finishing and stamping with their own trademarks, Reed & Barton supplied the trade with hollow ware. The first original Reed & Barton flatware pattern was the "Roman Medallion," designed by Henry G. Reed and patented by him December 29, 1868 (Fig. 4).

Reed & Barton currently has six patterns of silverplated flatware on the market.

Other flatware patterns had been patented. On December 4, 1844, Michael Gibney of New York secured the first design patent for flatware. Since electroplating had not at that time been perfected, it is safe to assume that his patent and several which followed were for coin silver. All the known examples bear out this premise.

It is difficult to determine, in some instances, whether a patented flatware design was to be made in solid silver or electroplate. It is only by finding marked examples that one may be certain, or by familiarity of the names of the designers and their affiliation with companies known to have made only electroplate.

The first design patent for flatware that was specifically for plated flatware was a medallion pattern patented by Luther and Norman S. Boardman, East Haddam, Connecticut, October 1, 1867.

Patent Office records of flatware designs, unfortunately, are not complete. Representative examples illustrated will give some idea of design trends (Figs. 5, 6). A better reference for this purpose is the chart of styles produced under the trademark "1847 ROGERS BROS." from 1847 to the present (Fig. 7).

About 1871 Robert Wallace started production of iron spoons which developed six years later into the manufacturing of a new type of silverplated flatware with cast steel as a base. By this process articles lighter in weight, yet of greater strength and elasticity were produced. The company also developed a method of plating steel with tin, which produced a metal protected from rust and wear, making it especially suitable for hard usage in Army, Navy, and work camps.

The best-known line of silverplated flatware produced by the Wallace company was marketed under the trademark "1835 R. WALLACE," first sold in 1897.

They sold their hotel flatware dies for silverplate to the International Silver Company in 1954.

It was in 1877 that the Oneida Community embarked on the manufacture of tableware. By 1878 the mill was turning out steel spoon blanks which were sold for plating to the Meriden Britannia Company.

The Wallingford branch of Oneida made ungraded, tinned, iron spoons in two patterns, called "Lily" and "Oval." These two iron spoons were the direct

5. Representative group of patented flatware patterns. *Above, left to right:* Design Patent No. 2,794, Luther & Norman S. Boardman. East Haddam, Conn., October 1, 1867; Design Patent No. 4,788, John M. Culver, Assignor to Hall, Elton & Co., Meriden, Conn., April 11, 1871; Design Patent No. 11,657, William Rogers, Hartford, Conn., Assignor to Watrous Mfg. Co., Wallingford, Conn., February 24, 1880; Design Patent 27,164, Sidney Smith, Bridgeport, Conn., Assignor to Holmes & Edwards Silver Co., Bridgeport, Conn., June 9, 1897. *Below:* Design Patent No. 27,165, Gustave Strohhaker, Wallingford, Conn., June 8, 1897 ("Plymouth" pattern); Design Patent No. 27,202, William Jameson, Niagara Falls, N.Y., June 15, 1897 ("Elberon" pattern made by Wm. A. Rogers, Ltd.); Design Patent No. 32,143, Samuel J. Large, Bristol, Conn., Assignor to Bristol Brass & Clock Co., Bristol, Conn., January 23, 1900; Design Patent No. 32,467, Austin F. Jackson, Taunton, Mass., April 10, 1900 ("La Mode" pattern made by Reed & Barton).

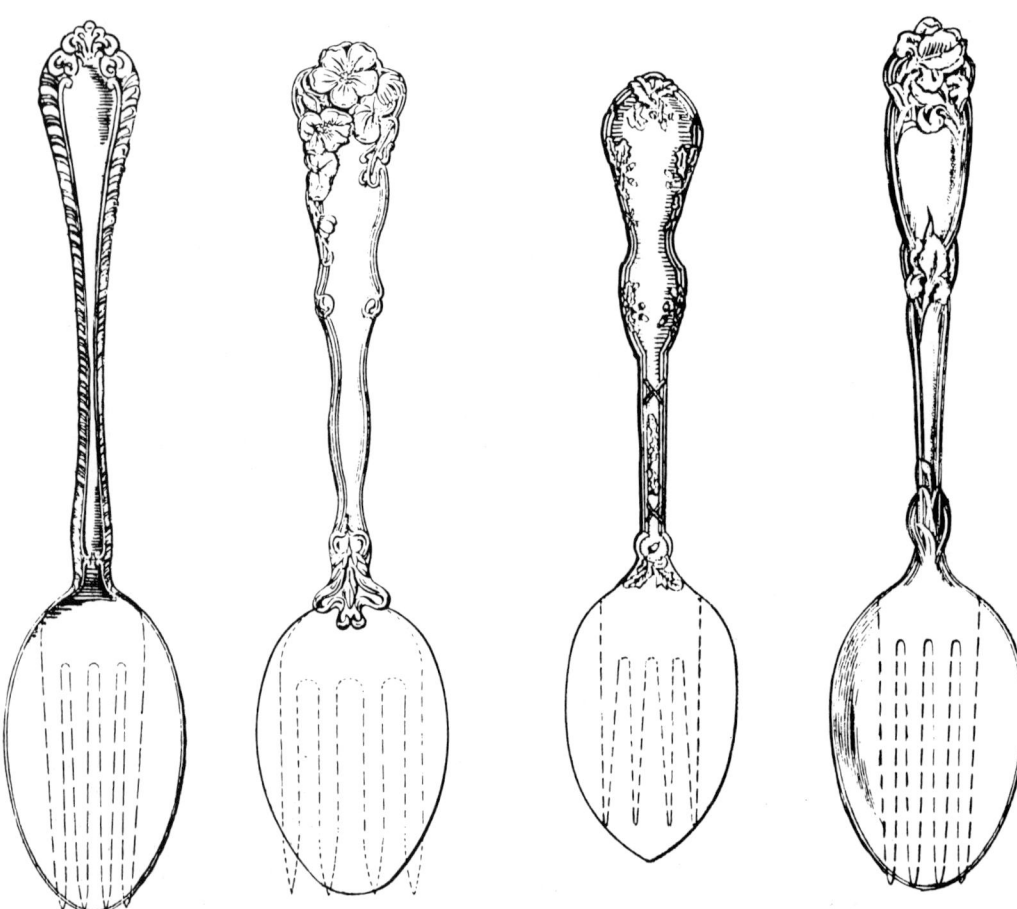

6. *Left to right:* Design Patent No. 32,914, Frederick Habensack, Sag Harbor, N.Y., Assignor to Fahys Watch Case Co., New York City, July 10, 1900; Design Patent No. 36,834, John Clulee, March 8, 1904 ("Berwick" pattern made by Simpson, Hall, Miller & Co., a division of International Silver Co., under the "(EAGLE) WM. ROGERS (STAR)" trademark); Design Patent No. 37,791, George P. Ittig, Bridgeport, Conn., Assignor to E. H. H. Smith Silver Co., Bridgeport, Conn., January 23, 1906; Design Patent No. 38,583, Frederick Habensack, Sag Harbor, N.Y., Assignor to Fahys Watch Case Co., New York City, May 28, 1907.

ancestors of the whole line of Community Plate.

Oneida's first silverware could not compete with the higher quality silver made by other companies. A decision was made to produce ware of a better quality and in a better-designed line. Their new design, called "Avalon," was exhibited in 1901 at the Buffalo Exposition (Fig. 8). In January 1902 their new line of Community Plate flatware was introduced (Fig. 9). At present Oneida Silversmiths produces about a dozen different silverplated flatware patterns.

Such patterns as "Plain," "Oval," "Tipped," "Olive," "Threaded," "Beaded," and other early ones were marketed by almost all silver manufacturers. Until the late 1860s probably most flatware blanks were made by the Rogers brothers and

7. Flatware patterns made under the "1847 ROGERS BROS." trademark.

847 ROGERS BROS.® AMERICA'S FINEST SILVERPLATE
MADE BY INTERNATIONAL SILVER COMPANY

This pictorial reference brochure illustrates the patterns made in America's Finest Silverplate since 1847. They are shown in chronological order with each pattern identified by name and the year in which it was introduced.

NEW!
KING FREDERIK
1969
(ACTIVE)

SILVER LACE 1968 (ACTIVE)
GRAND HERITAGE 1968 (ACTIVE)
ESPERANTO 1967 (ACTIVE)
GARLAND 1965 (ACTIVE)
MAGIC ROSE 1963
LEILANI 1960
REFLECTION 1959 (ACTIVE)
SPRINGTIME 1957
FLAIR 1955
HERITAGE 1953

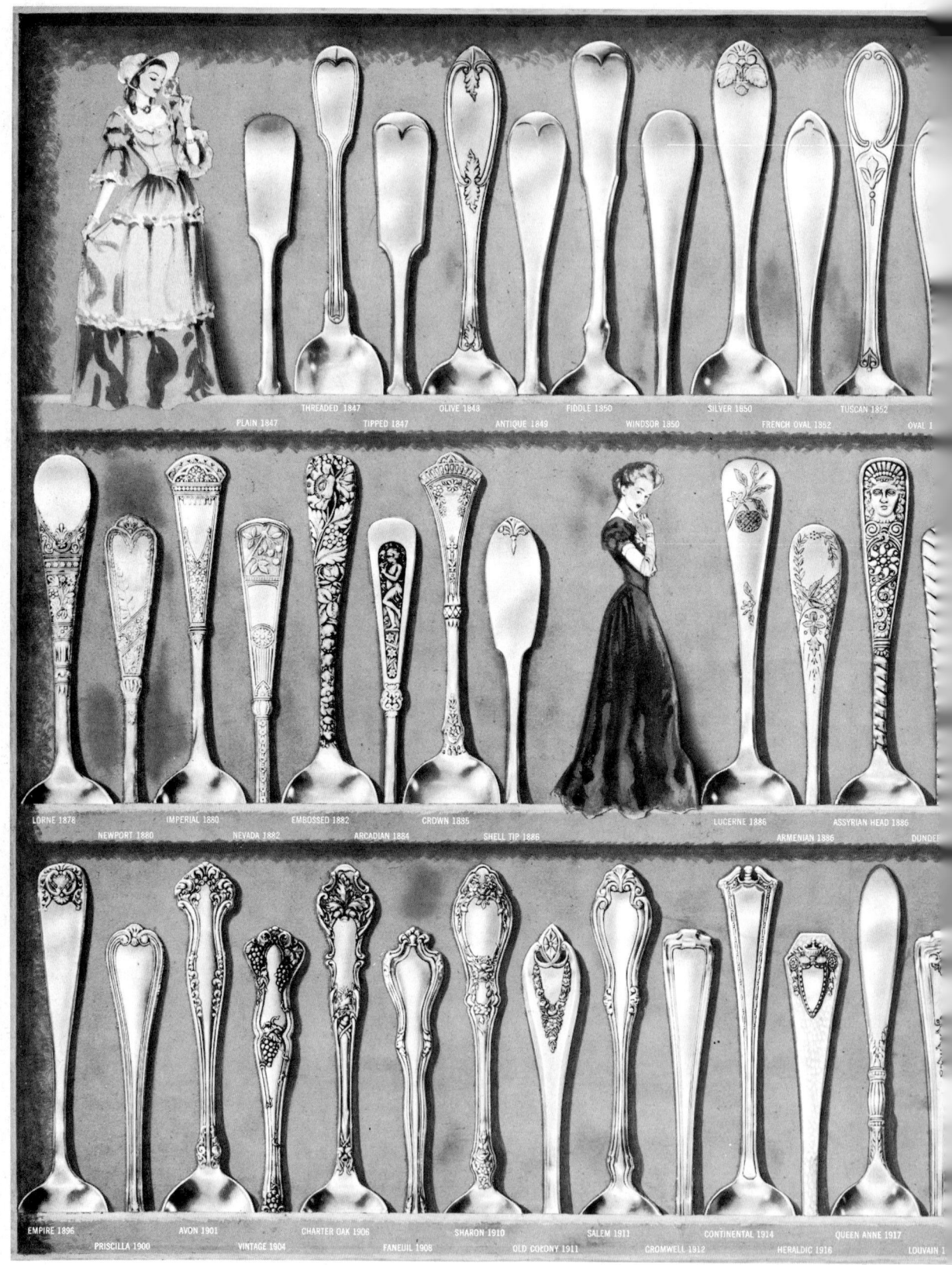

1847
AMERICA'S FINEST SILVERPLA

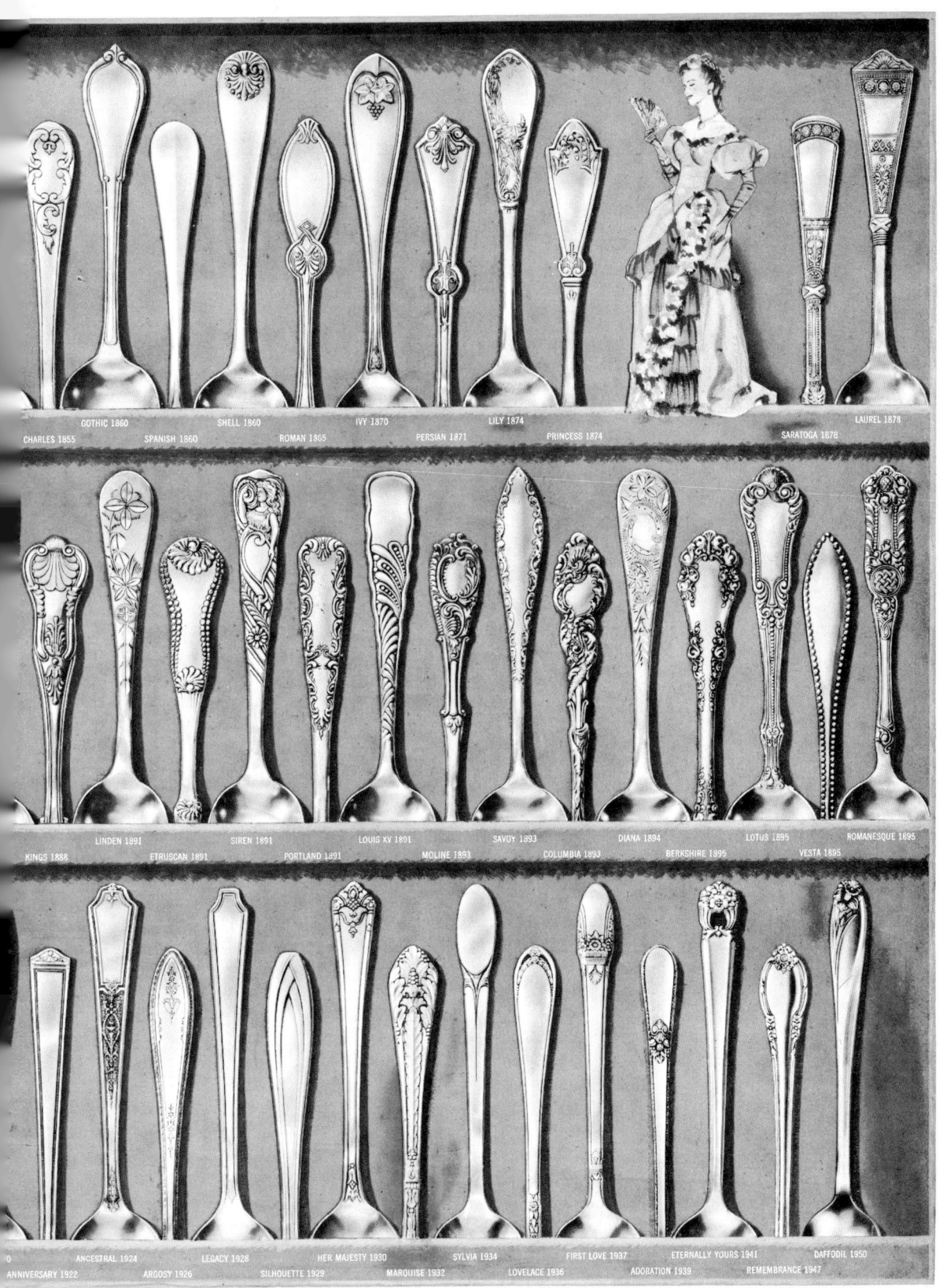

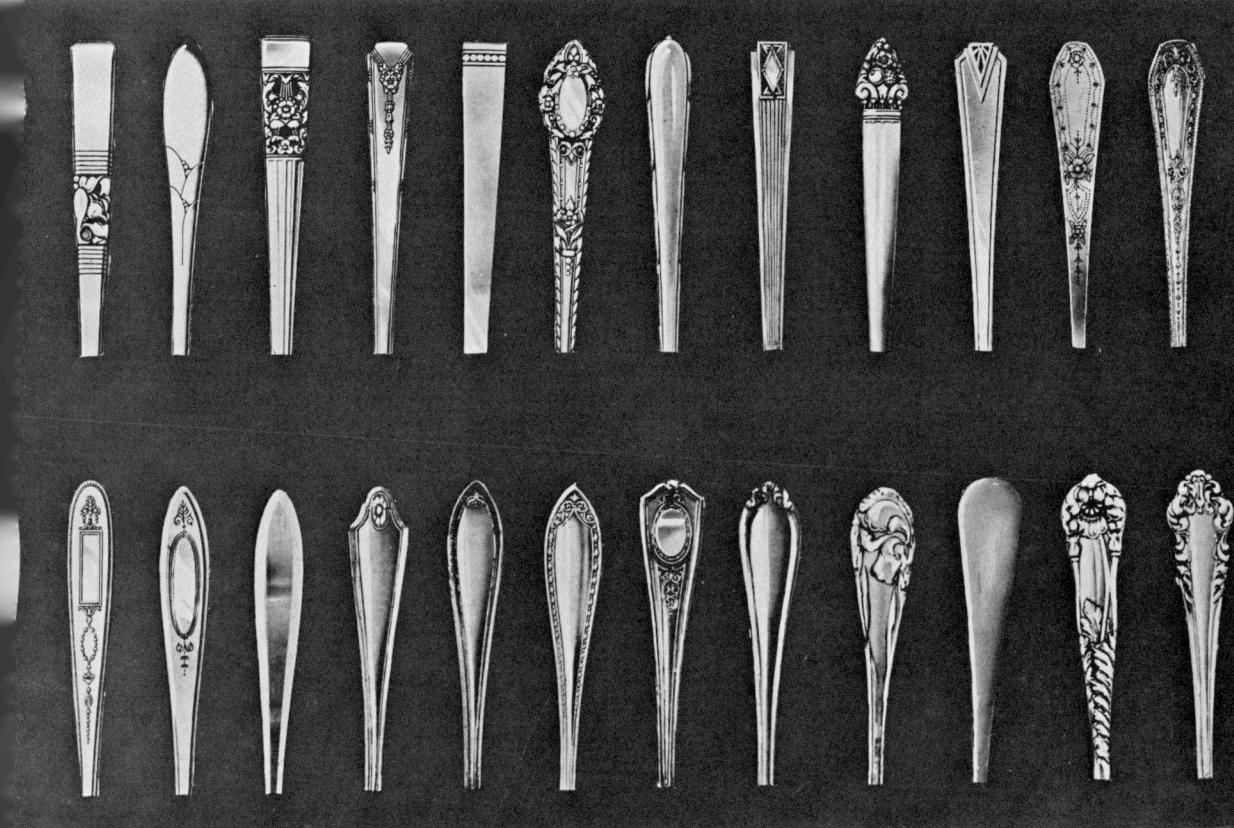

9. Community silverplate patterns from 1901 through 1949. *Top row, left to right:* 1. "Evening Star," 1949; 2. "Morning Star," 1947; 3. "Lady Hamilton," 1932; 4. "Coronation," 1936; 5. "Milady," 1940; 6. "Forever," 1939; 7. "Rendezvous," 1938; 8. "Berkeley Square," 1935; 9. "Noblesse," 1930; 10. "King Cedric," 1933; 11. "Deauville," 1929; 12. "Paul Revere," 1927; 13. "Hampton Court," 1925. *Bottom row, left to right:* 14. "Bird of Paradise," 1923; 15. "Grosvenor," 1921; 16. "Adam," 1916; 17. "Patrician," 1914; 18. "Georgian," 1912; 19. "St. Regis," 1911; 20. "Sheraton," 1910; 21. "Louis XVI," 1908; 22. "Classic," 1906; 24. "Flower de Luce," 1914; 24. "Windsor," 1902; 25. "Cereta," 1902; 26. "Avalon," 1901.

8. "Avalon," Oneida Silversmiths' first silverplated flatware pattern, introduced in 1901 at the Buffalo Exposition.

supplied to other manufacturers for silverplating (Figs. 10, 11).

Some designs were derived directly from English sources. Blanks were imported for silverplating and in other cases, though the blanks were made here, they were well-known English designs with only slight changes.

The "Kings" pattern, or its variations, was made in sterling by at least eight manufacturers, while in silverplate it was marketed by Gorham, International, National, Tiffany, Reed & Barton, Wallace Silversmiths, Wm. Rogers, and others. Slight variations in the design from one company to another may be noted (Fig. 12).

Pattern names have always caused confusion. Several companies manufactured entirely different designs which have been marketed under the same or

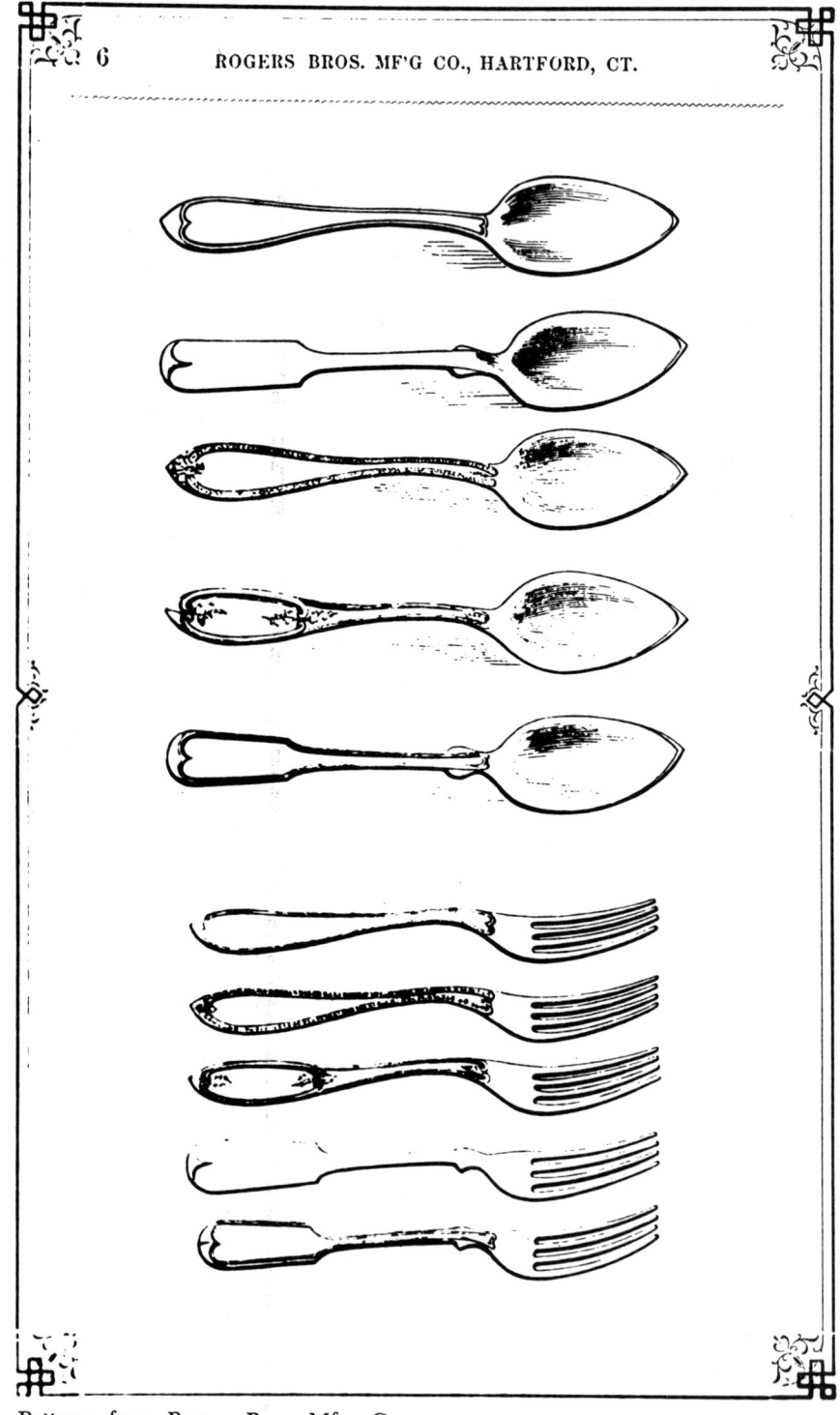

10. Patterns from Rogers Bros. Mfg. Co. catalog, 1860. *Spoons, top to bottom:* "Threaded," 1847; "Olive," 1848; "Beaded," 1855; "Tipped," 1847.

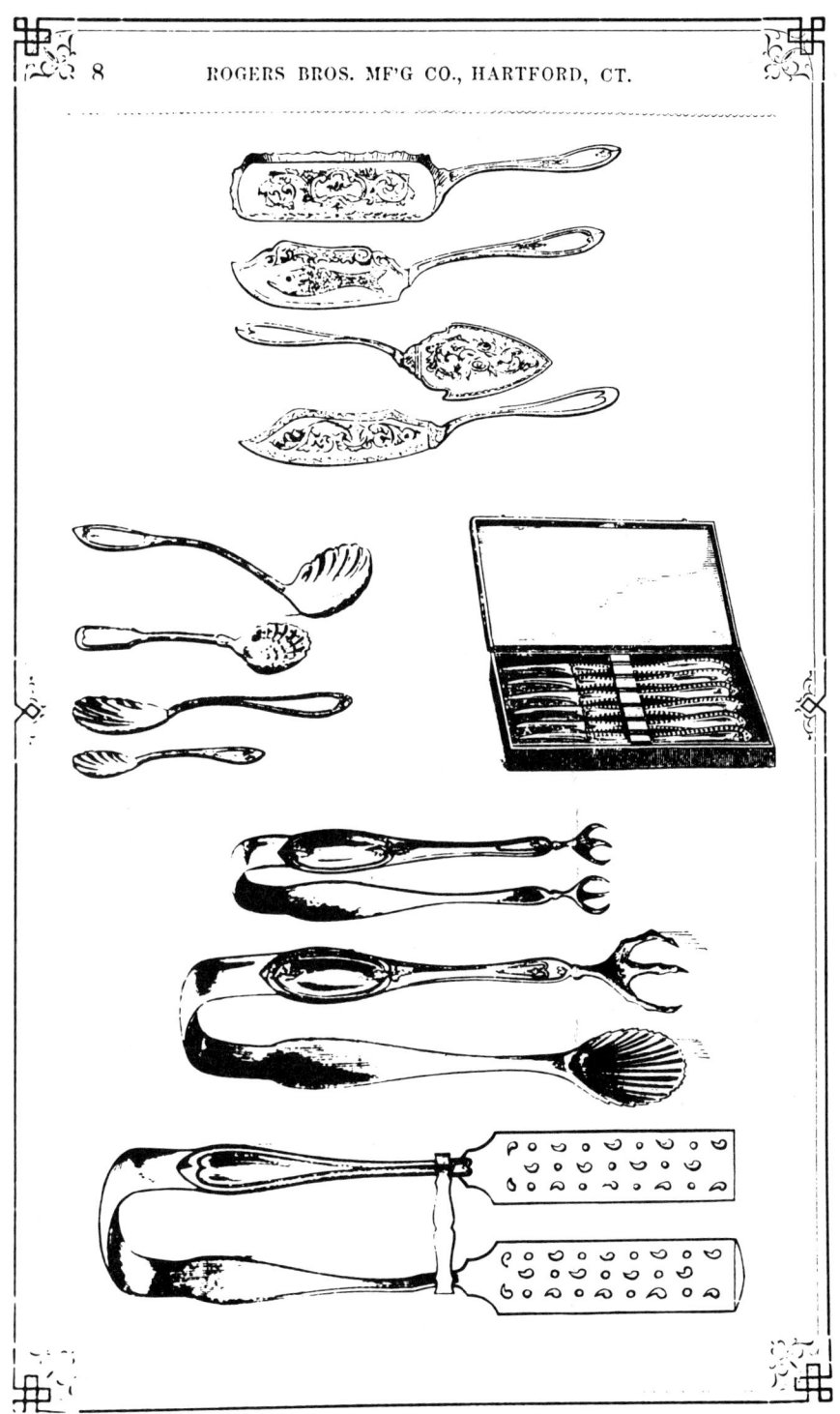

11. Serving pieces illustrated in Rogers Bros. Mfg. Co. catalog, 1860.

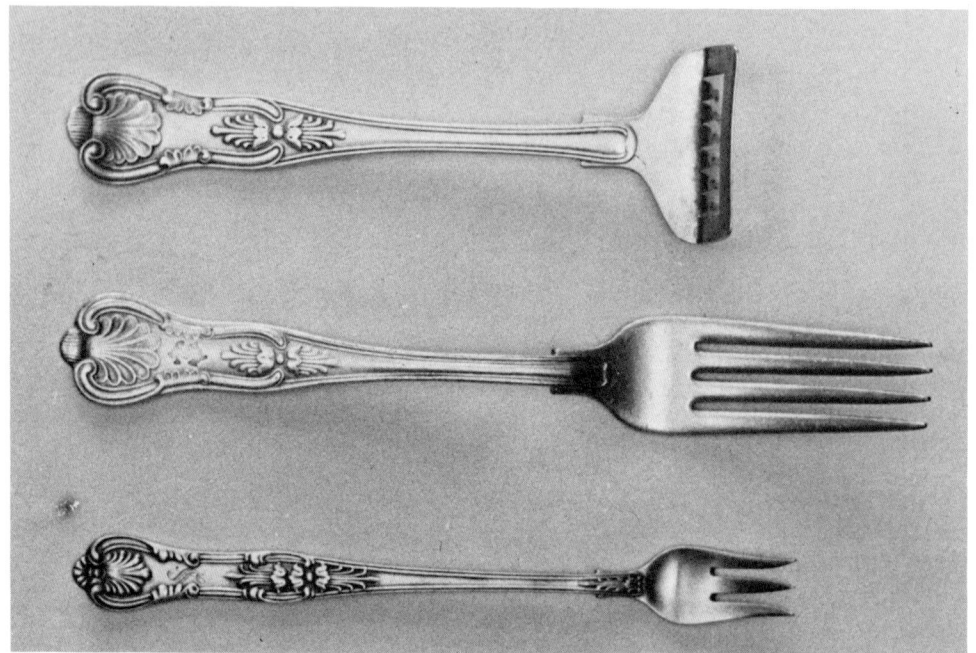

12. "Kings" pattern made by different companies, showing slight variations in a well-known pattern. *Left to right:* Tiffany & Co.: 1835 R. Wallace; Gorham "Anchor within a circle." The piece on the right is a combination corn scorer and scraper.

similar names. On the other hand, the "Berwick" pattern, for instance, made by Simpson, Hall, Miller & Company (a division of the International Silver Company) under the "(EAGLE) WM. ROGERS (STAR)" trademark was illustrated in the Warren-Mansfield Company (Portland, Maine) catalog of 1907–08 and called "Oxford." It was also illustrated in the Baird-North Company (Salem, Massachusetts) catalog for 1907 and called "The Diana." Many other examples have been noted. Retailers catalogs, especially, were prone to this sort of rechristening.

To add to this confusion is the fact that several patterns were made in both sterling and silverplate. This was true

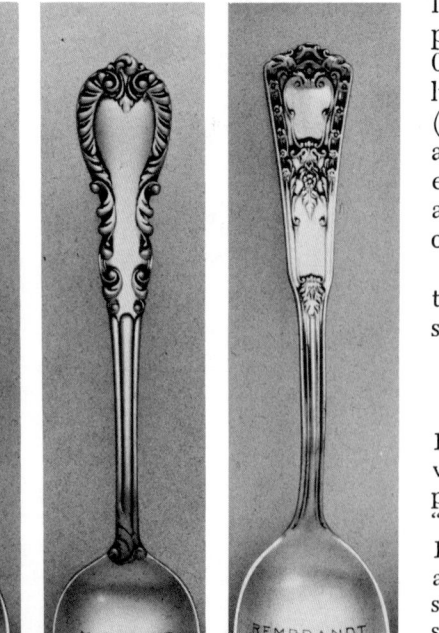

13. Three Reed & Barton patterns which were made in sterling and also in silverplate — "Luxembourg," "Majestic," and "Rembrandt."

14. *Left to right:* Silverplated child's fork and spoon made by W. A. Rogers; berry spoon made by the Gorham Co. Note the similarity in design.

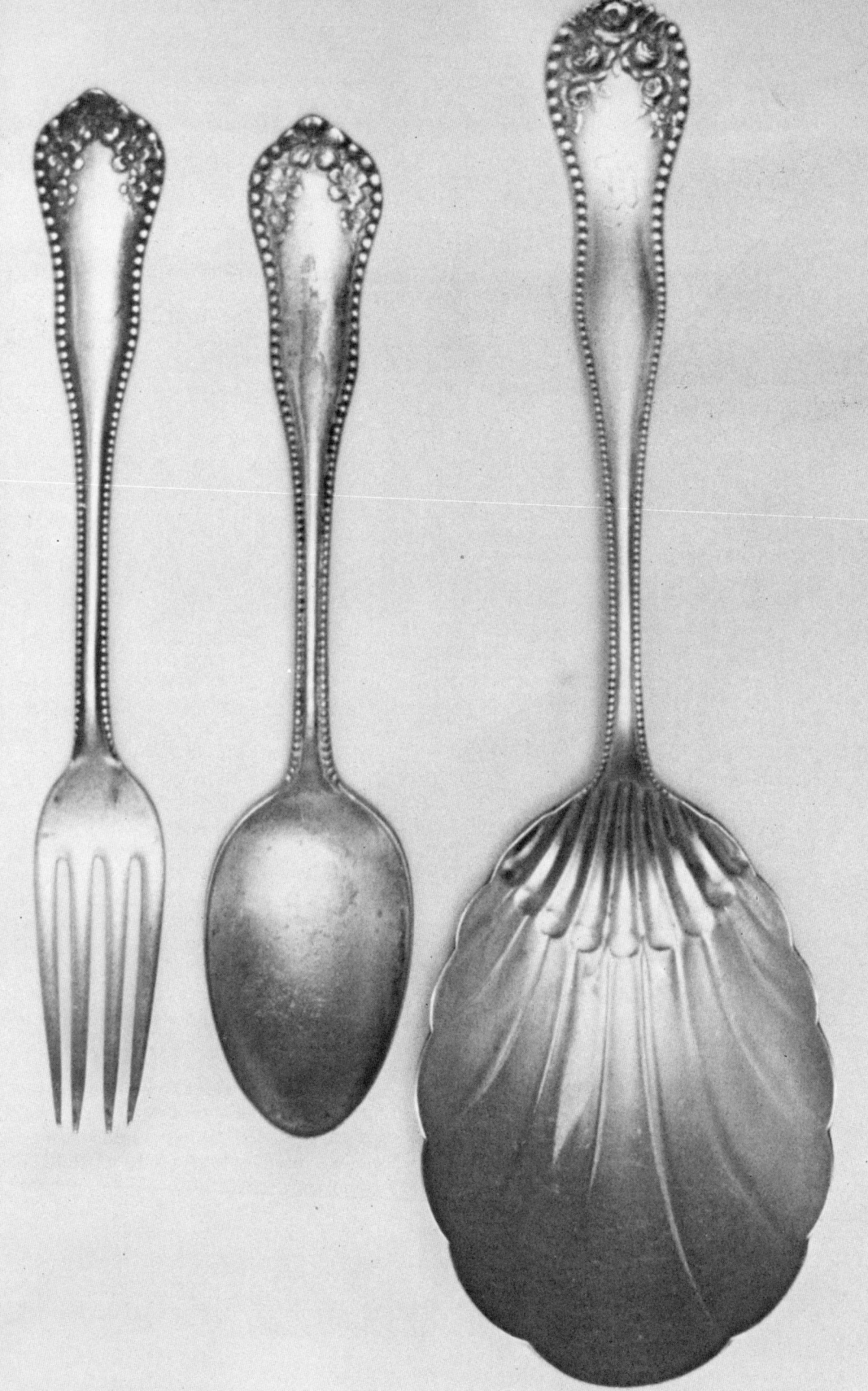

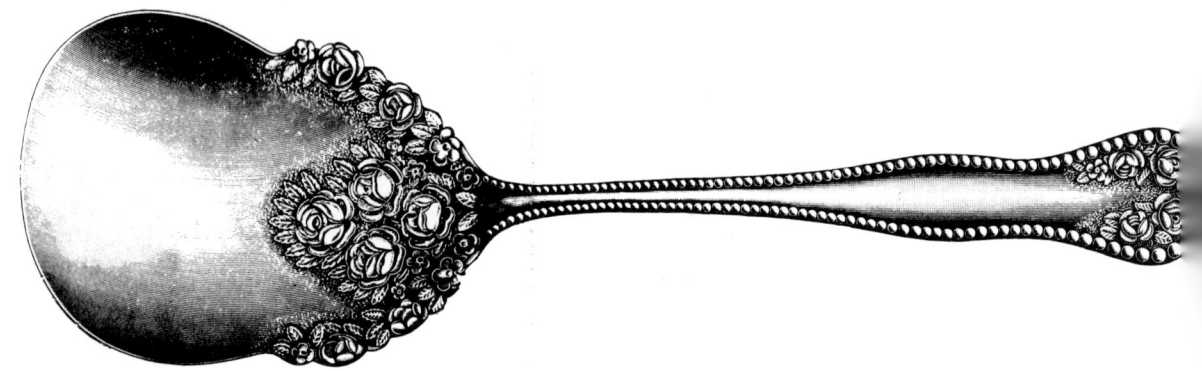

15. Berry spoon made by E. H. H. Smith Silver Co. of Bridgeport, Conn., in silverplate. This "York Rose" pattern is a rather obvious copy of the Gorham "Lancaster" rose pattern.

of "Plain," "Tipped," "Windsor," "Olive," "Beaded," "Oval," "Oval Thread," and others which were made by more than one company. The names were not always the same for both sterling and silverplate and often varied from one company to another.

"Embossed," "Tipped," "Shell Tipped," "Arcadian," "Newport," "Armenian," and "Lorne," all sold under the "1847 ROGERS BROS." trademark were also made in sterling silver.

The "Luxembourg," "Majestic," and "Rembrandt" patterns made by Reed & Barton were, according to them, made in both sterling and silverplate (Fig. 13).

There was much copying and near-copying of designs, especially the copying of favorite sterling patterns in silverplate (Fig. 14). Gorham's "Lancaster" pattern has a near duplicate in "York Rose" made in silverplate by the E. H. H. Smith Silver Company (Fig. 15). Note also the similarity of the child's set made by W. A. Rogers.

Victorian and Edwardian silversmiths created a tremendous variety of flatware pieces for the enjoyment of their patrons and to the consternation of the present generation. Early flatware patterns appear to have been limited mainly to spoons and forks, with knives being plain handled or omitted from consideration altogether. Only in the latter part of the nineteenth century were knives always included in the same pattern handle as the rest of the table service. The number of different serving pieces and the variety of forks and spoons was by then seemingly endless.

The styles of these forms varied greatly. Pickle forks had two to four tines which were straight or were curved inward or outward. Some had a cutting edge. Bar spoons were made in several lengths, varying from three and five-eighths inches to eight inches. Oyster forks had two or three tines which varied considerably in length. Like the pickle forks, these tines were either straight or curved. Place knives, forks, and spoons were made in at least three sizes. Pieces intended for the same use were given different names by different manufacturers.

CHAPTER XI

Care and Restoration

Care

Before the sixteenth century even city air was pure and did not cause silver to tarnish. The use of coal, and later of oil and gas, for lighting and heating released sulphurous gases into the air and tarnishing of silver resulted.

No great amount of detective work is necessary to disclose the principal causes of silver tarnish. A comparison of the rate of tarnish in wintertime when central heating units are in operation and summer when air conditioning is used, provides the clues. Heating in most areas is accomplished through the use of coal, oil, or gas, while air conditioning is usually electric.

Sulphur compounds in foods, such as eggs and salad dressings, and in rubber of all kinds are causes of tarnish.

Silver should be washed immediately after it comes in contact with salt as salt will leave pits which cannot be removed. Fruit juices contain acids which can pit silver. Plastic bags or glass liners should be used inside of bowls used for displaying fruit.

Silver used in flower displays needs to be protected from sap and acids also. Water in flower displays should be changed daily, of course, and silver containers rinsed thoroughly and wiped before refilling. Flowers should be removed at the first signs of wilting.

It is not possible to avoid entirely the agents that cause tarnish but it is comparatively easy to keep that lustrous sheen so much admired. Just as with sterling, silverplate should be washed immediately after use in hot soapy water and rinsed carefully before drying. This time-honored method cannot be improved. Soap, rather than detergent, is recommended because the latter often contains phosphorous or sulphur compounds. Rinsing is essential because silverware dried without rinsing will tarnish much more rapidly than pieces that have been rinsed.

Rotation of pieces in use will assure that every piece is kept clean and free from tarnish-causing agents. Tarnish cannot be prevented entirely but it can be retarded by daily use of silver and immediate washing which removes sulphurous oxidations before they become visible. Constant washing poses no threat of removal of silverplating. Rather, it imparts a patina that comes only through use.

Both sterling and silverplate, when washed constantly in a dishwasher will acquire an off-white or yellowish film—probably from the phosphates in the dish-washing compound. When this becomes noticeable it may be removed by a brisk rub with a rouge cloth or silver polish.

A tarnish deterrent can be devised for flatware by lining the storage drawer with Pacific Silvercloth.* Line the drawer completely, leaving a free length to be pulled over the silver from back to front of the drawer. This provides easy

* Pacific Silvercloth is available in drawer pads, silver chests, silverfiles, wraps, bags, pocketed rolls, and by the yard.

access and the Pacific Silvercloth may be folded back out of the way while flatware is being removed or replaced. A small piece of camphor in each drawer will also retard tarnish.

Hollow ware which is not in constant use may be stored by wrapping first in low-sulphite tissue paper and then tying in polyethylene bags, or wrapping in aluminum foil or one of the plastic wraps. The silver should not be in direct contact with any of these wraps but should always be wrapped first in tissue paper with a low sulphide content.

Silver collectors will find no joy in their possessions if they must be kept always stored away out of sight. Glass enclosed cabinets whose doors are dust and air tight are one solution. (A note of caution should be made. If a new cabinet is built, or an old one restored, avoid the use of latex and casein paints.) If one has been fortunate enough to inherit, or to find at auction, a glass enclosed cabinet, the installation of glass shelves at least one-fourth inch thickness and fluorescent lighting will provide an ideal home display. Small pieces of camphor may be tucked in corners to retard tarnishing.

In spite of all tarnish inhibitors and keeping silver clean, eventually it must be polished. The problem is to use the least abrasive polish and to use it only as necessary.

The writers have found Hagerty's Silver Foam one of the best for flatware and serving pieces in daily use. It is a light paste which is applied with a sponge, working polish into crevices. It rinses away easily and the foaming action removes the tarnish and polish residue. It does not clog the crevices of a deeply embossed design.

The same company markets a fork cleaner which is useful for dipping black-tipped tines which are the result of the sulphur in breakfast eggs or in the mayonnaise in salads. (Fig. 1). The tines are merely dipped into the liquid for a few seconds and rinsed immediately in clear water. This is a cleaner not a polish and, as with any other "dip," * there is a film which must be removed with a rouge cloth or silver polish.

Tarnish-Shield, made by the Minnesota Mining & Manufacturing Company and Silversmiths' Wash, made by W. J. Hagerty & Sons, applied according to directions, have both been found to be effective in retarding tarnish up to six months on pieces left exposed in the house. Most tarnish was readily traceable to heating operations since it occurred on ware in direct relationship to the proximity of heat outlets. This is something to consider in placement of silver displays. While these experiments conducted in one household do not constitute a scientific analysis, they may be considered indicative.

Hagerty's Silversmiths' Polish with Tarnish Preventive is especially useful for large pieces of display silver which cannot be easily immersed and for such pieces as felt-bottom candelabra and mirror frames which cannot be immersed at all (Fig. 2). The pieces should be polished thoroughly and the polish allowed to remain on for one minute to bond the tarnish barrier. The tarnish and residue can then be wiped off. Buffing with a soft cloth or Silversmiths' Gloves will restore the soft luster.

Frequent dusting with Hagerty's Silversmiths' Gloves (Fig. 3) was found to be a further deterrent to the tarnishing of articles which had been treated with Tarnish-Shield, Hagerty's Silver Foam, or Silversmiths' Wash. These gloves are especially useful as they eliminate the fingerprints which lead to tarnish. They contain a tarnish preventive so that each dusting imparts a new tarnish preventing bond.

* Chemical methods are cleaners, not polish, and must be followed by polishing. They should be used only on the plainest pieces for they remove the oxidation which defines the decorative details. Preferably they are reserved only for dipping fork tines or for cleaning pieces severely tarnished through long storage or neglect.

1. Hagerty's new Fork Cleaner does away with the black-tipped tines caused by the sulphur in eggs or in mayonnaise on salads. To restore the natural sheen of silver, follow up with Silver Foam or Silversmiths' Wash.

2. Hagerty's Silversmiths' Polish with Tarnish Preventive.

3. Dusting with Hagerty's Silversmiths' Gloves.

The International Silver Company markets its regular silver polish and a newer tarnish-preventive silver polish in applicator bottles. This is a "squeeze type" bottle with convenient applicator sponge built into the top.

The Gorham Company's paste polish comes in a wide-mouth plastic jar which is convenient for frequent use. A small sponge may be stored inside the top of the jar, making it even more convenient. Gorham also markets a tarnish preventive and silver cleaner impregnated on disposable cloths, six to a package. While these were found to be effective, each cloth can be used only once and then discarded, so that their relative high cost makes them less practical.

J. Goddard & Sons, Racine, Wisconsin. markets an effective paste polish with its own sponge in a separate compartment. This tarnish-preventive polish is excellent though somewhat more expensive than others. It is also not as readily available, but may be purchased in at least one fine jewelry store in most cities.

Several other polishes are on the market but were not tested for effectiveness or lack of scratch-producing qualities as were the above.

The W. J. Hagerty & Sons Company has placed on the market a Silver Spray containing a tarnish preventive (Fig. 4). This is not a lacquer but does provide an invisible monomolecular bond of tarnish preventive. Successful first application is dependent on the article being freshly cleaned and polished with Hagerty's Silver Foam or Hagerty's Silver Wash, followed by a thorough rinsing in hot water and drying with a lint-free cloth. Then, on a two-week schedule, the silver is sprayed to renew the tarnish preventive barrier. With Sil-

4. Hagerty's Tarnish Preventive Spray.

versmiths' Gloves it is spread evenly and buffed. The Silver Spray removes dust and leaves a lustrous shine that protects against tarnish.

In areas where the atmosphere is totally incompatible with tarnish prevention, lacquer may be applied. Jewelers and silverplaters can do this or have it done. Some change in appearance is to be expected as the lacquer surface does not have exactly the same light-reflecting qualities as unlacquered silver. The Metropolitan Museum of Art reports some success with Silversheeld made by Glenwood Products Corporation, West Englewood, New Jersey, and with Agateen, made by the Agate Lacquer Manufacturing Company Company, Long Island City, New York.

Restoration

A few dealers and collectors have been heard to remark that they would not have old silverplated pieces replated because it would destroy their value as antiques. This is utter nonsense. Electroplating "Old Sheffield Plate" would lower its value, it is true, as the original process of plating was entirely different. Replating old electro-silverplate, though, is simply to restore it to its original condition.

Just as in buying new silverplate, reliability of workmanship is to be sought.

5. 1. The customer is advised about prices and delivery dates. He is informed about the amount of time and labor that will be required. 2. An old candelabrum is examined to determine what parts are missing and the feasibility of finding or improvising an old part that is no longer made. 3. The hotel water pitcher being examined was badly dented and the handle had split open. A handle in stock is compared with the old to be sure it is the right kind. Next the pitcher will be placed in a tank of solution which will remove the old silverplate and oxide. Replating over oxide cannot be done because of the corrosion beneath it.

Reputable silverplaters take great pride in their ability to restore old silverplate. They are usually happy to take the time to explain what steps are necessary for complete restoration (Fig. 5).

By far the greater part of resilvering costs is the preparation of pieces not in the cost of the silver itself. Preparation of the surface of old silverplate is essential to satisfactory resilvering. Even old silverplate that has not been dented or broken must be stripped of all the old silver, perhaps marks of wear must be buffed away and then the piece made chemically clean to remove the oxide before resilvering. Better shops remove the handles from tea sets, etc., so that the buffing operation will not leave course areas around the surface where the handles join the piece. They are then resoldered in place before silverplating.

5 continued.
4. This old tankard has been stripped of its silver and oxide of tin. Here it is being examined to be sure all this has been removed so the new silver coating will adhere properly. Next it will be completely repaired and resurfaced. 5. A large bowl is removed from the plating tank. Now almost white, it will be restored to its silvery sheen by burnishing. 6. Inspection of articles ready for refinishing. 7. Replated articles being inspected before being returned. (*The Silver Lining*, June, 1963).

Dents can be removed, missing legs and mounts replaced, covers refitted and bases straightened. One of the most difficult aspects about repair is finding or making missing parts. So, in the case of damage, it is important to save any parts which become detached.

After replating, silverplate should receive the same care and attention given to new pieces. Careful and frequent washing with hot soapy water, thorough rinsing and drying are the best care for all silver. Dusting with a good silver polishing cloth or gloves each week will retard tarnish and the need for frequent polishing.

Glossary

Acanthus: A form of ornamentation taken from the acanthus leaf, originally used extensively on the Corinthian capital throughout the Renaissance period, sixteenth and seventeenth centuries.

Ajouré: A French term applied to metalwork which is pierced through, perforated, or openwork.

Alaska Silver: Base metal of secret composition. According to contemporary ads, "Its purpose is to imitate solid silver at a fraction of the cost." Subject to damage if left twelve hours or more in acid foods, fats, or grease.

Albata: Alloy of nickel, copper, and zinc, forming a silvery white metal; German silver, nickel silver.

Alchemy: A superior pewter used in the sixteenth and seventeenth centuries for making spoons and plates; an alloy of tin and copper.

Alcomy: An alloy of various base metals.

Alfenide: "Spoons made of alfenide similar to finest English white metal. Contains no brass or German silver." (Clipping dated March 18, 1878, source unknown.)

Alloy: A substance composed of two or more metals intimately united, usually intermixed when molten.

Alpacca: German silver and nickel silver are synonymous trade names of an alloy of copper, nickel, and zinc.

Aluminum Silver: A composition of aluminum and silver which is much harder than aluminum. It takes a high polish. Air does not affect the color. The proportion of ingredients varies. One of 3 parts silver and 97 parts aluminum makes an alloy similar in appearance to pure aluminum but is much harder and takes a better polish.

Annealing: Reheating of silver to keep it malleable while it is being worked.

Anvil: An iron block on which metal is hammered and shaped.

Apocryphal: Classical term for a fake.

Applied: Certain parts, such as spouts, handles, covers, etc., are sometimes made separately and applied with solder.

Argentine: An alloy of tin and antimony used as a base for plating; nickel silver; German silver; also "British plate"; known in China as "paktong." W. Hutton & Sons, Sheffield, England, said to have been "the first firm to manufacture spoons and forks from the newly-invented metal called Argentine, in the year 1833." (Bradbury, p. 338.)

Assay: The test made to prove that the metal is of the required quality.

Base Metal: An alloy or metal of comparatively low value to which a coating or plating is normally applied.

Beading: A border ornament composed of small, contiguous, beadlike, half-spheres. Popular in late eighteenth century.

Beakhorn: A sharply pointed anvil.

Bell Metal: A variety of "Old Sheffield Plate" consisting of an unusually heavy coating of silver, introduced in 1789 by Samuel Roberts.

Black Pewter: An alloy of 60 percent tin and 40 percent lead. Used for making organ pipes and candle molds.

Bleeding: Technical term applied to pieces of plate whereon the copper base is exposed.

Bobêche: Flat or saucerlike rings placed around candle bases to stop wax drippings.

Bright-cut Engraving: A particular form of engraving popular about 1790, in which the metal is removed by bevelled cutting tools. This gives a jewellike, faceted sparkle to the surface.

Bright Finish: Highly polished, mirrorlike finish produced by use of jeweler's rouge on a polishing wheel.

Britannia: A silver-white alloy composed largely of tin hardened with copper and antimony. Closely akin to pewter, yet differing in the higher proportion of tin, the addition of antimony, and the omission of lead, resulting in a more silvery appearance than is possible with the pewter mixture. It often contains also a small quantity of zinc and bismuth. A common proportion is 140 parts tin, 3 parts copper, and 10 parts antimony.

Bronze: An alloy chiefly of copper and tin.

Buffing: Removal of the outer layer of metal with a flexible abrasive wheel, exposing a shiny undersurface but imparting no additional hardness.

Burnisher: Tool with hard, polished working surface such as agate, for burnishing gold and silver.

Burnishing: Electrodeposits consist of a multitude of small crystals, with intervals between them, and with facets reflecting the light in every direction. The deposited metal is hardened by burnishing and by being forced into the pores of the underlying metal. The durability is thus increased to such an extent that, with the same amount of silver, a burnished article will last twice as long as one which has not been so treated.

Butler's Finish: Satin finish produced by a revolving wheel of wire which makes many tiny scratches, giving the article a dull appearance. Patented by James H. Reilly, Brooklyn Silver Co. Now produced by mechanical buffing and polishing with abrasives.

C: *(See Coin.)*

Cable: Molding like twisted rope, derived from Norman architecture.

Cast: Formed in a mold, *i.e.*, handles, ornaments, etc., are often cast separately.

Chafing Dish: One dish within another, the outer vessel being filled with hot water and in direct contact with the heat source and an inner container for food.

Chamber Candlestick: A tray candlestick in the form of a circular dish with a handle.

Champleve: Enameling by cutting troughs in the metal into which the frit (ground enamel) is melted; the surface is ground flush and polished.

Chasing: A cold modeling process of ornamenting metal by hand with small tools and punches forced into the metal with tappings by a small hammer.

Cloisonné: Enameling by melting the frit into areas defined by wire soldered to the surface to be decorated.

Coin: By 1830 "COIN," "PURE COIN," "DOLLAR," "STANDARD," "PREMIUM," or "C" or "D" were used to indicate 900/1000 parts of silver with 100 parts of copper added, the standard used for United States coins.

Commercial Silver: 999/1000 fine or higher.

Craig Silver: Similar to German silver. Used for making knives.

C-scroll: Usually applied to the shape of a handle in the form of a letter C; also called "single scroll."

Cutler: One who makes, deals in, or repairs utensils or knives.

Cutlery: Knives having a cutting edge.

D: *(See Coin.)*

Dish-cross: An X-shaped support for a dish, some with spirit lamps for warming food.

Dollar: *(See Coin.)*

Dolphin: The sea dolphin used as a sculptured or carved motif.

Domed: Spheroid form of cover, first used in 1715 on tankards, teapots, and coffeepots.

Domestic Plate: Silverware for home use.

Double-scroll: A sinuous line of S-shape, or composed of reverse curves, used especially in the design of handles.

Drawing irons: Metal parts of a drawing bench, through which silver is drawn.

Electrolysis: Conduction of an electric current by an electrolyte of charged particles.

Electroplate: Articles consisting of a base metal coated with silver by the process of electrolysis.

Electrotype: Copy of art object produced by electroplating a wax impression. Much used in the mid-nineteenth century to reproduce antique articles. Now employed in the production of facsimile plates for use in printing.

Electrum: A natural pale yellow alloy of gold and silver. Also, an imitative alloy of silver composed of 8 parts copper, 4 parts nickel, and 3 1/2 parts zinc.

Embossing: Making raised designs on the surface of metal from the reverse side, strictly applicable only to hammered work (repoussé).

Engraving: Cutting lines into metal with a scorper or graver.

EPBM: Electroplate on britannia metal.

EPC: Electroplate on copper.

Epergne: An elaborate centerpiece, especially for a dining table; an ensemble of cups and vases for holding fruits, flowers, etc.

EPNS: Electroplate on nickel silver.

EPNS–WMM: Electroplate on nickel silver with white metal mounts.

EPWM: Electroplate on white metal.

Etching: Surface decoration bitten-in with nitric acid.

Ewer: A jug or pitcher having a wide spout and a handle.

Feather Edge: Decoration of edge of spoon handle with chased, slanting lines. An engraved, decorative design.

Fine Pewter: A composition of 80 percent tin and 20 percent brass or copper. Used for making plates because of the smooth surface, attractive color, and strength.

Fine Silver: Better than 999/1000 pure. It is too soft for practical fabrication, and is mainly used in the form of anodes or sheets for plating.

Flagon: Large vessel for serving wine or other liquors.

Flash Plate: Unbuffed, cheap plated ware.

Flat Chasing: Surface decoration in low relief. Popular in England in early eighteenth century, and widely used in America from 1750 to 1785.

Flatware: Knives, forks, spoons, and serving pieces. May also be applied to plates, platters, and the other flat vessels.

Fluted: A type of grooving.

Forging: The shaping of metal by heating and hammering.

French-grey Finish: Produced by giving the article a light oxidation which is relieved with a steel crimped-wire wheel.

Fusion: An act or operation of melting, as the fusion of metals. Usually accomplished by the application of intense heat.

Gadroon: A border ornament radiating lobes of curved or straight form. Used on rims and feet of cups, plates, and other vessels from the late seventeenth century.

German Silver: A silver-white alloy consisting principally of copper, zinc, and nickle. During World War I this name was dropped by many and the term "nickel silver" used.

Gold Aluminum: A solid alloy used for flatware made by Holmes & Edwards Silver Company, Bridgeport, Conn. Marked with the trademark "WALDO HE" preceded by a symbol that was used by the Waldo Foundry which probably made the metal. Flatware made only in "Rialto" pattern, which was also made in silverplate.

Gold Plating: The covering of an article with gold.

Graver: Tool used to engrave silver.

Hallmark: The official mark of the English Goldsmiths' Company used on articles of gold and silver to indicate their genuineness.

Hollow Handle (H. H.): Handles made of two halves, soldered together. Knives especially need the thickness provided for comfortable use, controlled handle weight, and balance.

Hollow ware: A general term for articles in the form of hollow vessels, such as mugs, ewers, teapots, coffeepots, bowls, and pitchers.

Hollow ware Pewter: A composition of 80 percent tin and 20 percent lead, used for making teapots, tankards, coffeepots, and liquid measures.

Ingot: A bar of silver or other metal.

Katé: A Malayan weight equal to 11.73 ounces. Tea was sold by the "katde," which became "caddy"—hence, tea caddy. Also spelled **Kati.**

Lashar Silver: A process invented by Thomas B. Lashar of the Holmes & Edwards Silver Company, whereby the copper and zinc from the surface of nickel alloy was removed, leaving only the nickel exposed.

Latten: An alloy of copper and zinc; brass.

Limoges: Enamel painted on metal, covering the surface.

Maker's Mark: The distinguishing mark of the individual goldsmith or silversmith.

Malleable: Capable of being extended or shaped by beating with a hammer; ductile.

Matte Finish: Produced by light, evenly spaced punch marks, creating a contrasting dull surface. The matte finish is now often produced on silverplated wares by matte dipping before silverplating and then, after plating, by scratch brushing lightly with a crimped-wire wheel.

Matted Ground: A dull surface made by light punchwork, to secure contrast with a burnished surface.

Metalsmith: One versed in the intricacies of working with metals.

Nickel Silver: An alloy of nickel, copper, and zinc. This is usually 65 percent copper, 5 to 25 percent nickel, and 10 to 30 percent zinc. The best quality hollow ware is "18 percent" that is, it is 18 percent nickel, 22 percent zinc, and 60 percent copper. Flatware blanks are almost always 18 percent.

Niello: Deep-line engraving on gold or silver with the lines filled with copper, lead, and sulphur in borax, forming a type of black enamel which is fired and polished.

Non-tarnishing Silver: Produced by alloying silver with cadmium or by the application of a thin plating of rhodium or palladium on the surface. Used mainly for jewelry.

N.S.: Nickel silver.

Ormolu: "Ground gold," literally. Ground gold leaf used as a gilt pigment. Also, brass made to look like gold.

Oxidizing: Accented beauty of ornamentation by the application of an oxide which darkens metal wherever applied. Shadows and highlights are created which give depth and character.

Patina: Soft luster caused by tiny scratches that come with daily use.

Pewter: An alloy of tin and copper or any alloy of the low-melting-point metals, including tin, lead, bismuth, and antimony. Sad pewter is the heaviest, but not the best because of the high lead content. The higher the tin content, the better the pewter. Tin, with about 20 percent copper added, makes the finest pewter.

Pinchbeck: An alloy of copper or zinc used to imitate gold. Invented by Christopher Pinchbeck (1670–1732), London. Also called "Chapman's gold" or "Mannheim gold."

Pit Marks: Minute holes usually found on lead or soft metal borders.

Planishing: To make smooth or plain. Oval-faced planishing hammers are used to conceal hammer marks used in forming a piece.

Plate: Used in England and on the Continent when referring to articles made of precious metals.

Plique-à-jour: Translucent enamel without a metal backing, enclosed within metal frames, giving a stained-glass or jewel-like effect.

Premium: *(See Coin.)*

Pricking: Delicate needlepoint engraving. Pricked initials were often used on early pieces.

Pseudo Hallmarks: Devices used to suggest English hallmarks.

Pure Coin: *(See Coin.)*

Raising: Formation of a piece of hollow ware beginning with a flat circle of silver. It is hammered in concentric circles over a succession of anvils with frequent annealings.

Rolled Plate: *(See Sheffield Plate.)*

Rope-molding: A type of gadroon bordering made up of reeds and flutes slightly spiraled.

R. P.: Rolled plate.

Repoussé: Relief ornament hammered from the under or inner side of the metal. Usually given added sharpness of form by surface chasing of detail and outline. Has been practiced from early times. Popularized in this country by Samuel Kirk, about 1828.

Satin Finish: *(See Butler's Finish.)*

Scorper: Small chisel for engraving. The blades are of various shapes.

Sheffield Plate: True Sheffield plate was produced by fusing with intense heat a thin sheet of silver to one or both sides of a thick sheet of copper. The composite metal was then rolled down to the proper thickness for fabrication. Rediscovered by Thomas Bolsover (Bowlsover, Boulsover) about 1743. Frequently called "Old Sheffield Plate" to distinguish it from electroplate.

Silver Edge: An ornamental border of solid silver.

Silverite: "A combination of tin, nickel, platinum, etc." according to advertisements.

Silverplate: A base metal, usually either nickel silver or copper, coated with a layer of pure silver by electroplating.

Solid Silver: 925/1000 silver and 75/1000 alloy (copper).

Spinning: Process used for forming hollow ware. A metal plate is cut to proper size, placed against a chuck in a lathe, where pressure against it with a smooth, revolving instrument produces the desired form.

Stake: An iron anvil or tongue, on which a silver object is formed.

Stamping: Impressing of designs from dies into the metal by means of heavy hammers. Often followed by hand chasing to sharpen design details.

Stamping Trademarks and Stock Numbers: As early as 1867, the Meriden Britannia Company had a system of stamping nickel silver and silver soldered hollow ware with a cipher preceding the number. By 1893 nickel silver hollow ware with white metal mounts had as a part of the number two ciphers; that is, on a waiter with white metal, "00256," etc. This made it quickly understood by the number whether the piece was nickel silver, silver soldered, or nickel silver with white metal mounts.

Standard: *(See Coin.)*

Sterling Silver: 925/1000 fine, with 75/1000 of added metal, usually copper, to give it strength and stiffness. This is the standard set by the United States government in the Stamping Act of 1906, and any article stamped "sterling" is of assured quality. It appears on Baltimore silver, 1800–1814, and elsewhere after 1860.

Stoning: Polishing of silver with an emery stone.

Swaged: Shaped by the process of rolling or hammering.

Tempering: Strengthening of metal by heat.

Touch: Maker's mark, impressed with a punch.

Touchstone: A hard siliceous stone or modern square of Wedgwood on which a piece of silver or gold of known quality can be rubbed to compare its mark with that of a piece being assayed.

Trademark: Symbol or tradename by which a manufacturer may be identified. Widely used in this country as a guarantee of quality. A distinction should be made between trademark and hallmark, as required by English and other European countries.

Trifle Pewter: A composition of 60 percent tin and 40 percent lead. Of a darker color and softer than better grades of pewter, it was short lived. The alloy was altered to 83 parts tin and 17 parts antimony and was made into spoons, salt shakers, buttons, and similar articles which could not be finished on a lathe. Workers in this alloy were called "triflers."

Vermeil: Gold plating process developed in France in the mid-1700s. France banned production of vermeil early in the nineteenth century because the process involved the use of mercury. Present-day vermeil is produced by a safe, electrolytic process.

Victorian Plate: Silverplated ware made during the period from about 1840 to 1900 by the process of electrolysis.

Waiter: A tray on which something is carried; a salver.

White Metal: An alloy usually containing two or more parts of the following elements: tin, copper, lead, antimony, and bismuth. The color depends on whether lead or tin predominates; the more tin, the whiter the color.

Whitesmith: A planishing smith; a superior workman in iron, comparable to the armorer. Also a worker in pure tin of the "block" variety, not cast, but hammered and battered, planished and "skum." Originally, "whister."

Bibliography

Abbey, Staton. *The Goldsmiths and Silversmiths Handbook.* New York: Van Nostrand, 1952.

The American Heritage History of American Antiques from the Revolution to the Civil War. Edited by Marshall B. Davidson. New York: American Heritage Publishing Co., Inc., 1968.

The American Heritage History of American Antiques from the Civil War to World War I. Edited by Marshall B. Davidson. New York: American Heritage Publishing Co., Inc., 1969.

The American Heritage History of Colonial Antiques. Edited by Marshall B. Davidson. New York: American Heritage Publishing Co., Inc., 1967.

"American Manufacturers of Silver and Silver Plated Goods," *Jewelers' Weekly,* 4 parts, 1890.

"American Silver," *American Magazine of Art,* August 1919, v. 10, p. 400.

Antiques Journal, Kewanee, Illinois, 1897–

Antiques Magazine, New York, 1922–

Art Journal Illustrated Catalogue of the Industry of All Nations 1851, pub. in connection with *The Art Journal,* George Virtue, London, no date.

"The Art and Development of American Silversmithing," *The Jewelers' Circular and Horological Review,* Feb. 7, 1894.

"The Artistic and Practical Characteristics of American Silversmithing," *The Manufacturing Jeweler,* December 1884.

Avery, Clara Louise. *Early American Silver.* New York: The Century Co., 1930.

Beattie, W. R., "Celery Growing," U.S. Department of Agriculture Farmers' Bulletin No. 1269, Washington, D.C., revised, October 1944.

Bible, The Holy, King James Version.

Boger, H. Batterson, and Boger, Louise Ade. *The Dictionary of Antiques and the Decorative Arts.* New York: Charles Scribner's Sons, 1957.

Boswell, Victor R. "Our Vegetable Travelers," *National Geographic Magazine,* Vol. XCVI, No. 2, August 1949.

Bradbury, Frederick. *History of Old Sheffield Plate.* J. W. Northend, Sheffield, England, 1912; reprinted 1968.

Brunner, Herbert. *Old Table Silver.* München: F. Bruckman KG, 1964.

Buck, J. H. "Old Silversmiths of America," *The Jewelers' Circular-Weekly,* Pt. I, Philadelphia, July 6, 1904; Pt. II, New York, July 20, 1904; Pt. III, Boston, Aug. 3, 1904.

Bury, Shirley. "Silver and Silver Plate," in *The Early Victorian Period, 1830–1860,* Connoisseur Period Guides. New York: Reynal & Co., 1958.

"A Cincinnati Industry, Homan & Co., the largest manufacturers of fine silverplated ware in the city," *The Watch Dial,* July 1888.

Clark, Victor S. *History of Manufactures in the United States.* New York: Carnegie Institute of Washington, 1929.

"Contributions to the International Exhibition, Philadelphia," *The Art Journal,* 1877.

Copeland, Manton. "Sewing Birds Viewed by a Naturalist," *Bulletin of the Society for the Preservation of New England Antiquities,* Vol. XL, No. 4, April 1950, pp. 191–199.

"Current Styles in Solid Silverware," *Jewelers' Circular and Horological Review,* Sept. 26, 1894.

Dreppard, Carl W. *First Reader for Antique Collectors.* Garden City, N.Y.: Doubleday & Co., Inc., 1946.

Dreppard, Carl W., and Smith, Marjorie

Matthews. *Handbook of Tomorrow's Antiques.* New York: Thomas Y. Crowell Co., 1953.
Eighty Years' Progress of the United States. Hartford, Conn.: L. Stebbins, 1868.
Encyclopedia Americana. New York: The Americana Corporation, 1959 edition.
Fales, Martha Gandy. *Early American Silver for the Cautious Collector.* New York: Funk & Wagnalls, 1970.
"Fall Productions in Small Silver Wares," *Jewelers' Circular and Horological Review,* Sept. 26, 1894.
"Fall Styles in Silver Plated Ware," *Jewelers' Circular and Horological Review,* Oct. 3, 1894.
Flynt, Henry N., and Fales, Martha Gandy. *The Heritage Foundation Collection of New England Silversmiths, 1625–1825.* Deerfield, Mass.: The Heritage Foundation, 1968.
Gems of the Centennial Exhibition. New York: D. Appleton & Co., 1877.
Gibb, George S. *The Whitesmiths of Taunton, A. History of Reed and Barton.* Cambridge, Mass.: Harvard University Press, 1946.
"Gorham, America's Leading Silversmiths Since 1831," *The Contemporary Silversmith in Europe and America.* Saint Denis, Fance: Christofle, 1951.
Gorham Silver Co. *The Gorham Manufacturing Company Silversmiths.* New York: Cheltenham Press, 1900.
Gould, Mary Earle. *Early American Wooden Ware & Other Kitchen Utensils.* Springfield, Mass.: Pond-Ekberg Co., 1942; revised 1948.
Goyne, Nancy A. "Britannia in America, the introduction of a new alloy and a new industry," *Winterthur Portfolio II,* Winterthur, Del.: The Henry Francis Du Pont Winterthur Museum, 1965.
"Griswold Portrait Located; Waterman Data Sought," *Meriden Record,* Mar. 21, 1941.
Hagerty, John. "Early American Silver," *Design,* September–October 1941.
Hayward, Arthur H. *Colonial Lighting.* B. J. Brimmer Co., 1923. New edition, New York: Dover Publications, Inc., 1962.
Historical and Biographical Sketch of the Gorham Manufacturing Company. Reprint of booklet issued 1878; no date.
"History of the Gorham Manufacturing Company," extract from undated "flyer."
The History of the World's Columbian Exposition. 4 vols. New York: D. Appleton Co., 1898.
Hoving, Walter. "The History of Tiffany," *Christian Science Monitor,* Apr. 9, 10, 11, 1959.
"How America's $400 Million-a-Year Silver Manufacturing Industry Grew." *The Jewelers' Circular-Keystone,* Philadelphia: Directory Issue, 1965.
"How the Silver Plated Ware Industry Grew," *The Jewelers' Circular-Weekly,* New York, Feb. 5, 1919.
"How the Silver Plated Ware Industry Grew," reprinted from *Jewelers' Circular,* with revision. 1921.
Hughes, G. Bernard. *Small Antique Silverware.* New York: Macmillan Co., 1957.
Hughes, Graham. *Modern Silver Throughout the World, 1880–1967.* New York: Crown Publishers, Inc., 1967.
Humphreys, Mary Gay. "Maiden Lane of the Past and Present," *Jewelers' Circular and Horological Review,* Nov. 28, 1894.
Illustrated History of the Centennial Exhibition. New York: James D. McCabe, 1876.
Index of Trademarks Issued from the United States Patent Office, 1790–1893 and 1881 to present.
Ives, Halsey C. *The Dream City, World's Columbian Exposition.* St. Louis, Mo.: N. D. Thompson Pub. Co., 1893.
Jackson, Gifford. "Styling Cliché," *Industrial Design,* September 1962.
Jewelry Buyer's Guide. New York: Sherry Publishing Co., 1960.
The Jewelers' Circular & Horological Review. New York: D. H. Hopkinson. 1869–
The Jewelers' Circular-Keystone, Philadelphia, Pa.: Chilton Publication. 1869–
Jewelers' Circular-Keystone Brand Name & Trademark Guide. Jewelers' Circular-Keystone, Philadelphia: January 1965, January 1969.
The Jewelers' Circular-Weekly, 50th Anniversary Number. New York: Jewelers' Circular Pub. Co., 1919.
The Jewelers' Index. Philadelphia: Keystone Publishing Co., 1922 and 1931 editions.
The Jewelers' Weekly, New York: The Trade Weekly Co., 1896–1900.
Jobbers' Handbook, 1936–37.
Johnson J. Stewart. "Silver in Newark," A

Newark 300th Anniversary Study. *The Museum*, New Series, Vol. 18, Nos. 3 & 4. Summer-Fall 1966. The Newark (N.J.) Museum.

Keir, Robert M. *Manufacturing Industries of America*. Roland Press, 1928.

The Keystone Jewelers' Index. Philadelphia: The Keystone Publishing Co., 1922, 1924, 1931.

Kirk in U.S. Museums. Baltimore, Md.: Samuel Kirk & Son, Inc., 1961.

Klapthor, Margaret Brown. "Presentation Pieces in the Museum of History and Technology," Contributions from the Museum of History and Technology: Bulletin 241, Paper 47. Washington, D.C., 1965.

Langley, Henry. "Silverplating in California," *The Pacific Coast Almanac for 1869*, San Francisco, 1869.

Laughlin, Ledlie Irwin, *Pewter in America*, Vols. I and II. Boston, Mass.: Houghton Mifflin Co., 1940; also reissued Barre, Mass.: Barre Publishers, 1969.

Laughlin, Ledlie Irwin, *Pewter in America*, Vol. III. Barre, Mass.: Barre Publishers, 1971.

Lichten, Frances. *Decorative Art of Victoria's Era*. New York: Charles Scribner's Sons, 1950.

Luckhurst, Kenneth W. *The Story of Exhibitions*. London & New York: Studio Publications, 1951.

McClinton, Katherine Morrison. *Collecting American 19th Century Silver*. New York: Charles Scribner's Sons, 1968.

Marcosson, Isaac. *Anaconda*. New York: Dodd, Mead & Co., 1957.

May, Earl Chapin. *A Century of Silver, 1847–1947*. New York: Robert McBride Co., 1947.

Mebane, John. *Treasure at Home*. New York: A. S. Barnes & Co., Inc., 1964.

"Men Who Developed the Silver Plated Ware Industry," *The Jewelers' Circular and Horological Review*, Oct. 3, 1894.

Merrill, Charles White, "Silver Consumption in the Arts and Industries of the United States in 1930 and 1931," United States Bureau of Mines, Information Circular, July 1932.

Miles, John W. "Electro-Gold and Silver Plate," *Jewelers' Circular & Horological Review*, April, May, June 1883.

"Modern Silverware in Colonial and Old English Style," *Jewelers' Circular & Horological Review*, Oct. 9, 1895.

National Jewelers' Speed Book, No. 11, National Jeweler, 1930.

"New Fall Patterns in Flatware," *Jewelers' Circular & Horological Review*, Aug. 29, 1894; Sept. 12, 1894.

"New Process for Electro-Plating," *Jeweler, Silversmith and Watchmaker*, September 1877.

Official Descriptive and Illustrated Catalogue of the Great Exhibition, 1851, Vols. II and III. Spicer Bros.

One Hundred Years' Progress of the United States. Hartford, Conn.: L. Stebbins, 1871.

Ormsbee, Thomas Hamilton. "How Silver Spoons Were Made," *American Collector*, January 1939.

Parton, James. "Silver and Silver Plate," *Harper's New Monthly Magazine*, No. CCXX, Vol. XXXVII, pp. 432–448, September 1868.

Percy, Randolph T. "The American at Work, IV: Among the Silver-Platers," *Appleton's Journal*, New Series, No. 30 (December 1878).

Peterson, Arthur G. *Salt and Salt Shakers*. Washington, D.C.: Washington College Press, 1960.

Pleasants, J. Hall, and Sill, Howard. *Maryland Silversmiths, 1715–1830*. Baltimore: The Lord Baltimore Press, 1930.

Porter, Edmund W. "Metallic Sketches," *Taunton Daily Gazette*, Mar. 19, 1906, to Sept. 28, 1907.

Purdy, W. Frank. "Developments in American Silversmithing," *The Art World*. May 1917.

Rainwater, Dorothy T. *American Silver Manufacturers*. Hanover, Pa.: Everybodys Press. 1966.

Rainwater, Dorothy T., and Felger, Donna H. *American Spoons, Souvenir & Historical*. Camden, N.J., and Hanover, Pa.: Thomas Nelson & Sons and Everybodys Press, 1969.

Report of the Eighth Industrial Exhibition of the Mechanics Institute, 1871. San Francisco, 1872.

Reports of the United States Commissioners to the Paris Universal Exposition, 1867. Edited by William P. Blanke. Washington: Government Printing Office, 1870.

"Reproductions of Old English Silver Plated Ware," *Jewelers' Circular & Horological Review*, July 21, 1897.

Revi, A. Christian. *Nineteenth Century Art Glass.* Camden, N.J.: Thomas Nelson & Sons, 1959.

"Review of the New Fall Spoon Patterns," *Jewelers' Circular & Horological Review,* Sept. 26, 1894.

"The Rogers Manufacturing Company," *The American Jeweler,* March 1882.

William Rogers and His Brothers in the Silverware Industry. Philadelphia: Keystone Publishing Co., August-September 1934.

"The Wm. Rogers Manufacturing Co.'s Exhibit," *Jewelers' Circular & Horological Review,* Aug. 9, 1893.

Roth, Rodris. *Tea Drinking in the 18th Century America: Its Etiquette and Equipage,* Contributions from the Museum of History and Technology, United National Museum, Bulletin 225, Washington, D.C., 1961.

Saunders, A. F. "Three Periods of American Silversmithing," (1620–1800, 1800–1880, 1880–1925), *The Metal Industry,* April and August 1925; March 1926.

Schack, C. H., and Clemmons, B. H. *Review and Evaluation of Silver-Production Techniques,* Information Circular 8266, Bureau of Mines, United States Department of the Interior. Washington, D.C., 1965.

Schlesinger, Arthur M. *Learning How to Behave.* New York: Macmillan Co., 1946.

Selwyn, A. *The Retail Jeweller's Handbook.* New York: Chemical Publishing Co., Inc., 1950.

Silver, Economics, Metallurgy, and Use. Edited by Allison Butts. Princeton, N.J.: D. Van Nostrand Co., 1967.

"Silver, Just Silver," *Fortune,* July 1933.

Silver Standard. William G. Snow, Editor. Meriden, Conn., 1905-1912.

Silver (formerly *Silver-Rama*). Vancouver, Wash., January 1968–

"Silverware and Electro-plate Exhibits of the Gorham Company and Reed & Barton," *Frank Leslie's Historical Register of the United States Centennial Exposition, 1876.* New York: Frank Leslie's Pub., 1877.

"The Silverware Industry in America," *The Jewelers' Circular-Keystone,* New York: November and December 1946.

"The Silverware Industry, Early Workers in Silver," *The Keystone,* November 1899.

"The Silverware is from The Gorham Company which house leads all others," extract from the *Daily National Hotel Reporter,* Mar. 8, 1890, reprinted from *The Hotel Reporter,* December 1935.

Simpich, Frederick, "Pieces of Silver," *National Geographic Magazine,* September 1933.

Sniffen, Philip L. *A Century of Silversmithing, Reed & Barton Silversmiths.* Taunton, Mass.: 1924.

Snow, William G. "Early Silver Plating in America," *The Metal Industry,* New York, June 1935.

Snow, W. G. "Silver Plating in Connecticut—Its Early Days," *United States Investor,* May 18, 1935.

Spinning Wheel, Hanover, Pa., 1945–

"The Spoon Patterns of American Silversmiths," *Jewelers' Circular & Horological Review,* 22 parts beginning Apr. 10, 1895 and concluding Sept. 11, 1895.

Sterling Flatware Pattern Index, Philadelphia, Pa.: Jewelers' Circular-Keystone, No date; second edition, 1971.

The Story of Sterling. New York: Sterling Silversmiths Guild of America, 1937.

Stoudt, John Joseph. *Pennsylvania Folk-Art.* Allentown, Pa.: Schlecter's, 1948.

Styles in Silver. Philadelphia Museum Bulletin, Vol. XLI. No. 209, March 1946.

Tallis' History and Description of the Crystal Palace and the Exposition of the World's Industry in 1851. London, 1852.

"Charles L. Tiffany and the House of Tiffany & Co," *Jewelers' Circular & Horological Review,* Feb. 7, 1894.

"The Tiffany Exhibit at the World's Fair," *The Illustrated American,* May 20, 1893.

Tracy, Berry B. "The Decorative Arts (Silver)," *Classical America, 1815–1845.* The Newark (N.J.) Museum, 1963.

Trade Marks of the Jewelry and Kindred Trades, New York and Philadelphia: Jewelers' Circular-Keystone Publishing Co., 1869, 1896, 1898, 1904, 1910, 1915, 1922, 1943, 1950, 1965, 1969.

Tryon, R. M. *Household Manufactures in the United States.* Chicago: University of Chicago Press, 1917.

U.S. Tariff Commission. *A Survey of the various types of silverware, the organization of the industry and the trade in silverware, with special reference to tariff consideration.* Report No. 139, Second Series. Washington, D.C.: U.S. Govern-

ment Printing Office, 1940.
Vanderbilt, Amy. *Amy Vanderbilt's Complete Book of Etiquette.* Garden City, N.Y.: Doubleday & Co., Inc., 1952.
Wardle, Patricia. *Victorian Silver and Silver Plate.* Victorian Collector Series. New York: Thomas Nelson & Sons, 1963.
Watt, Alexander. *Electro-metallurgy.* New York: D. Van Nostrand Co., 1895.
Wells, Lester Grosvenor. "American Silverware Since Colonial Days," *Design,* November 1941.
Wenhem, Edward Gordon. *Practical Book of American Silver.* New York and Philadelphia: J. B. Lippincott Co., 1949.
Wertime, Theodore A. "Man's First Encounters with Metallurgy," *Science,* Vol. 146, No. 3649, pp. 1257–1267, Dec. 4, 1964.
Western Collector, San Francisco, 1963–
White, Benjamin. *Silver, its History and Romance.* New York and London: Hodder & Stoughton, 1917.
Wood, Violet. *Victoriana, A Collector's Guide.* New York: Macmillan Co., 1961.
The World of Science, Art, and Industry in the New York Exhibition, 1853–54. Edited by Prof. Benjamin Silliman, Jr., and Charles P. Goodrich. New York: G. P. Putnam & Co., 1854.

Index

Italic numbers refer to illustration pages. Place names are not indexed. The names of patterns are listed under "flatware patterns," "glass inserts patterns," and "hollow ware patterns," and *not* under each specific name.

To make this Index of greater value to the reader, the *items* manufactured by a company and discussed and/or shown in illustrations in this book are listed in alphabetical order under the company name. For example, Meriden Britannia Co. and Reed & Barton each has a long list of items; the reader would find a listing of page references only to the firm name of little interest.

A

acanthus decoration, 107, *107*, 455
Adam, Robert, style of, 91
Adams, Caleb Cushing (silversmith), 33
Adams, Chandler & Co., 252
Adams, John P. (jeweler), 33
Adams & Shaw, 33
advertising, early, 30, 60, 63, 66–71
agitation, in plating bath, 56
Allen, Grosvenor N. (designer), *124*
alloys, of gold, 58
  of silver, 39
amalgamation process, 17–19
America, The (model), 137
American Silver Co., 27
Ames Mfg. Co., N. P., 22, 32
  castor, 95, *170*, 171
"Anchor Rogers" trademark, 145, *146*
Anchor Silver Plate Co., 239
animal finials, 295, *299–300*
animal motifs, 253, *254*, 339
Apollo, bust of, *159*, 162
Apollo Silver Co., 247, 290
Appleton's Journal, teapot, 52–57, *53*
aquarium, Egyptian style, *161*, 162
Argand lamp, 407
"Art Deco" styles, 129–132
"Art Moderne" styles, 129–132

Art Nouveau, candlesticks, *422–424*, 425
  dresser sets, 370, *384–385*
  epergne, *206*
  mirrors, 385, *385*
  pin trays, 385, *386*
  tea service, 119–124, *121*, *122*
  vases, 162, *164–166*
ash holder, *392*
aspic dish, *236*

B

Babbitt, Isaac, 28
Babbitt, Crossman & Co., 28
Babbitt & Crossman, 28
Bächle, Amile (designer), *422*
Baird-North Co., 444
baking dishes, *293–295*, 294
Ball, Black & Co., 93
ball, teapot, 108, *108*
Bancroft, Redfield & Rice, 100, *101*, 223
bands, applied, 116, *117*
bar accessories, 282–283
Barbour Bros. Co., ice pitcher, *253*
Barbour Silver Co., 27
  plate, *273*
Barbour Silver Plate Co., Dutch reproductions, 60, *62*
  napkin ring, *345*

467

spoon holder, *304*
"Barge of Venus," 142–143, *142*
baroque style, 91
bar spoons, 446
Barton, Charles E., 29–30
base metals, 39–41, 52–53
   marking for, 72–73
baskets, *see* bread baskets; brides' baskets; cake baskets; sugar baskets
Bass, E. & J., *345*
bath, plating, 56
battery, galvanic, 21
Baur, Theodore (sculptor), 139, *139–140*
Beattie, William C. (designer), 31, 53, 93, 95, *138*, 138
Beckman, A. C., 351
beer pitchers, *283*
Benedict & Burnham, 39
Bennett, Charles A. (designer), *124*
Bennett-Merwin Silver Co., *124*
Bergen & Niland (glass cutters), 183
Berry, Henry (designer), 117, *120*
berry dishes, 184–198, *189–206*, color plate A
berry spoon, *445*, 446
"Big Bonanza" silver ore, 16
Biggins-Rodgers Co., 240
birds, as decoration, 111, *112*
Bisbee, I. (designer), 75
Bishop Museum, 148, 151, 153
Blackman, Jared C. (designer), 82, *84*
blanks, curved, *86*, 87
   for flatware, 44, 45, 46
   spoon, 82, *83*
Boardman, Luther & Norman S. (designers), *434*, 435
Bolsover, Thomas, 19
bonbon dishes, *302*, 302
Boon, Sanford (designer), 76, 77
Boon & Ormsby, 77
borders, beaded, 117, *119*
bottles, castor, 180, *181*
boudoir sets, *see* dresser sets
bouquet holders, *see* vases
bowl, forming of, 47
bowls, fruit, 184, 189, *189*
boxes, collar-button, *395*
   glove, 370, *372*
   handkerchief, 370, *372*
   jewel, 370, *371–378*

   pepper, 329
   sardine, 348, *349–350*
   stamp, *398*, *401*
   Victorian, 370, *371–378*
Boyle, Robert (inventor), 354
"Boy on a Dolphin" napkin ring, *341*
Brabrook, George (designer), 30, *89*, 89
Bradbury & Sons, T., 420
Bradel, William (designer), 79, *80*
Bradley & Hubbard Mfg. Co., lamp burners, 417
   sewing birds, 367
Brainard, Ellerson L. (designer), *422*
Brand(t), Hennig, 354
brass, as base metal, 40
bread baskets, 236, *237*
bread tray, *236*
brides' baskets, 184, *204–206*, color plates A, D
   prices of, 64
"Bright Plate" finish, 52, 456
Bristol Brass & Clock Co., *434*
britannia, 26, 28, 72, 456
   butter cooler, *241*, 242
   butter dishes, 241
   composition of, 20
   in spoon patent, 77, *77*
   introduction of, 20
Brockway, Josephus (designer), 75, 76, 77
Brown, M. (electroplater), 28, 29
Bruff, Thomas (designer), 75
brushes, sets of, 370, *382–383*
buffalo figurine, *160*, 162
"Buffalo Hunt, The," 139, *139*, *140*
burnishing, of teapot, 56
Butcher, R. (designer), 75
butler's finish, 52, 114, 456
butter cooler, *241*, 242
butter dishes, 236–248, *240–247*
butterflies, as decoration, 186, *189*
butter prints, 240
buttonhooks, 385, *387–389*
   as premiums, 65, *66*

C

cake baskets, 36, 221–232, *222–232*
call bells, on castors, 171, *172*, 180, *182*
   on spoon holders, 302, *306*, *310*, 311, *313*

camphene fuel, 407
candles, making of, 418
candlesticks, 418–428, *418–427*
capacity of utensils, stamp mark of, 97
card cases, 218, *220*, 221
card receivers, 205–221, *207–221*
cards, calling, 205–206
care, of silverplate, 447–451, *449–451*
Carson, Pirie, Scott & Co., *371*
cart, spoonholder shaped as a, 308, *309*
caskets, jewel, 370, *371–378*
casters, salt and pepper, 328–329, *331–334*
casting, 59, 60, *61*
   centrifugal, 60, *61*
   of hollow handles, 54
   of legs, 54
   shop, *44*
castors, 95, 170–187, *171–184, color plate B*
   individual, *347*, 348
   pickle, 64, *178*, 180, *183–187, color plate B*
   revolving, 172, *174–175*, 180
catalogs, early, 63
   identical, 73
celery, history of, 315, 320
celery baskets, *319*, 320
celery stands, 315, *316–319*, 320
centerpieces, *169*, 184, 186, 189, *189*
Central America, silver in, 15–16
"Century Vase, The," 138
Ceylon Tea Co. advertising spoon, 69–70, *71*
chafing dishes, 287, 290, *291*, 292
chasing of patterns, 29, *42*, 55
chatelaine bag, premium, 67
chatelaines, *391–392*, 392
Chatillon-DeMenil Mansion, 99, *100*
chief, statue of Indian, *159*, 162
Christofle (French firm), 21
Church, Joseph, 429
"Church & Rogers" trademark, 429, *431*
cigar lamp, *401*
classic style, 91, 92, 97–98, *98, 99, 100*
clip, napkin, *345*
close plating, 19
Clulee, John (designer), *436*
coal oil, for lamps, 415
Codman, William Christmas (designer), 122

coffeepots, "lighthouse," 114
   long-necked, 114–115
   self-pouring, 321, *322*
   size and shape of, 114, *115*
   straight-sided, 114, *116*
   see also tea services
coin-silver spoons, 22, 23, 429, *430*
cold-rolling of blanks, 85, *85*
Cole, John A., 429
"Collapsion Cups," 287, *288*
collar-button box, 395
"collars" on teapots, *109–111*, 111
Collins, Edward, K., 93, *95*
cologne bottles, *363–368*, 367, *370*
Colonial styles, 124, *124–126*, 127
Columbus Silver Co., 288
combs, 370, *382*
Commonwealth, model of the, 137
Community Plate, *see* Oneida Community
competition in selling, 30
compotes, *see* fruit dishes
Comstock Lode, 13, 16
condensed-milk-can holder, 349
Copeland, Dr. Manton (essay by), 367
copper, as base metal, 40
   in Old Sheffield Plate, 19, 40
copper-deposit process, 60
copying, of ancient pieces, 133
Cotton Exposition, International, 139
Cowles, William B., 22
Cowles & Sons, Whitfield (electroplaters), 22
Cowles Mfg. Co., 22, 23
cracker bowl, *283*
creamers, *see* dessert sets
Crossman, West & Leonard, 28
Crossman, William, 28, 29
cross rolling, of blanks, 47
cruet frames, 329
   see castors
crumb trays, 233, *236*
Crystal Palace Exhibition (London), 13, *90*, 92, 93, 95, 133, *134*
   (New York), 93, 95, *170*, 171
Culver, John M. (designer), *434*
cupellation process, 17
cups, 278, *284*, 286–290
   for clergy sick calls, 287, *290*
"curfew," defined, 354
cutting, of flatware blanks, 46

470 AMERICAN SILVERPLATE

D

decoration, incongruous, 31, 104
  of card receivers, 218
  of cake baskets, 227, 229
Defender, The (yacht), 153–154, *154*
Derby Silver Co., 27
  cake baskets, 229
  card receivers, 217
  dresser sets, 384
  napkin ring, 345
  syrup pitchers, 274
  tea service, 117, *120*, *121*
  water pitcher, 265
  water set, 264
design, for teapot, 52
  of flatware pattern, 41, *41–42*, 43
designs, dies for making, 46, *48*
desk sets, 398, *399*, *401–406*
dessert sets, 273, *274–276*
Deuster Wine Co., ad, 70, *71*
deYoung, M. H., 147
Dickinson, Charles (designer), 95, 97
dies, for shaping flatware, 46, *47*
  for shaping hollow ware, 54
  making of flatware, 41, 43
distribution of wares, 64–71
Dixon, James (designer), 28, 29
Dixon & Sons, James, 31, 95, 432
dog figurine, *160*, 162
dredge, salt, 329
dresser sets, 370, *379–387*
Dunkley & Woodman Business Directory, 30
Dunn, Leonard F. (designer), 85, *86–87*
Dutch influence, 91
Dutch reproductions, 60, *62*, 127, *127*
"Dying Gladiator" figurine, *160*, 162

E

Edwards, George Clark (designer), 321, *324*
egg, teapot shaped as, *109*, 110
egg-cup stand, 171, *176*, 177, 180
Egyptian motifs, 191, *198–200*
Egyptian style, *161*, 162
Eisenhardt, J. A., *313*
"Electroliers," 418
electrolysis, for plating, 17
electroplating, history of, 21–38
  of teapot, 55–56
Elkington, G. R. & H., 21

Elkington, Mason & Co., 90, 92
Elkington & Co., *134*, 432
Empire, French, style, 92
enameling, of castors, 183, *185*
engine-turning of designs, 29–30, 55
  cost of, 103
England, early silverplating in, 19
English designs, 29, 117, *119*
engraving, of design, 55
  cost of, 103
entree dishes, *292–293*, 294
epergnes, 140, *141*, 142, 143, 189, *190*, *205*, *206*
exhibition silverplate, 133–147, *134–147*

F

"Facetform," 132
Fahys Watch Case Co., *436*
Fairburn, William A. (inventor), 354
Fallows, James (designer), 81, *83*
fern dish, 67, *69*
Ferris, G. W. (inventor), 172
figurines, *159–160*
"Fine Arts Line" (Wilcox), 162, *167–168*
finials, berries and leaves, 119, *121*
  bird, 107, *107*, 111, *112*, 311, *314*
  butterfly, 311, *314*
  cone, 108, *109*
  cow, 242
  grape cluster, 104, *105*
  hunting dog, *102*, 102
  jumping horse, *150*, 151
  lion-head, 104, *106*
  lion with shield, *109*, 111
  pineapple, 101, *101*
  sphinx, *108*, 108
  strawberry, *98*, 100
finishes, types of, 52
finishing, of spoon handles, 49
Fish, Henry, H., 29, 30
Flagg, Asa F., 33
flagon, alcohol, 290, *291*
flatware, 429–446, *430–446*
  at World's Columbian Exposition, 146
  first Reed & Barton, 30
  patented processes in manufacture of, 74–89, *75–89*
  production of a pattern for, 41–52, *41–51*, 56
flatware patterns
  "Adam," *441*

"Arcadian," *446*
"Armenian," 146, *446*
"Avalon," *440, 441*
"Beaded," 92, 436, *442,* 446
"Berkeley Square," *441*
"Berwick," *436,* 444
"Bird of Paradise," *441*
"Cardinal," 325
"Cereta," *441*
"Classic," *441*
"Columbia," 146
"Coronation," *441*
"Cromwell," 146
"Denville," *441*
"Diana, The," 444
"Elberon," *434*
"Embossed," 446
"Evening Star," *441*
"Flower de Luce," *441*
"Forever," *441*
"Georgian," *441*
"Grosvenor," *441*
"Hampton Court," *441*
"King Cedric," *441*
"Kings," 146, 441, *444*
"Lady Hamilton," *441*
"La Mode," *434*
"Lancaster," 446
"Lily," 32, *435*
"Lorne," 446
"Louis XVI," *441*
"Luxembourg," *444,* 446
"Majestic," 325, *326, 444,* 446
"Medallion," 103
"Milady," *441*
"Monarch," 325
"Morning Star," *441*
"Newport," 446
"Noblesse," *441*
"Olive," 92, 432, 436, *442,* 446
"Opal," 146
"Oval," 32, *435,* 436, 446
"Oval Thread," 446
"Oxford," 444
"Patrician," *441*
"Paul Revere," *441*
"Pequot," 146
"Plain," 432, 437, 446
"Plymouth," *434*
"Raphael," *68*
"Rembrandt," *444,* 446
"Rendezvous," *441*
"Roman," 432–433, *432, 433*
"Roman Medallion," 30, *433,* 435
"Rose," 146
"Saint Regis," *441*
"Savoy," 325, *326*
"Shell," 146, 325
"Shell Tipped," 446
"Sheraton," *441*
"Threaded," 92, 432, 436, *442*
"Tipped," 92, 432, 436, *442,* 446
"Windsor," *441,* 446
"York Rose," 446
floor lamp, *414*
fluted edges, on glass, 200, *204, color plates A, D, E*
fluting, as decoration, *114,* 114, 116
Forbes, Marshall, 22–23
Forbes Silver Co., 27
Fork Cleaner (Hagerty's), 448, *449*
Fort Dearborn Watch & Clock Co., *400*
Fowler, Maltby (designer), 81, *83*
Fox, Andrew W., 22
Fox, Horace, 22
French Empire style, 92
French-grey finish, 52, 457
"French" plating, 19
frosted glass bowls, 198, *203*
fruit bowls (dishes), 184–198, *188–206, color plate A*
fruit knives, *396*
fruit stands, 184–198, *188–206*
furnace, electric, *43,* 44

G

Gale, William (inventor), 35, 75
Garfield, James A., pitcher presented to, *152,* 153
Gems of the Centennial Exposition, 141, 142
Georgian design, *123,* 124
"German" silver, *see* nickel silver
Germany, silver mines in, 15
Gibney, Michael (designer), 435
Gibson, John Jr. (inventor), 250, *253*
Gill, George (designer), 104, *106,* 108, *109,* 111, *183,* 183
glass inserts (liners), 155–158, 162, *167–169,* 170, 184, *308,* 308, 320, *color plates A, B, D, E*
glass inserts patterns
    "Daisy and Button," *color plate A*
    "Tree of Life," 189–190, *191,* 308, *308*

glass shades, for lamps, *410, 412–417, color plate C*
Gleason, Edward (designer), 171, *172*
Gleason & Sons, R., 171, *172, 173*
glove boxes, 370, *372*
Gloves, Silversmith's (Hagerty's), 448, *450*
goblets, 278, *285*
Goddard & Sons, J., 450
gold, colored, 58
gold inlaid process, 139
gold plating, of hollow ware, 52, 56
   tea service in, *110,* 111
Goodwin, Horace (electroplater), 22
Goodyear, C. (designer), *75*
Gorham, Jabez, 432
Gorham, John, 31, 432
Gorham & Thurber, 432
Gorham (& / Mfg.) Co., 30, 31–32
   berry spoon, *445*
   chafing dish cook book, 290
   flatware, *432,* 432–433, *444*
   fluted teapot, *114–119,* 114–117
   polish, 450
   salts, *327*
   tea service, *96,* 98
grades of plate, 146
   marketing of, 63–64
gravy boat, *349*
Grecian style, 95
Greece, silver mines in, 15
Green's Patent Vertically Revolving Castor, 172, *174*
Greenwood, Charles H. (designer), *124*
Griswold, Ashbil, 26, 63
Grosjean, Florian (designer), *79, 81, 82*
Gudebrod, Louis (sculptor), 147

H

Habensack, Frederick (designer), *436*
Hagenmacher, A. H., 39
Hagerty & Sons, W. J., 448–451, *449–450*
hairpin boxes, 370
hair receivers, *388, 389, 394*
Hall, Elton & Co., 27, 32
   cup, *287*
   flatware, *434*
   sugar basket, *275*
Hamil & Co., Charles W., *420*
hammered Grecian style, *126*
handkerchief boxes, 370, *372*

handles, of spoons, 77–82, *77–83*
   of teapots, 54
   selection of, 180, *182*
"hard metal" wares, 39
Hart, Hubert C. (designer), *88, 89*
Hart, J. H. & A. W., 162
Hartford Mfg. Co., 30, 73
Hartford Silver Plate Co., *217, 273*
Hartford Times, ad in, 362, *362*
Hart Mfg. Co., Lucius, *305*
Harper's Monthly, 49
Harper's Weekly, 30
Hattersley, William (designer), *95, 97*
Haukwitz, Godfrey (inventor), 354
Hawkesworth, Eyre & Co., *134*
Haynes & Lawton, 37, *38, 177,* 180
heat lamps, for entree dishes, 294
Herbene Pharmacal Co., *67, 69*
Hill, John (designer), 140, *243*
History and Technology, Museum of, *150,* 151
Hobbs, John H. (designer), 107, *107*
Holbrook, Edward, 33
hollow ware, at Columbian Exposition, 146
   operations in, 57–60
   plating of inside, 52
   production of, 52–60, *53–60*
hollow ware patterns
   "Adam," *125*
   "Americana," *130*
   "Arctic," *258*
   "Bearded Head," 107, *107*
   "Bearded Man," 107, *107*
   "Birth of the Rose," *384,* 385
   "Centennial," 107, *107*
   "Charter Oak," 104, *105*
   "Chippendale," *126*
   "Crocus," *265*
   "Denmark," *129*
   "Fern," *264*
   "Joanne," *127*
   "Marguerite," *121, 264*
   "Medallion," *102–103,* 103
   "Moss Rose," *261*
   "Paul Revere," *128*
   "Sanderson," *125*
   "Snow Flake," *262, 272*
   "Tara Hall," *130*
   "Venetian," *258*
   "Viking," 107, *107*
   "Winthrop," *131*

Holmes & Edwards, 27, 87, *87*
  flatware, *434*
  orange spoon, 321, *324*
Holmes & Tuttle Mfg. Co., 27
Holmes, Booth & Haydens, 321, *323*
Homan, Henry, 33
Homan Mfg. Co. (Silver Plate Co.), 33
  baking dish receptacle, *294*
  cake basket, 231, *232*
  hollow ware, *40*
  relish dish, *186*
  sick-call cup, *290*
  spoon tray, 315, *316*
  tea set, *123*
  vase, *165*
Hope Hose Co. of Philadelphia, carriage of, 134, *135*
hotel ware, 30, 64
Hull, John, 278
hummingbird figurine, *160*, 162
Humphrey, R. (designer), 81, *82*

I

Illustrated American Advertiser, 96
Indian chief, statue of, *159*, 162
Industry of All Nations, 90, 92, 95, *134*
ink erasers, *406*, 406
inkstand, Larkin premium, *64*, 66
ink wells, *402–405*
inlay, of solid silver, 87, *87*
  reinforcing, 52
inserts, glass, *155–158*, 162, *color plates A, B, D, E, 167–169*, 170, 184, 308, *308*, 320
interior plating, 56
international exhibitions, 133–147
International Exhibition (London), 95
International Silver Co. (INSILCO), 26, *26–27*, 435
  candlestick, *422*
  list of companies forming, 27
  polish, 450
  tea service, *128*
International Silver Co. of Canada, Ltd., Inc. 27
"in the metal" ware, 35, 36
iron, in spoons, 77, *77*
Isaacson, James H., 22, 23
Ittig, George P. (designer), *436*

J

Jackson, Austin, F. (designer), *434*

Jameson, William (designer), *434*
Japan, tea set presented to Emperor of, *138*, 138
Jepson, John (designer), *109*, 111
jewel caskets, 370, *371–378*
Jewelers' Circular and Horological Review, ads in, 33, 58, 326, *326*
Jewelers' Crown Guild, 65–66
Jewelers' Weekly, ads in, *145, 325, 395*
jobbers, 35, 36
Johnson, John D., 22
Judson, Whitcomb L. (inventor), 385

K

Kalakaua Yacht Club, 148, *149*, 151
Kann & Sons Co., 35, *273*
"Kate Greenaway type" figures, 329, 339, *345*
Kaufmann, Ernest (designer), 245, *245*, 253, *254*
Kelley & McBean, 69, *70, 361*
kerosene lamps, *409–417, 412–416*
Keystone, The, ads in, *123, 165*
Kilpatrick, Gen. Judson, tea service, 103, *150*, 151
Kirk, Samuel (silversmith), 36, *36*, 37, 104, *105*, 111
knife, of flatware patterns, 446
  orange, *325*, 325, *326*
  paper, 69, *70, 404, 406*
knife rests, 348, *348*

L

lacquer, 451
Ladies' Home Journal, ads in, 65, *66, 67*, 388
lamps, *407–418, 408–417, color plate C*
Langley, Henry (author), 36
La Pierre Mfg. Co., 27
lard-oil lamps, *407*, 408
Large, Samuel J. (designer), *434*
Larkin Soap Mfg. Co., premiums, *64*, 66
Lawrence, N. (designer), 250
Learning How to Behave, 217
Leavenworth, Seth H. (designer), *40*, 231, *232*
legs, of teapot, 54
Leonard, A. (designer), *98*, 100
Leonard, Gustavus, 29
Leonard, Horatio, 29
Leonard, Reed & Barton, 29, *171*
Leonard, Zephaniah A., 28, 29

liners, blue glass, 327
lines of ware, complete, 30, 73
liquor labels, 278, 282, 283, 397, 401
liquor sets, 397
Little, A. (designer), 74, 75
lotus blossom motif, 227, 228
Louvre, vase in the, 14
Ludwig, Adolph (designer), 238
Lyman's Patent Double Valve, 250, 251

M

machine-engraving, *see* engine-turning
magic castor, 171, *173*
Maltby, Stevens & Curtiss Co., 27
Manhattan Silver Plate Co., 27
manicure sets, 385, *386–387*
manufacture of spoons, described, 86–87
Manufacturing Jeweler, The, 400
Mappin & Webb, 171
mark, soldered on, 36
marketing methods, 63–72
marking, of ware, 72–73
Mars, statue of, *159*, 162
Mary Gregory type glass, 198, 331, *334*, 370
mask decorations, 223, *226*
mask feet, on teapot, 105, *106*, 107
Mason, John, patent by, 329
match boxes and safes, *352–361*, *354*, *361*
   souvenir of Columbian Exposition, 146, *147*
matches, invention of, 354
matte finish, 52, 457
Mead, John O., 21–22
Mead & Sons, 22
medallion-head decoration, *177*, 180
medallions, applied, 327, *327*
   on cake baskets, 223
   on tea service, *102*, 103, *103*
medals won by Meriden Silver Co., 140, *141*
memorandum tablet, premium, 66, *66*
Meriden Britannia Co., 25, *25–27*, 30, 73, 137
   berry dish, color plate A
   boxes, *375–378*
   "Buffalo Hunt," *139*, 139, 140
   butter dish, *245*, *246*, 247
   buttonhooks, *389*, *393*
   cake baskets, 36, 223, *225–228*, *231*
   candlesticks, *420*, *422–423*

card receivers, 207, *215–219*, 218
castors, 172, 174, *174*, *176*, 177, *color plate B*
celery stands, *316–317*
chatelaines, *391*, *392*
cigar lamps, 401
coffeepots, *104*
combs and brushes, 382
cook book, 290
crumb tray, 236
cups, *285–289*
Defender, The, 153, 153–154
desk sets, *402–403*, *406*
dessert sets, 276
entree dishes, *292–293*
figurines, *160*, 162
fruit knives, 396
goblets, 285
ice pitchers, 250, *251–257*, *256*, *263–264*
ice-water urns, *268*, 269
ink erasers, *406*
ink wells, *402–403*
lamps, *408–418*, *416–417*, color plate C
liquor labels, 282, 283, 401
manicure sets, *386–387*
match safes, *357–358*
medals won by, 140, *141*
moustache cups, 289
napkin rings, *337–346*, *339*
nut bowls, 301
orange spoon and knife, 325, *326*
pepper boxes, 329, *332*
puff box, *394*
pump pot, 321, *322*
punch bowl set, *277–278*
pyriform ware, 103, *104*
salts, *327–333*
salt shakers, 329, *331*
sardine boxes, *350*
sectional plating by, 51
sewing bird, *362*, 362
shaving brushes, *393*
shaving sets, 401
shoe horn, *406*
spoon holders, 302, *303–315*
stamp boxes, *398*, 401
syrup pitchers, *269–270*
tableware, 137
teapots, 101–102, *101*, *109*, 111
tea services, *103*, 104, *105*, *112*, *113*, *118*, *119*, *120*, *121*

toilet sets, *363–366*
toothpick holders, *357–358*
tureens, *298–299*
vases, *155*, 161, 162, *163–164, color plate E*
vegetable dishes, *296*
vinaigrettes, *390*
whisk broom holder, *394*
wine-bottle cases, *282*
wine coolers, *279–281*
Meriden Britannia Co., Ltd., 27
Meriden Flint Glass Co., 183
Meriden Silver Plate Co., 27
   card receivers, *217, 221*
   epergne, *141*
   mounts for plate, *168*, 170
   stand for bowl, 190, *191*
   spoon holder, *304*
   tea services, 119, *121, 125, 126*
   toilet stand, *363*
Middletown Plate Co., 27
   butter dish, *245*
   centerpieces, 140
   spoon holders, *304*, 311, *314*
   sugar bowl–spoon rack, 311, *312*
   tea service, 111, *112*
   toilet stands, *367*
Miller & Co., Edward (lamp burners), 417
Minnesota Mining & Manufacturing Co., 448
mirrors, *369*, 370
   advertising, 71, *71*
   Art Nouveau, *385, 385*
Mix, Garry T. (designer), 79, *81*
Mix, John (designer), 77, *77*
Mix, T. (designer), 75
Mix, William (designer), *74*, 75, 77, 78, 79
model of flatware, three-dimensional, 41, *42*
molds, reverse, 41
"Morgan" centerpiece, *169*
Morning Star, ship's trumpet of the, *152, 152–153*
motifs, unrelated, 253–254, *254*, *257*
mounts, for plate, *168*, 170
   white metal, *40*, 41
moustache cups, 287, *288–290*
mustard pot, *349*
musters, prizes at firemen's, 153, *153*

N

napkin rings, 67, 334, *335–347*, 339, 341, 348
National Stamping Law, 72
nature, motifs of, 93
New York Crystal Palace, 93, 95, 133–135
nickel silver, 29, 32, 39–41, 56–57
   furnace for melting, *43*, 44
North America, silver discoveries in, 16
Norwich Cutlery Co., 27
Noyes, John Humphrey, 32
nut bowls, *300–301*, 302

O

oil, for lamps, 407, 412–413, 416
"Old Jug," ad, 70, *71*
"Old Sheffield Plate," 18–20
Oneida Community Silversmiths, 32
   coffeepot, *124*
   flatware, *85*, *86–87*, *435*, *440*
orange holder, 326, *326*
orange knife, *325, 325, 326*
orange peeler, 321, *323, 324*
outfit for silverplating, 34
Overland Monthly, premiums, 67, *68*
Overton, Eugene (yachtsman), 148
oyster forks, 446

P

Pacific Coast Almanac for 1869, The, 36
Pacific Plate Works, 36
Pacific Silvercloth, 447–448
Paine, Diehl & Co., 321, *322*
Pairpoint, Thomas J. (designer), 138
Pairpoint Mfg. Co. (Corp)
   bonbon dish, *302*, 302
   bread tray, *238*
   butter dish, *246*
   cake baskets, *231*
   candelabrum, *424*
   castors, *186–187*
   centerpiece and compotes, *169*
   coffee sets, 114, *115, 116*
   dresser sets, *383*
   "Fine Arts" line, 170
   orange holder, *326*, 326
   syrup cup, *271*
   teapot, *122*
   tea set, *113*
   vase, *166*

palmette, as decoration, *114*, 114
Panama-Pacific Exposition, 147, *148*
paper knives, 69, *70*, *404*, 406
paperweight, 144, *144*
papier-maché, shell of, 250
Paris International Exposition, 139, 145
Paris Universal Exposition, 134–137
Parker & Casper Co., 27, *223*, *225*
Parkin, William (designer), 30, 104, 105, *106*, 172, *174*, 223, 227
patents for processes, 30, 75–89, *76–89*
patio process of silver extraction, 17
pattern numbers, 72
peacock, on castors, *178*, 180
Peck, Deforest H., 27–29
peddlers, 63
pedestal-footed teapot, 104, *105*
peeler, orange, 321, *323*
"pelican in her piety" motif, *109*, 110–111
People's Home Journal, 67, *69*
pepper boxes, 329
pepper shakers, *see* salt shakers
Perkins, J. (designer), 75
Persian design, 114, *115*
petroleum, 407, 412
pewter, 20, 39, 72
Philadelphia Centennial Exhibition, *110*, 111, 137–145
photography in advertising, 63
Pick & Co., Albert, *124*
pickle castors, *178*, 180, *183–187*, color plate B
pickle dishes, *186*
pickle forks, 446
picture frames, 370, *379*
pin trays, Art Nouveau, 385, *386*
pitchers, for ice water, 153–154, *153*, *233*, 233, *248–268*, 248–263
  syrup, 269–270
  tilting, *152*, 153
  whiskey, 283
  see also tea services
plate, cut-glass, *168*
plateaus, mirrored, 236, *240*
"plating," defined, 18
Pleadwell, William E. (designer), 89, *89*
points, of greatest wear, 82–89, *84–89*
polish, 448, *449*, 450
polishing, of edges, 46, *48*, 49
  of teapot, 56
Pomona art glass, 183

Poole Silver Co., 425
Porter, Edmund (author), 28
Porter, William, 28
Poseidon, decoration, 191, *201*
Pratt, Benjamin, 29
Pratt, William H., 22
premiums, *64–71*, 66–71
presentation silverplate, 147–154, *149–154*
prints, butter, 240
production methods, 41–57, *41–51*
"Progress Vase," 137
projections, at points of wear, 83, *84*
puff boxes, 370, 379, *394*
pump pots, 321, *322*
punch bowl sets, 273, 277, 278, *278–279*
purse, premium, 67
pyriform tea services, 103, *104*

Q

quail, figurine, *160*, 162
quadruple plate, marking of, 73
quality, stamping of ware for, 73
Queen City Silver Co., *239*, *386*

R

racks, for spoons, 302, *303*, *306–308*, *313*
ram's head decoration, 104, *105*, 186
receivers, card, 205–221, *207–221*
receptacles, for baking dishes, 293–295, *294*
Redfield & Rice, 100, 223, *226*, *304*
Reed, Henry, 27, 29–30
Reed, Henry G. (designer), *100*, 100, *109*, 110
Reed & Barton (R & B), 27–31
  ash holder, *392*
  at Philadelphia Centennial, 137
  baking dish, *295*
  bar accessories, 282–283
  boudoir sets, *372*
  butter dish, *243*
  cake baskets, *227–228*, 229, *230–231*
  candlesticks, *419–421*
  card receivers, *208–214*, 218
  casting operations, *61*
  castors, 171, *178–179*, 180
  celery stands, *318–319*
  coffeepots, *109*; *see also* tea services
  cups, *284*, *288*
  desk sets, 399, *404–405*

dresser accessories, 379
epergne, 189, *190*
factory, *31*
flasks, *397*
flatware, *434*, 435, *437–439*, *444*, 446
hollow ware operations, *57–60*
ice pitchers, 256, *258–263*
ice-water urns, *266–267*, 269
ink wells, *404–405*
jewel boxes, *374*
lamps, 417–418
lines of ware, 73
liquor sets, *397*
match safes, *359–360*
mirror frames, *369*
napkin rings, *335–336*, 339
nut bowls, *301*
paper knives, *404*
patent for reinforcing, *89*, 89
salt dishes, 329, *333*
salt shakers, 329, *333*
shaving cup, *392*
spice dishes, *282*
spoon holders, *306–311*, 311, 314
spoon warmer, *334*
syrup pitcher, *272*
teapots, *53*, 99, *100*, 100, 105, *106*, *109*, 110
tea services, 94, 108, *108*, 110, 116–117, *118*, *129*, *130*, *131*, *138*, 138, *272*
toilet stands, *368*
toothpick holders, *359–360*
tureens, *299–300*
vases, *155–158*, 162
vegetable dishes, *297*
vinaigrettes, *390*
Reed Silver Co., 31
refining of silver, 17
reinforcing of wear points, 82–83, *84*, 87, *87*, 89, *89*
relish dishes, *186*
Renaissance designs, 91, 103, 124, 133, 191, *197*
repoussé work, 55, 92, 111, *112*, 117, *119*
reproductions, Dutch, 60, *62*, 127, *127*
resist, in multi-color ware, 59
restoration of silverplate, 451–453, *451–453*
Ridgeway, J. (designer), 75
riveting, of spoons, *81*, 81, 83
Robinson, George C. (designer), 83, *84*

Rochester burners, for lamps, *412–415*, 416
Rockefeller, John D., 412–413
Rockford Silver Plate Co., *64*, 66, 295
rococo style, 91, 92, 103, 118, *120*
Rogers, Asa, 22, 23, 25, 26, 429
Rogers, Simeon, 23, 25, 26, 429
Rogers, William (Wm.), 22, 23, 25, 26, 429
  flatware, *434*, 445
  match box, 354
  reinforcing patent, 83, 84
"Rogers, Wm." trademark, 429, *431*
Rogers, Wm. A., Ltd., *434*
"Rogers, Wm. Jr." trademark, 429
Rogers & Bro., 27, 30, 73
  cake basket, *204*
  flatware, 429
  orange knife and peeler, 321, *324*, 325
  trademark, 429, *431*, 432
Rogers & Bros., C., 27
"Rogers & Co., A. Jr." trademark, 429, *431*
"Rogers & Co., Wm." trademark, 429, *431*
"Rogers & Cole" trademark, 429, *431*
Rogers & Hamilton Co., 27
  orange spoon, 325, *326*
Rogers & Mead, 22
"Rogers & Son, Wm." trademark, 429, *431*
Rogers Bros. Mfg. Co., 22–27, *23–24*
  baking dish, 294
  cake baskets, 222
  flatware, *442–443*
  spoon holder, 302, *302*
  teapot, *97*, 98
"Rogers Bros., 1847" trademark, 429, *437*
Rogers Cutlery Co., 27
Rogers Mfg. Co., Wm., 27, 73
  napkin ring, 345
  pepper box, 329
  pickle castors, 145, *146*, *color plate B*
  vase, *color plate E*
Rogers Mfg. Co., Ltd., Wm., 27
Rogers Silver Co., F. B., vegetable dish, 297
Rogers Silver Co., J., spoon holder, *314*
Rogers, Smith & Co. 27, 73
  cake basket, *223*
  card receivers, *217*

lamps, *416, color plate C*
napkin ring, *345*
spoon holder, *304, 305*
rolling mill, *44–45*
  patent for, *76, 77*
rotary castor, 171
rotation of articles in plating bath, 49, *50,* 51–52
Royle,–(designer), 321

S

salt dishes, *176,* 177, 327–331, *327–333*
salt shakers, 328–331, *331–334*
Sanderson, Robert, 278
sandwich plate, *236*
San Francisco Plating Works, 38, *38*
sardine boxes, 348, *349–350*
satin finish, *see* butler's finish
Schlesinger, Arthur M., 217
scratch-brushing, 59
"Sculptureform" style, 131
Sears, Roebuck & Co., catalog prices, 64
sectional plating, 51, *51,* 146
setter dog figurine, *160,* 162
sewing birds, 361–362, *362,* 367
shakers, salt and pepper, 328–329, *331–334*
  self-righting, 331, *333*
shaping of hollow ware, 54
shaving cups, 287, *288–289, 392*
shaving sets, 401
Shaw, Frank (designer), 33
Shaw, Thomas (electroplater), 33
Shaw & Co., Thomas, 33
"Sheerform" style, 131
Sheffield Silver Co., *247*
shells, for hollow ware, 54
Sheridan, Joseph (designer), *86,* 87
Sheridan Silver Co., *292, 293*
shoe horns, *406*
sifters, sugar, 331
silver, alloys of, 16
  biblical references, 14
  history of, 13–17
Silver Foam, 448, *449*
Silversmith's Gloves, 448, *450*
Silversmith's Polish, 448, *449*
Silversmith's Wash, 449
Simpson, Hall & Co., 111
Simpson, Hall, Miller & Co., 27
butter dish, *246*
dessert set, *274, 275*
flatware, *436, 444*
napkin rings, *339, 342–343*
sardine boxes, *349*
spoon holder, *304*
teapots, *108,* 108, 118, *120*
water cooler, 140
Simpson, Samuel, 23, 32
Simpson Nickel Silver Co., 27
"skyscraper" style, 129
Smee, Dr. Alfred (inventor), 21, 22
Smith, George W. (designer), 100–101, *101*
Smith, Patterson & Co., *291*
Smith, Sidney (designer), *434*
Smith, Sumner (electroplater), 22
Smith Silver Co., E. H. H., *436, 446*
soda fountains, 143
"soft metal" wares, 39
soldering, of trimmings, 55
South America, silver discoveries in, 15–16
souvenirs, 146, *146–147,* 287, *290*
Spain, silver mines in, 15
Sperry, Albert A., 22
Sperry, Alfred W., 22
Sperry, Egbert W., 22
Sperry, William, 22
sphere, teapot shaped as a, 108, *109*
sphinx, decoration, 189, *189*
spice dishes, *282–283*
spinning room operations, 54
"Spirit of the West, The" (sculpture), 147, *148*
spoon boat, *311,* 311
spoon bowls, advertising, 69, *70*
spoon holders, 64, 302–315, *303–316*
spoons, orange, 325, *326*
  patented processes in manufacture of, 74–89, *75–90*
  premium, 70, 71
  souvenir, 145, *146*
spoon trays, *311,* 311, 314–315, *315*
spoon warmers, 334, *334*
spot plating, 49, *50*
spouts, shaping of, 54
Spray, Silver (tarnish preventive), 450, *450*
Springfield Silver Plate Co., 36, 223, *225*

"sprinklers," salt and pepper, 67; *see also* shakers
"spun" wares, 39
squaw, statue of Indian, *159,* 162
stamp boxes, *398, 401*
stamping (swaging) of flatware, 48, 74, 75, *76,* 77
  of hollow ware, 28
Standard Silver Co. of Toronto, Ltd., 27
standards, of plating, 72
stands, card, *see* card receivers
  flower, 162
  fruit, 184, 190–191, *191–205, color plate D*
  toilet, *363–368,* 367, 370
Steffin, Albert (designer), *122, 166,* 238
"Stepform" style, 129
sterling silver inlays, 52
Sternau & Co., S., *291*
Stimpson, James H. (designer), *241,* 242, *243,* 248, 248–250, *249–250*
Stohr, Samuel (designer), 147
storing, of silverware, 448
strap-work, *108,* 108
"Streamform" style, 129
Strohbaker, Gustave (designer), *434*
styles, blending of, 13
  development of, *90–131,* 91–131
sugar basket, *275*
sugar bowls, *36,* 311, *314; see also* dessert sets
sugar dish, *37; see also* sugar bowls
sugar tongs, 146, *147*
sulphur compounds, 447
swaging (stamping), patents for, *74,* 75, *76,* 77
swing bottle, 97, *99,* 100
swing coffee urn, *99,* 100
syrup pitchers, 269, *269–274, 273*

T

tablewares, 171–320, 349, *351*
tanks, operation of plating, 46, 49, *50–51,* 51–52
"Taperform" style, 129
tarnish, *see* care, of silverplate
Tarnish-Shield, 448
Taunton Britannia Mfg. Co., 28–29, 171
Taunton Silver Plate Co., 205
teapot, from *Appleton's Journal, 53*
  patent drawing of Reed & Barton's first, *100,* 100
  self-pouring, 321, *322*
teapots, *see* tea services
tear-drop design, 129
tea services, styles of, 91–131, *93–131, 272*
teaspoons, *see* flatware; spoons
tea strainers, 349, *351*
"Tempest, The" (fire engine), 153, *153*
thimble holders, 370, *379*
Thurber, Gorham, 432
Tiffany & Co., 33, 137, 145, *444*
Tiffany & Young, 33
tilters, for pitchers, 250, *252–262*
toilet stands, *363–368,* 367, 370
toothpick holders, 354, *354–361,* 361
toy dishes, premium, *67,* 67
trademarks, 72–73
  Guild, 65
  on flatware, 73
  Reed & Barton's, *100*
  Rogers (various companies), 429, *431,* 432
Trans-Mississippi Exposition, 139
Transpacific Yacht Club, 148, *149*
trays, bread, 232–236, *233–239*
  child's, *284*
  crumb, 233, *236*
  pin, 385, *386*
  sandwich, 232–236, *232–233*
triple plate, marking, 73
trumpet, ship's, *152,* 152–153
Tufts, James W., 71, *71,* 143, *144*
tureens, 295, *298–300*
Turkish design, 114, *115*
two-color plating, 56

U

urns, ice-water, 263, *266–268*

V

Van Bergh, Frederick (designer), 117, *120*
Van Bergh Silver Plate Co., 117, *120*
Vanderbilt, The (model), 137
vases, *90, 92, 95,* 154, *154–158, 161–169,* 162, 170, *color plate E*
  Art Nouveau, 162, *164–166*
  bud, on napkin rings, 339
  on castors, *179,* 180, *182*

on toilet stands, *368*, 370
Victorian, 162, *163, color plate E*
Vasseur, Herman (designer), 108
vegetable dishes, 294, *296*, 297
Venetian chased decoration, 116–117, *118*
vertically revolving castor, 172, *174*
Veterans Association of Connecticut, *150*, 151
Vickers, James, 20
Victorian styles, 95, 162, *163–164, color plate E*
Victor Silver Co., *164, 274, 380–381*
Viking Brand hollow ware, 31
vinaigrettes, 389, *390*, 392

W

waiters, *see* trays
Walker, John (inventor), 354
Wallace, Robert, 32, 39, *85*, 85, 435, *444*
Wallace, Simpson & Co., 32
Wallace & Co., R., 32
Wallace & Sons Mfg. C., R., 32
Wallace Silversmiths, 32
Warner, William A. (designer), *87*, 87
Warren-Mansfield Co., 444
waste bowl, *35*
Watch Dial, The, ad in, *33*
Watchmaker & Jeweler, The, ad in, *253*
Watchmakers' and Jewelers' Guild, 65
watch stands, 370, *379*
water-cooler, multi-fauceted, 140
Waterman, Charles (inventor), 361
Watrous Mfg. Co., 27, *434*
Weber, Henry (designer), *122*
Webster & Bro., E. G., 27
Webster & Son, E. G., 27
  Dutch reproduction, *62*
  napkin ring, *345*
  spoon tray, 314, *315*
  teapot, 116, *117*
Webster Mfg. Co., 27
  syrup pitcher, *273*
  teapots, 105, *106, 107*
Webster-Wilcox division of INSILCO, 127, *128*, 426–427
Weintraub, M. (designer), *127*
welding, of flatware, *88*, 89
West, William A., 28, *29*
whale oil, for lamps, 407
whisk broom holder, *394*

White, LeRoy S. (designer), 82, *83*
white gold, 58–59
white metal, 20, 39–40, 56–57, 60, 72
Whitney Museum, 147
Wilcox, Dennis C., 26
Wilcox, Horace C., 26, 63, 250
Wilcox & Co., H. C., 26, 27
Wilcox & Evertsen, 27
Wilcox Britannia Co., 27
Wilcox Silver Plate Co., 27
  aspic dish, *236*
  bread tray, *236*
  butter dish, *246*, 247
  cake basket, 225, *227, color plate A*
  castor, *color plate B*
  centerpiece, 186, 189, *189*
  "Fine Arts" line, 162, *162, 167–168*
  fruit dish, *196*
  hair receiver, *389*
  jewel box, *373*
  lamps, *412–413*, 418
  moustache cup, *290*
  napkin rings, *345*
  orange cups, 321, *325*, 325
  spoon holders, *304*, 308, *310*
  trays, *237*
  vase, *162*
Wilde, Henry (inventor), 49, 51
Wilkinson, George (designer), 31–32, 138
wine-bottle cases, 278, *282*
wine coolers, 278, *279–281*
wine stands, *177*, 177
wire-strengthened spoons, 78–81, *78–82*
wolf and grouse figurine, *160*, 162
Woodman-Cook tea set, 116, *118*
Work-woman's Guide, 339
World of Art and Industry, The, 134, 135
World's Columbian Exposition, 145–146, *146–147*
World's Fair (1853–54), *134, 135*
Wright, John (inventor), 21

X

XII plating, *51*

Y

Young & Co., Otto, 355

Z

Zisser, Paul R. (designer), *239*